Rupert
Murdoch

RODNEY TIFFEN is emeritus professor in Government and International Relations at the University of Sydney. A leading international scholar of media, his books include *News and Power* (1989); *Scandals: Media, Politics and Corruption in Contemporary Australia* (1999); *Diplomatic Deceits: Government, Media and East Timor* (2001), and numerous other publications on mass media and Australian politics. His most recent book, with Ross Gittins, is *How Australia Compares* (2nd ed. 2009). He worked with the Media Monitoring Project as an observer during the 1994 South African election, conducted three reviews of Radio Australia, and worked with the independent Finkelstein Inquiry into the media in 2011–12.

Rupert Murdoch

A Reassessment

RODNEY TIFFEN

NEWSOUTH

A NewSouth book

Published by
NewSouth Publishing
University of New South Wales Press Ltd
University of New South Wales
Sydney NSW 2052
AUSTRALIA
newsouthpublishing.com

National Library of Australia
Cataloguing-in-Publication entry
 Author: Tiffen, Rodney, author.
 Title: Rupert Murdoch: a reassessment / Rodney Tiffen.
 ISBN: 9781742233567 (paperback)
  9781742241494 (ePub/Kindle)
  9781742246420 (ePDF)
 Notes: Includes bibliographical references and index.
 Subjects: Murdoch, Rupert, 1931 – Influence.
  Directors of corporations.
  Newspaper publishing.
  Mass media – Influence.
  Corporate power.
  Scandals.
 Dewey Number: 070.92

Design Josephine Pajor-Markus
Cover design Xou Creative
Cover image Peter Macdiarmid/Getty Images
Printer Griffin Press

All reasonable efforts were taken to obtain permission to use copyright material reproduced in this book, but in some cases copyright could not be traced. The author welcomes information in this regard.

This book is printed on paper using fibre supplied from plantation or sustainably managed forests.

Contents

Acknowledgements

Douglas Adams begins one of his comic science fiction novels with the observation that in no known language is there the phrase 'as pretty as an airport'. It is also likely that in no known language is there the phrase 'as exciting as living with a writer'. My deepest thanks in the writing of this book are, as always, to my wife Kathryn, who not only read the whole draft, but lived uncomplainingly, indeed cheerfully and supportively, through its long gestation.

My next greatest thanks are to my friends Peter Browne and Ross Gittins, who also read the whole manuscript and gave me careful and constructive feedback, which improved the book greatly. Mark McDonnell, a leading financial analyst, will not agree with all the judgements in the book, but generously read and gave helpful advice on the business chapters. David McKnight, Chris Masters and Nick Davies were kind enough to give me feedback on individual chapters.

I am grateful to Murdoch watchers in Sydney, Melbourne and London who helped with insights and information, including Eric Beecher, Brian Cathcart, Neil Chenoweth, Nick Davies, Bruce Dover, Roy Greenslade, Bruce Guthrie, Charlotte Harris, David Hayes, Martin Hickman, Brian MacArthur, David McKnight, Stephen Mayne and Dimity Torbett. I made a research visit to New York, but my period there coincided exactly with Hurricane Sandy, and all the meetings I had arranged fell through. I do not blame Rupert Murdoch for this, however.

Again I am grateful for the collegiality of the departments of Media and Communications and Government and International Relations at the University of Sydney, especially Graeme Gill, and of media scholars more generally, especially David Rowe,

Acknowledgements

Paul Jones, James Curran, Howard Tumber and Jeremy Tunstall.

I would also like to thank Sarah Shrubb, Emma Driver, Geraldine Suter and especially Phillipa McGuinness at NewSouth Publishing. All these people helped improve the book, but any remaining errors are, of course, mine, except that all complaints about punctuation should be directed to Ross Gittins.

Finally, I would like to thank my parents, Gladys and Leslie Tiffen, for an inheritance beyond riches, and our children, Paul and Ruth, who are unlikely to inherit a family company.

Murdoch family tree

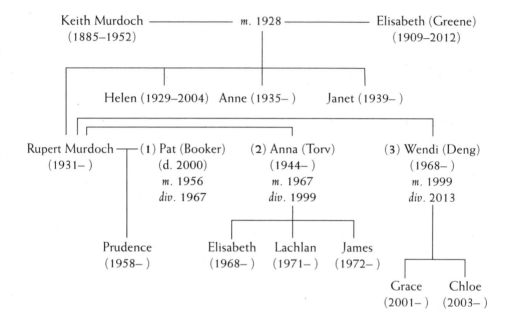

Keith Murdoch ——————— *m.* 1928 ——————— Elisabeth (Greene)
(1885–1952)   (1909–2012)

Helen (1929–2004)   Anne (1935–)   Janet (1939–)

Rupert Murdoch ——(1) Pat (Booker)   (2) Anna (Torv)   (3) Wendi (Deng)
(1931–)   (d. 2000)   (1944–)   (1968–)
                      m. 1956   *m.* 1967   *m.* 1999
                      div. 1967   *div.* 1999   *div.* 2013

Prudence   Elisabeth   Lachlan   James
(1958–)   (1968–)   (1971–)   (1972–)

                                          Grace   Chloe
                                          (2001–)   (2003–)

Murdoch company names

Rupert Murdoch's first company in Australia was called News Limited.

His British operations from 1968 on went under the name News International.

His American and his global company went under the name News Corp.

In 2013, News Corp split its operations in two, with one part operating as Twenty-First Century Fox and the other retaining the name News Corp, often referred to as 'the new News Corp'. The Australian operations are now called News Corp Australia.

1

The passing of the Murdoch era?

16 October 2013 marked Rupert Murdoch's 60th anniversary as a director of News Limited.[1] Since 1953, although his formal titles have changed at various times, he has been in charge. Such business longevity may be unique. It is hard to think of any other corporate head who has had such a long tenure.

Murdoch's record is extraordinary at both ends of the age spectrum. He is still running a company in his eighties, a time when most chief executives have long since retired. Likewise, he gained control at the tender age of 22 as a result of the death of his father Sir Keith Murdoch, who had been the dominant figure in Australian journalism for three decades. Although Sir Keith had been head of Australia's largest newspaper group, the Herald and Weekly Times, his actual ownership of newspapers was much more limited. Rupert's inheritance was restricted to one afternoon newspaper in the South Australian capital, Adelaide.

When Rupert arrived at the Adelaide *News*, television had not yet begun in Australia, geostationary communication satellites did not exist, and of course no one could even envisage the internet. The movement from a single newspaper in Australia's fourth (now fifth) largest city to a multi-media empire with global reach is by any measure a remarkable business success story.

According to the *Financial Times* Global 500, in June 2012 News Corp ranked 120th among the world's corporations by market value, with a total of $54.2 billion, one ahead of the National Australia Bank.[2] It was the second-ranked media company, behind Walt

Disney (ranked 57, value $86.7 billion), and a long way ahead of the third-ranked Time Warner (183), although some other corporations, particularly those classified as IT and telecommunications, have expanded into media areas.

News Corp differed from the other leading global media corporations in two crucial respects. The first was that its roots – and still much of its public profile – lay in newspapers, and so in a medium where politics and the potential for political bias and conflict were ever-present.

The second was that, far more than any of the others, News Corp was the personification of its principal owner, its actions inevitably associated both in the public mind and in reality with Murdoch himself. 'For better or worse, [News Corp] is a reflection of my thinking, my character, my values,' said Murdoch in 1996.[3] He stands in direct descent from the most controversial press barons in Anglo-American democracies, such as Britain's Beaverbrook and Northcliffe and America's Hearst and Pulitzer, relishing political power as much as commercial success, ruling internally with an iron fist and externally exciting controversy and gossip.

Murdoch, however, has a presence in several countries and across different media that Northcliffe and Hearst could never have imagined. He is the largest press proprietor in both Britain and Australia. In Australia his titles comprise around two-thirds of daily metropolitan circulation, a concentration of control not matched by any proprietor in any other democratic country. In Britain, he has both the biggest-selling daily paper, the *Sun*, and the most famous quality title, *The Times*. In both countries, he is the key player in the pay television market. In the United States his media assets include the *Wall St Journal* and the *New York Post* newspapers, one of the four free-to-air television networks, a major movie studio, and a large presence in cable TV channels, including Fox News. In Asia, he has the Star satellite television service (now split into four companies), and he has various holdings in Italy and other

European countries. His companies go beyond newspapers, television and film into magazines, book publishing (HarperCollins), pay TV decoders and supermarket inserts.

He renounced his Australian citizenship in 1985 to become a US citizen, prompting *New York Times* columnist William Safire to refer to him as a symbol of something new: global man, equally at home in Sydney, London and New York.[4] Ironically, at the same time, he is regarded as a foreigner everywhere, and is perhaps in that way as well the ultimate embodiment of globalisation. Most Americans still refer to him as Australian, while in Australia his domination of the country's newspaper industry is even more controversial because he is a foreigner. In England, he was dubbed the 'dirty digger' in the early 1970s, and his Australian-ness is a recurring theme in commentary. British journalist Michael Leapman, for example, thought that Harry Evans, when editing the *Times* in 1981–82, 'was trying to show Murdoch that he could be as ruthless and spiteful as any Australian'.[5]

Had Murdoch retired a decade ago, he would have been one of the media's most controversial figures because of his journalism and his political entanglements, but seen as an outstanding business success. These themes had been fairly constant since the 1970s, when author Thomas Kiernan judged that his great success in building the London *Sun* 'cemented his reputation as a brilliant international business and financial manager. At the same time, however, it increasingly drenched him in a self-perpetuating odour of moral and ethical disrepute.'[6]

Since then there have been frequent invocations of both themes. The business achievements are praised: 'no other Australian has had a greater impact on the world business stage' thought former Australian Prime Minister John Howard;[7] 'without doubt the most remarkable Western businessman since the Second World War', judged Channel Four investigative journalists Robert Belfield, Christopher Hird and Sharon Kelly.[8] But the criticisms of his papers' journalism have been equally strong: most spectacularly, the *Columbia Journalism Review* editorialised that his *New York Post* appealed 'to the basest passions and appetites of the hour', and thought the matter was so grave that the paper 'is no longer merely a journalistic problem. It is a social problem – a force for evil.'[9] Most bitingly, the British playwright Dennis Potter said 'no man [was] more responsible for polluting the press and, in turn, polluting political life', and famously named the cancerous tumour that was killing him Rupert.[10] Most humorously, *Chicago Sun-Times* columnist Mike Royko, who defected to the *Chicago Tribune* when Murdoch bought his former paper, thought that 'no self-respecting fish would be seen dead wrapped in a Murdoch newspaper'.[11]

So, until recently, the typical judgement might have echoed that of Theodore Kheel, a New York lawyer, who acted both against and for Murdoch. Kheel famously said, 'Rupert Murdoch is very good at what he does. The question is: is what he does any good?'[12] Now, however, the question will also be how good has he been at it? Now the journalistic and political critiques are even stronger, and judgements on business criteria are also more mixed. Several factors have fed the change, but the single most important one was the UK phone hacking scandal.

Rupert Murdoch's world changed forever on 4 July 2011. On that day the *Guardian's* Nick Davies published an article saying that the *News of the World* had tapped teenage murder victim Milly Dowler's phone. The scandal had been building – very slowly and far from surely – for almost five years, since August 2006, when *News of the World* reporter Clive Goodman and private investigator Glenn Mulcaire were arrested for having tapped the phones of members of the Royal Family and their staff. Goodman and Mulcaire pleaded guilty, issued apologies, and in January 2007 were sentenced to prison. But News International portrayed it as the work of a single rogue reporter. However, the investigative work of Davies and the editorial courage of the *Guardian;* the work by the lawyers for civil litigants, who had been victims of *News of the World* phone taps; the efforts of some members of a House of Commons committee; and eventually – in contrast to their culpably shoddy work early – the investigations by the London police, all destroyed the single-rogue-reporter fiction.

The Milly Dowler story opened the floodgates. Since then, News Corp has been engulfed in the biggest media scandal in any English-speaking country in living memory. It triggered what veteran journalist and newspaper historian Roy Greenslade called 'the most astonishing 14 days in British press history, with daily shock heaped upon daily shock'.[13] Politicians competed with each other in the ferocity of their denunciations. News International closed the *News of the World*, and in the face of opposition from all three major political parties abandoned its attempt to raise its ownership of satellite broadcaster BSkyB from 39 to 100 per cent, which would have been the largest deal in Murdoch's history. On successive days, London's chief police officer and one of his deputies resigned. Rupert and James Murdoch were forced to appear before a parliamentary committee, televised live, in what Rupert called the most humble day of his life.

The scandal revealed that Murdoch's London tabloid papers had engaged in phone tapping on an unprecedented scale, had bribed police, were at the centre of a web of political patronage and punishment, and had engaged in a systematic cover-up in which many senior executives lied. By late 2012, when the Leveson Report was published, 90 people had been arrested and were awaiting criminal prosecution,[14] and News International had paid damages in at least 72 civil cases.[15] The Leveson Inquiry, instituted by the Cameron Government to examine the scandal and the issues it raised, held oral hearings for around nine months, and heard from 337 witnesses, including the current prime minister and three of his predecessors, and other political and media figures, before publishing a 2000 page report.[16] Events are still unfolding, and will affect the future of the Murdoch empire.

The scandal will now be central in defining Murdoch's career and legacy. It sharpened previous critiques of Murdoch's journalism and political influence. British Labour Party MP Tom Watson said the scandal showed how Murdoch's company 'came to exert a poisonous, secretive influence on public life in Britain, how it used its huge power to bully, intimidate and to cover up, and how its exposure has changed the way we look at our politicians, our police service and our press'.[17] The grubbiness and amoral cynicism of the journalism, the scale of the illegality and invasions of privacy, the timidity of the politicians, police and others in the face of Murdoch's power more than confirmed what his fiercest critics had believed. In addition, it has thrown a sharp new light on the governance and organisational culture of News Corp, and encouraged a more critical perspective on some of its business strategies.

The continuing fallout from the scandal suggests that in some sense the height of the Murdoch empire has passed. The personal power exercised by Murdoch may have peaked as well, and it is still to be seen how the corporation will adjust to a possible post-mogul phase. This moment of transition offers an opportunity to reassess Rupert Murdoch.

Unlike most books on Murdoch, this one is structured analytically rather than chronologically, to explore major themes. The second chapter traces the building of his empire, and later chapters analyse his business strategies, his politics, his journalism, his relations with governments, and his road to scandal.

There is no shortage of information about Rupert Murdoch. There are at least a dozen books, many of them excellent, of which Murdoch, or some part of his career, is the central subject. There are also several memoirs and journalistic accounts where he figures substantially. Moreover, there are tens of thousands, probably hundreds of thousands, of newspaper and magazine stories, as well as radio and TV programs, which contain material on Murdoch. Unlike some other Murdoch books, this one is not based on interviews or close acquaintance with central figures; it is a distillation of the abundant material already on the public record.

This book aims to examine all of Murdoch's long and varied career: to give due attention to all three countries – Australia, the UK and the US – where he is a major journalistic player, to go up to the British phone hacking scandals and their aftermath, but also to go back decades to probe formative and interesting episodes. It seeks to trace how his political attitudes, his business strategies and his attitudes to journalism have developed.

The first challenge for anyone seeking to analyse Murdoch is the sheer length and complexity of his career. He has packed into one lifetime more conflicts and controversies than a dozen other media proprietors might manage. Journalist James Fallows, reviewing Murdoch's career in 2003, remarked, 'I was surprised to be reminded of how many dustups Murdoch has been involved in.'[18] Any book must therefore be selective. This one concentrates on his politics and journalism, rather than, for example, his entertainment businesses. Even here the range is impossibly large, as Murdoch's journalistic outlets cover many types in several countries. This book focuses on where Murdoch has been most directly involved, and on the areas that best illustrate his priorities and worldview, or have had the greatest impact.

A second difficulty is that despite the richness of what is publicly available, there are gaps, because Murdoch's *modus operandi* is secrecy. Even though the primary democratic purpose of news organisations is increasing public transparency, and News Corp is a public company, Murdoch prefers to operate beyond public view. He exercises personal control over his empire through telephone and face-to-face conversations, usually without any documentary record, so no outsider has access to these interactions.

Both he and the politicians he deals with are loath to put their dealings on the public record even though these politicians have placed great importance on their relations with Murdoch. He was the first media proprietor to visit David Cameron after he became Prime Minister in 2010, but at Cameron's request he came and went by the back door.[19] Margaret Thatcher often expressed in private her great admiration for Murdoch and gratitude to him: 'Rupert is magnificent.'[20] After she was ousted from the Tory leadership, Murdoch played a central role in the publication of her memoir, through his company, HarperCollins. Despite this, her memoir contained 'not a single reference to Rupert Murdoch'.[21] Similarly, the memoirs of Bob Hawke,[22] John Howard[23] and most other leading Australian politicians make only the most minimal references to their governments' dealings with Murdoch. When Lance Price, a spin doctor for Tony Blair, wrote his memoir about the experience, the book had to get Cabinet clearance: 'The real surprise was that no fewer than a third of [the government's] objections related to one man – not Tony Blair or even Gordon Brown, as I might have expected, but Rupert Murdoch.'[24]

In this book, when important conversations occurred with only Murdoch and one or two other people present that is indicated in the text. Occasionally, however, it is impossible to decide between contradictory accounts. Murdoch had told several people, and affirmed under oath before the Leveson Inquiry,[25] that after the *Sun* very publicly withdrew support from the Brown Labour Government on 30 September 2009, the prime minister telephoned him and said, 'Your company has declared war on my government and we have no alternative but to make war on your company.' Brown denied that any such conversation occurred, and supported this with the log of his telephone calls from the Cabinet Office.[26] Leveson declined to try to resolve these contradictory claims,[27] and no outsider can do so with certainty.

The single most prolific source of information on Murdoch is his own public statements. But these need to be treated with caution. Murdoch's statements about his intentions or directions have proved an unreliable guide to his actions, although this can be the case with any business figure engaged in takeover activities and keen to confuse his competitors. Neither are his general sentiments a good guide. In 1977, he told *More* magazine that:

> it would be a pity if I grew any bigger in Australia ... If I were to grow bigger and take over one of the other groups ... that would be against the public interest ... The fewer there are, the worse it is.[28]

This noble sentiment did not prevent him in the next two years from mounting an abortive takeover bid on the Herald and Weekly Times company, or from successfully taking over that company in 1987, raising his share of national daily metropolitan newspaper circulation from around one-quarter to almost two-thirds. In November 1977 he said that he didn't 'think that a newspaper should own outside interests'.[29] But in 1979 he became a half owner of an Australian airline.[30] In 1979, he said that 'to buy the *Times* would be a highly irresponsible thing to do for your shareholders',[31] but within another couple of years he had bought it.

He said that he disapproved of Britain introducing a national lottery, because 'it offends my Presbyterian instincts'.[32] He had managed to overcome such instincts, however, when the Wran Labor Government in New South Wales approached him in 1979 to take part in a consortium to market Lotto.[33] The government's rationale was that these groups' superior marketing skills would make Lotto more successful. In return, the companies received a government-guaranteed high profit,[34] a prospect which no Presbyterian could resist.

Similarly, Murdoch's career is littered with what others have called broken promises or commitments that were not honoured. As early as 1960, Robert Falkingham, the Fairfax company treasurer, was warning his boss, Rupert Henderson, not to sell Murdoch the Sydney *Daily Mirror*, because Murdoch 'has proved that he is not a man to honour his agreements'.[35] Many of his major acquisitions – from the *News of the World* in 1969[36] to the *Wall St Journal* in 2007[37] and several in between – have been followed by claims of betrayal and broken promises. Murdoch has often counter-charged, claiming bad faith on the part of his critics and the necessity of acting as he did, or pointing to the loopholes and fine print he had crafted that allowed him to do as he had done.

There are also cases of Murdoch lying about the past. In 2012, such a case was put clearly on the public record during the Leveson Inquiry. In 1981, in the lead-up to his takeover of the *Times* and *Sunday Times*, Murdoch was very keen that the British Government not refer his planned takeover to the Monopolies Commission. He denied, including to the official historian of the *Times*, that there had been any direct contact between himself and Prime Minister Thatcher. However, the Thatcher papers, released in 2012, show that they met over lunch in the crucial period, and that Murdoch followed up with correspondence. At the crucial Cabinet committee meeting, Thatcher argued that Murdoch's takeover did not require a referral under the Fair Trading Act, and the committee agreed.[38] At the Inquiry, the News International barrister argued against the suggestion that Murdoch had suffered a conveniently selective amnesia, and said it was simply that Murdoch did not remember events of 31 years ago.[39]

In 2007, while acquiring the *Wall St Journal*, he indignantly denied that in 1994 he had removed the BBC from his Asian Star satellite service in order to please the Chinese Government. 'I don't know how many times I have to state that I did not take the BBC off Star TV for political reasons; nor have I ever given any sort of political instructions, or even guidance, to one editor of the *Times* or the

Sunday Times,' he said.[40] Murdoch's move in 1994 was preceded by considerable speculation that he was about to do so. One Australian newspaper, for example, reported in March that Guo Baoxing, of China's Ministry of Radio, Film and TV, had told Star to drop the BBC, while Murdoch had told the *Economist* that the BBC caused him a lot of headaches with the Beijing Government because of its critical coverage, and that he had threatened to drop it.

Afterwards Star TV's chief executive, Gary Davey, said the decision was taken for purely commercial reasons. Three months later, however, Murdoch told his biographer, William Shawcross, that he had pulled the BBC in the hope of soothing bad relations with Beijing: 'I was well aware that the freedom fighters of the world would abuse me for it.' The Chinese leaders 'hate the BBC', Murdoch said. In 1995 he told US journalist Ken Auletta, 'the BBC was driving [the Chinese leaders] nuts ... It's not worth it. We're not proud of that decision [but] it was the only way.'[41] US journalist Jack Shafer concluded that it was only in 2007 that Murdoch returned to promoting the fiction that removing the BBC wasn't for political reasons, and indignantly denying what in the 1990s he had readily admitted.

The role of political expedience in these public statements is clear. But what are we to make of the following revealing example from the diary of Woodrow Wyatt, a confidant of both Murdoch and Thatcher? Thatcher rang Wyatt in 1986 to say she was about to announce that Marmaduke Hussey would be the next Chairman of the BBC. Wyatt was shattered, because he had a low opinion of Hussey. Murdoch's reaction was just as strong: 'Has she gone mad? What a disastrous appointment.' But when Wyatt raised the topic with Thatcher, she said, 'I wouldn't have done it if I hadn't had a strong recommendation from Rupert', and was amazed that Murdoch was now criticising it privately. Wyatt then went back to Murdoch, who denied recommending Hussey; however, when pressed, 'he seemed evasive and giggled a bit'. Wyatt concluded that 'she is telling the truth and not Rupert'.[42]

Here Murdoch is engaging in a pastime he seems to relish: venting his low opinion of people. According to Leapman, 'Murdoch is never happier than when running down journalists and businessmen – equally those who work for him and those who do not – in outspoken and sometimes vulgar terms.'[43] Here he is apparently lying – in private to a close friend – because he enjoys the game, enjoys playing both sides of the street.

A further difficulty in weighing evidence lies in the mythmaking about Murdoch by both his admirers and his critics. Many Murdoch employees loudly proclaim his abilities, but sometimes their tales are unreliable. For example, Vic Giles, who was brought over from the London *Sun* to New York in early 1974 to help Murdoch launch his sensational weekly newspaper, the *National Star*, was very impressed by the quality of Murdoch's contacts. He said that while he was doing a headline for a story on Nixon, Murdoch said it was wrong, and rang the White House. Nixon immediately rang back, and confirmed Murdoch's account. Murdoch then told his journalist: 'You're wrong, Dickie says it's this way.' According to Giles, although Murdoch had only been in the States a couple of months, 'he knew everybody. He was talking to Carter and LBJ as if they were his bosom buddies.'[44] Murdoch may have been talking to former President Johnson in early 1974 as if he were his bosom buddy, but it would be worrying if he heard anything in reply, as LBJ had died in January 1973. Equally, it would have taken improbable prescience for Murdoch to be bosom buddies with the future president Jimmy Carter, as the then Governor of Georgia still had almost no national profile.

While not questioning the strength of the 'Rupert-Dickie' relationship that Giles attests to, it seems unusual for the President to personally answer a query from a national magazine which still had negligible circulation and no political credibility. The closest the *National Star*, which specialised in UFOs and stories of the bizarre, had come to a political scoop in its early days was its revelation that 'if all the Chinese jumped up and down in unison, the vibrations would cause a tidal wave that could engulf America'.[45]

The legacy of Ozymandias

And on the pedestal these words appear:

'My name is Ozymandias, King of Kings:
Look on my works, ye mighty, and despair!'
Nothing beside remains. Round the decay
Of that colossal wreck, boundless and bare,
The lone and level sands stretch far away.

Percy Bysshe Shelley, 1817

No corporate figure in the contemporary world has been as intent on securing his business legacy as Rupert Murdoch. Despite News Corp being a public company in which the family has only a minority of the shares, he has long been intent on a dynastic succession. The phone hacking scandal has probably destroyed this fantasy.

However, the corporation, per se, has recovered spectacularly well from the scandals. In July 2011, its share price was $14.96; in April 2013 it was up to $31.54.[46] It has been buoyed by several factors, including a share buyback, and an increasing confidence that the scandal would not cross the Atlantic. One of the scandal's more bizarre consequences was the News Corp Board negotiating a settlement of $139 million with a group of American shareholders who sued it. The entire cost was covered by an insurance policy that 'protects corporate boards from this type of litigation',[47] and the money was distributed to all shareholders, including the Murdoch family.[48]

The scandal crystallised a sentiment already strong among investors that, in the words of the *Economist*, 'newspapers are not central to what News Corporation does ... but newspapers are central to who Mr Murdoch is'.[49] The scandal reinforced the view, made ever stronger by the impact of the internet, that the now financially marginal newspaper tail was wagging the entertainment dog. When considering earnings per share, Bloomberg data showed News Corp, on an adjusted basis, increasing from $0.71 in Financial Year 2005 to $1.41 in Financial Year 2012 – a very respectable performance. However, when compared with two other American media giants, it is rather less so: across the same timeframe, Time Warner increased from $1.05 to $3.29 and Walt Disney from $1.21 to $3.08.

In June 2012, Murdoch announced that News Corp would split into two – a large and profitable entertainment and media company and a small, much less profitable, and more politically contentious publishing company. Although Murdoch vigorously denied that the split had anything to do with the scandal,[50] US writer Michael Wolff judged that 'until the phone hacking scandal came to dominate every aspect of News Corp's corporate consciousness, hell would have had to freeze over before Rupert would have let his papers go'.[51] Nevertheless, Murdoch's email to News Corp's 50,000 employees, headed 'we will wow the world as two', was decidedly upbeat. Murdoch declared that the company had decided to restructure because of its 'increasingly complex' asset portfolio:

> We must realign and reorganise in this moment of opportunity. Over the years, I have become accustomed to the noise of critics and naysayers ... and pretty thickskinned! Remember what they said when we started Fox Network, Sky, Fox News and the *Sun*? These experiences have made me more resilient.[52]

News Corp shares reached their highest levels for five years on the news. The reason most business analysts applauded the demerger was their belief that, in *New York Times* reporter Amy

Chozick's words, 'in effect, News Corporation had evolved into a successful entertainment company with a newspaper problem'.[53] New York stockbrokers were referring to the two parts as GoodCo (the entertainment part) and BadCo (the publishing side). David Carr, another reporter from the *New York Times*, said that creating a separate division to allow newspaper businesses to grow and reach their full potential 'is a little like the engineer of a locomotive unhitching the caboose and telling the people marooned there that they were now free to travel toward any destination they desire'.[54] A cartoon in the *Economist* was the most succinct – it pictured the media wing as an eagle and the publishing company as a turkey. In December 2012 it was revealed that if the publishing arm had been a stand-alone company that year it would have lost $2.08 billion.[55]

In 2013 it was announced that the publishing arm would keep the name News Corporation, with Robert Thomson as CEO and Murdoch as Executive Chairman, while in the entertainment division Murdoch would be both Chairman and Chief Executive, with Chase Carey as Chief Operating Officer. The split was not as neat as the headlines suggested. The publishing division included not only newspapers, book publishing and educational products, but also the pay TV service Foxtel. So the Australian operation will continue as a single entity, on the curious grounds that Australia is so far away.[56] Many of the newspapers were currently losing money (the *Times* and *Sunday Times* was losing £50 million a year, the *New York Post* $100 million a year, and the Australian newspapers were in a steep decline). However, unlike most of its publishing competitors, the new company would begin life with a $2.6 billion cash balance.[57] Nevertheless it is clear that News Corp newspapers have been insulated from the effects of the internet in recent years by cross-subsidy from what will in future be the entertainment division.

At each stage of his career Murdoch has had observers guessing, often wrongly, about his next move. No one would have predicted a few years ago that News Corp would split as it has. This move doubles the questions about Murdoch's future strategies, influence and legacy. As Ozymandias testifies, few people, no matter how mighty they once seem, bequeath quite the future they intend.

2

Building the empire

From Adelaide to Hollywood and almost to Beijing

Bob Hawke's prime ministerial memoirs recall a 1983 dinner in Geneva he had with Rupert Murdoch and Paul Keating. Murdoch was regaling them with his plans for making a fortune from satellite television in Europe. 'As the dollar signs continued to dance in [Murdoch's] eyes' Hawke became bored, and asked, 'Rupert, will there ever come a stage in your life when you reckon you've made enough money and got enough power [and instead enjoy life and your family and our] beautiful, fascinating globe?' 'Murdoch looked at me as if I was slightly deranged' and resumed talking about his business plans.[1] Indeed, when this conversation occurred, Murdoch's empire had not yet reached half its eventual size. This chapter outlines the major moments in its expansion.

Adelaide inheritance to Australian national player

Appropriately, the beginning of Murdoch's career was surrounded by conflict. His father, Sir Keith, died in October 1952, at the age of 67. On Friday, 3 October, at the Herald and Weekly Times Board meeting, he had survived a showdown following growing tension with his deputy (and designated successor) John Williams. Williams had hoped Murdoch would be dismissed but instead *he* was; this was followed by a heated exchange between the two.[2] Murdoch died from a heart attack the following night and the Murdoch family never forgave Williams. The company reinstated Williams. On the following day, Sunday, he used a blowtorch to open the safe in Sir Keith's office, apparently to see what private transactions his former boss had been engaging in.[3] In an admirable display of multi-tasking, Williams was at the same time preparing the Monday papers' memorial tribute to Sir Keith. On Tuesday he delivered the eulogy at Murdoch's funeral.[4]

The settlement of the estate took several months, and, because of a combination of debt and death duties, it amounted to considerably less than expected. However, Keith had held a controlling interest in two newspapers. His widow, Elisabeth, felt compelled – much against Rupert's wishes – to sell the *Courier-Mail* shares to the Herald and Weekly Times, but insisted – against the company's and the trustees' wishes – that Rupert be given the chance to be publisher of the Adelaide *News* and the *Sunday Mail*.

By the time Rupert arrived in Adelaide to take up the reins of his new, but small, operation, he had graduated from Oxford with third class honours, and then worked as a subeditor at the *Daily Express* (while staying at the London Savoy). The Herald and Weekly Times immediately declared war by starting a Sunday newspaper to compete with the *Sunday Mail*, the most profitable part of Rupert's operation. Rupert's pugnacity was immediately on display in a defiant front page editorial that denounced the 'interlopers'. The two Sunday papers competed fiercely for two years before a truce in December 1955 re-established a Sunday monopoly: ownership of the *Sunday Mail* was split in half, but crucially, the name, management control and the printing contract all remained with Murdoch – 'Not bad for a 24-year-old who was supposed to be a babe in the woods,' he told author Tom Kiernan with some pride a quarter of a century later.[5]

The *News*, meanwhile, was prospering. The editor, Rohan Rivett, had been brought in by Sir Keith Murdoch, and had greatly improved the paper. Rivett had been captured in Singapore, and his book *Behind Bamboo*, describing the experience of being a prisoner of war under the Japanese, had been a bestseller. Later he had been the London correspondent for the Herald and Weekly Times, and had acted as a friend and mentor to Rupert during his early years at Oxford. At first Rohan and Rupert were close allies, and for a time Rupert was content to leave the journalistic side to Rivett, while he learnt the commercial ropes.

Murdoch, however, was already impatient to expand:

I'd never lived in a city as small as Adelaide … I don't mean
that against Adelaide, but if you were brought up in media, in
a city the size of Melbourne, and you saw the life ahead of you
in Adelaide, it was hard not to be ambitious, to think of a wider
frame.[6]

The only newspaper on the market was a Sunday paper in Perth. Murdoch bought it, paying more than most thought it was worth, and then used a team from his Adelaide paper to revive it. Freed from the professional presence of Rivett, Murdoch had a chance to exercise his tabloid tastes, and he quickly increased the paper's circulation.

Then Murdoch won one of the two commercial TV licences in Adelaide and set about learning the TV industry, but his ambitions in this field went largely frustrated for the next few decades.

His next big step, in 1960, was into Australia's largest city, and here his entry was aided in an extraordinary way by one of his competitors. In the 1950s, the Sydney newspaper market had two competing morning papers – the *Sydney Morning Herald* (owned by Fairfax) and the *Daily Telegraph* (owned by Frank Packer) – and two competing evening papers – the *Sun* (Fairfax) and the *Daily Mirror* (owned by the failing Norton company). Fairfax bought the *Daily Mirror* from Norton for fear that it would fall into Packer's hands, or give the Melbourne-based Herald and Weekly Times a Sydney base, but could not bring itself to close the paper. In the first of several deals in which established media owners underestimated him, Fairfax chief executive Rupert Henderson then sold the *Daily Mirror* to Murdoch. Henderson expected Murdoch to fail, but within half a dozen years the *Mirror*'s circulation was overtaking the *Sun*'s.[7]

The move into Sydney had brought Murdoch into direct competition with Packer and Fairfax. He had established a beachhead earlier by buying a suburban newspaper chain, and the three companies competed fiercely for a short time before profitably dividing the contested territory between them.[8] The first showdown between the Packers and Murdoch, however, was resolved by a bloody and spectacular brawl, involving an improbable cast of characters. The Packers, denied access to the *Daily Mirror*'s printing press, sought to fill the gap by acquiring the Anglican Press, which was in financial trouble. Impatient with the legal processes, Sir Frank's sons, Clyde and Kerry, both of whom had been amateur boxers, gathered several others and forcibly took possession of the building. The Anglican Press was run by one of Sydney's great eccentrics, Francis James: the son of a clergyman, he had been shot down over Germany in World War II, and now used the back seat of a Rolls Royce as his office. When told of the Packers' occupation of the building, he immediately rang Murdoch. While James organised some of his friends, Murdoch rang the sports editor of the *Sunday Mirror*, Frank Browne, a former professional boxer, who had the dubious distinction, in 1955, of being one of only two Australians ever jailed for contempt of parliament. Browne gathered four big 'bruisers', to use James's description. The party set about recapturing the Press building, at about 1.00am, and an almighty brawl followed. The Packers lost, and fled, bruised and battered, while James led the victors in a prayer of thanks. Murdoch had also dispatched a photographer to the scene and the front page of the next day's *Daily Mirror* recorded the Packers' humiliation.

Murdoch's next encounter with the Packers did not go so successfully. The Menzies Government decided to issue a third commercial TV licence in the major cities, and Murdoch lobbied publicly for the new Sydney channel.[9] When he failed to get the Sydney licence, he embarked on a plan that was audacious, but that surely would have failed if allowed to run its course.[10] He took control of the channel in Wollongong, a city south of Sydney. He outbid the Sydney channels and bought several American programs, and urged two million people in Sydney's suburbs to redirect their antennas away from Sydney and towards Wollongong.

Packer thought the best course was to make a deal with Murdoch, so he sold him shares in Channel Nine. However, a couple of years later, in April 1967, he did a 'reverse share transaction', so that instead of his newspaper company having control of the TV station, the opposite was the case. This severely diluted both the value and the voting strength of Murdoch's shares: their strength went from 25 per cent to 10 per cent.[11] He was quoted as saying privately that 'while I was honeymooning in London [with second wife Anna], I was raped in Sydney', and that Packer 'must be the biggest crook in Australian newspapers, but equally he is the cleverest'.[12]

While he was stalled in television, Murdoch's next move in newspapers was revolutionary. In 1964 he began what was possibly the most pioneering journalistic enterprise of his whole career, one which greatly improved the standard of Australian political journalism. Murdoch began Australia's first general national newspaper, the *Australian*. It was an idea whose time had almost come. Because of the problems of timely distribution across such a vast continent, and because in earlier generations advertising markets and perhaps readers' news interests were so strongly local, no one had ever envisaged a national newspaper. Australia's first daily business newspaper, the *Australian Financial Review*, had also begun, and the effect of both it and the *Australian* contributed greatly to a reinvigoration of Australian journalism. As usual, Murdoch's motives were mixed and hard to determine. No doubt there was some genuine idealism. According to Kiernan, his mother had told him that she didn't care how much money he made, but he 'must publish something decent for a change'.[13] The paper also gave him considerable kudos and political leverage,[14] and it is notable that he has maintained his commitment to it even though it has rarely made a profit.

Characteristically, however, Murdoch's own role was more problematic than this indicates.[15] It was imperative for the new paper to establish a strong Canberra base, but Murdoch's premature boasting to the owner of the *Canberra Times*, Arthur Shakespeare, resulted in the latter selling that title to Fairfax, which meant that when the *Australian* was launched, it faced a much more formidable local competitor.[16] Although the *Australian* was one of Murdoch's most visionary enterprises, several of his decisions compromised its quality journalism.[17]

Murdoch completed this phase of his Australian newspaper expansion in 1972, when he purchased the *Daily Telegraph*, the only newspaper owned by the Packer family.[18] The Packer sons, Clyde and Kerry, finally persuaded their father that the company's future lay in television and magazines. Although the price was high relative to the market value,[19] the purchase gave Murdoch parity with Fairfax in Sydney, both having a morning and an afternoon paper. Now there were only three proprietors of Australian metropolitan daily newspapers: the Herald and Weekly Times owned papers accounting for around half the circulation; the Fairfax company, the most patrician of the proprietors, owned most of the nation's quality newspapers, and accounted for a quarter of the circulation; and the newcomer Murdoch now also had papers accounting for about a quarter of the circulation.[20]

Although Murdoch had become a major media figure in Australia, in the late 1970s his position in television was still peripheral.

Australian television was structured as a series of metropolitan markets, and in the biggest centres there were three competing commercial channels. Government policy stipulated that one company could only own two TV stations, but the reality was that ownership of the Melbourne and Sydney channels was crucial and that the provincial stations, while having some locally originated programs, overwhelmingly acted as subordinate members of a de facto national network. Murdoch still lacked a Melbourne or Sydney channel.

The Ten network, the late starter (in 1964 compared with 1956 for the others), was the perennial third place getter in commercial TV ratings and advertising revenue. In early 1979, Murdoch, in a series of stockmarket raids, moved to become the major shareholder in Sydney's Channel Ten. By this time, because of the virulent anti-Labor bias of his newspapers since 1975, everything Murdoch did was controversial. The Labor Party opposed allowing Murdoch to own the licence on the grounds that he did not fulfil the requirement that an Australian TV licence holder had to be an Australian resident: Murdoch spent only around 40 days a year in Australia. Murdoch was telling the tax authorities that he was a US resident, while telling the broadcasting authorities that he was an Australian resident.

Although he told the Australian Broadcasting Tribunal that he had no plans to acquire Ten's sister station in Melbourne, within three months he was making moves in that direction. The channel was then owned by Ansett airlines, Australia's second domestic carrier. Murdoch's move led to a prolonged conflict, as Reginald Ansett resisted, and others, including Robert Holmes à Court, the Australian oil company Ampol, and Peter Abeles of TNT, also circled, buying small packets of shares which they hoped to increase. Eventually Holmes à Court, having been double-crossed by Ansett, dropped out, ceding control to a partnership between Murdoch and Abeles. The complications continued, with revelations about the warehousing of shares, secret deals, and major groups having no regard for the law. Eventually, after an appeal to the Administrative Appeals Tribunal, Murdoch emerged as a co-owner with Abeles of an airline as well as of Melbourne's Channel Ten.[21]

Over less than two decades Murdoch had moved from being a minnow to owning one of the four largest media companies in Australia. There was little immediate scope to expand further. The country was now too small for his ambitions. His next targets had long been international, specifically in Britain.

The most famous newspaper publisher in the world 1968–81

In 1968, Murdoch had no significant holdings outside Australia. By 1981, he was 'the best-known newspaper publisher in the world'.[22] In between, he had transformed the London newspaper market, first by purchasing the Sunday *News of the World*, then by making the *Sun* the biggest-selling newspaper in the country, and finally by purchasing the *Sunday Times* and the *Times*. His notoriety in the US had become almost as great, most importantly in 1976, when he acquired the *New York Post* and *New York* magazine in quick succession.

His first British acquisition was the biggest-selling newspaper in the English-speaking world. The Sunday *News of the World* had a circulation of 6.2 million, and with its mix of sensationalism and Tory prejudices, had long been a British institution. It 'had been more or less controlled by the Carr family since 1891',[23] although in an increasingly self-indulgent way by Sir William Carr. Conflict inside the Carr family made it vulnerable to takeover. When Murdoch was alerted to this, around October 1968, the most likely outcome looked to be a takeover by Robert Maxwell, a Czech-born British citizen. The *News of the World* editorialised against him in racist terms:

It would not be a good thing for Mr Maxwell, formerly Jan Ludwig Hoch, to gain control of this newspaper ... which is as British as roast beef and Yorkshire pudding ... This is a British newspaper, run by British people. Let's keep it that way.[24]

'Who is Rupert Murdoch?' Maxwell asked when told of the new player entering the field.[25] He was soon to find out, as the two media tycoons fought several battles over the next two decades. Murdoch entered the fray publicly as an ally of the Chairman, William Carr, and with the help of a shrewd adviser, Lord Catto. In January 1969 Maxwell was defeated, partly because his financial position was in reality much weaker than was publicly apparent.[26] Murdoch was later to say, 'I could tell that the establishment wouldn't let Maxwell in.'[27] However, William Carr's rescuer quickly became his hunter. Within six months Murdoch had forced him to resign and replaced him as Chairman, and a year later, after a prolonged trial of strength, he fired the editor, Stafford Somerfield – and had to pay out the last several years of his contract. This kind of skilful jujitsu and broken promises stuck 'to him as a kind of signature',[28] and has often been brought up in others of his dealings.

Murdoch did not change the nature of the *News of the World*. It was already nicknamed 'News of the Screws', and his conflicts with Somerfield had nothing to do with journalism. Years later he joked: 'I sacked the best editor of the *News of the World*. He was too nasty even for me.'[29] It remained the biggest-selling paper in Britain, until it was closed ignominiously in July 2011 because of the phone hacking scandal.

Murdoch was determined to break into the daily newspaper market as well, particularly because he owned a press that could be used to print one, and was contemplating starting a new title. A takeover opportunity soon arose, however. The IPC company, the only pro-Labour newspaper proprietor and owner of the biggest-selling tabloid, the *Daily Mirror*, had acquired a failing trade union-owned newspaper, the *Daily Herald*, and had re-launched it as the *Sun* in 1964. But it did not find a market. IPC had promised to keep it alive for seven years, but it was proving a major drain on profits: its sales kept falling, probably to around 800,000 in 1969.[30] Again Maxwell was the frontrunner as purchaser, but the unions preferred Murdoch and the company didn't believe Maxwell had the necessary funds. Murdoch solved IPC's problem at what for him was a bargain price.[31]

The first edition of the new *Sun* appeared on 17 November 1969. It became Murdoch's greatest newspaper success. Starting from a base circulation of less than 1 million, it reached 3.5 million by the end of 1975[32] and at the beginning of 1978 it passed the *Mirror*, which had been the country's top-selling newspaper since 1949.[33] It has maintained that position ever since. Its circulation peaked at over 4 million during the 1980s and into the 1990s,[34] but by 2012 it had declined to just above 2.5 million.[35]

While Murdoch was carving out this success in British tabloids, he was becoming increasingly disillusioned with British society. His affection for it had never been strong, even in his student days. But now he saw it as a country in decay, weighed down by its several establishments: not only the traditional hierarchies of class, but also the 'liberal' establishments of the universities, the BBC and quality press, which made life difficult for him. He found dealing with the trade unions increasingly frustrating. Such feelings reached a peak with some personal tragedies. When the Murdochs were out of the country in January 1970, one of their friends was kidnapped while she was driving their car. She was then killed. The criminals' target was Rupert's wife Anna Murdoch. Later that year she was (blamelessly) involved in a fatal car accident.

The Murdochs moved to New York in 1973.[36] 'New York, he [sensed, was] his kind of town'[37] – without snobbery, fast moving, deal oriented – and it has been his home, except for a brief unhappy period in Los Angeles, ever since.

In that year he made his first American acquisitions, the two daily newspapers in San Antonio, Texas – because they were available and he could afford them.[38] The Hearst company had the biggest newspaper in the city.[39] The monopoly morning paper continued much as it had been, but he took the afternoon paper down-market, improving its circulation to some extent. Its most infamous headline was 'Killer Bees Head North'.

In 1974 he started a weekly sensational tabloid newspaper, the *National Star*, to compete with the *National Enquirer*. It was sold at supermarkets, and had a style that paid only lip service to actual news reporting. At first it failed to make an impact, but some years later, after it first dropped the 'National' from the title and later introduced colour, it did better. By the late 1980s it was Murdoch's most profitable American publication.[40]

Murdoch remained virtually unnoticed in America until he bought the daily *New York Post* newspaper and the weekly magazine *New York*. These gave him a strong presence in the country's largest city. 'The cover of *Time* showed King Kong with the face of Rupert Murdoch bestriding the rooftops of Manhattan: "Extra!!! Aussie Press Lord Terrifies New York".' *Newsweek*'s cover had a mock newspaper front page with a picture of Murdoch, and the headline 'Inside: Aussie Tycoon's Amazing Story! – Press Lord Takes City'.[41]

New York magazine's editor and publisher, Clay Felker, was a famous New York identity, and had befriended Murdoch when he came to live in the city. However at the moment when Felker was vulnerable to losing his magazine because of over-spending, his friend Murdoch, whom he thought might help, instead moved to take control. Felker, with the anger of the betrayed, told Murdoch he would fight him tooth and nail. Murdoch replied, 'Teeth and nails are fine but it's money that wins this kind of scrap.'[42] Felker mobilised the staff against Murdoch, and 40 of them left, amid much fanfare,[43] but after the pyrotechnics ended, Murdoch was in control. As a result he also acquired the profitable weekly newspaper the *Village Voice*. Despite his forceful interventions elsewhere, Murdoch, after an initial rebuff,[44] never again tried to interfere at the *Village Voice*, whose whole appeal was to a left-liberal and counter-culture constituency Murdoch had no sympathy for. In 1985 he sold it at a handsome profit.[45]

The far more important move was the purchase of the afternoon daily newspaper, the *New York Post*, for just over $30 million from its long-time owner, Dorothy Schiff. He radically repositioned the previously staid and liberal paper into a sensationalist and editorially right-wing one. This was very different from any newspaper New York had known for some generations, and it attracted a huge amount of critical comment. The *Columbia Journalism Review* called him 'a sinister force' in our lives, and for the chief editor of the *New York Times* he was 'an evil element'.[46]

The *New York Post* still figures centrally in Murdoch's affections, but he never made it a commercial success. In 1988 he was forced to sell it because of the cross-media laws, and in the 11 or so years he had owned it, biographer Jerome Tuccille estimates that he lost around $150 million.[47] According to his publicist, he wept real tears in February 1988 when the sale was completed.[48] Less sentimentally, *Village Voice* journalist Alexander Cockburn likened it to Dracula selling his coffin.[49] Although Murdoch told Tuccille that he had put the *Post* completely behind him, as 'a nightmare chapter of my life',[50] when the paper was on the verge of closing in 1993 he lobbied strenuously to get it back. Supported by the urgings of the journalists, Democrat Mario Cuomo and others he was given a waiver from the cross-media laws, because of the jobs that would be lost with closure, and rebought it. He then moved to again put his ideological stamp on the paper and his name appeared on the masthead as editor in chief.[51] By 2007, according to Wolff, the paper was losing $50 million a year,[52] and by 2013 one report said it was losing $100 million annually.[53]

Murdoch never became the force in American newspapers that

he was in Australia and Britain. But he did make some further important purchases, although both were also later sold. The Boston-
based *Herald American*, owned by Hearst newspapers, was failing and
about to close when Murdoch negotiated to buy it in December
1982. Although he drove hard bargains with the unions, he was
broadly welcomed as the paper's saviour. He changed the name
back to Boston *Herald*, and increased its circulation, finally selling it
in February 1994 – because of cross-media ownership rules – when
he wanted to acquire a Boston TV station. His 1984 purchase of the
Chicago Sun-Times was far more controversial, with several journalists leaving in very public protest. He sold it in 1986 as part of his
move into American television, making a pre-tax profit of around
$70 million.[54]

Murdoch already owned the biggest-selling newspaper in Britain. Now he set his sights on the country's most famous quality
newspaper. The history of the *Times* is central to the rise of an independent, quality press in England, and it retained a unique prestige.[55] However, for decades it had been running at a loss, kept
afloat by the generosity of Lord Thomson. The losses were compounded when the typesetters went on strike in late 1978; the closure lasted almost a year. In late 1981 Thomson put the loss-making
Times on the market, threatening to close it completely if no deal
were reached.[56] Its stablemate, the *Sunday Times*, was operating profitably. Eventually Murdoch was deemed the preferred buyer,[57] and
as we shall see in Chapter 9, the Thatcher Government eased his
passage.

One factor which made the deal sweeter – but of which, according to Murdoch, both he and the Thomsons were unaware[58] – was
that purchase of the *Times* would bring with it a 5 per cent holding
in the news agency Reuters. Reuters, begun as a privately owned
venture by Julius Reuter in 1851, had been constituted as a trust
between its member news organisations during World War II, and
all the British national newspapers had a share in it.[59] It had gradually

been transforming itself, and its huge investment in infrastructure and its international base had seen it develop into a much bigger and potentially more profitable enterprise, with financial data eventually dominating in terms of revenue. Its members were increasingly keen to realise its financial value. By buying the *Times* Murdoch doubled his shares in Reuters. Reuters was later floated, very profitably for its member organisations.[60]

Press baron to multi-media mogul – the 1980s explosion

When Murdoch gained control of the *Times* he was a few weeks shy of his 50th birthday, and he had been head of his company for just over a quarter of a century. Over-simplifying, the first half of this period he had spent becoming a major player in Australia, and the second half he had devoted to becoming a major newspaper publisher in Britain and America. However, far from being content with his lot, Murdoch was about to undertake some of the most dramatic moves in media history. His most spectacular were into film and television, but he also made bold moves in newspapers. For good measure he expanded in magazines (unsuccessfully) and book publishing (successfully). 'The value of Murdoch's empire – measured in terms of assets owned – was placed at $1.52 billion in 1984' and five years later was more than six times that figure.[61] In what was, throughout, a manic career, this is the single most manic period. In this decade he transformed his empire again: from one based principally in the UK and Australia to one with its centre of gravity in the US; from a company that was principally a newspaper publisher to one centred in broadcasting and film. But his dynamism almost brought him undone: he accumulated such debt that the company almost went bust. In the end he prevailed, and became an even bigger player in the world's media.

Although nearly all the other moves considered below contributed to Murdoch's later debt crisis, one contributed substantially to his bottom line. From a contemporary vantage point, the destructive power which trade unions used against Fleet Street newspapers, an industry that was far from buoyant, is difficult to believe. It stemmed from the inherent vulnerability of newspapers, where even a short industrial action can disrupt the tight production and distribution schedules and so inflict great financial damage. Printers were often earning more than journalists, and the efficiencies offered by new technologies were simply banned by some unions. Over-manning and 'Spanish practices' (ie rorts) were rife. Such defiance of economic gravity could not last forever, but it was Murdoch's ruthless and skilful moving of his Fleet Street papers to Wapping that decisively ended it. Like the other Fleet Street companies, Murdoch loathed the unions, a feeling which became more acute with the financial burdens of acquiring the *Times*. 'If it's the last thing I do, I'll make the goddamn unions pay dearly for their idiocy,' he told Kiernan.[62]

Murdoch bided his time. The plant being built at Wapping was said to be for a new newspaper title, the *Post*, which of course never eventuated, and the secrecy regarding its true purpose was maintained. According to Roy Greenslade, there were four conditions that allowed Murdoch to move when he did. The first was the money which had come from the Reuters float. The second was the huge prices which central London real estate was commanding, which made it an attractive proposition for newspapers to develop 'green fields' production sites further out and profitably dispose of their London real estate. Within a decade no newspaper had its headquarters in Fleet Street. The third was that new press proprietor Eddie Shah was planning to launch a non-union paper outside London, which threatened to bring the cheap competition the existing papers had long feared. Fourth was the Thatcher Government's 1984 Trade Union Act, which made strike action subject to secret ballots and made it more difficult for unions to support other unions on strike.[63] Moreover, through his friend Woodrow Wyatt, Murdoch had secretly secured the agreement of an outside union, the electricians' union (the EEPTU) to produce the papers.[64]

When everything was ready, he became completely intransigent in his negotiations with the Fleet Street unions. They then did exactly what he wanted and went on strike, which allowed him to sack them. With a mixture of carrot and stick, he persuaded the journalists to move to Wapping. Although many felt conflicted, and some had qualms about crossing a picket line, overwhelmingly they chose to go.

On 25 January 1986 four million newspapers were produced at Wapping.[65] 'Fortress Wapping' was a newspaper factory surrounded by 4 metre-high spiked steel railings topped by barbed wire.[66] For a year, pickets, often violent and abusive, remained, and there were many TV news stories on the clashes between picketers and police. On the first anniversary of the move, the largest-ever crowd – 13,000 – gathered. Of 1000 police on duty, 168 were reported injured, as were many demonstrators.[67] But this was the protesters' last gasp. Murdoch – seizing the moment offered by technological change and favourable political and financial environments – had won.

Murdoch's Wapping victory took a severe internal toll, although Murdoch remained largely oblivious to this. *Sunday Times* editor Andrew Neil felt that his relations with his 'staff were strained almost to breaking point.'[68] In the aftermath of victory, morale plummeted. Bruce Matthews, Murdoch's most senior manager in London, found Murdoch 'a very sour man' who made matters much worse whenever he visited London.[69] Despite doing such good service for Murdoch in the move, Matthews was soon dispatched. Other senior managers involved, John Dux and Gus Fischer, also thought Murdoch's visits were acutely counter-productive, that he was 'a lousy manager', and felt burnt by their assistance to him during Wapping.[70] The EEPTU head, Eric Hammond, had assisted the move to Wapping in the expectation that his union would be the main representative of the workers there, but instead Murdoch saw his chance to keep it entirely non-union,[71] and once victory was achieved, Hammond too was dispatched, disappointed.[72]

Murdoch's main interest in his British newspapers now was to support his American film and television ventures. A rival newspaper executive calculated that Murdoch's costs were reduced by £80 million a year by the move to Wapping; some analysts calculated that as a result the *Sun* was making a profit of £1 million a week.[73] Murdoch did not use this huge boost in his cash flow to gain a great competitive advantage over the competing British newspapers; instead, with one exception, he channelled it across the Atlantic. The exception was that in 1987 he purchased Eddie Shah's *Today* title, a mid-market tabloid which pioneered the use of colour printing and computerised editing. But it never made a profit and he closed it in November 1995.[74]

At the same time, Murdoch was radically restructuring his empire in Australia, but unexpectedly this almost proved to be a financially ruinous move. In September 1985, in order to hold a TV licence in the US, he had taken American citizenship, but in so doing – at least according to any straightforward reading of the law – he became ineligible to hold a TV licence in Australia. Murdoch's timing was good, as changes to media ownership laws by the Hawke-Keating Government made his exit from Australian television much more profitable (see Chapter 8). (Remembering Murdoch's debt crisis a few years later, it should be noted that this was the third large, unexpected cash injection he received in the 1980s, after the Reuters float and the post-Wapping profits.) The sale of the Ten network helped to fund his audacious move to buy the Herald and Weekly Times (HWT), Australia's largest newspaper publisher, the company where his father had once been managing director. Since that purchase, Murdoch has had a dominating position in Australian newspapers.

Murdoch thought that his high pre-emptive bid for the Herald group would be decisive, and ultimately it was, but en route there were very expensive complications he had not anticipated. In 1979, he had bid for the company but failed (profitably). At that time the HWT Board had resisted, and the Melbourne *Herald* editorialised:

> Mr Murdoch's papers always respond in unison – as though to some unseen divine wind – as they pursue their relentless campaigns in favour of current Murdoch objectives – particularly his political ones. Every journalist in Australia knows that.[75]

This time the HWT Board welcomed Murdoch's bid, and what 'every journalist in Australia knows' did not rate a mention. However, as a defensive response to Murdoch in 1979, HWT and its subsidiaries in Queensland, South Australia, Western Australia and Tasmania had developed a series of cross shareholdings. Robert Holmes à Court took some strategic shareholdings, especially in Queensland Press, sufficient to give him veto power. Belfield et al. estimated that Holmes à Court cost Murdoch A$1 billion,[76] while Neil Chenoweth estimated that Holmes à Court's flanking move doubled Murdoch's cost to $3.6 billion.[77] The financial disaster for Murdoch had ongoing complications, because 'A subsidiary company cannot hold shares in its parent.' This trapped Murdoch in his quest for control of the whole group. He came up with 'his most desperate plan yet'. His family company, Cruden Investments, paid $600 million for 56 per cent of Queensland Press. But Cruden had no means of repaying this, and even servicing the interest was going to be a problem – 'it had become a debt problem waiting to happen'.[78] The problems may have been manageable, if not for the October 1987 stockmarket crash.

That month *Forbes* magazine, in its annual rich list, had put Murdoch as the 8th richest person in America, valued at $2.1 billion, mainly based on his shares in News Corp. But by the time the magazine hit the streets Murdoch was no longer a billionaire. On Wednesday, 21 October, the Commonwealth Bank, worried about the loan to Cruden Investments, even took a lien over the Murdochs' penthouse in New York. Conveniently, Queensland Press (its new Murdoch family members absent) bought 42 million News Corp shares from Cruden Investments. The HWT Board decided to buy the Cruden stock at $16 a share, what they said it was worth, even though on the open market they could have paid around $12.80, so paying around $93 million more than the market price – a better deal for Cruden than for other Queensland Press shareholders. Australian regulators looked hard at these decisions over some years, but in the end decided not to prosecute, the strong recovery of the News Corp share price in later years taking the heat out of the issue.[79]

This was Murdoch's first big debt crisis, and it passed completely beyond public view. At the end, the American citizen had moved out of Australian television, and instead acquired a dominant position in Australian newspapers, his titles accounting for almost two-thirds of daily metropolitan circulation.

Murdoch's first move into entertainment in America was in films. He had helped to finance *Gallipoli*, a film about Australia's first major military involvement in World War I, the disaster of which Murdoch's father had been centrally involved in disclosing. Murdoch's involvement in the movie had been partly for sentimental reasons, but he was impressed by the financial riches which followed. 'Do you realise,' he said to Kiernan, '[that] a single picture like this can clear more than a year's worth of *Suns*?'[80] As Tuccille notes, 'The artistic and commercial success of *Gallipoli* sharpened Murdoch's appetite for more of the same.'[81] In a preliminary sortie, he had become a shareholder in Warner Brothers in 1983, but Warner's defensive moves effectively blocked him from going further. It led to litigation, which Warner won, but which Murdoch and his team fought with such 'extraordinary legal invective' that one judge described it as 'a corporate form of feudal warfare',[82] and Warner decided to settle on generous terms. Murdoch walked away bitter, but richer by more than $40 million.[83]

Twentieth Century Fox proved a more affordable and more welcoming proposition. It had been bought by Marvin Davis and Marc Rich in 1981, but Rich had then fled the country to avoid arrest on fraud and tax evasion charges (he was pardoned by Bill Clinton in one of his last acts as President in January 2001). Davis bought out Rich's half for $116 million, and in 1984 sold it to Murdoch for $250 million, which included a capital injection for the ailing company. The company was, however, starting to improve under the leadership of Barry Diller.[84]

This was but a prelude to an even more dramatic move. Murdoch had known John Kluge, the principal figure in Metromedia, since the mid-1970s. Metromedia owned and operated small but profitable independent TV stations in seven major cities,[85] which made up around 22 per cent of the American viewing audience.[86] Murdoch paid $650 million in cash and assumed Metromedia's $1.3 billion of debt.

Originally the purchase of Metromedia was to be with his partner in Twentieth Century Fox, Marvin Davis. But at a crucial moment Davis pulled out, and the acrimony between them was such that they could not continue together in the movie venture either, and eventually Murdoch bought him out, for $325 million.[87] This severing of an unsatisfactory partnership was beneficial long term, but it added very considerably to Murdoch's short-term outlays. Murdoch has often proclaimed himself a gambler, and said he is energised by risk. But now he had effectively 'gambled his entire media empire on his 20th Century-Fox-Metromedia acquisition'.[88]

Although in the mid-1980s Murdoch's empire was still dominated by newspapers, he already had a considerable history in television. He had been a player in Australian television since the late 1950s, at first a minor one and from 1980 a central one, and had grounded himself thoroughly in the industry's economics. Although often overlooked, he had a short but successful period running London Weekend Television (LWT). Murdoch had been humiliated in an interview on London Weekend TV with David Frost, and a year later he bought a large holding in the struggling company.[89] Murdoch enjoyed the 'challenge of reviving failing institutions', and despite official rules to the contrary, he was very directly involved in managing the TV company.[90] He 'believed that if he could pump some "really commercial thinking" into LWT' and overcome 'its highbrow approach to television programming', 'he could save it', and indeed he soon returned it to the path of profitability.[91] He sold out at a profit in 1980 in order to finance his Australian TV purchase of the Ten network,[92] which under his direction was also operating profitably.

Nevertheless it was a huge step from his previous experience to the ambition he publicly proclaimed in October 1985: to start a new network of affiliated stations, and in the long term to become the fourth network in American television. The essential logic of US television had remained the same for decades. There were three major networks – the youngest, ABC, had been formed in 1948 – and the relationship between networks and their affiliates was the key to competitive position. However, the number of TV channels in most markets exceeded three, so there was scope for competitive manoeuvring beyond these three. There were technological, regulatory and commercial factors that made a challenge more possible in the second half of the 1980s, but it was still a challenge from which most businesses would have shrunk.

Murdoch moved to integrate his TV operations and Twentieth Century Fox under a new corporate umbrella, Fox Inc., with Barry Diller as CEO.[93] For Murdoch, the films that Twentieth Century Fox had already made were as important as the ones it would make in future. The library was a source of programming for his own channels and he could sell from it to others.

The Fox TV network was slow to develop, beginning with programming just for weekend evenings, and expanding a night at a
time over the next few years. For several years it made a loss, and
there was considerable instability in its programming and management. Eventually, however, it had a run of programs that made an
impact: *Married – with Children; The X Files; Beverley Hills 90210; Melrose
Place;* and above all, *The Simpsons.* (In the 2000s, its biggest hit was
American Idol.) The turning point, the 'deal [which] validated Fox',[94]
was when it bought the rights to the US National Football League
in 1993, outbidding CBS, and winning a range of new affiliates, so
that its reach to the US market expanded greatly. In 1994, Murdoch
claimed Fox was the top network;[95] a more accurate claim would
have been that by then it made sense to talk of four rather than
three networks, with Fox fourth by most measures – but this was
still a very considerable achievement.

The success of Fox was a classic Murdoch triumph. In less than
a decade he had broken the mould of what seemed the eternal and
inevitable three-network competition.[96] His risk-taking had been
vindicated. Some programming was original, such as the animated
Simpsons; all of it was cheap to produce. Then came the knock-out
blow – the football rights. Fox's current affairs and 'reality' programs,
such as *A Current Affair, Cops* and *America's Most Wanted,* were dubbed
'tabloid television' by their critics. But they were the epitome of
the Fox approach: cheap to make and aiming for an audience not
usually attracted to the 'high-brow' current affairs on the other networks. No one could accuse Fox of being elitist.

Not nearly as revolutionary were Murdoch's moves into book
publishing. The book industry had consisted of a series of independent publishers, but their amalgamation into larger companies
was widespread through the 1980s.[97] Murdoch was a prominent
player in this trend. He already owned Angus & Robertson books
in Australia; he had started to acquire Collins Books in the UK; and
then in March 1987 he bought Harper & Row in the US, paying

far more than others had thus far ventured,[98] three times the value of Harper's assets and over 50 times its annual profits. Then he launched a full bid for Collins Books. Although resisted by the then director, Ian Chapman, who felt personally double-crossed by Murdoch's move, he succeeded. In early 1989, he merged the two companies.[99] He had paid more than the market expected, but the new entity, HarperCollins, has been a central player in English-language book publishing ever since.

Murdoch's even more expensive moves into American magazine publishing were much less successful. There were two transactions, one before and one after his move into American film and broadcasting. The first came in 1984 when he acquired Ziff-Davis magazines for the considerable sum of $350 million.[100] In the end, as part of his debt reduction program in the 1990s, he disposed of most of this stable profitably.[101] The second move was in October 1988, when he shocked American media circles by purchasing Triangle Publications for $2.8 billion.[102] News had debts of over $4 billion, and most analysts thought it was already over-stretched. He disposed of nearly all the titles in the early 1990s, at a loss. He kept the biggest, and most well known, *TV Guide*, which he retained for a decade: it had the advantage of giving Fox the prominence due to a fourth network. So, though Murdoch had been a major player in American magazine publishing for a moment, by the end of the 1990s he was completely out of the industry. The purchase of Triangle Publications was, simply, a disastrous failure.

In June 1988 Murdoch announced that he would be setting up a satellite venture in Britain called Sky. The launch of Sky is explored further below, but it was an important element in the developing debt crisis that almost undid Murdoch's whole empire.

So in a tumultuous few years, and surrounded by sharp political conflict, Murdoch's boldness had fortified his position in British newspapers and given him dominance in Australian newspapers. Also, he had established a substantial presence in US television and film and in book publishing, and was poised to enter the new industry of satellite broadcasting. Much of this had been not simply risky, but reckless. Murdoch had acquired debts that endangered his whole empire.

In Chenoweth's view, 'Murdoch had never been able to afford his great move in 1985–86 to buy Twentieth Century Fox, the Metromedia television stations and to launch the Fox network.'[103] In addition, his Australian acquisitions had proved far more expensive than he had envisaged; his book publishing acquisitions were expensive in the short term; his 1988 magazine purchases were expensive and ill-advised; and any profits from his satellite ventures seemed at best far in the future.

By late 1990, life for News Corporation 'had become a mesmerizing sequence of near-death experiences'.[104] In August Standard & Poor's gave News Corp's debt rating a Triple C plus, the equivalent of junk bond status.[105] When a Channel Four documentary (by Belfield, Hird and Kelly) on its problems was broadcast, the share price fell 20 per cent in a day.[106] A series of short-term debts were coming due, and News was unable to pay. On 6 December, a Pittsburgh bank owed $10 million by News at first refused to roll over the loan. When told that meant News would go out of business, the loan officer persisted. When Murdoch spoke to the officer again, other banks had interceded and the loan was rolled over.[107] In December 1990 'News needed to reschedule $7.6 billion of debt held by 146 institutions around the world.'[108]

This was a staggering figure, and Murdoch's empire came very close to collapsing in ignominy. The key factor that saved Murdoch was the difficulty and cost to his creditors of letting him collapse. The structure of News Corp was so complicated, spread through so many countries, including several tax havens, each with its own laws and procedures, and the structure of the debt was so complicated, with so many competing claims against the company, that no creditor could be assured of receiving proceeds from the sale of any particular assets, and all would face years in court very expensively sorting out the mess. The problem was so large that one Citibank leader, William Rhodes, even thought there was 'systemic risk if the [rescue] deal fell through' and he talked to financial authorities in three countries about the problem.[109]

Two banks, Citibank and Samuel Montagu, led the consortium of major lenders that effectively saved Murdoch, and in the end also rescued their investments, with what they called a Debt Override Plan. Nevertheless there were still a couple of months of uncertainty, until all the banks signed on – 'the domino effect of even one tiny default ... would trigger cross defaults which would overwhelm the group'. The leading banks enforced two lines: 'We are where we are' and 'Nobody gets out.'[110] By 10 January 1991, the most important 27 banks had signed an agreement running to more than 300 pages. There was to be an extra bridging loan of $600 million; an upfront fee of 1 per cent of the amount outstanding; interest rates were to be raised by one percentage point; and News had to reduce its debts by $2 billion over the next two and a half years.[111]

Murdoch was now on a firmer leash than ever before. For example, in November 1991 it was reported that News Corp would 'need to raise about US$1 billion (a year) for the next nine years to keep up with its revised schedule of loan repayments'.[112] Nevertheless, within 28 months, he had replaced all the earlier debt with long-term debt and some capital raisings,[113] and had disposed of some assets. However, whereas in 1990 the Murdoch family effectively owned 46 per cent of the shares, by 1993 their share was closer to 33 per cent.[114]

The Debt Override Plan had given Murdoch certainty, and he had survived. He had, said Canadian newspaper publisher Conrad Black in a description which Murdoch liked, bet the company and won,[115] even if that victory had ultimately been delivered by his bankers.

1990s – Positioning in a global, multi-channel television industry

In 1990, the dominant mode of receiving television in most countries was via an analog, terrestrial signal, which meant there was relatively limited spectrum available. By 2000, the dominant modes were digital, and via cable or satellite. The multi-channel environment, the growth of subscription television, and much more crossing of national borders, either directly by satellite, or through international trade in programs, all marked substantial differences between the beginning and the end of the decade. By 2000, Hollywood made more than half its movie earnings from international sales.[116] For Murdoch, the key challenge of the 1990s revolved around satellite and subscription television. This is the only area where Murdoch was in the vanguard. He had been interested in the potential of satellites since the early 1980s. Although the reality never matched his probably impossible ambitions, by the end of the decade Murdoch's first-mover advantage had added considerably to his empire.

None of Murdoch's early satellite investments – in South America, the US or the European one that he was enthusing about to Bob Hawke over dinner – became substantial or profitable operations: 'As with other Murdoch ventures, enthusiasm and ambition ran ahead of the product.'[117] He took a higher risk and made a more determined commitment in 1988 with Sky, to operate on the Astra satellite from Luxembourg. He gave up his hopes of pan-European profitability, recognising that people want to be entertained in their native language, and focused his efforts on Britain.

In June 1988 in London he announced his intention to launch a four-channel service in grand terms: 'We are witnessing the dawn of an age of freedom for viewing and freedom for advertising.'[118] As discussed in Chapter 9, this brought him into direct conflict with British Satellite Broadcasting, which in December 1986 had won a heavily contested tender to become the country's first – and, it expected, only – satellite broadcaster.[119] Both companies bled money at an amazing rate. According to Chenoweth, News spent around £550 million on the venture and the BSB syndicate spent around £850 million.[120] In November 1990, the two companies merged. Both desperately needed the merger, but if the BSB partners had learnt of News's debt crisis, they may have been tempted to make fewer concessions, or even not do the deal at all.[121]

No cash changed hands, and in theory the merger was on equal terms. But several aspects favoured Sky. The merged operation used the Astra satellite. Moreover, the CEO was Sky's, New Zealander Sam Chisholm. Over the next several months, as he folded two loss-making organisations into one leaner operation, the casualty toll may have been as high as 3000 employees.[122] The post-merger civil war soon had a clear victor: 'Initially Sky occupied 17 out of the top 30 positions. Within a short time they occupied all but one.'[123]

Another lasting advantage to News was that encryption was to be performed by the company NDS, of which News was a part owner. The film companies had refused to supply their programming to a satellite service unless the signal was encrypted. NDS had solved these problems for Murdoch, and a close association developed, despite one of its key figures being a fraudster, and the Israeli-based company having its own turbulent internal life.[124] Decades later the company became the focus of charges that it had acted as a pirate outfit against Murdoch's competitors.[125]

The big turning point occurred in 1992, when BSkyB secured exclusive rights to televise the English Premier League. Viewers now needed to subscribe to watch football live, and they did so in their hundreds of thousands. 'By 1996, BSkyB's grip on pay TV in Britain had become unshakable. It was Britain's third largest media business, bigger than many film studios.'[126] BSkyB saw further enormous growth late in the decade when it gave away digital set-top boxes for free,[127] turning the technical change into a marketing triumph.

BSkyB was to be the forerunner of other delivery platforms and control of programming around the world, but Murdoch's global ambitions have met with only mixed success. He has been active in South America, while in Australia – amid the chaotic policy making on pay TV[128] – he has stayed close to the incumbent telecommunications carrier Telstra, succeeding in the end by creating a Foxtel monopoly.

Murdoch's biggest and most important such venture was in Asia. In 1993 he bought almost two-thirds of the Star satellite, for over $500 million. This was by far his biggest deal since the rescue by the banks, which is perhaps why he sold the very profitable Hong Kong newspaper, the *South China Morning Post*, to pay for it.[129] The Hong Kong-based service had been started by Richard Li in 1990. According to William Shawcross, 'the footprint of Star's satellites covered all Asia and the Middle East ... about three billion people'.[130] Its audience was much less impressive than its footprint. Of its five channels, four were in English, and probably only a couple of per cent of people within its reach had English as a first language. The service was also of limited appeal to advertisers, who had only the sketchiest data on who was watching. In 1996 Star lost $100 million,[131] but in 2005 it reported a profit 'well over $100 million', with 70 per cent of its revenues coming from India.[132] Star was helped greatly by the coming of digitisation, which meant that the number of channels expanded enormously: 'By 2000, it comprised 30 broadcast services in seven languages potentially reaching 300 million viewers in 53 Asian countries.'[133] In 2012 it broadcast 60 services in 13 languages, and claimed a daily audience of 120 million viewers.[134] However, Murdoch never realised the dream he pursued with such vigour: to penetrate the Chinese domestic market via Star.

Although the 1990s began with Murdoch in such deep debt that his corporate survival was partly a matter of luck, he not only consolidated his spectacular 1980s expansion, but with a combination of first-mover advantages, promising long-term strategy and a willingness to sustain short-term losses, he had navigated his way into the more global and multi-channel TV environment as well as anyone. Typically, his almost infinite ambitions had not been realised, and he had some important setbacks and failures. However, in News Corp's annual report for 1997 he could accurately proclaim that 'no company in the world can match News Corporation in its ability to maximize its own product across multiple distribution platforms around the world'.[135]

American fireworks 1997–2003

On 24 February 1997 Murdoch started a fight with the US cable operators, proclaiming satellite the way of the future. Next day, 'investors dumped cable stocks in droves, ... wiping out more than $1 billion in market value for the cable TV market'.[136] This declaration of war, a war that Murdoch lost, had two sources. First, Murdoch saw an American satellite TV service as a key to his global satellite plans and corporate development. Only the American market offered the economies of scale that would allow him to undertake huge global enterprises. The second source was his launching of Fox News the previous year.

Murdoch knew that the only way for Fox News to succeed was to get sufficient carriage on the cable systems around the country, most particularly on the Time Warner system in New York. Normally cable operators paid a small fee per subscriber to channels they featured,[137] but very occasionally payment went in the other direction. The most that any new channel had thus far offered a cable company for carriage had been $1.20 for every subscriber. Murdoch offered an unprecedented $11 per subscriber to carry his new channel. Murdoch had shaken hands with Time Warner chairman Gerald Levin on a deal to carry Fox News, but after Ted Turner protested, Levin reneged. Murdoch responded in style. In

October 1996 News Corp launched a $2 billion law suit against Time Warner. New York Mayor Rudy Giuliani leapt into action on Fox's behalf. The conflict also brought on a spectacular slanging match between Murdoch and Turner, which raged for years. Turner likened Murdoch to Hitler, called him slimy and a disgrace to journalism, and promised to squish him 'like a bug'. Murdoch's *New York Post* headline asked readers 'Is Ted Turner nuts? – You decide', and said he must have gone off his lithium.[138] Eventually Time Warner carried Fox.

In February 1997, when he announced that cable was a declining platform and the future was satellite, Murdoch thought he was speaking from a position of strength, about to conclude a deal with Charlie Ergen and EchoStar. Murdoch's view reflected his own immediate position, and his long-term preference for satellite over cable. But it probably had particular validity at that time in the US, as cable had developed there earlier than in most countries, and its many local monopolies still relied on old analog systems whose capacity was much less than the latest digital technologies could provide. The 'Cable King' John Malone, for example, in his local monopolies, had 'spent as little money as possible upgrading his cable systems'.[139]

All this was occurring in a corporate environment marked by unprecedented mergers, as large corporations sought synergies in the more global and digital era. These media behemoths, or mega-media corporations, seemed to be the only way to thrive, perhaps even to survive, in the future, and leading players in previously distinct industries – film, television, cable, telecommunications, manufacturing, computing – came together: 'It was as if no single company wanted to be left without a partner in this new and uncertain age.'[140] All three of the main US networks entered into merged entities: ABC Disney; NBC Universal; CBS Viacom.[141] The biggest of them all came on 10 January 2000 when 'AOL paid a stunning $165 billion to buy Time Warner', 'the largest merger in history and the most striking testament to the influence – and inflated values – of the internet'.[142]

For News Corp this was a period of 'almosts' – they almost joined with MCI; they almost joined with EchoStar; they almost joined with General Motors (GM) and Hughes Electronics; they almost joined with Microsoft.

The single most important attempted partnership was with GM and its subsidiary Hughes Electronics, to gain control of the DirecTV satellite service. In 2000, GM announced its intention to divest itself of its satellite business, and on 6 February 2001, Murdoch thought he had an agreement:[143] 'The Sky Global/DirecTV combination represented Murdoch's bid to create the largest global media platform of all time.'[144] This deal took, he said, 'the first 90 per cent of the [weekly] meeting time' of his top executives,[145] and until the last moment he was confident it would happen.[146] It failed largely because his potential partners were deterred by Murdoch's approach:

> News Corp has one of the most aggressive corporate cultures in
> the world. For five decades Murdoch had run News as a one-man
> show. In that time he had never had a successful partnership ...
> The News execs had been bagging their opposite numbers at
> Hughes for weeks. Hughes expected a partnership. What they
> got was a boarding party.[147]

In October 2001, when GM sold DirecTV to EchoStar, it looked as if Murdoch had been locked out of the US satellite market.[148] But after this deal was shot down by the Federal Communications Commission (FCC) on anti-monopoly grounds,[149] Murdoch was finally able to realise his ambition. Other potential buyers having disappeared, Murdoch became the largest shareholder in DirecTV at a much reduced price in April 2003. He was rhapsodic:

the benefits will be felt almost immediately – in the competition it will offer cable, [and] the richer services it will provide to American viewers … We are forging what we believe will be the premier diversified entertainment company in America today … [The] completion of the DirecTV transaction will mark the culmination of a long-time pursuit by our company of providing the missing link in a global satellite television platform that will span four continents and encompass 23 million subscribers.[150]

While the satellite ventures grabbed the most attention, Murdoch had also laid the foundations for what would continue to be a growth area for his empire – the development of specialist channels. While Fox News has probably generated most controversy, for its rabidly pro-Republican bias, it has also become a major profit centre, the single most important driver of the substantial growth in News Corp's income from cable networks.[151] With the sporting rights he already owned, Murdoch was well placed to set up a sporting network, and Fox Sports has become one of the two biggest sportscasters globally. Other specialist channels followed – National Geographic, Fox Family Channel – as well as movie and entertainment channels. These are now large contributors to News Corp profits.

Empire in transition – the 2000s

In the last two decades of the 20th century, News Corp grew spectacularly. Its assets increased from $1 billion in 1980 to $20 billion in 1990 and to $38 billion by 2000 – one of the most dramatic corporate expansions in media history. In the 21st century this rate of growth slowed, but was still substantial, to $54 billion by 2010.[152] Similarly, the structural trends inside News Corp have been towards incremental change, rather than revolutionary upheaval, as had been the case in previous decades. The relative share of newspapers and magazines in News Corp's operating income declined steadily from 90 per cent in 1980 to 71 per cent in 1990, to 45 per cent in 2000 and to only 11 per cent in 2010.[153] According to the *Financial Times*, broadcast television was only 1 per cent in 1990, shot up to 39 per cent by 2000 and then shrank back down to 5 per cent in 2010. Films have become ever more important, from around 8 per cent in 2000 up to 29 per cent in 2010, although the share of films shows more year-to-year volatility.[154] The main growth area has been in cable networks, which on the *FT*'s figures grew from 4 per cent in 2000 to 48 per cent in 2010.

News Corp – at least since the end of Murdoch's US satellite wars – has been a more orthodox large corporation. It has shown greater financial caution. It was so relatively cashed up that in 2011–12 it carried out one $5 billion buyback of shares, and then announced another.[155]

While its overall business performance has been solid, there are three areas where Murdoch either retreated from his driving ambitions or where new ventures failed (all explored at length in Chapter 4).

From 1993, Murdoch invested a lot of money and effort in China, not only via Star, but in a whole series of enterprises. He assiduously wooed key figures in the Chinese Government. But at a media conference in New York on 16 September 2005, he admitted that News Corp had 'hit a brick wall in China'. The trend towards opening up had gone into reverse, he said, with the authorities now 'quite paranoid about what gets through'.[156] The next two years saw News selling off or greatly reducing its stake in its Chinese properties. The world's most powerful media mogul's time in China appeared to have 'come and gone'.[157]

The second retreat was at least as great. After striving for almost a decade to gain DirecTV, within three and a half years he surrendered the great prize. The central reason for this reversal lay in the consequences of another key move Murdoch had made. In

April 2004, Murdoch announced that he wanted to change the domicile of the company from Adelaide to Delaware. Senior executives thought that relocating the main company from the Australian stock exchange to the NASDAQ was logical because the bulk of the company's activity was in the US and the move might help raise the price of News Corp shares.[158] There were some protests in Australia, as it was felt that Delaware's less stringent regulatory requirements offered fewer protections to shareholders, but in October 2004 Australian shareholders approved the move.[159] One complication was that once the company was listed on the US S&P 500, making it more possible for US index fund investors to buy, it would be delisted from the S&P ASX 200. This would cause many Australian fund managers to sell their holdings. This created a price dip, as Australian institutions sold out in a rush before US institutions bought in. John Malone seized the moment. By November 2004 he had 19 per cent of the voting shares, second only to the Murdoch family's 30 per cent.[160]

In order to remove Malone from News Corp's share register, Murdoch sold him DirecTV.[161] Elsewhere, News Corp continued to see satellite as central to its strategy. It kept developing Star in Asia. In Australia in 2012, Foxtel became a 50/50 split between News and Telstra when News bought out the quarter share owned by James Packer's company. It also made a de facto national monopoly official when it bought out Austar – with which it had amicably split territories and programming agreements for some years.[162] In Britain, it sought to raise its stake from 38 per cent to 100 per cent ownership of BSkyB, which, in dollar terms, would have been the single biggest transaction in its corporate history. However, it was thwarted by the phone hacking scandal. In contrast, in order to remove what he saw as the continuing threat of Malone, Murdoch gave up his US satellite ambitions.

Murdoch's third failure – an area in which he was far from alone – was in the internet, the great force transforming media businesses in this period. News Corp, like all other media companies, is still strenuously devoting its energies to the challenges of the internet, its revolutionising of consumers' media habits and its threat to intellectual property values. But on the way it made some bad investments, most obviously MySpace, which it bought for $580 million in 2005 and sold for $35 million in 2011.[163]

Murdoch's last big acquisition of the period was of Dow Jones and the *Wall St Journal* in 2007. He offered $60 a share, a 67 per cent premium on Dow Jones's share price.[164] After three months of agonising, the Bancroft family, owners of the *Journal* over the last century, sold it to him for a total of $5.83 billion. Although this gave Murdoch the most authoritative financial newspaper in America, and so perhaps helped him position for business journalism more generally, the decision made little business sense. Less than two years later, News Corp wrote down its value by more than half, to $2.8 billion.[165]

So, while the 21st century has not been a period of dramatic new acquisitions and radical growth for News Corp, Murdoch's huge and complicated media empire continued to expand incrementally. By 2013 – excluding services that operate only on a regional basis, such as those in Asia and Latin America – News had operations in more than 20 countries. Its most important markets, since its retreat from China, were in the US, Britain and Australia, but it also had operations in Italy, Germany, in around 10 East European countries, in Papua New Guinea and Fiji.

For decades some analysts had seen weakness, not strength, in News Corp's diversity, thought the whole lacked coherence and argued that without Rupert's energy holding it together, News Corp would not survive.[166] In the mid-1990s, finance journalist Kevin Maney put this view strongly: 'There is only one true global media baron. Too bad his company could be destined for oblivion.' When Murdoch 'is no longer there, the company will most likely be no longer there either'. It was difficult to predict what would happen to this 'worldwide media hodgepodge' when it is 'Murdoch-less'.[167]

Since the 2013 split in the company, these questions have been more often asked about the publishing company, News Corp, rather than the entertainment company, Twenty-First Century Fox. In an era of rapid change, no forecasts about the future of media companies can be made with any certainty, although the two companies are probably as well placed as any of their competitors to meet the coming business challenges. Whatever the future, the six-decade journey from a single afternoon newspaper in Adelaide to a global multi-media power is one of the most remarkable in corporate history. In the process, one individual, starting with a modest inheritance in 1953, achieved a net worth of $11.2 billion by 2013, to become the 91st ranked billionaire on the planet.[168]

3

Midas of the media
Murdoch's business strategy

Murdoch was depressed when his parents 'ordered him off to Oxford'.[1] He had assumed he would follow his father into the Australian newspaper business, although he had not yet developed strong ambitions to do so. He was enrolled in philosophy, politics and economics, but his real focus of study was tabloid newspapers. After graduating, he spent some months subediting on the *Daily Express*, under chief sub Ted Pickering, whom he later praised as 'my first great mentor'. His months in what he called Beaverbrook's brothel left him with 'an abiding admiration for the craft of the London subeditor'.[2] By the time Murdoch left England in 1953 he had developed strong ambitions – he wanted to be a publisher of tabloid newspapers, to return to Fleet Street, and one day to own the *Daily Mirror*, then at the peak of its powers.

He spent the next decade and a half developing his Australian empire, and learning all aspects of the newspaper business. He loved the subediting side, and would spend Saturday ripping apart his Perth *Sunday Times*, reorganising it, and 'ordering stories to be rewritten with more urgency, color, and exaggeration; thinking up sensational, blaring headlines; cleaning up the paper's layout and dirtying its tone'.[3] Then, through the 1960s, he honed his skills in Sydney, one of the few cities in the English-speaking world to have competing afternoon newspapers. It was not only news presentation, however, that interested him; it was the marketing and production aspects as well. When he returned to Fleet Street and the *News of the World*, the printers told him it 'was impossible to print a tabloid on presses configured for a broadsheet, [but] he dumb-founded them by showing how it could be done'.[4]

Murdoch was ready – and the situation was propitious – for his first and most important success, the one on which his future scope for expansion rested. The London *Sun*, which he acquired in 1969, became 'the single largest source of Murdoch's publishing profits and the pillar of his capacity to borrow money'.[5] As author Piers Brendon noted, 'Murdoch loved the *Sun*, which tripled its circulation [to 3 million] within four years and in 1978 overtook the *Mirror*.'[6] Ever since, it has been Britain's top-selling newspaper.[7]

'Murdoch knew precisely what kind of paper he wanted the *Sun* to be.'[8] It was aimed at what he saw as the gap that had opened in the market because the *Mirror* 'was getting above its readers, trying to push them up-market against their will'. He would provide 'a tabloid modeled on the *Mirror* of the 1940s and 1950s, before it had become seized by ideas above its station',[9] had become 'preachy and teachy', bogged down by liberal earnestness,[10] gentrified.[11] He was determined not to have 'any of that up-market shit in my paper'.[12]

The formula by which Murdoch and his first editor Larry Lamb pursued this has become famous. The most notorious ingredient was the emphasis on sex; in particular the regular topless page 3 girl, who first appeared on the paper's first anniversary, in November 1970.[13] The paper looked for any opportunity to be risqué, such as having pussy week, which was about cats:

> The *Sun* was saucy, even naughty, but it was all good clean fun.
> The sex material was informative and amusing and, unlike porn,
> was not designed to induce the 'leer and the snigger'.[14]

The slogan was 'make it breezy, not sleazy'.[15] When Roy Greenslade, a subeditor on the paper, re-read the files decades later, he found a 'relentless use of sex':[16]

> There was a sexy book of some kind serialized every week, such
> as *The Sensuous Woman*. The women's department, Pacesetters,
> churned out endless features on the theme of how to have better
> sex lives.[17]

There was a radical change in news priorities, with traditional
notions of news being downgraded, and areas Murdoch and Lamb
believed were of greatest audience appeal highlighted. In 1968,
coverage of sport and show business made up 33 per cent of the
Sun's editorial space, but 30 years later that proportion had nearly
doubled, to 63 per cent.[18] (For the *Mirror* the corresponding per-
centages were 31 and 52.) While sport and crime had long been
staples of tabloid journalism, the new ingredients were celebrity
and television. In Piers Brendon's view:

> The tabloid dealt in fantasy as much as fact, especially when
> conjuring up melodramas about the lives of the stars of television
> soap operas. But, Murdoch made the *Sun* snappy, pithy, sexy. He
> got what he wanted, a 'tear-away paper with a lot of tit'.[19]

In Lamb's view, the readers would get the headlines and basic facts
from the television and 'look in their *Sun* for entertaining gossip'.[20]
This was also a mantra of Murdoch at this time: because of television, newspapers were more and more about entertainment.[21] This
allowed them to invest much less in journalists than their competitors. As authors Peter Chippindale and Chris Horrie note, 'With
only 100 hacks, the new *Sun* was ludicrously lightly staffed compared to papers like the *Express* and the *Mirror*, which had more than
400.'[22] As well as employing fewer reporters, Murdoch has always
been notoriously stingy with news-gathering expenses. John Lisners
remembered 'Rupert's penny pinching ways' on the Adelaide *News*:

'Go nowhere. Cover everywhere. Pay nothing.'[23] He was able to do this because there was over-staffing at other papers, and because he took reporting responsibilities less seriously than they did. He also economised on accommodation: the staff of the *Sun* was squeezed into the *News of the World's* Bouverie Street premises.[24]

While Murdoch was frugal with many expenses, he increased the expenditure on promotion and marketing enormously. Indeed the *Sun* was a pioneer in advertising newspapers on television. This was already a common practice in Australia, but was still virtually unknown in Britain, and Murdoch's big investment in marketing brought large circulation gains.[25]

Beyond this, however, the *Sun* connected with its readers. Its humour and cheekiness were a large part of its appeal,[26] and the paper was good at self-promotion. When a library in Sowerby Bridge decided not to have the *Sun* on display any more, the paper played it up. It offered to pay for new library rods and provide free copies. It also put on a competition where first prize was a free weekend in Sowerby Bridge, and second prize was a whole week.[27] When an article in the *Financial Times* about the paper's circulation success referred to the Soaraway *Sun*, the paper adopted it as its marketing slogan.[28]

According to writer Michael Wolff:

> The *Sun*, with profit margins as high as 60 or 70 per cent, [became] the most significant part of his business and [remained] so for nearly 20 years … the *Sun's* success has transformed even Murdoch's idea of the tabloid. He feels he has found the secret.[29]

It is a secret that did not travel as well as he hoped. In particular, he was unable to repeat his British success in America. He did increase circulation in some of his papers, when he substantially increased their promotional budgets. American newspapers derive an even higher proportion of their income from advertising than do British tabloids, but his down-market approach was less attractive to advertisers. At one stage the *New York Post*, for example, had 20 per cent of newspaper sales in New York, but only 7 per cent of the advertising. There is a famous but probably apocryphal story that when Murdoch tried to get Bloomingdales to increase its advertising, an executive replied, 'But Rupert, your readers are our shoplifters.'[30]

Indeed sometimes the Murdoch formula was counter-productive. When he bought *TV Guide*, he thought the magazine's mid-market journalism was 'far too cerebral',[31] and took it down-market. During the 10 years that News Corp owned it, circulation fell from over 17 million to below 13 million.[32] Nevertheless, the rise of Murdoch's *Sun* is perhaps the most stunning business success in the history of English-language newspapers in the last several generations.

There is no doubt that Murdoch had a special feeling for tabloid newspapers, and enjoyed being part of them: 'The energy you feel in a good newsroom comes from speed, good reflexes, and that highest Murdoch standard, a lack of pretense.'[33] Today, as newspapers are under such threat from the internet, Murdoch is seen by many as their champion.

It would be wrong to over-romanticise this, however. His liking for newspapers has always co-existed with an ambivalent attitude to journalists; indeed his career has been peppered with frequent expressions of dislike – 'I despise all journalists';[34] 'You know what journos are like, particularly journos overseas. They're bone idle.'[35] When he was told that a *News of the World* journalist had dropped dead, Murdoch is said to have responded, 'Well, it wasn't from overwork.'[36]

To use the journalistic cliché, Murdoch may have ink in his veins, but it should be stressed that it is subeditors' rather than reporters' ink. He has consistently under-invested in reporting. Just as the *Sun* employed far fewer journalists than its competitors, Murdoch's Sky News was similarly lean. In 1989 it broadcast 14.5 hours a day with a staff of 260 and a budget of £30 million, while ITN did 6 hours of news each day with a staff of 930 and a budget of £64 million.[37] His Fox News Channel, for example, employed fewer than half the journalists than did its rival, CNN. At the time of the Iraq War, for example, Fox News had 6 overseas bureaux and CNN had 31. Where Fox News had 1250 employees, CNN had 4000.[38]

While competition can be a constructive force, it also generates destructive emotions, exemplified by some of the sentiments expressed by Murdoch and his employees. From the mid-1990s onwards, the *News of the World* newsroom 'was extreme, even by Murdoch's standards', as he exhorted them to 'smash its closest competitors, the *People* and the *Sunday Mirror*'.[39] Former *Sun* editor Kelvin MacKenzie said that what he likes about his *Daily Mail* rival Paul Dacre is that 'each day he arrives at work determined to crush the life out of his rivals'.[40] In a 2007 visit to Melbourne, Murdoch complained that the *Sunday Herald Sun*, which was selling around 600,000, 'should be selling a million by now'.[41] When his executives said Melbourne could be a one-newspaper town in five years, Murdoch replied through gritted teeth, 'That has to be our goal.'[42]

Television, movies and sport – just other businesses

As Murdoch moved into television, he took similar approaches. He had thrived in situations of circumscribed competition, where inefficient, financially self-indulgent practices had developed, where there was thus scope for cutting costs, and where, at least in his eyes, the competitors' product had lost touch with its audience. This was the case not only with his greatest success, the *Sun*, but with his assault on the three-network system in US television. In both cases he had the advantages of an outsider. He was not a prisoner of the past, inhibited by ingrained assumptions which prevented established competitors from seeing alternatives. In both cases he was able to introduce cheaper and more audience-oriented products.

Many people directly involved in media are focused primarily on the intrinsic merits of the content – they want to make a great movie or TV program or produce great news reporting. Many of Murdoch's contemporaries at Oxford were interested in journalism, but most were probably interested in reporting and writing, and in quality papers. Murdoch, by contrast, was most interested in tabloids, and in production and presentation, in what made a paper attractive to an audience. His interest in film and television programs was similar: less in the intrinsic merits of what was on the screen and more in the total value chain and how it would appeal to an audience. 'Murdoch's idea of a successful TV businessman was his friend, the cable king, John Malone. Malone understood that the real media business was about distribution, leverage, monopoly.'[43]

Murdoch was always on the search for the consumer tipping points – what will be the critical factor that will make affiliated television stations change their network allegiance? What will entice consumers to subscribe to a pay television service? During the 1990s, his answer was sport. In 1992, as noted in Chapter 2, BSkyB won the rights to English Premier League, outlaying 'what then seemed the astronomical sum of £304 million'. It was Sam Chisholm's decision, and many had doubts, but within weeks BSkyB had signed up one million new subscribers.[44] It went from a £47 million loss in 1992 to a £62 million profit in 1993.[45]

The next year brought the single most important turning point for Fox TV, as it outbid CBS for the rights to American football, the NFL.[46] 'The NFL deal validated Fox' and enabled it to win a wide range of other sports broadcasting rights.[47] In October 1996 Murdoch told shareholders at the News Corp annual meeting: 'We intend to ... use sports as a battering ram and a lead offering in all our pay-television operations.'[48] 'Sports programming commands unparalleled viewer loyalty in all markets,' he said.[49] By 1997, the company was paying more than $1 billion a year for sporting rights.[50] Murdoch's approach to sport was simple – you need to have what the audience wants, and then you monopolise it.[51]

Of course, not all of these paid off so dramatically, and as competitors caught up the cost of the 'battering rams' escalated greatly, so that in 2002, News Corp's chief operating officer, Peter Chernin, admitted that they had 'clearly ... overpaid' for sporting contracts that year.[52] Murdoch had produced a massive 'redistribution of wealth from media groups to professional sports',[53] and in the process, television income had become central to sports budgets.[54]

In his review of the rise of live sports broadcasting, Michael R. Real says the two most influential figures were Roone Arledge and Rupert Murdoch.[55] Their contributions could hardly have been more different. Arledge, the head of sports broadcasting at the American ABC network, was intent on bringing the drama, struggle and human emotion of sport to TV viewers, and pioneered, for example, the instant replay. Murdoch's interest was because 'sports had the greatest marketing power'.[56]

Just as 'Murdoch may be the first person to come to Hollywood who has no interest in the movies or stars or show business itself',[57] so he is also, among people centrally involved in the sports-media complex, the one least interested in sport. The adolescent who hated organised sport, the adult who disliked being a spectator, let alone a participant,[58] except when he was betting at horse races, had become the media businessman who saw sport as an unparalleled commercial opportunity. When he bought the Los Angeles Dodgers baseball team in 1998 (sold 5 years later without great on-field success),[59] it was reported that 'he had never been to a game of baseball'.[60] Nor does he take a great interest in the other sports he is involved in. When he visited the News Corp-owned rugby league team, the Melbourne Storm, he asked coach Craig Bellamy whether the coach was allowed to talk to the players at half-time, perhaps thinking it had rules like rugby union had had in his youth, when such interaction was not allowed.

Murdoch's lack of interest in a product has sometimes led to miscalculations. News Limited in Australia did great damage to both its finances and its reputation with its attempt to go outside the established rugby league competition and start its own 'Super League'. The attempt cost it at least $500 million in the short term. In the long term it led to Murdoch having to share Fox Sports with Packer, another major financial penalty.

When News Limited became co-owner of the new, merged competition, its lack of appreciation of the traditions and emotional attachments led it into new blunders. It excluded the South Sydney Rabbitohs, who had won 20 premierships but struggled in recent seasons. The result was a series of legal cases, eventually won by the Rabbitohs. The club had a march of support, which the *Financial Review* estimated involved 80,000 fans, at the time the biggest demonstration in Sydney since the end of the Vietnam War. Murdoch's *Daily Telegraph* added its own insult by reporting the march on page 65.[61] The belief that supporters' loyalties and emotions can be easily overridden and redirected shows a degree of contempt, as well as a lack of interest and knowledge.

A unique mix of temperament and skills

Murdoch told his biographer, Tom Kiernan, that from the beginning he knew that 'newspapering was like any other business: Expand or perish!'[62] A policy of expansion may seem a commonplace of business strategy, but Murdoch's appetite for expansion seemed infinite. Each achievement was but the forerunner to the next: at a party celebrating the first anniversary of the London *Sun*, he amazed Roy Greenslade, then a subeditor on the paper, by asking, 'Where should I expand next?'[63] 'The guy is just ... insatiable,' exclaimed Clay Felker, the former publisher of *New York* magazine, still angry more than a decade after being one of Murdoch's victims.[64] One of Murdoch's competitors, Lord Stevens of Express Newspapers, thinks, 'He's got the appetite of a snake. He'll swallow a sheep if it's passing.'[65] To an anonymous admirer, 'trying to stop him being predatory is like trying to turn a vulture into a vegetarian'.[66]

Murdoch is unusually impervious to the personal vanities and status rewards that so many other media moguls value. He is not interested in recognition by what he calls the Establishment. It is unthinkable that he would have done what Conrad Black did – reorganise his empire in order to become a member of the House of Lords. In Wolff's view, Murdoch:

> has no interests outside his work: not sport (he may be the only Australian man not interested in sports), not culture, not reading, not movies. He has no social aspirations either. Money itself isn't even that compelling to him. He's eerie, or scary, in his lack of lifestyle desires and need for approval … His penuriousness, his aversion to pretense, his disdain for grandness or affectation or – his worst, most damning word – elitism, is the DNA of his company.[67]

For Wolff, this gives him a clarity of focus and perception in business:

> Most, perhaps all, of the entrepreneurs attracted to Britain and rising in it are looking for a broader kind of approval – they have major social aspirations – whereas Murdoch is only market driven … Britain is something to take advantage of, not to be a part of.[68]

Similarly, 'It's seldom happened, perhaps never happened, that Hollywood, with its charms and blandishments, fails to seduce (usually fleece and seduce)',[69] but Murdoch has remained immune.

However else he is remembered, Murdoch will always be known as a deal-maker extraordinaire. Some of the most celebrated of today's entrepreneurs have built their corporations around one or a few major innovations, such as Bill Gates at Microsoft and Steve Jobs at Apple. Murdoch has overwhelmingly grown his empire through acquisitions.

Deal making fits Murdoch's strengths and temperament. He loves the game; the thrill of the chase; the buzz of the deal. On topics he is interested in, Murdoch is an information sponge, willing to listen to the advice of anyone. He is also a lover of gossip. His 'intelligence service is the best in Fleet Street';[70] he 'would talk to anybody who had a good piece of information for him;'[71] 'Murdoch without a telephone was like an alcoholic without a drink';[72] 'Murdoch, a reluctant socializer, is a brilliant networker. He's one of the early geniuses of the form.'[73] Wolff found, during many months of interviewing Murdoch, that:

> the most reliable way to hold his interest was to bring him a rich nugget. His entire demeanor would change. He'd instantly light up. He'd go from distracted to absolutely focused.[74]

He not only scans the business horizon for opportunities, but for information about the vulnerabilities of his competitors and potential targets: 'Assessing his competitors is the one place where Murdoch is systematically analytical rather than reflexive and instinctive. He loves to analyse other people's weaknesses.'[75]

In Murdoch's first big deal in Britain, the purchase of the *News of the World*, a bitter Robert Maxwell correctly observed that Murdoch had caught 'a big fish with a very small hook'.[76] Murdoch manoeuvred brilliantly, first to join with Carr to see off Maxwell, then to dispose of Carr. Similarly, he was able to purchase the *Sun* at a bargain price because he saw and exploited the impossible situation that Cudlipp's IPC was in, committed to a paper that could only be a drain on their finances. Murdoch had a possible course of action – to compete with their major title, the *Daily Mirror* – that was not available to them.

Wolff observed that one of Murdoch's strengths as a deal-maker is 'the courtship'. 'Whereas other businessmen run the numbers, Murdoch deals with personalities.'[77] This was particularly the case with his purchase of *New York* magazine. When Felker offered Murdoch a stake, Murdoch immediately guessed that Felker would be doing the same to others, and thus that the company was in play. Murdoch prevailed though his decisiveness and through his money, but in addition:

> The striking thing is not the disputatiousness, irascibility and egocentricity of the *New York* magazine board – although, even for a media company board, it is rather extreme – but that Murdoch is able to corral and manage them.[78]

This points to another of his less obvious deal-making strengths. Takeover situations are often charged with high personal drama. Murdoch has been able:

> to deal with, and prevail in, highly personal, profoundly emotional transactions in which the stakes are not just financial but deeply related to ego, turf, and family. This impatient man has an extraordinary tolerance for the ambivalence of non-rational players – and a keen eye for their weaknesses.[79]

Of course Murdoch prevailed in many deal-making situations simply by being the highest bidder. This was sometimes the result of his competitiveness and his gambler's love of the adrenalin of risk. But equally, he had a keen grasp of what was the main game and what merely a sideshow, of what would bring value in the long run. At his best and most visionary, this means that Murdoch has seen potential that others haven't, has seen how what seems an isolated transaction fits into his larger jigsaw. So, by most accounts, News:

had overpaid for Star TV, but did so because Murdoch was convinced he had at least a two-year head start over his rivals, who would have to wait until new satellites were launched before they could begin broadcasting.[80]

Similarly, he was willing to pay a 'transformation premium' in 1985 for Kluge's six television stations[81] because they were all in major markets and could be the foundation for a fourth network. When he was acquiring Twentieth Century Fox, he was buying not just a movie studio, but a film library and production facilities that would aid his television ambitions.

On the other hand, it is easy to exaggerate how strategic Murdoch's actions are. He once claimed:

> A lot of people claim they have ten-year plans or five-year plans or something. But basically, the most successful businesses are opportunistic and you take your opportunities when they come.[82]

Murdoch has often had the capacity to move more quickly than his competitors,[83] making decisions aided only by a small team of advisers. This is a testament to his ability to hold all the key factors in his head, but also to a governance structure where all power is vested in him. When News Corp and Pearson were both interested in acquiring Star TV, the Pearson negotiators needed time to consult their board, but Murdoch made the deal to purchase 64 per cent for US$525 million 'in a matter of hours. Murdoch didn't bother to inform his own board until later that the deal had been done.'[84]

As well as an unerring eye for the weaknesses of his adversaries, and for what will clinch a battle, he also has a keen grasp of the locus of control; of when he moves from being supplicant to supremo. Then he displays an unashamed willingness to use that control as he wishes, unencumbered by any promises he has previously made. During negotiations he distinguishes clearly between what can and what cannot be enforced later, what has lasting importance and what has only temporary nuisance value. Although he has often been angered by journalists protesting at the prospect of his takeover, he has also known that such protests are not usually going to affect either the outcome or the long-term viability of the acquisition.

Deal-making involves a particular set of skills: early and accurate intelligence; clarity of perception and priorities; suppleness in negotiations across both material details and the emotional, non-material aspects of the deal; and decisiveness. Finally, it involves a clear perception of what counts now and what counts next, not what used to count. As Murdoch advised one of his Fox executives after a show was cancelled, 'cut your losses, and don't look back'.[85]

Beyond his skill at the transactions themselves, what distinguishes Murdoch's decisions and deals is his willingness to take on risks that most businesses and individuals would shrink from. He has often described himself as a gambler.[86] Others have talked of 'his addiction to risk'.[87] It is easy in retrospect to underplay what radical leaps into the unknown some of his decisions have represented. Partly, of course, this was because of the sums of money involved – some of these ventures could have sunk his whole empire. In other cases it involved a step into the unknown: most obviously with his satellite ventures in Britain and Asia. Sometimes it involved taking on seemingly all-powerful opponents or breaking a long-established mould.[88]

Sometimes what seems obvious in retrospect was very uncertain at the time. The moment was ripe for embattled British newspapers to confront the industrial problems that were costing them so much money, but Murdoch alone 'possessed the resources and ruthlessness – or as admirers said, "the guts and tenacity" – to spearhead a revolution of inestimable benefit to the newspaper industry'.[89] And if things had gone wrong in Murdoch's move to Wapping, at the very least it would have severely damaged his cash flow at a critical period.

As important as his willingness to take large risks has been his 'sometimes startling persistence'.[90] Either because he does not wish to admit defeat or he does not want to give satisfaction to his competitors (whom he often refers to as enemies), Murdoch has kept going when it seemed he must give up, and eventually has prevailed. He did this in the 1960s with the *Australian*, when even he felt at times that it was within weeks of closing. In 1988, the Fox television network was hemorrhaging money so badly that News Corp's financial director told reporters that if the losses continued News would have to dump the new network, although the following day he claimed he had been misreported.[91] Murdoch also kept going with his Sky satellite service to the UK. If his competitor, BSB, had known the full extent of his problems, they probably could have driven him out of business. But a combination of bluff and courage meant he was able to secure a compromise on favourable terms.

While courage and persistence are universally admired traits, Murdoch's distinctive flavour also comes from his combativeness. Competition and conflict are central in his motivations. Bruce Dover found, when working with Murdoch, that he 'loved nothing better than proving the naysayers wrong'.[92] He is often the target of fierce criticism, but usually Murdoch is 'energised' by 'blatant declarations of hostility'.[93] Any conflict also becomes a precedent: 'when someone's trying to run you down you try to protect yourself, so that, the next time, someone else doesn't try to run you down'.[94]

Indeed conflict is so central to Murdoch's world view that Wolff concluded: 'If you are against him, then you are his enemy and he fights you – it becomes binary. Sometimes it seems that he creates enemies just because it simplifies the world.'[95] After his takeover of the *Wall St Journal*, he and central executives, thinking about their place in history, were toying with branding for News Corp. Murdoch's 'preferred branding statements for News were about kicking dirt in people's faces. His true message was that he was the winner.'[96]

The competitiveness can help focus organisational targets and energies. As long ago as 1959 Murdoch was determined that his Southern TV would beat rival Channel 7 to be the first to broadcast in Adelaide, and he did whatever it took to win that race.[97] In a similar scenario, he won the race to be the first satellite broadcaster in Britain, even though it involved going to air with many unsolved technical problems, and in the short term led to horrendous financial losses. So he took on 'his weak-willed establishment competitors', confident that he could bear more pain than they could.

But combativeness can be counter-productive. As Chapter 2 showed, Murdoch's attempted partnership with GM collapsed because of their well-founded wariness of his style and intentions. 'Rupert is so aggressive that he doesn't really make a good partner,' said John Malone when trying to helping him during a dispute in 1997.[98] Moreover, declarations of conflict energise opponents as well as one's own side. Murdoch is always suspicious, even paranoid, about what his competitors are doing and whether or not they can be trusted. He broke ranks with the other two New York publishers during an industrial dispute, hoping to gain an advantage, but it merely cemented their hostility towards him.[99] So when, in April 1982, he announced that he wanted to buy his main New York competitor, the *Daily News*,[100] and said that the two papers were engaged in 'a dance of death which must end with the disappearance of one or both newspapers',[101] the response was predictably defiant. Its then owner, the Chicago Tribune company, denounced the bid as 'a transparent attempt to destroy and shut down' the *News*, and the newspaper published the statement under the headline 'Trib to Rupert: Drop Dead'. Murdoch's risk-taking, determination and combativeness have often fuelled his success, but they have also often fuelled opposition to him.

Monopoly muscle and vertical integration

In Murdoch's own view, as told to a US congressional committee in 2003, 'my life has been built, and my business, [on] starting competition and starting up against other people and providing diversity'.[102] In 1979, when the Australian Broadcasting Tribunal had initially blocked his application for the Channel Ten licence, Murdoch wisely decided to come to Sydney and appear himself. I was in the Sydney hearing room that day, and remember vividly the power of Murdoch's anger. The Chairman, Bruce Gyngell, was often left floundering as Murdoch made his accusations. His anger served his strategic purpose, and if it was feigned, it was brilliant acting. He proclaimed his patriotism, among other claimed virtues:

> Who else has risked his every penny, his reputation and his career in fighting for what he believes is right for this country?[103]

> My life has been spent fighting them [the other major media companies], starting with a very small newspaper.[104]

> A previous conservative government brought in a special law to protect those monopolies [Fairfax and the Herald and Weekly Times] and to make certain that outsiders like myself could never get as much.[105]

He attacked the 'gutter campaign' against him by the Fairfax press, 'trying to paint me as a crazed tycoon who cannot be trusted with a TV company'.

As late as 2008, when he was addressing a Washington public meeting about his purchase of the *Wall St Journal*, he disarmed the audience by saying:

> Is all media in one hand bad for democracy? Absolutely. We are a tiny fraction of the media landscape. There are millions of voices

out there. We certainly don't have any monopolistic effect.
Everything I have done in my life has been to create competition
... We want to give people choices. The more choices, the better
it is. To think that the media is concentrating is ignoring the
facts. It is being fragmented in a thousand ways. I would agree
with you that that's good. It doesn't suit my business, but ...[106]

Murdoch's self-portrayal – as the challenger of establishments,
who achieves success with lean and mean structures while building
market share by giving audiences what they really want and not
what 'elites' think they ought to want – has long outlived its reality.
It's 'yesterday's cliché'.[107] Now he has elite connections and support,
deeper pockets than his competitors, and all the advantages of a big
company over smaller companies. In the early part of his career, he
was often the entrepreneurial outsider who deployed novel strategies to build market share; the later part has been more about lever-
aging size and monopoly power.

The size and diversity of the Murdoch empire means that he can
cross-subsidise (and cross-promote). News Corp can sustain losses
for a period – or forever – in order to drive competitors out of business. In September 1993, Murdoch cut the price of the *Times* from 45p
to 30p. Its circulation increased at the expense of that of its rivals,
and when the *Daily Telegraph* followed it down to 30p in May 1994,
Murdoch cut the price again, to 20p. Viewed in isolation, this made
no business sense. About 15p of the price went to cover distribution,
and production cost 16p a copy, so despite advertising income, every
issue it sold was costing money. The paper lifted its circulation from
354,000 before the cut to 670,000 at the end of 1995.[108] But the first
nine months of the price war cost the company £45 million. Over
the five years to 1998, Chenoweth estimates, the price cuts cost the
Times £150 million.[109] However, unlike its competitors, such losses
did not 'imperil its existence'.[110] This was a classic case of squeezing
competitors through predatory pricing; survival depended not on

the merits of the particular products, but on total corporate size.

An important aspect of Murdoch's later business strategy has been the concentration on vertical integration. Dover notes that 'Murdoch was a total believer in vertical integration, by which you produced and owned not just the content, but the means to distribute and redistribute in every territory in which you operated.'[111] In subscription television he increasingly aimed to control the delivery platform (the hardware, either satellite or cable), the individual channels shown on the service, and finally the production facilities that make the programs. The key advantage in vertical integration is that pricing can be discretionary: one can charge a greater or lesser amount to different suppliers to skew the choices available to consumers – supermarkets do this when they accept a smaller margin on their own brands. In the extreme, it can allow a company to exclude competitors, and thus deny consumers the opportunity to choose.

In pay television, the negotiation between channels and delivery platforms is rather arcane and, importantly, the public has no direct involvement. In 2010, there was a fierce dispute between Cablevision and News Corp. Cablevision ran an advertisement in the *New York Times* accusing News of demanding extortionate amounts for some channels and threatening to pull all its channels off the air.[112] A few weeks later, Cablevision surrendered, but not gracefully. Its public statement complained:

> In the absence of any meaningful action from the Federal Communications Commission, Cablevision has agreed to pay Fox an unfair price for multiple channels of its programming, including many in which our customers have little or no interest.[113]

In this case, because News had channels that Cablevision wanted, it could pressure Cablevision to accept and pay for others that it did not want.

Murdoch found himself in a much more precarious position in 1996, when Time Warner initially refused to carry his new Fox News service because Ted Turner did not like the idea of the network carrying a competitor to his CNN. This was a public humiliation for Murdoch, but even more importantly, he had already spent $300 million and had committed to hundreds of millions more in the coming months. He thought he needed 25 million subscribers to be viable and had less than half that.[114] After some fiery public controversies and law suits, Time Warner agreed to carry the new channel.

Soon after, Murdoch again found himself vulnerable, when his satellite plans collapsed. Though he had insulted the cable operators, he had to come crawling back to them. The consequence was that 'most of the large cable companies were giving Murdoch a slow no on carrying his channels'.[115] These were years of great stress and crisis for Murdoch.

The master manipulator of the process was John Malone, who, by the 1990s, had grown into the biggest cable operator in America. Al Gore had dubbed him the Darth Vader of the industry.[116] Malone hadn't 'mustered some of the most impressive profit margins in the business by coddling the subscriber base'.[117] As new cable channels were launched, they needed access to subscribers and Malone 'drove a tough bargain. He demanded that cable networks either allow [him] to invest in them directly, or they had to give [him] deep discounts on price.' He made a series of strategic partnerships, with both cable operators and channels. Malone's idea 'was to collaborate even with your enemies – especially with your enemies – to avoid the large and costly fight of real competition'.[118] There were accusations that Malone went beyond tough business practices into shutting out rivals. The Home Shopping Network charged that it could not get access on his network because it was a direct competitor with the QVC network, part-owned by Malone.[119]

Murdoch has also – since his late 1990s mishaps – become better at either being the gatekeeper himself or in alliance with it, as in DirecTV and BSkyB, or having channels that are so valuable that no cable operator will be willing to be without them. The subscription television industry rewards bigness.

The difficulties in competing with a corporation with the financial strength and attitude of News International were vividly demonstrated in a case that dragged on through the final years of the Blair and Brown Governments. In 2006, the newly formed Virgin Media, growing out of the cable company NTV plus Richard Branson's Virgin group, was negotiating a merger with ITV. The new group's cable operations would have the potential to provide much tougher competition for BSkyB's satellite service. Before these negotiations were consummated, 'James Murdoch swooped in ... and bought 17.9 per cent of ITV, seriously lousing up the Virgin Media deal.'[120] This made BSkyB ITV's largest shareholder. Murdoch paid 135p a share, for a total cost of £940 million. Over the next three and a bit years, first the Office of Fair Trading, then the media regulator Ofcom, the Competition Commission, then the Competition Appeal Tribunal and finally, in January 2010, the Court of Appeal all ruled that BSkyB would have to substantially reduce its stake in ITV.[121] ITV shares were then trading at 51p a share, so when reducing its stake to 7.5 per cent, News made a loss of around £340 million.[122]

Although a partnership between BSkyB and ITV would have been beneficial to News, nearly all observers thought that News would not be allowed to keep the shareholding it had purchased. However, the key was not the outcome but the time it took. By normal business criteria, it was a bad investment. News had bought at a premium, and eventually had to sell at a substantial loss. But its key aim had been to prevent the emergence of a more powerful competitor, and in this it succeeded. It was, almost literally, buying time.

When interviewed in Australia during this protracted process, Rupert Murdoch:

said concern about media ownership was an issue '10 years out of date' and described as 'paranoid' a decision by regulatory authorities to investigate the 17.9 per cent stake he took in commercial television network ITV.[123]

However, this dismissal of ownership as irrelevant was belied by the very fact that News had made such a large purchase with the principal aim of stopping ITV and Virgin Media from merging. It showed that he still viewed ownership issues very seriously indeed.

Perhaps News thought it would be able to retain its stake. Possibly it did not foresee the fall in the ITV share price. Either way we have a corporation willing to risk losing a couple of hundred million pounds, and deliberately putting itself in breach of the law, in the view of most observers, in the knowledge that by the time the legal processes were exhausted it will have thwarted the plans of its competitors. This is a long way from Murdoch's self-portrayal as the entrepreneurial outsider taking on the establishment.

4

Midas's lost touch
The business case against Murdoch

In March 2000, Murdoch was diagnosed with prostate cancer. The following month, the news leaked, and News shares fell $10 billion.[1] In contrast, in May 2012, when a British Parliamentary Committee judged that he was not a fit person to run BSkyB, 'the market's immediate response was to mark up News Corp stock', because it signalled that Murdoch's hold on the corporation was weakening.[2] Indeed some analysts then talked of the Murdoch discount; most spectacularly, Bloomberg analysts asserted that News Corp, before the split, was worth at least 50 per cent more without Rupert Murdoch.[3]

For the first several decades of his career, most people in business and the media had underestimated Murdoch. When he made his first foray into London, taking a share in the *News of the World* in 1968, the owners, the Carr family, according to Murdoch, expected that he would be 'a Sancho Panza to Carr's Don Quixote'.[4] According to Wolff, in New York in the mid-1970s, most assumed Murdoch was 'easy pickings' and 'classic dumb money'.[5] His extraordinary success then created an aura of genius and a sense that he had the Midas touch – not least among his own publications and employees. He became 'the best businessman Australia has ever produced', according to the *Australian*'s media columnist Mark Day in 2011,[6] with 'the super-human energy of a 35-year-old', according to a colleague.[7] When Wolff interviewed Rebekah Wade (now Brooks), then editor of the *Sun*, she told him with great intensity that she had considered Murdoch from all angles, and her conclusion was that he was 'a genius'.[8]

However, this energetic genius essentially failed to conquer the last two big business frontiers he confronted – China and the internet. These failures are understandable given the difficulties involved, but they undermine any idea of Murdoch infallibility, and in each case aspects of Murdoch's style and decisions contributed to the failure.

When Murdoch bought Star TV in 1993, his vision was for Direct to Home (DTH) satellite broadcasting, paid for by sub-scription and advertising, and his primary target was to capture viewers in the world's largest emerging market: China. China was not only the most populous country in the world, but one in the midst of unparalleled economic growth, fuelling an ever-expand-ing consumer market. Star has proven to be a very good long-term investment, especially in India, but it failed miserably to deliver on Murdoch's Chinese ambitions.

Famously, Murdoch began badly. In a speech in London, on 1 September 1993, five months after purchasing Star, Murdoch pro-claimed that 'advances in the technology of telecommunications have proved an unambiguous threat to totalitarian regimes every-where'. Coming a few years after the violent suppression of demon-strators at Tiananmen Square, this comment seemed directly aimed at the Chinese Government. According to Dover, who was then working for Star, when the reports of Murdoch's speech reached Beijing, Premier Li Peng was incandescent with rage.[9] Dover and Star's CEO, Gary Davey, joked that 'word for word, Murdoch's remarks were probably the costliest ever uttered by an individual'.[10] Within months, the Chinese Government had banned the sale and use of satellite dishes anywhere in China.[11] As Dover observed, 'Star TV was a business without a revenue stream.' Advertisers, not want-ing to displease the government, stayed away.[12]

In many ways the main narrative in the next decade was Murdoch trying to woo and reassure the Chinese Government that allowing his company, a foreign broadcaster, unfiltered access to the Chinese population would not be a threat to political control. This led him into several actions which properly attracted condemnation in the West. He banned the BBC from the Star satellite. He reneged on a HarperCollins contract to publish a book by Chris Patten, the last British governor of Hong Kong, and it became a bestseller for another company. He spent close to $1 million to secure the rights to Deng Rong's boring and poor-selling hagiography of her father, Deng Xiao-Peng.[13] He disparaged the Dalai Lama,[14] and maintained a determined agnosticism about human rights abuses. He told business journalist Wendy Rohm in 2001:

> I don't know. It's the popular thing to say that China abuses
> human rights. Their answer is there are plenty of human rights
> abuses in this country. And in every country.[15]

Murdoch sought to build goodwill and strategic relationships through a variety of avenues, including a pioneering joint internet venture with the *People's Daily*[16] and extensive television co-productions with Chinese companies. In Dover's view, Murdoch was 'an extraordinary catalyst of change in China'.[17] But News Corp's investment in local television production did not lead to the strategic advantage it had anticipated. News had 'underestimated how quick the Chinese were at cloning anything that looked like a successful format and just how deep were their pockets'. At the time, in 2003, there were over 600 terrestrial TV stations, plus many cable operators, in China, and no effective protection of copyright. One reality dating program, for example, generated 200 copy-cat versions.[18]

But free access for households to DTH satellite did not materialise.

To the extent that Murdoch failed in China because of factors under his own control, it was that he was too impatient and aggressive. By 1998, he was hopeful of a meeting with President Jiang Zemin, but in a meeting with the Education Minister, he lost patience and demanded the Chinese Government lift the ban on DTH satellite television. That meeting quickly ended, and the meeting with Jiang did not eventuate.[19] Murdoch then removed Davey and Dover from Star's leadership and installed Gareth Chang, a Chinese-American, who seemed to offer hope of more immediate and tangible progress. But 18 months later, Chang was also gone.[20] Dover felt that the Chinese like continuity of relationships, a slow building of trust and understanding, and that Murdoch's changes of personnel put his cause back substantially.[21]

In particular, navigating towards business opportunities in China involved operating in the grey area, the nowhere land between what Chinese authorities would deem to be according to the law and what would obviously constitute a breach.[22] In 1996, the President of the *People's Daily*, Shao Huaze, in a friendly conversation, advised Murdoch that: 'Giants who seek to walk in China need to learn to tread lightly.'[23] This was advice that Murdoch seemed congenitally incapable of following. As Dover notes, 'When operating in the grey sector it also helps if you have what the Chinese call an umbrella, a person in authority who can provide a degree of protection.'[24] In the last years of Jiang's reign, Murdoch and his executives were increasingly confident that they had the highest umbrella in the land, and became increasingly brazen. Instead of stepping lightly, 'Murdoch was stepping on toes everywhere.'[25]

Star was distributing its channel beyond what had been officially approved, and was illegally collecting subscription revenue. Even worse, it was bragging about it.[26] This prompted competitors to complain about the company being given special treatment and about the breaches it was committing. In early 2005, Murdoch believed 'he was on the brink of a spectacular breakthrough in China'.[27] Instead, by the middle of the year he was subject to an official crackdown. He admitted defeat and retreated from his Chinese ambitions.

These ambitions were probably unrealistic anyway. His 'approach to China ... was steeped in a sort of colonial mindset – [he seemed to feel] that somehow the Chinese would welcome a white man bearing gifts'.[28] He was focused on his international competitors and on the issues of state control and official access, but Chinese commercial interests had other plans: they captured the market for themselves.[29] In the end, in terms of its own business interests, 'News Corp's China adventure [was] a huge disaster.'[30]

Murdoch took the iniative in trying to advance his Star interests in China. With the internet, on the other hand, he had no choice but to react. Early on, he was an internet sceptic,[31] believing it was a passing fad; that stocks were overvalued and that it would destroy more businesses than it created.[32] In 1996, he had the chance to scoop up AOL for $5 billion, but Microsoft head Bill Gates advised him against it. It later went up to $150 billion – 'It was a pretty serious opportunity we missed there,' Murdoch commented later.[33]

As the internet frenzy increased, he started to fear that he was missing out. In 1999–2000, at the very peak of the internet bubble, the company, led by James, made a series of purchases in the US. By the end of 2000 they were all 'failing or defunct'.[34] James and Wendi then spent $150 million on 20 internet businesses in Asia, but 'within a year, none of these investments would be worth a fraction of the value paid for them' and 'within two years all but a couple had disappeared completely'.[35] Rupert was unrepentant, telling his October 2000 AGM that unlike his media rivals, he had never been taken in by the dot com revolution in the first place,[36] and that News Corp was less hurt by the bursting of the bubble than others.[37]

The bursting of the bubble was temporary, and internet developments quickly gathered pace again. Through the early 21st century, the Murdoch rhetoric about the coming challenge was well pitched:

The winners will be those who capitalize quickly on changing opportunities. The challenge is to move early and innovate often. This is not always a comfortable path, but it is the only one which will lead News Corp to success in the global market of the 21st century.[38]

Similarly, he made the right noises about transforming established media, saying that too many newspaper executives thought the business was only about print:

In the coming century, the form of delivery may change, but the potential audience for our content will multiply many times over … Our real business isn't printing on dead trees. It's giving our readers great journalism and great judgement.[39]

His leading executives proclaimed similar ambitions. News Limited CEO John Hartigan thought: 'We have the opportunity to move from setting the agenda each morning … to actually owning the agenda. All day. Every day.'[40]

But the achievements have not matched the rhetoric. All established media have found it hard to deal with the destruction of intellectual property values which the internet threatens. But Murdoch entered the new century with some particular and idiosyncratic misconceptions, which made News Corp's task more difficult. Murdoch was convinced that:

the television is going to play a bigger part in people's lives than the PC … The fact is, particularly with the satellite, you can build a very intelligent set-top box with a TiVo recorder or whatever; you can do a lot of things.[41]

He also thought that 'the most profitable use of television advertising so far' would be when viewers could purchase products by just clicking on the screen.[42] It is easy to make fun of these expectations, but few saw the nature of the transformations clearly at that time.

In 2005, News Corp started to again make large internet-related investments. Characteristically, Murdoch proclaimed that News Corp must transform itself into a 'digital powerhouse',[43] and forecast that News Corp could rival Yahoo and Google, 'given time'. He reiterated this grandiose claim in 2008.[44] He formed Fox Interactive Media, and three days later it bought the company that owned the social networking site MySpace for $580 million. A couple of months later Fox Interactive Media entered the video game market, buying IGN for $650 million. After spending $1.3 billion, Murdoch declared, 'we now have the most potent combination of relevant content and critical audience mass to forge a real and profitable presence on the Web'. But these investments did not prosper.

MySpace looked to be a success for some time. In 2007, Murdoch told an audience:

> You were all laughing at me for buying MySpace. What's that worth today? It's worth more than twenty times what we paid for it.[45]

In the same year, he scornfully observed that 'Facebook is infinitely smaller than MySpace.'[46] But in fact MySpace fell steadily behind Facebook, and News Corp sold it for $35 million in 2011, a $540 million loss.[47] The noteworthy feature here is not only the losses that News Corp made, but the triumphalism that accompanied them.

News Corp continued to experiment. It launched *The Daily*, the first newspaper made specifically for the iPad, in February 2011. Its cost structure appealed to Murdoch – 'no paper, no presses, no trucks'.[48] But *The Daily* closed in late 2012 – in Wolff's judgement, it had been 'a tone deaf, middle-market paper on a tablet'.[49] News Corp has some profitable websites, and some of its media products have made at least partially successful adaptations to the internet, but these do not come close to compensating for its losses thus far.

Leading Australian business journalist Alan Kohler was scathing about Murdoch's internet performance:

> Poor News Corp. At the front line of one of the greatest revolutions in history, in which great opportunity wrestles daily with horrendous value destruction, and the company is cursed with a leader who was born 79 years ago, in the Great Depression.[50]

But perhaps the problems run deeper than just age. Murdoch's business strategies are not well suited to the speed and fluidity of the new environment. The established Murdoch model was one of expensive acquisitions – newspapers, TV, major film studios, satellite – which then offered a strategic stronghold in industries where the parameters were well known and stable. In the digital world start-up enterprises are easier, and the environment – in terms of technology, consumption patterns and profitability – changes much more quickly. Murdoch tried to conquer the internet by throwing money at it, but News had no consistent strategic vision.

Murdoch sought to penetrate the world's biggest emerging market, China, and to cope with the media's biggest challenge, the internet. He devoted great money and corporate energy to them, but in both cases the result was mediocre. Although in both cases failure can be partly attributed to his managerial shortcomings, both presented very difficult and complex challenges, and many companies besides News Corp similarly failed.

However, there are two areas – personal and political indulgences – where Murdoch failed his shareholders, and these failures are much less excusable. Murdoch's personal indulgences involve placing his immediate control and dynastic ambitions for his family above the interests of other shareholders; his political indulgences have centred on his support for right-wing causes, and especially on keeping newspapers for this purpose rather than because of their shareholder value. Both types of indulgence have become ever more expensive.

In his attitudes to the British monarchy, Murdoch has always been a republican, but in corporate life he has remained a monarchist. In 1998 he announced that his oldest son, Lachlan, would take over from him – 'The children selected him. It was their vote,'[51] he said. In the eyes of the *Economist*, and many others, 'the interests of the family and those of the firm [we]re diverging'.[52]

The least expensive aspect of this has been direct nepotism. 'I'm a great believer in nepotism,' Murdoch told a business associate,[53] and he has certainly put his belief into practice. There have been transactions and decisions involving each of Murdoch's three children by his second wife, Anna. James had dropped out of Harvard to start a hiphop record label, Rawkus Records, with two friends. News Corp bought it for an undisclosed sum in 1998 (and James has worked for News Corp ever since). The label closed in 2004.[54] Whether James received an appropriate sum for Rawkus Records cannot be judged because of the secrecy, but News Corp's previous interest in hiphop had been limited.

That transaction passed with little notice, unlike the much larger purchase in February 2011 of his daughter Elisabeth's TV production company Shine, for A$628 million, 16 times its most recent annual profit. Shine was a much more obviously successful company, making programs such as *Masterchef*, and had programming that News Corp wanted. Nevertheless, a lawsuit by shareholders accused Murdoch of 'rampant nepotism', and of treating News Corp 'as a wholly-owned family candy store'.[55]

Lachlan left the company in 2005, but still receives a pension payment, which was $2.42 million in 2012.[56] News Corp has not made any acquisition from him, but according to the *Australian Financial Review*, it refrained from one in 2010 because of him. The

Australian office, led by Hartigan, had done all the preparatory work to bid for the Ten network, and was about to do so when the deal was stopped dead by the New York office: Ten was off limits, because Lachlan was interested in buying into it.[57] In each of these instances it could be argued that Murdoch family interests and News Corp shareholder interests diverged, but none of them involved a substantial (by the measure of News Corp's total size) cost.

The much more expensive and important conflicts between family control and shareholder value occurred because of the way in which family ownership of shares declined as a percentage of total shareholding after the debt crises of 1987 and 1990. One strand of this involved Queensland Press (see Chapter 2). Murdoch, in order to rescue himself from the crisis following the purchase of the Herald and Weekly Times in 1987, had the Murdoch family directly invest in Queensland Press. This produced some transactions where the main beneficiary was unclear. The first was when Queensland Press purchased some News Corp shares at higher than the then market rate, which helped News Corp in its debt crisis. The Australian Securities Commission investigated the transaction, but did not mount any prosecutions.

The last occurred as part of the 2004 garage sale in which the various cross-holdings around News Corp and the Murdoch family investments were cleaned up as Murdoch shifted the corporation's headquarters from Australia to the US.[58] When Queensland Press was bought by News Corp in 2004, Murdoch family interests were the main beneficiaries, and there was some criticism of the price paid, 'pitched more than $500 million higher than comparable multiples for listed Australian newspaper companies'.[59] As a final twist, just before the purchase, the Murdoch family companies were transferred from Canberra to Bermuda, a move that would save tax and stamp duty payments. But part of the deal specified that any variation in stamp duty payable would be met by News Corp.[60]

Thus other News Corp shareholders finally said a fond farewell to the complications arising from Queensland Press in 2010, when News Corp made a $77.6 million payment to cover the costs of the extra taxation due when Australian tax authorities ruled against the Bermuda contrivance.[61]

The other main strand was the introduction of tiered shareholdings. All existing shareholders retained their voting rights, but Murdoch now raised new capital without diluting control by offering non-voting shares.[62] Such dual classes of shares are unpopular with shareholder associations and others who think that they depart from the basic principle of the stock exchange, that control of a public company should be proportionate to the share of capital invested. But Murdoch defended it: 'It has led to long-term stability in management, which has enabled us to take bigger risks than other people,' he said in 2007.[63]

In 2004, an even more controversial move compounded the dual shareholding setup. John Malone took advantage of the temporary dip in the share price, when Australian institutions sold off their holdings following the corporation's move to the US, raising his stake to 19 per cent of the voting stock. Although this was still considerably below Murdoch's 30 per cent, Murdoch immediately imposed a 'poison pill' provision. Poison pill schemes typically:

> allow existing shareholders to buy more stock at a discounted rate, thereby diluting the value of individual shares and the predator's holdings. They effectively eliminate the takeover premium in a company's share price ... They are hated by shareholders.[64]

This made it difficult for Malone to raise his stake above 19 per cent and for any outsider to build a stake larger than 15 per cent.[65] There was a strong reaction among institutions, and an even stronger one when, in 2005, despite an initial, explicit promise not to do so, the board extended the poison pill beyond its original 12 months. A group of superannuation funds sued Murdoch and News Corp over the extension.[66] Alan Kohler declared that 'News Corp is nothing but a badly performing business run by untrustworthy people.'[67]

As Chenoweth observed, Malone and Murdoch had 'been the closest and most dangerous of friends' for 20 years.[68] Malone was 'probably the only man in the world ... [Murdoch] fear[ed]'.[69] After making the desperate poison pill move, Murdoch made an even more desperate one to get Malone off his share register. In December 2006 the two made a deal whose essence was that Malone gave up his shares in return for ownership of the US satellite broadcaster DirecTV.[70]

The need to do such a deal existed principally in Murdoch's mind. From what is publicly available, Malone made no threatening or disruptive moves during this period, except at one point where he opined that it would be beneficial for all shareholders if Murdoch focused a 'little bit more on shareholder returns and a little less on empire building'.[71] This seems insufficient grounds for author Paul La Monica to assert that 'perhaps most importantly, the deal meant that Murdoch and other News Corp executives no longer needed to worry about meddling from Malone'.[72] That single statement seems to be the sum total of Malone's 'meddling'.

Murdoch had always said that winning control of DirecTV would be 'a company-transforming deal'.[73] For six years, Murdoch's major priority had been to control it, and finally, in 2003, after many setbacks and a long law suit, he achieved his goal. In Wolff's words, 'It is, he [said], the absolute necessary synthesis of all that he's worked for – and it has finally all come together.'[74] And then, a mere three years later, in his 'marvellous, bravura way, Murdoch [declared] DirecTV to be irrelevant to his interests and goals and [gave] Malone a good deal on it ... No looking back.'[75]

Malone got a better deal than other News Corp shareholders. In the years since, DirecTV has been a great success. Its revenue grew from \$14.8 billion in 2006 to \$27.2 billion in 2011; its subscriber base went from 16 million to 20 million; and its operating profit margin has stayed at around 15 per cent.[76] Assuming that News could have managed DirecTV as well as Malone did, News Corp shareholders were denied a growing and lucrative revenue stream. The deal had been in Murdoch's interests, not theirs.

His political indulgences have also become more expensive. The least expensive have been his direct political donations, extensive as these have been, and usually towards the far right of the political spectrum.[77] The most expensive have involved his subsidising of newspapers to advance his political aims. Murdoch has often claimed that his 'newspapers are run to make profits. Full stop.'[78] Some have defended him on these grounds:

> Murdoch's motivation for owning newspapers is profits first and politics second ... When people go off about him bringing in ideological brethren and saying that he's an ogre, I think that's completely unfair. He's there to make money.[79]

But there is abundant evidence to the contrary. Clearly newspapers mean more to him than just their dollar value. He told Ken Auletta that the thing in his business empire that gives him most pleasure is 'being involved with the editor of a paper in a day-to-day campaign. Trying to influence people.'[80] After he had to dispose of the *New York Post* in 1988, he said, 'I feel depressed. This will be the first time I've lived in a city with no newspaper going on around me.'[81] After he regained the chronically loss-making paper in 1993, it was clear he would never voluntarily dispose of it.

He told the staff that 'I am not here as some fairy godmother to pour money into the paper.'[82] But in fact he did precisely that. The paper was losing \$50 million a year by 2007, according to Wolff, and in 2011, reports put its losses at around \$80 million a year.[83] 'It is almost impossible to exaggerate how determined and how wrong-headed Murdoch is with the *New York Post*,' says Wolff.[84] In London, the *Times* and the *Sunday Times* have also run at a loss for a number of years.[85] When Wolff suggested to Robert Thomson, then editor of the *Times*, that the *New York Post* may have lost more money than 'any other media enterprise in history', Thomson responded 'I would not underestimate the *Times* in that regard.'[86]

Then, in 2007, Murdoch made an acquisition which defied business logic. He bought Dow Jones, publisher of the *Wall St Journal*, for $5.6 billion. The company had been trading at around $35 per share; Murdoch offered $60. None of the Dow Jones advisers 'had ever seen quite such an overvalued offer'.[87] In February 2009, it wrote down half its value.[88] Nor were there any grounds to be surprised by this disaster. Shortly before, the attempt to sell the Tribune company, publisher of the *Chicago Tribune*, 'had dragged on for almost a year', a 'painful warning sign for would-be newspaper investors', and what had started as an auction degenerated into a fire sale, securing far less than any of the bankers involved had originally thought it would.[89]

News Corp shareholders should be doubly angry about the sale of DirecTV to Malone, because part of the urgency surrounding that deal arose from Murdoch's thinking that if Malone were still a shareholder when Murdoch bid for Dow Jones, he would vigorously oppose it.[90] In other words, Murdoch had to do one bad deal for shareholders (DirecTV) to free him to do what turned out to be another one (Dow Jones).

Wolff notes:

> Part of the curiousness of the takeover was not just that Murdoch seemed to have no immediate Murdoch stamp to put on the *Journal*, but also that he seemed in fact to have no specific plan at all for it.[91]

Whatever Murdoch hoped to gain by ownership of the *Journal*, it was not profits. It may have been ego, the satisfaction of winning a prize he had long wanted. It may have been a platform from which to attack what he saw as the citadel of the liberal media, the *New York Times*. When the *Wall St Journal* launched a New York metropolitan section in 2010, Murdoch told the editors he wanted to damage the *New York Times*.[92]

So part of Murdoch's business epitaph now will be that he probably produced the greatest loss-making newspapers in history, and with Dow Jones produced perhaps the most dramatic write-down in US media history. Midas had certainly lost his touch.

5

From Lenin to Palin
The making of a radical conservative

I'm worried about my son Rupert. He's at Oxford and developing
the most alarming left-wing views.

Sir Keith Murdoch, letter to Hugh Cudlipp, 1952[1]

Yesterday was the 29th anniversary of the Great Teacher [Lenin].
We stood to attention for one minute in front of THE BUST on
the mantelpiece and drank several toasts – and then settled down
to some good reading of adulatory Russian poetry.

Rupert Murdoch, letter to Rohan Rivett, Christmas 1952[2]

Today, Murdoch's views are predictable – those of the extreme
right wing of the US Republican Party. His social anchors are with
people who share those beliefs, and his political preferences are
overwhelmingly for right-wing parties, and within those parties for
the more right-wing leaders and factions. It was not always thus.
He has moved across the political spectrum, from Vladimir Lenin to
Sarah Palin. As is well known, during his Oxford years he kept a bust
of Lenin on his mantelpiece. For the next two decades, his political
views ranged widely, often inconsistently, but from the mid-1970s
he has consistently manifested a right-wing ideology – although

90

sometimes tempered by commercial and political pragmatism.

How red was Red Rupe, the nickname given to Murdoch by his fellow Oxford students? According to Tom Kiernan, fellow students recalled Murdoch as a 'wild-eyed pretend radical', and felt that the nickname signified more about his political style than his substance, but Murdoch insists that he matured into a sincere and deep-thinking radical during his Oxford years.[3]

Although any sign of incipient Bolshevism disappeared with his departure from Oxford, in the following years Murdoch's political beliefs were an inchoate mix of rebelliousness, an admiration for movers and shakers, and a concern for the underdog. There was an anti-establishment attitude, especially against what he saw as lazy, undynamic establishments, and most especially against establishments such as Robert Menzies' Australian Government and Thomas Playford's South Australian Government, both of which combined conservatism with a refusal to embrace him and his ambitions. But there was also a fluidity about his views which meant that he was often influenced by strong individuals. There was also a keen eye for the gap in the market. From the early 1950s until the early 1970s he found himself on the Left side of the political spectrum as often as the Right.

One strong strand during these decades was his nationalism. This was no doubt fanned by his early years in England and whatever slights – real or imagined, deserved or undeserved – he suffered there. He disliked Australians 'who embraced everything that was English and rejected everything that was Australian'. As late as 2005 his passionate anti-colonialism was still evident:

A long time ago, the British always thought in terms of their empire and were pretty patronizing toward us Australians, pat you on your head and say, 'You'll do well', and when you do do well they kick you to death.[4]

In 1972, in the lead-up to Gough Whitlam's Labor Party victory, the first for the party in 23 years, Murdoch gave voice to the emerging nationalist mood in Australia:

> Australians are no longer content that their country will go on being inevitably, irreversibly, or without protest, a metal quarry for Japan, a pastoral lease for distant investors, a province for Madison Avenue, or a South Pacific windbreak for French nuclear scientists ... They are no longer content to be a pale echo of great and powerful friends, to be a secondhand society, a reflection of another hemisphere and sometimes another age. They are seeking a fresh, vigorous Australian identity of their own.[5]

Whitlam could not have put it more eloquently.

Perhaps his nationalism helps to explain why, around 1970, Murdoch said, 'I tended to be more on the conservative side when I was in England, more in the liberal camp when in Australia.'[6] Nevertheless, in the British election in 1970 the Murdoch papers supported the re-election of Harold Wilson's Labour Government, and in Australia in 1972 they strongly supported the election of the Whitlam Labor Government. However, by 1975, having relocated to New York from London in 1973, his views had solidified into the strongly conservative ideology he has maintained ever since. According to Murdoch, he 'turned into a pretty strong free market type conservative' because of 'the most searing experience of my life': dealing with the Fleet Street unions.[7] The changes go much further than this, though.

Murdoch's attitudes to the Vietnam War illustrate his changing views. He was an opponent early on. Influenced by senior editorial staff at the *Australian*, particularly Douglass Brass,[8] the national paper was the sole voice among morning papers editorialising against the Government's commitment of troops in April 1965:

The Menzies Government has made a reckless decision on
Vietnam ... That decision is wrong ... It could be that our
historians will recall this day with tears.[9]

But later, Murdoch's views, in George Munster's words, 'followed
the line of his federal political allies'. In the 1969 election, endorsing the Gorton conservative Government, the paper argued that
'thoughtful voters' would support its approach to the 'over-riding
problem' of defence. Soon afterwards though, the revelation of the
My Lai massacre had the *Australian* powerfully covering its horrors,
and editorialising in favour of withdrawal from Vietnam.[10]

Through the 1970s, as Murdoch's views became more conservative, Denis Cryle concluded that the *Australian* 'gradually forsook
its earlier liberalism for Cold War rhetoric'.[11] As the Australian
public moved from hawkish to dovish views, Murdoch moved in
the opposite direction. By the end of the war, in 1975, Murdoch
was mobilising against the Whitlam Government, and domestic
political controversies dominated its coverage, castigating the government and 'the Left', for example, over their lack of planning for
the exodus accompanying the end of the war.[12] An indication of the
paper's reduced intellectual capacity was its failure even to attempt
to reflect on the course of the war; perhaps this was because by
then it was a topic that Murdoch, increasingly adopting the foreign
policy views of US Republicans, was reluctant to consider.

Perhaps the sharpest change in Murdoch's thinking was in relation to social class and inequality. He continued to view 'all inherited privilege with suspicion',[13] but his earlier professed sympathies
for the underdog and underprivileged all but disappeared in his
increasing hostility to the welfare state. By 1974, Murdoch – in
Kiernan's words – had concluded that:

The more a capitalist nation 'gave' to its populace, the more the
succeeding generations expected and demanded, until eventually

there was nothing left to give without bankrupting the nation's capital base. It was an insidiously destructive psychology that had to be stopped before it did to the rest of the English-speaking world what it was doing to England itself. Richard Nixon and his Administration represented America's last best hope to reverse the trend.[14]

For Murdoch in the 1990s, it was 'a sorry fact that the media as a whole ... unquestioningly embrace a welfare state which divides and embitters our society without helping the truly poor and needy'.[15] In the late 1980s, as some of Thatcher's more determined supporters wanted to extend their 'revolution', Murdoch's *Times* and *Sunday Times* gave considerable prominence to people arguing for a 'return to stigmatizing the poor who were responsible for their own situation' and about the monster of the underclass being created by the 'poverty industry'.[16] Such views appeared as late as the 'Britain is broken' themes of the *Sun* in the lead-up to the 2010 election. Once, when *Sunday Times* editor Andrew Neil and Murdoch were discussing the 'need for the radical reform of welfare', Neil said that there still had to be some sort of basic provision, safety net, for everyone. 'Yeah, yeah, maybe,' growled Murdoch, 'but it should be very low.'[17]

Neil concluded, from his countless discussions with Murdoch, that he 'is much more right-wing than is generally thought but will curb his ideology for commercial reasons'.[18] Part of this is his whole-hearted embrace of the virtues of the market – 'I love the free market. It's certainly been very good to me. I think you'd have to admit, it's been very good to the world.'[19] But Murdoch has never been a simple conservative. He once said, 'the greatest compliment that was ever paid to me was by Ian McGregor, the Chairman of British Steel, who said: "There are only two radicals in this country – Margaret Thatcher and Rupert Murdoch."'[20] Wolff found that Murdoch became much more animated and forthcoming in interviews when asked about being a change agent, a phrase Murdoch then kept repeating.[21] One of his closest confidants, US economist Irwin Stelzer, opined, 'I hate to say that money doesn't matter, because money always matters, but I think Rupert mainly sees himself as a kind of anti-Establishment revolutionary.'[22] Conveniently, all groups opposing Murdoch soon become re-cast as 'establishments' – soon there were not just the royal establishment and the banking and business establishments, but also the Left establishment, the journalist establishment, and the trade union establishment.[23]

The 'conservatism' that Murdoch embraces has little to do with the conservatism coming down from Edmund Burke, celebrating the wisdom of the traditions and institutions handed on through generations, cautious that change will have unintended consequences, that subtle balances will be upset, leading to things becoming worse rather than better. Rather, conservative politics becomes redefined as advocacy for change, and 'radical' is a term of praise.[24]

The crudity of Murdoch's politics

Not even its most ardent advocates would claim that Twitter is a medium that invites expansiveness and the considered appraisal of competing views. When the evergreen octogenarian Murdoch embraced Twitter in 2012, his tweets offered insights into his attitudes that did not enhance his reputation for political sophistication.

He began the year by insulting the British – 'maybe Brits have too many holidays for broke country!',[25] and later denounced their government for supporting the euro, 'must be mad',[26] and for being about to wreck the English countryside with 'uneconomic bird killing windmills. Mad.'[27] His views on Australian politics were equally unflattering: 'Gillard once good education minister, now prisoner of minority greenies. Rudd still delusional, who nobody could work with. Nobody else?'[28] 'Weird place mucking up great future.'[29]

In American politics, as the 2012 Republican primaries began he was an enthusiast for the Christian evangelical candidate Rick Santorum, as the 'only candidate with genuine big vision for country'. [30] His judgements on President Obama were consistently negative. 'Just saw [the anti-Obama documentary] 2016. Truly scary if no answer. Every voter should see and decide for self what future they want for America.'[31] And it would be a 'Nightmare for Israel if Obama wins ...',[32] while the 'White House [was] still lying about Benghazi.' [33] Moreover, referring to a bill about regulating the internet, Murdoch charged that 'Obama has thrown in his lot with Silicon Valley paymasters who threaten all software creators with piracy, plain thievery',[34] and responded to the resulting controversy by saying that 'Piracy leader is Google who streams movies free, sells advts around them.'[35] Murdoch was despairing of politicians everywhere – 'To hell with politicians! When are we going to find some to tell the truth in any country? Don't hold your breath.'[36]

Murdoch had told a British parliamentary committee during the phone hacking scandal in July 2011 that it was the most humble day of his life. By 2012, he had recovered. When some people acting for phone hacking victims pushed for reforms, he tweeted: 'Told UK's Cameron receiving scumbag celebrities pushing for even more privacy laws. Trust the toffs! Transparency under attack. Bad.'[37] At the same time, he thought 'Any shareholders with complaints should take profits and sell!'[38] When the scandal surrounding the pay TV security company NDS broke in March, he thought 'every competitor and enemy piling on with lies and libels'.[39] 'Enemies have many different agendas, but worst old toffs and right wingers who still want last century's status quo with their monopolies.'[40]

The biggest controversy was to greet his commentaries on the Middle East. When, late in the year, there were conflicts between Israel and Hamas, Murdoch asked, 'Can't Obama stop his friends in Egypt shelling Israel?'[41] The question was built on a series of incorrect assumptions,[42] but an even bigger critical storm greeted his next venture: 'Why is Jewish-owned press so consistently anti-

Israel in every crisis?'[43] Peter Beinart commented, 'Give Murdoch credit: He's packed a remarkable amount of idiocy and nastiness into 140 characters.'[44]

Even allowing for the constraints of the medium, Murdoch's tweets have been notable as much for their style as for their content. He has first class access to inside information and gossip grapevines, and frequent contact with leading figures in government, business and media. Yet his tweets contain blatant errors and simplifications, and rarely acknowledge any shades of grey. What is most striking is the crudity of his views, and his dismissive contempt for others, evident in the intolerant way he constructs opponents' opinions and motives. The way he expresses his beliefs has consequences for the way his tabloids, in particular, frame political conflicts, and for the way he makes his views known internally to his editors and senior journalists.

The most complete account of how Murdoch dealt with a strong editor who had political views different from his is from Harold Evans, editor of the *Times* in 1981–82. Murdoch had an arsenal of unflattering labels for his critics and for the contributors he disapproved of: 'the chattering classes', 'bloody pinko Islington liberals', 'pissing liberals', 'limp-wristed left-wing layabouts and stuck-up, self-important, expense-padding Trotskyites'.[45] 'Murdoch would jab his finger at the paper and say, "What do you want to print rubbish like that for?"' A journalist accurately reporting evidence given to the inquiry into the Brixton riots in 1981 was labelled 'a commie'.[46]

At that time, neither Thatcher's nor Reagan's economic policies were going well. After Professor James Tobin of Yale University won the Nobel Prize for economics, Evans commissioned an article from him, which talked about the risky experiment of monetarism. At dinner Murdoch berated him:

'Why d'ya run that stuff?'
'Well, it's timely.'
'It's timely and it's wrong. What does he know anyway?'

'He won the Nobel Prize.'
'Intellectual bullshit.'

Evans's wife, Tina Brown, commented that 'she had never seen anyone so hunched up with anger' as Murdoch. Evans said that he would like to have engaged Murdoch in a political discussion, but found that he 'had no relish for anything more than a couple of colliding assertions ... He got restless or tetchy with any attempt to engage him further.'[47] According to Evans, Murdoch's 'tone was assertive and hostile to debate'.[48]

Murdoch's simplistic approach is seen most clearly in his views on international conflicts. In 1982, after Israel's invasion of Lebanon, he told *Sunday Times* editor Frank Giles that Ariel Sharon was 'a man of action'. But, said Giles, what if the action is wrong or misguided? 'That's not the point,' said Murdoch. 'He gets things done.'[49]

On every international conflict that has arisen since the end of the Vietnam War, Murdoch has been, usually vociferously, on the hawkish side. Moreover, he has typically expressed contempt for those who even consider other options. Witness the calculated insult he gave to Australian Prime Minister Malcolm Fraser at a dinner following the 1981 budget. Fraser's Cabinet had been hesitating over sending an Australian contingent to the Middle East in a peacekeeping role. Murdoch seized Fraser's upper arm and exclaimed for all to hear: 'Show a bit of muscle, Malcolm, show a bit of muscle.'[50]

In the 1980s, when Thatcher was negotiating with Beijing over the future of Hong Kong, which was to revert to China in 1997, Murdoch told Neil that he wanted his papers to take a stronger line:

She should hold out, make no concessions and tell the Chinese that there's a Trident submarine off their coast: If the Red Army moves into Hong Kong they should be left in no doubt that we'll nuke Beijing ... though I suppose we could fire a warning nuke into a desert first.[51]

Just as ludicrously, Murdoch has twice favoured the idea that Australia should acquire nuclear weapons. He did so first in 1967, reflecting an aggressive Australian nationalism, and then again in 1984, embracing the Reagan agenda against the Soviet Union.[52]

Murdoch was a late convert to Cold War views, but an extremely zealous one. Hugo Young, then deputy editor of Murdoch's *Sunday Times* but soon to leave the paper, said that any 'reports from El Salvador which allowed for any possibility that US foreign policy was in error were clearly potent evidence that the Commies had the *Sunday Times* in their grip ... a term of abuse that I personally heard more than once'.[53]

During the 1980s Murdoch was slow to understand the changes that Mikhail Gorbachev was making in the Soviet Union. He tried to convince Collins book publishers (not yet fully owned by him) not to publish Gorbachev's memoirs, which had been considered a publishing coup. 'He's still a communist, you know,' he told company head Ian Chapman, and when Chapman said he was going ahead with the contract, Murdoch replied, 'Well Ian, if you're content to be an arm of Soviet propaganda, go ahead and publish.'[54] Murdoch's *New York Post* had proclaimed Gorbachev 'a worthy heir to Stalin', and *Post* columnists wrote as if both glasnost (the domestic loosening of government control) and rapprochement with the West were fakes.[55] As David McKnight commented, 'neo-conservatives seemed utterly unable to understand events in the Soviet Union'.[56]

The end of the Cold War did nothing to temper Murdoch's approach to international conflicts, especially in the Middle East, where his unwavering support for Israel is matched by his stereotyped views of Islam. One day over lunch he ventured to Wolff that 'Muslims have an inordinate incidence of birth defects because they so often marry their cousins.'[57] This kind of simplistic and one-sided view matches his view of race relations in America in the 1970s, where he thought that 'the energy and prosperity of industrious white America was being drained by the tremendous black problem'.[58]

On the eve of George W. Bush's invasion of Iraq in 2003, Murdoch opined that 'We can't back down now where you hand over the whole of the Middle East to Saddam.' This nonsensical claim – one not even advanced by any member of the Bush administration – was followed by one of his worst predictions: 'The greatest thing to come of this to the world economy ... would be US$20 a barrel for oil.' He was not worried about the protests around the world against the coming war:

> We worry about what people think about us too much in this country [the US]. We have an inferiority complex, it seems. I think what's important is that the world respects us, much more important than they love us.

However, he didn't produce any evidence of how the invasion was increasing the world's respect for America.

As the war bogged down in 2004, Murdoch remained upbeat, contending that the 'only real problem in Iraq' was confined to 'one small part where the Sunnis are, which were the people who supported Saddam'. (Sunnis comprise around one-third of Iraq's population and form the majority in the capital, Baghdad.) And even in November 2006, he had no regrets: 'The death toll, certainly of Americans there, by the terms of any previous war, are [sic] quite minute.'[59]

The unwillingness to acknowledge past errors or to admit the complexity of some of the issues is consistent with Wolff's very critical view of Murdoch's political approach:

> A vital element in understanding his political consciousness is understanding its shallowness.

[He is] compulsively drawn to ... action [and] opportunity.

He's a poor debater (although he can raise his voice and pound the table).

Neither is he 'conventionally smart', which Wolff considers part of the reason he seeks to belittle and demonise intellectuals: 'If you're not with Murdoch, even on a modest point, you're a liberal'; in the past, you were a 'commie'.[60]

This picture is consistent with the recollections of one of his student contemporaries:

He was grossly impatient and brooked no disagreement ... He took a dictatorial approach to his politics, and if you dared to disagree with him on some minor point he would banish you from his small circle. He was a debating bully and would often resort to ad hominem attacks when his logic and clarity of language faltered ... He had all the answers and if you didn't go along with him you were nothing. You were a 'putrid little shit', or some such expletive.[61]

The big difference between the student and the media proprietor is that the latter has power. It suggests he gets his way less by seeking to persuade than by imposing his opinion. The cognitive style is similar, though. He does not engage with contrary views; instead he applies generic, dismissive labels both to those holding them (commie, anti-American, liberal) and to their arguments (mad), and simply does not deal with uncomfortable contrary evidence. It is the mindset of someone with a largely closed worldview. He puts his views in a way designed to shut down discussion rather than open or permit debate.

Murdoch's former Australian CEO, John Menadue, said he 'was, and still is, a frustrated politician. He can't leave politics alone.'[62]

While it is no doubt true that he relishes being a player in the political game, he would not survive as a politician, with its collective discipline and its public accountability. Murdoch's political ambitions would be undone not only by his radical conservatism – which is a long way from the mainstream of at least Australian and British politics – but by the crude way he expresses his views. As a democratic politician, he would be much more accountable for the poor predictions and outrageous comments he has made than he is as a media proprietor.

6

The enthusiastic player
Murdoch's early political involvements

While Murdoch's ideological dispositions place him at the far right of the political mainstream, it is wrong to explore his politics exclusively as an abstract set of beliefs. Their expression has been tempered not only by political and commercial pragmatism, but also, and even more, by his wish to be a player. Murdoch enjoys wielding power and being seen to wield it. Menadue, who worked with Murdoch for seven years, thought that what drove him 'was not making money, as useful as that was, but gaining acceptance by and then influence with people in positions of power'.[1] He likes being an insider, privy to the gossip around the personal dramas of politics. He relishes the sense of shaping events, and his publications have cultivated his image as a king-maker. No other company has ever run a headline like 'It was the *Sun* wot won it', as News International did after John Major's 1992 election victory.

Typically, however, Murdoch's aspirations are marked by double talk. When the *New York Times* put it to him at the time of the Iraq War in 2003 that he was the most powerful person in English-language media, for example, he replied, 'that is flattering but it's just not true. Maybe it would be if I tried to impose my views but I just don't do it.'[2] 'You can demonise me by using the word "power",' he said to Shawcross, 'but that's the fun of it, isn't it? Having a smidgeon of power.'[3] He told prominent journalist Trevor Kennedy, 'you wouldn't be human if you didn't enjoy the influence. I should say that one's influence is greatly over-rated', especially by politicians, 'who are forever calling and looking for favours and looking for one's approval'.[4]

In private, however, he is less proper and less modest. When dealing with politicians, Munster thought, Murdoch likes to foster the impression that he could deliver them an advantage they could not get otherwise.[5] When Labour's Ken Livingstone 'said on television that his party's defeat in the 1987 general election had been caused by media lies and smears, Murdoch cried out delightedly: "That's me!"'.[6] After the *New York Post* splashed a story that the parents of the 1984 Democratic nominee for Vice President, Geraldine Ferraro, had been arrested but never convicted for illegal gambling in the 1940s, Ferraro spoke emotionally of her mother's pain at the smear, and angrily denounced Murdoch as a rich and well-connected powerful man 'who does not have the worth to wipe the dirt under [my mother's] shoes'. When this was read out to a party at Murdoch's house, the 'editors whooped and laughed, and Murdoch poured more champagne'.[7]

In 1993, during a dispute with Buckingham Palace over the *Sun's* having published the Queen's Christmas letter two days early, his confidant Woodrow Wyatt was urging on him the need to make a rapprochement. But Murdoch became angry. Wyatt, exasperated, recorded in his diary:

> I am beginning to wonder whether [Rupert] hasn't gone absolutely Citizen Kane. He was shouting away telling me how important he was and how he has a great media empire … and telling me he had more power than the government in England.[8]

Murdoch's aspirations to be a player for its own sake were clear with his first big campaign in America, supporting Ed Koch to become mayor of New York in 1977. Within a year of owning the *New York Post*, according to Wolff, Murdoch:

entirely [altered] the political landscape in New York. In a
precise calculation, he [decided] to use the *Post* as an instrument
to elect somebody – he [understood] that it doesn't really matter
whom, just that the *Post* be responsible.[9]

Some of Murdoch's editorial mobilisations have been driven by his
political beliefs or strong passions – such as for Thatcher and Reagan
– but the ideological stakes in the New York mayoral election were
not great. Murdoch decided to support Koch, an underdog, first
for the Democratic nomination and then in the election, and the
Post went all-out in his cause. Academic and journalist Mitchell Stephens found that once the *Post* had endorsed Koch (in a front page
editorial), there were no unfavourable stories about him at all from
then until after the election. Mario Cuomo, a more liberal Democrat and earlier the favourite, lamented:

> The *New York Times* is perhaps the single most credible newspaper
> in the world. But when they endorse you, you get one column on
> the editorial page. With Rupert he turns the whole paper over to
> you.[10]

Another politician on the receiving end, Mayor Abraham Beame,
was more graphic: 'No New Yorker should take Rupert Murdoch's
New York Post seriously any longer. It makes *Hustler* magazine look
like the *Harvard Law Review*.'[11]

On 27 September 1977, citing a lack of freedom to express any
opinions contrary to the paper's policy, 50 of the paper's 60 reporters walked off the job, indicating their disquiet over slanted news
coverage.[12] That coverage, recalled former *Post* journalist Frank
Rich, was:

> tilted in favour of Ed Koch and Carol Bellamy, both then
> unabashed liberal Democrats, running for mayor and City

Council president. It was the *Post's* journalistic corruption
that enraged those reporters, the editorials run as news stories
(including on page one), the endless parade of fawning features
on the favoured candidates, not the fungible ideology of
Murdoch's opportunistic partisanship.[13]

However, playing such a role in Koch's victory established Murdoch as a king-maker. Koch remained grateful,[14] and according to Murdoch, seldom made a move without consulting him.[15] Murdoch had established himself as a central player in the city's politics.

From very early, Murdoch had a thirst for direct political involvement. A year after the 1955 Labor Party Split, a great Australian political cataclysm that saw the formation of a right-wing anti-communist group, the Democratic Labor Party, Murdoch and his editor Rohan Rivett secretly sought to entice Labor's most promising rising star in South Australia, Don Dunstan, to join the breakaway party with the promise of favourable publicity.[16] Wisely, Dunstan refused; he later became one of the great reforming Labor premiers.

In the first decade or so of his career, Murdoch's political antennae were often poorly attuned. In 1961, Menzies had been prime minister for 12 years and his political dominance seemed assured, but, confounding initial expectations, that election was one of the closest ever. In the end the Liberal/Country Party Coalition hung on by one seat, and that final seat was close to a dead heat. Murdoch maintained his papers' support for the conservative government, and was so bored that he departed for the US during the campaign. His greatest coup was to get a photo of Labor leader Arthur Calwell leaving the Fairfax newspapers' building.[17] In a cheeky story, the *Mirror* reported the meeting between Calwell and Fairfax chief Rupert Henderson as 'the strangest and least attractive wedding of the season ... the flowers were pink, by request'.[18]

Then, in 1963, when Menzies had recovered his political

dominance, Murdoch swung his support to Labor, giving them financial as well as editorial support. He had developed a relationship with Calwell, who commented that had Murdoch given him money in 1961, he wouldn't have needed to in 1963.[19] During the campaign, Murdoch's *Daily Mirror* had a front page headline 'Top poll tips Labor'.[20] Fortunately for its reputation, the 'top' polling organisation was not named – a substantial swing against Labor brought a comfortable victory to the Coalition.

Murdoch's most substantial political relationship thus far then developed: with John McEwen, the deputy prime minister and leader of the Country Party.[21] Nicknamed Black Jack, McEwen was a dynamic but controversial figure in Australian politics: his strategy for promoting the country's economic development centred on high tariffs, with large public subsidies going to agriculture and mining. Murdoch was still out of favour with Menzies, however. One of Murdoch's favourite stories was 'how McEwen had smuggled him out of his parliamentary suite when Menzies' imminent arrival was announced'.[22]

Following the death by drowning of Menzies' designated successor, Harold Holt, in December 1967, there was a leadership vacuum in the Liberal Party. Its deputy leader, William McMahon, was an enemy of McEwen, and represented the more free trade, free market tendency within the government. The Coalition was in danger of splitting when McEwen, then acting prime minister, made a public statement that he would not accept McMahon as prime minister. Murdoch wanted to support McEwen as the new prime minister – 'the best man for Australia!' – but the editor of the *Australian*, Adrian Deamer, refused to endorse such a political impossibility: the Liberals would never have accepted a Country Party member as leader of the government.[23]

However, Murdoch and McEwen had more tricks in store before the 9 January leadership vote. The *Australian's* first editor, Max Newton, was now a publisher of industry newsletters, a lobbyist in Canberra, and very close to McMahon. Newton was estranged from Murdoch, and had referred to him as 'a whippersnapper from Adelaide'. One of Newton's clients was the Japanese trade organisation JETRO. On the evening of 5 January 1968, McEwen met with Murdoch, and gave him a package of material from the Australian Security and Intelligence Organisation (ASIO) about McMahon. Afterwards, Murdoch rang Newton, and said 'this is the whippersnapper from Adelaide. I suggest you read my paper tomorrow.' Next morning the *Australian's* headline read 'Why McEwen Vetoes McMahon: Foreign Agent is the Man between the Leaders'. Based on the ASIO file,[24] the newspaper had conjured Newton's perfectly normal commercial relationship with the Japanese trade organisation into a threat to national security, and used this to damage McMahon. A couple of days later it published – again presumably via ASIO – the contract between Newton and JETRO in full. McMahon withdrew from the leadership ballot and an underdog candidate, John Gorton, became prime minister.[25] This was Murdoch's first big political coup.

The 1969 election saw a strong swing to Labor under its new leader, Gough Whitlam, but not a win. However, the problems inside the government mounted to such a degree that in March 1971 Gorton was overthrown and replaced by McMahon. Gorton and his supporters were far from reconciled to the new leadership, and their continuing hostility provided a stream of stories. The Coalition Government was in disarray and decay.

The oddest couple

By late 1971 Whitlam already felt sure he would win the next election. While foreign policy had been an electoral minus for Labor in previous elections, it now looked to be a plus. First, the Vietnam War was opposed by an increasing number of Australians, and second, Whitlam had taken a major political risk by going to China as opposition leader and promising to establish diplomatic relations. His risk was rewarded because, as he left, it was revealed that US National Security Advisor Henry Kissinger was making a secret trip to China, presaging a coming historic visit by Nixon, which took place the following March.

Murdoch was attracted to the prospect of a left of centre government ending 23 years of conservative rule. Backing Whitlam would be supporting an almost certain winner, and his victory would help modernise Australian politics. Laurie Oakes and David Solomon argued that 'by the time the [1972] campaign got under way, Murdoch was an integral part of the "It's Time" [Labor's slogan] machine'.[26] Murdoch himself said 'I was close to [Whitlam] at the time, or certainly very friendly to him.'[27] His support went considerably beyond editorials – in Menadue's words, 'Murdoch was up to his ears in the campaign', and was in very frequent contact with Labor's primary tacticians, Mick Young and Eric Walsh. He contributed around A$75,000 to Labor, although almost four-fifths of this was via advertisements in his own publications.[28] Whitlam enthusiastically adopted some of Murdoch's suggestions, such as appointing Dr 'Nugget' Coombs as a personal economic adviser, and having a referendum to allow Australians to choose a new national anthem to replace 'God Save the Queen'.[29] But not all his suggestions were so welcome. Murdoch took it on himself to draft what he thought should be Whitlam's final campaign speech, and 'eventually some ideas and lines were used, and Young got Whitlam to thank Murdoch for his input'.[30]

Three years later, in 1975, Murdoch was determined to get rid of the government he had been so keen to see elected in 1972. This was one of the most dramatic years in Australian political history. A series of scandals resulted in the resignations of two senior ministers, and in October the opposition blocked the supply of money to the government for the first time in Australian history. They were able to do this only because convention had not been followed in replacing two Labor senators with senators from the same party. Whitlam refused to call an election, and a deadlock and constitutional crisis followed. Eventually the Governor-General intervened, withdrawing Whitlam's commission and swearing in opposition leader Malcolm Fraser as caretaker prime minister. In the subsequent election, the Coalition parties won a smashing victory.

A small industry has developed around explaining the rupture between Murdoch and Whitlam. The Labor side posits two ulterior motives for Murdoch's changed allegiance. The first is that Murdoch wanted to be appointed High Commissioner in London, and Whitlam refused. To appoint the 'dirty digger', as the magazine *Private Eye* had dubbed Murdoch, as Australia's ambassador to the Court of St James certainly would have invited ridicule, and it is hard to imagine that Murdoch would have remained patient in the position for very long. Murdoch has since denied ever seeking it, or says it was a joke. But Menadue – who was directly involved – confirms it, although he adds that as far as he could tell, Murdoch 'carried no grudge for the knockback'.[31] The other one concerns the refusal of the government to allow the development of a bauxite mine in Western Australia owned by a consortium in which Murdoch was a prominent member. Cabinet rejected their proposal for development in March 1974,[32] but Murdoch's papers were strictly impartial in the election held two months later, in May.

On the Murdoch side, three explanations have been proffered but none is satisfactory. According to Kiernan, 'Murdoch would later claim that Whitlam's inept handling of the budget deadlock … caused him to turn against the Labor prime minister.'[33] But this fails the test of timing, because his anti-Labor attitudes predated that deadlock by many months. In 2013 a US embassy cable released by the US National Archives and published by WikiLeaks reported that in a November 1974 meeting between Murdoch and US Ambassador Marshall Green, Murdoch's disillusion with Whitlam was already clear. He told Green that 'he expects to support the opposition in the next election', which he thought would occur within a year because the opposition would block supply; others of his predictions proved less accurate. He also criticised the government's economic management, especially its 1973 tariff cut.[34]

Murdoch claimed later that he had come to vehemently oppose Whitlam because the government was introducing a 'European type of socialism which caused ruin and misery in other countries'.[35] This is a very imaginative construction of the Whitlam Government's policies, and overlooks the fact that during the 1970s many Western European social democracies were doing considerably better economically than Anglo-Saxon countries.

Murdoch gave a third reason, which Kiernan seems to accept. Soon after Labor was elected on 2 December 1972, the Nixon administration began carpet bombing Hanoi and Haiphong harbour, and in 11 days US planes 'dropped more bombs over North Vietnam than in all of the previous three years'.[36] This followed the proclamation by Henry Kissinger, days before the US election six weeks earlier, that 'peace [was] at hand', prompting euphoria in the US and around the world. Such heavy and indiscriminate bombing when peace was supposed to have been achieved prompted deep disillusion and protest around the world, not least in the US itself. The Labor Party had long been opposed to the war, and some of the most prominent anti-war ministers publicly denounced the US in strong terms. Whitlam remained publicly silent, but wrote a letter to Nixon which departed from the traditional Australian stance of unquestioning compliance, and caused great indignation in Washington.[37] There was also a ban placed by maritime trade unions on US shipping in protest.

According to Kiernan, the US State Department and the US embassy in Canberra – whose competence was illustrated by its forecast that McMahon would win the 1972 election – thought that Murdoch 'had been instrumental' in Whitlam's victory and called on him to get Whitlam to end the shipping boycott. However,

Whitlam refused Murdoch's urgings. In Kiernan's view, 'Murdoch felt both betrayed and embarrassed – betrayed by Whitlam's refusal to do his bidding and embarrassed that the refusal had damaged his standing with the Nixon Administration.'[38] If this is an accurate reflection of Murdoch's thinking, it betrays a failure to understand the depth of anti-war feeling in both the Labor Party and the trade union movement. Whitlam knew it would have been a fool's errand to intervene in the shipping ban as he would have simply been rebuffed and this would have damaged his credibility. Nor does Murdoch seem to appreciate the reasons why the bombing brought such disgust. Finally, it fails the test of timing: if this episode did have such an effect on Murdoch, it did not show in his newspapers until a couple of years later.

Three reasons together seem to explain the depth of Murdoch's falling out with Whitlam and Labor. The first is that in these years, the now New York-domiciled Murdoch's politics were solidifying into a very right-wing view of the world. The second is that like many business figures, he was extremely critical of the Whitlam Government's economic management. While Whitlam had the misfortune to be in government as stagflation struck the Western world, there are valid claims that his government did not respond well or coherently.

The third reason concerns their awkward personal relationship. Although Murdoch had been close to the Labor campaigners in 1972, he and Whitlam were never personally close. Murdoch later said he 'never really liked Whitlam personally. I always thought he had a dreadful intellectual arrogance about him.'[39] 'The chemistry was never there,' judged Menadue, who tried to bring them together.[40] At a July 1971 dinner the conversation was 'polite but cool', although Whitlam was surprised by Murdoch's opening gambit – 'How do we get rid of this government at the next elections?'[41] In September 1971 Gough and Margaret Whitlam spent a night at Murdoch's farm Cavan, which Whitlam described as one of the most 'excruciatingly boring' nights of his life. Menadue thought 'The relationship stuttered forward in a fairly desultory way.'[42] In 1972, with Murdoch still keen and Whitlam's staff equally keen, a cruise on Sydney Harbour was arranged – 'Do I have to come?' asked Whitlam, but he did, and the evening went well.[43]

After the election, Murdoch hosted a victory dinner whose guests included Katherine Graham of the *Washington Post*. Although the evening was a great success, again it had been difficult to persuade Whitlam to attend – 'Comrade, I am not a national exhibit,' he protested.[44] Thereafter personal meetings were few and far between. After seeing Murdoch in London during Easter 1973, Whitlam 'peremptorily cancelled several planned meetings', finding Murdoch's expectations distasteful, and asserting that he was too busy to spend time with Rupert.[45]

But his biggest snub to the publisher came in September 1974 in New York. Whitlam's press secretary, Eric Walsh, always keen to bring the two together, had arranged a dinner. But that morning, Whitlam bumped into David Frost, the English TV personality. Whitlam and Frost had done some interviews together and had developed a warm personal relationship. Murdoch, in contrast, had in 1969 been subjected to the most humiliating TV interview in his life by Frost, and had vowed to take his revenge. The interview occurred after Murdoch's *News of the World* had published some new memoirs by Christine Keeler, reviving the Profumo scandals of the early 1960s, and Frost attacked Murdoch's motives in reviving the affair.[46] Murdoch had been expecting an easy chat, but instead was subjected to an onslaught. According to Wolff, Frost adopted a 'sarcastic, prosecutorial, and sanctimonious' tone without any pretence to impartiality, in front of an audience that was predominantly against Murdoch. However, Frost's motives were as base as Murdoch's – he wanted to make his 3-week-old show the centre of attention, and his grilling of Murdoch helped it 'catch fire'.[47]

In an insult which Murdoch would have found doubly

galling, Whitlam cancelled his dinner with Murdoch and dined with Frost instead. A breakfast meeting for the next morning was hastily arranged, but Murdoch was understandably angry. Whitlam was carelessly allowing a political enmity to assume great and damaging dimensions.

1975 and all that

In 1975 Murdoch mounted what veteran Canberra correspondent Mungo MacCallum called 'the most extraordinarily ruthless and one-sided political coverage I think any of us can remember',[48] and what former editor and writer Donald Horne called vendetta journalism.[49] Murdoch's editorial mobilisation was very crudely exercised. During the election campaign, when unemployment figures were released the paper used raw instead of the usual seasonally adjusted figures to make the government look worse.[50] The *Daily Mirror* headline of the first edition of 26 November had 'Gough's Promise: Cheap Rents'; the second edition was changed to 'Gough Panics: Cheap Rents'.[51] Reporting on the affair of leading Labor figure Jim Cairns and Junie Morosi, the paper published a photo of the two having breakfast on a hotel balcony, but it did not show Mrs Cairns, who was also present.[52]

One News Limited journalist told me in the early 1980s that:

[T]he real rot set in in August 1975.

It was very rugged on the *Australian*. They changed a lot of my stuff.

Bruce Rothwell was sent out to take charge of the paper. He was mad, mad, mad.

It was all totally unsubtle; very ham-fisted.

> Working for Murdoch is a good exercise in understanding the
> politics of the media. I knew I had to put my own professional
> standards above my love for the job … Before I took the job, I
> said the only way I can take this job is that I'm ready to be sacked
> that night. If not, then they've got me.

During the campaign Murdoch journalists staged the first strike
in Australian history over editorial issues.[53] On 28 October 1975,
76 members of the Australian Journalists' Association (AJA) who
worked on the *Australian* expressed concern that the paper had
become a laughing stock. They protested against the 'blind, biased,
tunnel-visioned, ad hoc, logically confused and relentless' way
policy was affecting news coverage:

> We can be loyal to the *Australian*, no matter how much its style,
> thrust and readership changes, as long as it retains the traditions,
> principles and integrity of a responsible newspaper. We cannot
> be loyal to a propaganda sheet.[54]

Murdoch wrote back: 'If you insist on providing ammunition for
our competitors and enemies who are intent on destroying all our
livelihoods, then go ahead.'[55] In a meeting with the striking journalists Murdoch asked what was wrong with that day's paper. Robert
Duffield praised the *Sydney Morning Herald*'s better treatment of a
story. 'You dare to show this paper to me?' said Murdoch. 'These
people are our enemies, trying to destroy us.'[56] Political stories by
Canberra journalists were being rewritten in Sydney and appearing
under the byline 'Our political staff'.[57] Several of the paper's senior
journalists resigned in the following months. The exodus was so
large that one used to joke that they wanted to have a reunion of
the former political correspondents on the *Australian*, but the Melbourne Cricket Ground was booked that day.

Many critics, such as MacCallum and Horne, were Labor

sympathisers, and Murdoch's standard response was to say that the charges of bias simply reflected the bias of the critics. One of his editorial managers, Brian Hogben, complained about the lack of professionalism of the journalists at the *Australian*, saying that they were all Whitlam fans. In contrast, one political journalist felt that the 'lack of professionalism rested with the editorial executives in Sydney', who 'were not prepared to maintain editorial independence' and were 'wilful and reckless in their determination to slant the news'.

Years later, when Murdoch was attempting to take over the Herald and Weekly Times, the same Brian Hogben now felt that journalistic professionalism made concerns about concentration of media ownership irrelevant:

> If, in the case of Rupert Murdoch, who is the popular villain of the piece, every word which appears in his papers is slanted, twisted and corrupted, you are saying by implication that every one of those hundreds and hundreds of journalists [in News Limited] is dishonest and a coward, that they're no better in fact than Adolf Eichmann, the Nazi who was just obeying orders when he gassed millions of Jews. And I am damned sick of that sort of slander perpetrated against hundreds of people who I know and respect.[58]

In fact, Hogben's comments in 1975 highlighted how the slanting of news can occur even while most journalists are still seeking to properly carry out their role.

Playing to win

Although politicians seem to live in fear of Murdoch and so curry favour with him, it may be that they, and Murdoch, and his critics, have an exaggerated view of his power. One can understand the feelings of Murdoch's targets and the humiliation they feel from negative coverage. US journalist Richard Cohen wrote of Murdoch's *New York Post*, 'The paper mugs its enemies for the sheer fun of it – over and over again. This repetition gives it a sort of torque that no politician can ignore.'[59] This is true, but it is another matter to extrapolate from, say, a battered reputation, even from an individual career being ruined, to an election result. The *Economist's* Bagehot column noted in 2003 that:

> The *Sun* can boast that since 1979 the party it has supported has always won. But that probably says more about Mr Murdoch's readiness to jump ship at the right time than about the *Sun's* ability to influence the votes of its readers.[60]

According to Wolff, writing in 2008, Murdoch had been reluctant to jump to the Tories, 'but knew he was, however begrudgingly, going to have to',[61] and later he did. Perhaps this suggests a need to be on what was expected to be the winning side. Political leaders are always keen to make a sure thing even surer, and have remained keen for his support in elections they almost certainly would have won anyway.

In the 1970s Murdoch claimed that 'we single-handedly put the [Whitlam] Government in office', and his American biographers, Kiernan and Wolff, seem to accept this boast.[62] However, the claim collapses as soon as the electoral data is examined. Whitlam achieved the biggest swing in 1969, when Murdoch opposed him. In two-party preferred terms (a measure in Australian elections that takes account of swings to the two major parties after the distribution of preferences from minor parties and independents), there was a huge swing, of 7.1 per cent, in 1969, and a further swing of 2.4 per cent in 1972.

At this time, Murdoch's papers accounted for around a quarter of daily metropolitan circulation. He had a strong presence in New

South Wales and a negligible presence in Victoria. In 1972, Whitlam secured a bigger swing in Victoria (5.5%), than in New South Wales (3.8%).[63] As noted above, Whitlam was already supremely confident of winning before Murdoch came on board. It is impossible to quantify what Murdoch's support contributed in votes, but it clearly was not a central factor.

After his alienation from the Whitlam Government, Murdoch also claimed, 'But now we're not happy with them, and if they don't straighten up we'll bloody well get rid of them.'[64] Labor supporters have always been bitter about their treatment by Murdoch in 1975. Moreover, in his biography of Murdoch, which is largely sympathetic, Tuccille is of the view that:

> in 1975 his newspapers' attacks on Gough Whitlam ... were
> instrumental in toppling the Labor Party government from power
> ... *The Australian*, a money loser since its inception, had finally
> paid Murdoch back in political capital. If he had had any doubts
> about its influence prior to the campaign of 1975, they were
> permanently laid to rest from that moment on.[65]

Again the electoral data does little to support the claim. The swing against Whitlam was strong everywhere (7.4% in two-party preferred terms, the biggest in any election since World War II, with Whitlam's 1969 swing being the second largest). But again it is at least as large in states where Murdoch had a negligible presence as in those where his newspapers had high circulations. It is important to note also that whatever political capital the *Australian* earned in 1975, it also alienated a large part of its readership, and did itself considerable commercial damage. The *Australian*'s circulation had risen to 153,000 in 1974, but with its anti-Labor mobilisation, it dropped to 118,000 by 1977, and as late as 1982 had barely risen (119,000).[66]

There are many levels of political effect, beyond affecting

voters' opinions. One level involves changing the perceptions and decisions of the main participants, and here, including by his own account, Murdoch may have been more influential. Twenty years later, Murdoch told journalist and author Paul Kelly:

> [M]y concern at the time was that Malcolm Fraser, having taken the country to the brink, might lose courage and back off. Maybe if the *Australian* hadn't been so firm on the constitutional issue then Fraser might have lost courage.[67]

In the following years Murdoch's papers remained stridently anti-Labor. Although not as celebrated as 1975, the next plausible candidate for an election where the Murdoch press may have affected the outcome was the 1980 federal election. This was a very close election, with Labor winning 49.6 per cent of the two-party preferred vote. The polls had been close ever since 1978, with Labor more often ahead.[68] Against the expectations of many observers, Labor's lead seemed to increase during the campaign, and as late as the last week polls showed Labor ahead. It was an election where it was said that 'an unusually large number of voters made up their minds very late'.[69] This time Labor failed to secure as big a swing in New South Wales (2.8%) as in Victoria (5.8%), although of course other factors may also have been at work. Murdoch journalists told me in interviews that 'an element of hysteria crept into the organisation' as Labor looked likely to win, and 'people in the media like myself were under a fair amount of pressure to find some bullets'. Especially in the last week of the campaign, the news priorities and orientations of the News Limited papers were very much in line with what the Coalition Government would have wished.[70] Again, it is impossible to have any certainty or to quantify impacts, but in such a finely balanced and uncertain election, there was more scope for a media organisation to affect the result.

There have been many later occasions when the Murdoch press has been on the losing side. It supported Hewson against Keating in 1993, and the day after the election, according to Keating, Murdoch apologised, saying, 'we got it wrong; correction – Ken [Cowley] got it wrong'.[71] At the risk of reading too much into this apology, it seems to imply that their news coverage and support were coloured by their expectations about the result. In 1999, the Murdoch press, plus public statements by Rupert and son Lachlan Murdoch, supported Australia becoming a republic, but the referendum failed.

It is impossible to quantify the impact of Murdoch's editorial positions on public opinion, let alone on election results. The absence of definitive evidence of direct effects means that views about how press coverage interacted with other factors must remain tentative. Murdoch's fantasies about his political prowess should not be accepted, but neither does this mean his support is irrelevant.

7

The passionate player
Thatcher, Reagan and beyond

Of all the political leaders he met before and since, none inspired in Murdoch the attachment he had to Reagan and Thatcher. Their leaderships coincided with the most dramatic growth in his empire, and both were right-wing leaders whose governments, in both rhetoric and practice, marked sharp departures from previous conservative governments. His commitment to them coloured the reporting by all his news outlets.

Murdoch's entry into British politics was less than spectacular. When he bought the *Sun* in 1969, one of his promises to Hugh Cudlipp, the former owner, was that it would continue to support Labour. He stuck to this position initially, and supported Harold Wilson's re-election in 1970, although the paper adjusted with no evident disappointment to the Tories' surprise victory under Ted Heath.[1] At the election in February 1974, it abandoned its commitment to Labour and very tepidly endorsed Heath. Its editorial, 'The Devil and the Deep Blue Sea', concluded that 'in spite of the record, Ted's Tories look the better bet'.[2] Instead Wilson formed a minority government in a hung parliament, and then called another election for October, which he won. This time the *Sun* ducked a choice between the two major parties, saying, 'We're sick of the Ted and Harold show' and advised readers to vote for the best candidates.[3] So, at each of its first three elections, Murdoch's *Sun* had failed to support a winner.

Politics was not a big part of the *Sun* as it grew to become the

121

biggest circulating paper in the country. Its appeal lay in sex, human interest, crime, sport and show business. But readership of the *Sun* overlapped significantly with what has often been a strategically important part of the British electorate: people who are working class but socially conservative. When Britain was a much more working-class country than it is now, the great Conservative Prime Minister Benjamin Disraeli saw the importance of wooing these people, whom he called 'angels in marble'[4] – those whose political support, by economic position, would be inclined to the left, but for whom other appeals, such as nation, race and order, were of greater concern and led them to vote conservative. In the 1970s the somewhat more affluent members of the working class, for example those working in skilled manual occupations, were seen as the key to electoral success; they were heavily represented among *Sun* readers.[5]

The newspaper only became stridently political in the late 1970s, although editorially it had largely been on the Tories' side since Thatcher became leader in February 1975.[6] This to some extent reflected Murdoch's own shift to the right, but the paper also responded to and amplified the increasing public frustration with strikes and disorder. It rode and fanned a populist wave in campaigning against the decaying Callaghan Labour Government. *Sun* headlines such as 'Winter of Discontent' and 'Crisis? What Crisis?', making fun of (and distorting) a statement by Callaghan, fed straight into the Conservatives' electoral strategy. In the lead-up to the election, *Sun* editor Larry Lamb became a regular visitor to Mrs Thatcher's house to offer informal advice, and he was knighted afterwards. On polling day, the *Sun* published an unprecedented 1700-word editorial. The headline read: 'Vote Tory This Time. It's the Only Way to Stop the Rot'.[7]

However, it was not just 'this time'. Murdoch continued his support for the Conservatives until after the 1992 election. His support was very much for Thatcher personally and he took her side against the 'wets' inside her own party as well as against Labour. Former Murdoch editor and Tory supporter Andrew Neil later wrote that:

> news stories were told from a Thatcherite perspective, features geared to further Thatcherite ideas ... At election time, Tory tabloids turned themselves into the publishing arm of Tory Central office. The newspapers were full of powerful, skillful, constant propaganda for the Tory cause.[8]

Through these years, the *Sun*'s support was often manifested less in positive coverage of Thatcher's domestic policies than in negative coverage of her opponents: critical coverage of 'loony Left councils',[9] trade unions and the Labour Party were recurring features. In the 1982 election, the *Sun* had a headline 'Do you seriously want this old man to run Britain?' with a photo of Labour leader Michael Foot, and warned that he was a 'willing dupe' of the ruthless Left.[10] The Tory press generally, but the Murdoch press most of all, embraced Thatcher's re-conquest of the Falkland Islands from the Argentineans, and in the process made her a conquering heroine. During the 1987 campaign, according to Woodrow Wyatt, 'Rupert said they are doing two shock issues in the *Sun* about what it would be like under Labour and about Britain being great again.' When Wyatt told Thatcher she said, 'Rupert is marvellous.'[11] Murdoch approached the election more as a campaigner than a journalist. This was also true of his approach to Thatcher's greatest crisis up to that time.

Westland – managing appearances and realities

'We've got to get her out of this jam somehow. It's looking very bad.'[12] Thus Murdoch expressed his worries to Wyatt as the Westland crisis was building to its climax. Ten days later, on 24 January 1986, as Thatcher faced a House of Commons urgency motion,

she said, 'I may not be Prime Minister by six o'clock this evening.'[13]
'That was the measure,' said Hugo Young, 'of the disillusionment
she knew to be present in the Conservative Party.'[14] The previous
Friday her Industry Secretary, Leon Brittan, had resigned, saying he
had made regrettable errors, and Thatcher said those errors were
made without her knowledge. An emergency debate was scheduled
for the Monday; the prime minister survived, but with her credibility severely dented.

When it began, there was no indication that Westland would
develop into such a crisis.[15] The company, Britain's last helicopter
manufacturer, was in great financial trouble. Sir John Cuckney was
installed to rescue something for Westland's bankers, and favoured
selling it to a partnership of the American company, Sikorsky, and
the Italian company, Fiat. The British Defence Secretary, Michael
Heseltine, one of the government's highest profile ministers, met
Sikorsky representatives in September 1985 and 'concluded that
the Sikorsky deal, though nice for the banks, did nothing for Westland's shareholders, and nothing for the British taxpayer who had
put large sums into Westland'.[16] He lined up a consortium of three
European companies, and his Cabinet colleagues seemed favour-
ably disposed.[17] Believing he had Thatcher's support, Heseltine
publicly endorsed the plan.

In December, Heseltine professed great shock when it seemed
to him that Thatcher had 'suddenly, and unaccountably, reversed
herself … [and was now] vigorously promoting' the Sikorsky-Fiat
bid.[18] Tension between them mounted. In Heseltine's view, denied
by Thatcher, a meeting for a key group of ministers had been
scheduled for 13 December and then not held. The failure to meet
convinced Heseltine that 'something very wrong had happened'.[19]
Early in the New Year, Heseltine thought Thatcher had made a
misleading public comment, and countered with his own version
in a letter to the European stakeholders. The Department of Trade
and Industry, on the authority of the minister, Brittan – and, many

suspected, with the knowledge of Thatcher and her office – then leaked the parts of a government legal opinion that claimed there were 'material inaccuracies' in Heseltine's letter. Thatcher's office gave anti-Heseltine briefings to journalists. Murdoch's *Sun* did the leakers proud, with its headline, 'YOU LIAR', and its report that 'Battling Maggie' had caught Heseltine in a devious Euro-scam.

The Cabinet's law officers, Sir Patrick Mayhew and Sir Nigel Havers, were incensed that their advice had been leaked and distorted for factional purposes, and that they were now embroiled in scandal.[20] At the subsequent Cabinet meeting Heseltine resigned after a clash with Thatcher, throwing the government into a deeper crisis. He darkly hinted that there was 'something extremely fishy about all this'. Brittan put in a series of clumsy performances both in public and in party meetings, and he also soon resigned.

Murdoch's involvement went far beyond colouring the reporting to put a pro-Thatcher view. Sikorsky was an arm of United Technologies Inc., and since 1984, Murdoch had been a member of that company's Board, recruited by his friend, its head, Harry Gray.[21] At that time Gray was hoping to sell its Sikorsky helicopters to the Australian Government, and within a year he succeeded.[22]

On Sunday 19 January 1986, in the midst of the crisis and five days before Murdoch planned to begin publishing at Wapping, Murdoch had lunch with Thatcher at the prime minister's country residence, Chequers. After the lunch, Murdoch rang Wyatt with the idea that he would get United Technologies to buy shares in Westland to fix the vote in favour of the Sikorsky-Fiat option – in the end, the future of Westland would be decided by its shareholders.[23] Just before the crucial meeting, buyers from Switzerland, Panama and Australia bought Westland shares and all voted for that bid. The Australian buyer, later revealed as Peter Abeles' TNT, bought almost 5 per cent of Westland's shares, just below the threshold at which shareholdings had to be publicly declared. Abeles was not only Murdoch's partner in Ansett Airlines, but had just 'signed a

£1-million-a-week contract with Murdoch to handle the distribution of all News International's papers out of Wapping'.[24] The new shareholders sealed Sikorsky's victory. As Bruce Page observed, this sudden rush of share buying was barely explored in the press.[25] In 2006, on the 20th anniversary of the crisis, Heseltine demanded a fresh investigation. He said that despite a House of Commons Committee recommending it in 1986, no investigation had been carried out.[26]

The bottom line was that Murdoch never wavered in his support for Thatcher over Westland, and Thatcher never wavered in her support for Murdoch over Wapping.

The end of the Thatcher era

In 1990, Thatcher suffered a series of political disasters[27] leading to a mounting sense of dissatisfaction inside the Conservative Party, but Murdoch and the *Sun* remained staunch supporters. As the Conservative MPs took the vote that resulted in her demise, a *Sun* columnist wrote:

> So the back stabbers have won. The tin pot Judases and two-bob
> traitors of the Tory party turned on the woman who had kept
> them in power for 11 years. What a gutless rabble.[28]

The editor, Kelvin MacKenzie, wrote an open letter to Tory MPs to support 'Maggie the Lionheart', and reminded them that 'it was OUR readers who put YOU in office'. After her loss, the *Sun* devoted 24 of its 48 pages to her.[29]

The papers soon rallied, and set about the task of getting John Major re-elected against Labour's Neil Kinnock in 1992. This was the election where the paper itself proclaimed 'It was the *Sun* wot won it', and it is often seen as the campaign where the tabloids' partisan bias was at its peak. The *Sun*'s campaign climaxed in their famous election day front page with Kinnock's head in a light bulb, and the rest of the page taken by the headline 'If Neil Kinnock wins today, will the last person to leave Britain please turn out the lights'. The day before it had run nine pages on the election, each headed with the slogan 'Nightmare on Kinnock Street'. Earlier it had pursued such themes as Kinnock being too influenced by his wife – 'Is Glenys a Red in Neil's Bed?'[30]

After the election, according to Wyatt's diary, 'Rupert rang in a great state. What an appalling campaign it had been and how they were lucky to have got in and how they had been helped by the *Sun*.'[31] Thatcher and, most rhapsodically, Tory Treasurer Lord McAlpine, thought the role of the press was central:

> The heroes of this campaign were Sir David English, Sir Nicholas
> Lloyd, Kelvin MacKenzie and the other editors of the grander
> Tory press. Never in the past nine elections have they come out
> so strongly in favour of the Conservatives. Never has the attack
> on the Labour Party been so comprehensive.[32]

In a rare bipartisan consensus, Neil Kinnock and many on the Labour side shared this view. It should be remembered, though, that all these sources had an interest in denying credit to Major for his victory.

But 1992 was the high tide of Murdoch's (and the other Tory tabloids') support for Major. Once the threat of Labour had been seen off, the *Sun's* nostalgia quickly came to the fore: 'Quit now Major and bring back Maggie', it urged before the 1993 Conservative conference. Major's promise to uphold family values was taken as a licence to explore the sexual peccadillos of Tory MPs, while a series of financial scandals, including 'cash for questions', meant that Major suffered at least 34 separate instances of so-called sleaze stories. The *Sun's* columnist Richard Littlejohn called it 'a sleazy dishonest administration led by a political pygmy'.[33]

Reagan

Murdoch moved to New York in 1973, and his politics gravitated very quickly towards the right wing of the Republican Party. In particular, Murdoch 'was at once fascinated and astonished by Watergate. In his view, the affair constituted a perverse abuse of the American news media's power.'[34] For most people in the media, Watergate 'is a myth of David and Goliath, of powerless individuals overturning an institution of overwhelming might',[35] of news media making power accountable by revealing truth. On the 40th anniversary, the two key reporters, Bob Woodward and Carl Bernstein, affirmed the importance of holding Nixon responsible for his misdeeds,[36] but Murdoch was 'aghast at the press's politicking' against Nixon.[37] He told a friend, 'the American press might get their pleasure in successfully crucifying Nixon, but the last laugh could be on them. See how they like it when the Commies take over the West.'[38] He thought the news media's behaviour in the Watergate hearings was 'reckless, irresponsible and self-defeating', and believed that:

> the new cult of adversarial journalism has sometimes been taken to the point of subversion ... It's a disgrace that we can and do read thousands upon thousands of words about our national defence and our foreign policy every day without so much as a nod of recognition to the enormous risks to our freedom that exist today.[39]

Murdoch thought Nixon devious and unsavoury, but felt that that was what politicians needed to be in the real world. 'If anything brings about the downfall of this country, it'll be the Democrats acting in league with the press,' he said.[40]

In 1980 he was firmly in the Reagan camp. Prominent Republican Jack Kemp enthused that 'Rupert Murdoch used the editorial page, the front page and every other page necessary to elect

Ronald Reagan president.'[41] Murdoch 'took as much credit for [Reagan's victory] as he possibly could', and claimed that the *Post* had 'delivered New York state to Reagan'.[42] Perhaps there was a kernel of truth in the claim, but it should also be remembered that since 1993, when Murdoch regained control of the *Post*, New York has gone Democratic in every presidential election despite the *Post*'s strident support for the Republicans, in 2012 voting 63%–36% for Obama over Romney.

When Murdoch 'bought the *Chicago Sun Times* in 1983, the journalists were told that they could not criticise Reagan directly. If there had to be criticism, it had to be directed at his aides.'[43] Even towards the end of Reagan's presidency, when his political fortunes were at a low ebb, and he was under pressure for both illegality and incompetence in the Iran-Contra scandal, Murdoch did not falter in his support. Eric Beecher was then editing the Melbourne *Herald* for Murdoch, and Murdoch wanted its Washington correspondent, Geoffrey Barker, replaced because Murdoch considered him anti-Reagan. Afterwards, Murdoch served as a trustee of the Ronald Reagan Presidential Foundation.[44]

According to Murdoch's editor of the *Sunday Times*, Andrew Neil:

> I was able to regularly criticize Margaret Thatcher, even though he adored her. Criticizing Ronald Reagan was a more risky business: Reagan was Rupert's first love.[45]

On the only occasion when his two loves were in conflict – when Reagan invaded the tiny Commonwealth island of Grenada following a coup there – there was no doubt where Murdoch stood. He told Wyatt that Thatcher was 'just childish', that she was 'out of her mind', 'desperately over-tired' and 'not listening to her friends'.[46] He told Kiernan:

Reagan's Grenada action has to do with the freedom of the
Western world, including England's. Thatcher had no business
opening her mouth. I'll see she pays for it.[47]

Apart from that episode there was room to embrace both.

The invasion of Grenada also exemplified just how fully Murdoch had embraced Reagan's foreign policies. The *New York Post* claimed that the coup in Grenada posed a 'clear threat to peace in the entire Caribbean area – and by extension, in all of Central America'. Grenada, it said, was 'a Soviet forward base'.[48]

Murdoch's passionate anti-Communism and his support for Reagan led him to join a project that most would have considered a conflict of interest. Reagan appointed Charlie Wick, a friend of Murdoch who later became a member of the News Corp Board, to head the United States Information Agency. Wick recruited an informal group, including Murdoch, to 'Project Democracy', a campaign against Soviet 'disinformation and propaganda' in Europe, using slush funds raised outside Congress. Countering Soviet disinformation was easily stretched to opposing any views critical of Reagan's policies (such as his wish to deploy nuclear weapons in Western Europe).[49] Participating in a government's black propaganda exercise is something most media figures would baulk at.

When it came to conflicts between Reagan and the media, Murdoch knew which side he was on. His negative views of the American press, which had started to crystallise during Watergate, solidified under Reagan. He told Kiernan:

Reaganism represents a positive change in American thinking
… It has the support of the people, but not the national press.
The press here is sitting around doing its usual thing, sneering at
Reagan and waiting to pounce on him the moment he stumbles
… The whole Reagan package needs much more support by the

press. If no one else will provide it, we'll bloody well have to do the job.[50]

He accused the press of 'attempting to change the political agenda' and of ignoring 'the traditional values of the great masses of this country'.[51]

It is notable just how readily and scathingly Murdoch attributes bias to other news organisations. It is also notable just how frequently he invokes the refrain about liberal media bias without ever offering any supporting evidence. From this time on, Murdoch has frequently made offhand comments denigrating elite US media, especially the *New York Times*. Sometimes it is flippant. He joked in front of a crowd of admiring CEOs that 'I'd love to buy the *Times* one day. And the next day shut it down, as a public service.'[52] And another:

I think that Arthur Sulzberger [publisher of the *Times*], over the years, has made it very clear that he wants a very liberal paper, and that he wants a staff that reflects that community. For five years, he didn't want any white heterosexual men hired.[53]

At other times, it is deadly serious. After taking control of the *Wall St Journal*, Murdoch told a meeting of its senior editors that they had to 'figure out how to cripple, really cripple, the *New York Times*.'[54]

Adrift

Through the 1980s, Murdoch was riding high, with his heroes in power. But he was much less enamoured of their two successors. George H.W. Bush and John Major were the type of managerial conservatives he disliked. Bush was never strong on what he dismissively called 'the vision thing'.

Murdoch was politically adrift. He tended to frame this as a search for worthy leaders. But the larger truth is that the Reagan and Thatcher projects were politically exhausted. They had collided with socio-political realities and with public opinion.

At this time, Murdoch's move into US television meant that he was also adrift in terms of having no press presence, and so he did not have an overtly political profile. This alienation led him into bizarre positions. In 1988, when George H.W. Bush was certain to win the Republican nomination, Murdoch supported the tele-evangelist Pat Robertson. Robertson's 1988 candidacy was itself a minor miracle, given that earlier he had predicted that the world would end in 1982. God made several revelations to Robertson denied to other mortals: for example, that the Russians again had missiles in Cuba. Robertson also argued that feminism encouraged women to 'leave their husbands, kill their children, practise witchcraft, destroy capitalism and become lesbians'. When a deal he was doing in Scotland collapsed, he attributed it to how strong homosexuals were in that 'dark land'. Murdoch, however, claimed Robertson 'was right on all the issues'.[55]

In 1992, Murdoch again could not bring himself to support the orthodox conservative George H.W. Bush, and instead embraced the third-party candidate Ross Perot,[56] whose populist economics included high protection (in contrast to Murdoch's free trade views) but also – more appealingly to Murdoch – large cuts in government spending. Murdoch told Wyatt not to 'underestimate [Perot]. I know him quite well. He is a very tough businessman. He has got bags of money ... If there were an election tomorrow, he'd win it.'[57] Ironically, the 18.9 per cent of the popular vote Perot won came mainly from people who would otherwise have supported Bush, and so helped Bill Clinton win the presidency.

So after Reagan and Thatcher, in both the US and the UK, Murdoch found himself estranged from their mainstream conservative successors. He solved this problem in two very different ways. He resolved his post-Thatcher doldrums by a return to the political mainstream, supporting the election of Blair's Labour Party in 1997. He resolved his post-Reagan doldrums by becoming more sectarian. In 1995, he started the *Weekly Standard*, which became the standard bearer for the 'neo-Cons' and their foreign policy views.[58] Most importantly, in 1996 he started Fox News which, as we will see in Chapter 11, became an important player in Republican politics. In the US Murdoch cast his lot with the far right elements in the Republican Party.

With varying degrees of fear and favour

Quality journalism depends on an ecumenical scepticism and a willingness to report newsworthy developments no matter who may be helped or hurt. Murdoch – at least regarding Reagan and Thatcher – has a partisan mentality, quite the reverse of this. He could rarely, if ever, see any validity in critical news stories about either. 'You're always getting at her!' he said to Harold Evans, who thought that Murdoch 'hated "balance" and "objectivity" and kept calling for more "conviction", which, Evans thought, meant more Tory cheerleading'.[59] *Times* editorial writer Richard Davy recalled that Murdoch always complained that the *Times* 'didn't stand for anything, whereas we always thought it stood for reasoned argument and liberal values'.[60] Wolff put it most strongly: 'The entire rationale of modern, objective, arm's length, editor-driven journalism … [Murdoch] regarded as artifice if not an outright sham.'[61]

One of the tactics Murdoch and his representatives use, when confronted with accusations of bias, is to talk about the biases of those making the charges, to change a discussion about journalism into a discussion about the politics of their critics. But such a strategy cannot account for the *Wall St Journal* journalists who, against their own career interests, mobilised against Murdoch becoming their owner.[62] The *Journal* had perhaps the most conservative editorial line and op-ed pages of the major US newspapers. The journalists' fear was not that Murdoch would make the paper's editorial outlook more conservative, but that editorial views would impinge directly on the reporting and selection of news. Seven journalists, responsible for coverage of China, wrote a joint letter to the then controlling shareholders, the Bancroft family, urging them not to sell to Murdoch:

> Our China team won the Pulitzer Prize for international reporting this year for a series of stories detailing the consequences of China's unbridled pursuit of capitalism ... It is an important example of the coverage that we fear would suffer if News Corp takes control. News Corp Chairman Rupert Murdoch has a well-documented history of making editorial decisions in order to advance his business interests in China.[63]

The problematic aspect of Murdoch's political journalism is not his preferences, although the degree of uniformity among his publications is greater than it is in many other companies, and in Australia and Britain his share of voice presents a problem for democratic pluralism. What has made Murdoch so controversial is the way his editorial support has been manifested: it has reached crudely and deeply into news judgements and the presentation of stories. Of course there has been considerable variation between news outlets and countries. Sky News in the UK and Australia is much more balanced than Fox News in the US, for instance. The opinion pages of the *Times* and the *Australian* show much more diversity than do those of his tabloid newspapers. There are also periods of greater or lesser editorial mobilisation, and there are issues where most Murdoch papers take a strong view and those where they do not. This book is 'biased' towards periods and issues where Murdoch has been most actively and directly involved, where editorial mobilisation has been strongest, and has led to the most one-sided reporting, and thus it under-represents the amount of good journalism carried out in titles he owns or has owned.

One key when considering these issues is to move beyond a dichotomous – completely unbiased vs totally biased – discussion, to degrees of partisanship. As with other areas of life, there is a tendency to obliterate crucial distinctions. Take corruption: no society is completely free from corruption, but this should not obscure the real and important differences in the degree and nature of corruption in different societies and at different times.

Nevertheless, some things are clear. Murdoch's perceptions of media bias – from Watergate through the Reagan years and beyond – are very different from those of most journalists. And in terms of almost any professional criterion – accuracy, balancing competing views, presentations of news, judgements of newsworthiness – the *New York Post* was more biased in the way it covered the news during the Reagan era than its New York competitors, and subsequently Fox News has performed at a less professional level than its competitors.

In the UK, from the arrival of Macmillan in 1957 to the departure of Wilson in 1976, the general trend was towards more muted press partisanship, but from the late 1970s, this was put into sharp reverse, and Murdoch was a central factor in the reversal. According to scholar Jeremy Tunstall, Thatcher 'probably received more press adulation from more national newspapers than did any other British Prime Minister after Winston Churchill's wartime premiership ended in 1945'.[64] At the end of the Thatcher period, driven by many factors, not least Murdoch's *Sun*, the quantitative advantage of the Conservatives was at a peak – with pro-Conservative papers having a three to one circulation advantage[65] – and, according to prominent British journalist and former News International editor Brian MacArthur, in 1992, 'the popular press have never been quite so biased as they are today, nor so potent a threat to standards of political debate'.[66]

8

The dominant player
Murdoch ascendant

When John Howard was elected Australian prime minister in March 1996, Murdoch had just celebrated his 65th birthday. He was at a very different stage of life from when he had been an enthusiastic participant in Gough Whitlam's 1972 'It's Time' campaign. He was head of a global media empire, and determined that politicians should court him; it was long past the time when he would ingratiate himself with them.

The most spectacular wooing was by Tony Blair when he and Alastair Campbell went halfway round the world, to Hayman Island, off the Queensland coast, to attend a gathering of senior Murdoch executives. Irrespective of what Blair said at the conference, this was a public political courtship, a demonstration of a willingness to bury the Labour resentments of past mistreatment. For Piers Brendon, it was 'the most humiliating odyssey ... since Henry IV abased himself before the Pope at Canossa'.[1] Campbell, however, 'was never in doubt that it was a good thing to do'.[2]

In August 2008, David Cameron emulated Blair when Murdoch's son-in-law Matthew Freud flew him to Greece to join Murdoch for drinks on his yacht *Rosehearty*.[3] According to Peter Oborne, 'Cameron's first meetings with Murdoch went poorly.' He quoted a 'leading News International figure' who said, 'We told David exactly what to say and how to say it in order to please Rupert. But Cameron wouldn't play ball. I can't understand it.'[4] So the upper echelons of both the Conservative Party and News International thought this meeting on Murdoch's yacht crucial; in contrast, in testimony to the Leveson Inquiry, Murdoch professed not even to remember it. Leveson concluded that Murdoch:

> regarded the lengths to which Mr Cameron had gone to meet
> him as not unusual and one got the feeling that Mr Murdoch was
> well used to political leaders seeking him out: a telling indicator
> of the power and importance of one of the biggest media
> proprietors.[5]

Murdoch would never admire any new leaders as much as he had Thatcher and Reagan. Partly it was that Murdoch tended to judge new leaders by how they measured up to his idealised versions of those two, and most were found wanting. Also, he was now dealing with politicians considerably younger than himself. Tony Blair was 22 years younger; David Cameron 35 years younger – indeed Cameron was roughly an age peer of Murdoch's children, Elisabeth and James, and moved in their social circles.

Murdoch's more recent approach to being a political player reflects his greater power and his range of experience, but also differs in the three countries. It is likely that President Obama spent much less time worrying about Murdoch than prime ministers Cameron and Julia Gillard. This is partly because Murdoch's share of news media is much less significant in the US than in Britain and Australia. It is also because the stance of his American outlets rarely varies: Fox News, the *New York Post* and the *Wall St Journal* will never support the Democrats against the Republicans.

There is a paradox here. Murdoch's centre of gravity – in business, social relationships and political attitudes – is now more than ever in the US. Commercially and emotionally, Britain and Australia mean less to him, but they are the two countries in which he wielded greatest power. Perhaps this explains his more high-handed attitude towards Australian and British political leaders.

Most Murdoch papers strongly supported Howard's election in 1996, but Murdoch then related to Howard with a degree of coolness, bordering on arrogance. In the years up to 2001, his papers often treated the prime minister with disdain. One source of tension was Murdoch's wish to change media policies. After profiting enormously from the cross-media 'reforms' introduced by the Hawke Government (see Chapter 9), Murdoch was now keen to re-enter Australian television, but there were two policy obstacles – the cross-media rules, which Murdoch had supported at the time, and the ban on foreign companies owning Australian television licences. There was no prospect of the Howard Government being able to change either policy, as the government did not have control of the Senate, but this did not lessen Murdoch's impatience. In 1998, Murdoch criticised media regulations, saying, 'I think the individuals involved in making decisions are overawed by some of the existing players', implying that the government was too keen to placate Packer. Then he likened the Howard Government's approval of 'monopolies' in television to the recently fallen corrupt regime of President Suharto in Indonesia.[6]

The one political issue where Murdoch was at odds with Howard was the referendum to replace the Queen with an Australian head of state. The proposal was rejected, but Murdoch's role in supporting the case for change attracted criticism from the monarchists. Senior Liberal Nick Minchin said that Murdoch, a US citizen, should understand that this is a matter for Australians to determine; this is a point he never made when Murdoch was supporting the Liberals in election campaigns. He thought that 'Mr Murdoch should be embarrassed by his newspapers' outrageous propaganda campaign.'[7] Lachlan Murdoch, then 28, speaking from the US, criticised Howard's conduct of the issue, and seemed to endorse Costello as Howard's successor. 'Howard was absolutely

appalled,' said one senior minister, who also noted that, with decisions about digital television about to be made, this was a bad time
for the Murdochs to annoy the prime minister.[8]

Indeed Murdoch saw the opening up of the digital spectrum as
an opportunity to re-enter television. News Corp was not eligible
for a normal TV channel, so the Murdoch press focused on the possibility of gaining licences to permit 'datacasting', a concept that
gained prominence for a couple of years – when it suited Murdoch
interests – and then disappeared without trace. A Murdoch business
journalist, Mark Westfield, thought that 'Howard ... singled out
News Limited as a demonic force seeking to ravish the Australian
public in pursuit of its commercial interests.'[9] In 1999, Murdoch
again 'let fly at the Prime Minister over what he [believed was]
unfair treatment being dished out to News Ltd'. According to journalist Steve Lewis, this explained 'why the government has been
copping it in the neck from the Murdoch press ... The ferocity of
the News Ltd campaign cannot be ignored.'[10]

From September 2001, Howard's and Murdoch's agendas
coincided. As Howard's electoral fortunes improved, and as he
strongly supported US actions in the 'war on terror', the Murdoch
press settled into solid support. Even then there was a degree of
coolness in Murdoch's public comments that the prime minister
would have found galling. After Howard gained a Senate majority in 2005, media policy changes were again politically possible.
Murdoch, for whom Australia was now a much lower priority,
was less than gracious in his public advice: 'Tear up everything,
and make it an open go for everybody, otherwise leave it alone,'[11]
he dismissively commented. When Howard was making a tri-
umphal American tour in 2006, Murdoch made the unwelcome
prediction that he would retire 'on the top of his game' later in
the year. Given that Murdoch himself was nine years older than
Howard, raising the topic of retirement was dangerous territory.
Former Victorian premier and dedicated Costello foe Jeff Kennett

issued the obvious riposte: 'He should practise what he preaches.'[12]

Although the Murdoch press has overwhelmingly supported the conservative side of politics, in both Britain and Australia, sometimes it has not. Perhaps that is why Australian Labor leaders have remained keen to woo Murdoch. No contemporary Labor leader would repeat Whitlam's sentiment that he was too busy to bother with Rupert. A meal with Murdoch – with a few platitudes offered to waiting reporters afterwards – has become one of the staples of Australian political leaders' visits to the US.

Murdoch has only supported the non-conservative side when it was clear that they were going to win. So each time this has served Murdoch's goal: being, and being seen to be, on the winner's side. The Blair and Hawke-Keating Governments were led by centre-left, dynamic leaders who were economic modernisers, and who, crucially, had shown they were amenable to dealing with Murdoch.

Murdoch's editorial support for UK Labour was always qualified and tepid; it endorsed a conservative agenda on most policy issues. In contrast, his support for conservatives has sometimes been whole-hearted and embracing. As David McKnight notes, 'His support for Blair did not involve the vicious slurs and raucous jeers against the Tories that the *Sun* had directed against Labour.'[13] Murdoch was always much keener on Margaret Thatcher than he was on the Conservative Party generally, and often his papers were critical of other Conservative politicians,[14] but he expressed his disapproval of the Labour Party much more stridently. Thus in 2003 he praised Blair's 'courageous and strong' support for the Iraq War, because 'it's not easy doing that in a party which is largely composed of people who have a knee-jerk anti-Americanism and are sort of pacifist'.[15] While the *Sun* and the *Times* supported Labour in 1997, 2001 and 2005, the *Sunday Times* supported the Conservatives at each election.[16]

There has been an interesting contrast between Murdoch's British papers and his Australian ones. In Britain, announcements of

Murdoch editorial support seem designed to further the Murdoch mystique, to proclaim that his media are a political force which it is important to have on-side. In the 2005 election, as Roy Greenslade notes:

> The Sun, which has never been noted for its reticence, presented its decision to support Tony Blair as if it were a matter of supreme national import. What was infinitely more fascinating was the fact that the rest of the media treated it in similar fashion.[17]

Then, at a most strategic moment, designed to maximise the impact of the announcement, when Gordon Brown was to deliver his speech to the Labour Party conference, the Sun declared on the front page that it was backing David Cameron.

Similarly, Murdoch's annual London summer party was an ostentatious show of his power. Most prominent people in Britain wanted an invitation and felt obliged to attend, whatever they felt about Murdoch and his papers. When Murdoch was asked at the Leveson Inquiry whether Prime Minister Gordon Brown attended the previous summer party, Murdoch replied: 'Yes, I think so. Most people did.'[18]

In contrast, in Australia his papers have taken different stances in different elections. When asked about Australian politics, he some-times defers to his editors – 'Ask my editors,' he modestly replies, even though this suggests, to veteran journalist Alan Ramsey, 'a more tolerant Rupert Murdoch than any of us remember and most of us would ever believe'.[19] However, when a Liberal victory has been likely, they have often unanimously been on the winning side. Clearly, there is political value in the empire appearing to dis-play some internal diversity. It makes it harder for critics who are describing the dangers to democracy in such a media behemoth, and provides useful exceptions to situations when all editorials sing in unison, such as in support of the Iraq War.

In the months leading up to the 2007 election, it appeared certain that Kevin Rudd would defeat Howard. This presented a dilemma for Murdoch and his editorial upper echelons. As Eric Beecher has observed, Murdoch rules by phone and clone, and senior editors overwhelmingly share his conservative ideologies. On the other hand, they did not want to be on the losing side. According to the editor of the *Australian*, Chris Mitchell, it was still difficult to persuade Murdoch to endorse Rudd.[20]

The *Australian*, *Daily Telegraph* and *Courier-Mail* all advocated a vote for change, while the *Herald-Sun* and the *Advertiser* stuck with the Coalition. Some of the pro-Labor editorials were among the gentlest ever emanating from a Murdoch publication. The *Daily Telegraph* began: 'This is an unusual editorial in that it praises the leadership and legacy of our current prime minister – and calls for him to be removed.' (Contrast this with its front page anti-Labor editorial on the first day of the 2013 campaign – 'Kick this mob out'.)[21] Interestingly, in 2007 the news coverage in these papers showed very little correlation with their editorial support for Labor. It was more balanced than in some other election campaigns, but the last-minute coverage of the polls in all of them seemed to be showing a wish for a swing back to Howard.[22] Whatever party is editorially endorsed, the news priorities and commentary remain consistently skewed towards conservative agendas.

This is partly because Murdoch's political ideology was now more consistent and stable. In 1999, he described himself to William Shawcross as leaning towards a libertarian outlook, meaning 'as much individual responsibility as possible, as little government as possible, as few rules as possible. But I'm not saying it should be taken to the absolute limit.'[23] Sometimes this finds coherent and eloquent expression as a vision for a better society, such as in his Boyer Lectures for the ABC.[24] At other times it simply becomes a default position against government intervention and a basis for anti-politician populism.

If anything, Murdoch's attachments to political leaders have become more contingent, his political ideologies more entrenched. Whichever party is in power in Britain, there are unlikely to be any stories in the Murdoch press, particularly the *Sun*, praising the European Union. John Major called the *Sun* 'the house magazine of England-against-the-world',[25] and Alastair Campbell, formerly Blair's director of communications and strategy, described a lunch he and Blair had there as being like a British National Party meeting.[26] An article by Blair publicly distancing himself from a pro-European stance – headlined 'I'm a British patriot' and promising that Labour would not allow Britain to be absorbed into a 'European superstate'[27] – was the precursor to what the *Sun* called its 'historic announcement' that 'the *Sun* backs Blair'.[28] If Blair seemed to waver on the issue, the Murdoch papers were quick to bring him into line. In 1998, when the paper thought Blair might have desired to scrap the pound and join the euro, its headline asked, 'Is this the most dangerous man in Britain?'[29]

Murdoch has been a constant voice for the view that Britain should look more towards the US and less towards Europe. In the US, he has been a constant voice for hawkish foreign policies, and in Australia and Britain his publications have been a constant voice for supporting US actions. This was most prominently and importantly on display in the Iraq War.

Operation Iraqi Freedom

The three English-speaking countries comprising the 'Coalition of the Willing' which invaded Saddam Hussein's Iraq in 2003, are the three countries where Murdoch has the largest journalistic presence. Andrew Neil told a House of Lords inquiry that 'there were more discordant voices [on Iraq] in the Bush administration than there were in the Murdoch empire'.[30] According to author Robert Manne, in 2002 the Hobart *Mercury* had initially deviated from the company's hard line on Iraq, but later conformed. A journalist on the paper told him that the newspaper had been instructed by head office to alter its position.[31] While McKnight and McNair found that Murdoch's editorial writers in all three countries marched in unison, the papers they studied showed more variation in how much diversity was found on the opinion pages. The *New York Post* and the *Sun* had almost none, while the *Times*, the *Australian* and the *Herald-Sun* displayed a variety of viewpoints.

More than a decade later, it is hard to recapture the belligerence and military over-confidence in the US in 2002–03. The shock and anger following the 9/11 attacks and the apparent success of the military action in Afghanistan fed a thirst for more. 'Neo-Con' T shirts in Washington proclaimed, 'Wimps go to Baghdad; real men go to Tehran'. When Fox News's most popular presenter, Bill O'Reilly, was talking to an anti-war academic, O'Reilly said, 'We'll take care of [North Korea] after Iraq.' The academic started to reply, 'Really, and when the Saudis ... ?' 'They're after that,' interrupted O'Reilly.[32] CNN's leading correspondent, Christine Amanpour, said the news media generally, including her own organisation, had been intimidated by the Bush administration and 'its foot soldiers at Fox News', and this had led to self-censorship and a reluctance to ask hard questions.[33]

In 2002–03, the Murdoch press reported with absolute certainty that Iraq had weapons of mass destruction (WMD) and that Saddam was linked with Al Qaeda's terrorism. 'He's got them. We know he's got them,' declared the *Sun*.[34] Nine days after September 11, the *New York Post* reported that 'Saddam's fingerprints' were all over the attacks.[35] As McKnight notes, 'Over the next 18 months, the paper continually called for an attack on Iraq, its editorials twice urging that the Palestinian leader Yasser Arafat also be included as a target.'[36] On at least four occasions, the *Sun* falsely claimed that Iraq had a nuclear bomb or was making one.[37] After the British released a dossier on Iraqi WMD in September 2002 the foreign editor of the *Australian*, Greg Sheridan, proclaimed: 'The Blair dossier should transform the debate over the Iraq threat. Either Tony Blair is a monstrous liar or Saddam Hussein is. Take your pick.'[38] In the week leading up to the war, the *Sun* told its readers that 'a huge chemical weapons factory has been discovered'.[39]

Apart from the certainty about the evidence and the stridency of the calls for military action, the other notable aspect of the Murdoch press was the scathing disparagement of anyone who expressed doubts or caution or warnings about a pre-emptive strike. When France and Germany opposed military action, the *New York Post* branded them the 'Axis of Weasels', a phrase that became a refrain on Fox News.[40] The *Post* also had targets closer to home: Pentagon officials expressing caution were the 'surrender lobby', there were the 'predictable defeatists from the State Department and the *New York Times*',[41] and the senior American politicians, including George H.W. Bush's Secretary of State James Baker, who formed the Iraq Study Group, were 'Surrender Monkeys'.[42] The *Post* also charged that the chief of the UN weapons inspectors, Hans Blix, had deliberately covered up convincing evidence of Iraq's WMD program.[43]

Murdoch's London *Sun* was equally strident. It mocked the 'UN weasels' for going 'soft on Iraq' and said that 'anti-war critics were "traitors" and "naïve pawns of the men who struck America"'.[44] In March 2003 it attacked 'the weasel voices of the wobblers' who should 'belt up'.[45] While there was more variety on the opinion pages of the *Australian* and *Herald-Sun*, their chief staff columnists were among the most hawkish. The *Herald-Sun*'s Andrew Bolt thought that opponents of the war were, 'in effect, pro-terrorist'.[46] On 9 September 2002, Bolt wrote sarcastically: 'Let me spell it out slowly for [Labor politicians] Crean and Rudd: Saddam. Won't. Let. In. Inspectors.' When inspectors were admitted, two weeks later, he did not apologise.[47] More than three months after the invasion, Sheridan still thought 'WMD doubts are ludicrous' and said that hawkish US official John Bolton 'had provided him "almost as an afterthought" with the "sensational" evidence that would prove the existence of Saddam's WMD'.[48] As Manne noted, throughout the period leading up to the invasion, Sheridan – like many other Murdoch columnists – used adjectives such as 'bizarre', 'absurd' and 'preposterous' to describe opposing views.[49] Similarly, Manne thought the *Australian*'s editorials were an 'attempt to create an atmosphere where cautious considerations of facts and arguments were seen as examples of stupidity, or as the betrayal of the national interest, or as ideological blindness'.[50]

When it looked as if the defeat of Saddam would bring a quick triumph, the Murdoch press was rhapsodic. McKnight observed: 'The *Sun*'s columnist Richard Littlejohn gloated that "the Not in My Name" crowd and the Starbucks Strategists got it hopelessly, ridiculously wrong.'[51] The *Australian*, with the headline 'Coalition of the Whining Got it Wrong', editorialised:

> Never underestimate the power of ideology and myth – in this
> case anti-Americanism – to trump reality. But at least we know it
> is not love, but being a left-wing intellectual, that means never
> having to saying you're sorry.[52]

It particularly criticised former WA Labor premier Carmen Lawrence, who predicted a possible three million refugees and perhaps half a million Iraqis killed. This was wrong 'by a factor of 400' mocked the paper, although since then Lawrence's forecast has proved tragically nearer the mark. For Sheridan:

> The eagle is soaring. The bald eagle of American power is aloft,
> high above the humble earth, and everything it sees is splendid.
> For as it soars and swoops it sees victory, power, opportunity.[53]

Against the initial expectations of those supporting the invasion, the easy defeat of Saddam did not lead to peace in Iraq, but to a disastrous, draining and bloody series of conflicts. Honest, intelligent publications such as the *Economist*, which had supported the invasion, later conceded that the war had taken a course they had not predicted. The magazine continued to give the war qualified support, but openly acknowledged its political and humanitarian costs.

Neither Murdoch nor his papers indulged in much retrospective musing about the fact that Saddam's WMD were never found – this had been the public rationale for the war, after all – nor about why the original optimism about post-Saddam Iraq had been proven so wrong. One might have thought that this was particularly required given the intolerant way they had treated all the war's critics and doubters, who had actually been correct. Indeed, failure did not dim the ferocity of their rhetoric: when the British Parliament voted down the Blair Government's attempt in November 2005 to acquire powers to detain 'terrorist suspects' for 90 days without trial, the *Sun* reported it under the headline 'TRAITORS'. Its report began 'Treacherous MPs betrayed the British people last night by rejecting new laws to combat terror.'[54]

In 1852, in the lead-up to the Crimean War, the editor of the *Times*, John Delane, made one of the great declarations about the democratic role of the press. The press, he said:

> can enter into no close or binding alliances with the statesmen of the day … [Rather,] the first duty of the press is to obtain the earliest and most correct intelligence of the events of the time, and instantly, by disclosing them, to make them the common property of the nation … The press lives by disclosures.[55]

The parade of false claims in 2002–03 regarding Saddam's possession of WMD – Iraq importing aluminum tubes for nuclear purposes, importing uranium from Niger, the defector 'Curveball's' claims of biological weapons, meetings between Iraq and Al Qaeda

– and the alleged race against time for the West to forestall his imminent aggression constitute one of the most remarkable propaganda blitzes in modern democracies. It was difficult for even the most vigilant news media to penetrate the falsehoods.

The result was that the US and its allies mounted a pre-emptive war against Iraq and their stated reasons for doing so proved to be a fiction. The gravity of this has rarely been apparent in the Murdoch press. Responsible newspapers such as the *Washington Post* and *New York Times* later reflected publicly on their journalistic failings during the period. The Murdoch press did not. But they had failed Delane's first test for journalism. Murdoch's close alliance with 'the statesmen of the day' had interfered with his papers' commitment to accurate disclosure. They were part of the noise rather than part of the signal. They had served their proprietor better than their readers.

Agenda journalism

In one of the last issues of the *Sun* edited by Rebekah Brooks, the front page consisted of the faces of the 207 British soldiers killed in Afghanistan, with a large headline across the middle, reading 'Don't you know there's a bloody war on?'[56] The 'strap' at the top said 'Message to Politicians Failing Our Heroes', and 'The *Sun* Says' editorial began near the bottom of the page.[57] The multi-page splash was accompanied by a cartoon of a wounded soldier with the caption 'Abandoned'. The article was peppered with extreme, totalistic claims:

Our leaders are pretending the war isn't happening.

Mr Brown and his ministers are missing in action.

[The Ministry of Defence is] groaning with third-rate penpushers, riddled with petty turf wars and empire building and paralysed by indecision.

The *Sun* assumed for itself the mantle of speaking for Britain's war dead, even though its attention to the war in Afghanistan since 2001 had hardly been steadfast. Most of the claims in the story would be strongly contested, but the paper did not even pretend to report alternative views. Instead those in authority were subjected to blanket condemnation.

The fact that the sheer arrogance of the headline and story is not necessarily seen as shocking is indicative of just how much expectations have changed. In the 1970s, US scholar Bernard Roshco argued that 'the history of the American press can be seen as an account of how it continually enlarged its conception of the information it could properly publish'.[58] This is an optimistic view of how the scope of official secrecy has been reduced, and, sometimes more problematically, how what used to be considered private has been opened to public scrutiny. While in many ways this trend has continued since then, perhaps equally important have been the news media's increasing sense of their own rights and decreasing sense of inhibition about how they should cover the news.

The idea of presenting both sides and allowing the reader to decide is observed less and less in the tabloid press. Increasingly, stories are presented in ways that cue the reader as to how they should respond. On 2 August 2013, much of the press anticipated that the Rudd Government was about to announce a plan to impose a levy on banks for savings deposit insurance, to replace the free insurance the banks received from the government on all savings accounts up to $250,000, itself introduced to maintain confidence during the global financial crisis. The *Herald-Sun's* front page announced 'Rudd bank tax will hit you', illustrated by a woman staring forlornly into her empty wallet, bulging shopping bags hanging off her arms. The *Daily Telegraph* photoshopped a picture of Rudd and Treasurer Chris Bowen dressed as bank robbers, with a headline 'Rudd plans to pinch Aussies' savings'. The costs and benefits of such a policy move could be debated, but what is evident here is that neither paper's presentation gives any credence to arguments for such a decision. It is this type of presentation that made the Labor Government feel it could get no oxygen for its policies in the Murdoch press.

Sometimes one-sided presentations were compounded by sheer misreporting. There were reports that before the 2011 federal budget Murdoch had called his senior Australian editors to a meeting at his ranch in Carmel, California, to workshop their coverage of the Gillard Government.[59] Whether or not this was true, and whatever was said, the *Daily Telegraph*'s coverage of the 2011 federal budget was particularly misleading. It pictured a caricature of Treasurer Wayne Swan as a pickpocket 'reaching into the pockets of an honest, unsuspecting family',[60] 'victims of Labor's war on middle-class welfare … mercilessly assaulted by yesterday's Federal Budget'. It then calculated how much the 'carbon tax' would add to their annual bills: power (A$300); food ($A390) and petrol ($A150).

One major problem with this was that there was no 'carbon tax' in the 2011 budget. It was to be introduced in the following budget, and no one knew what its level would be. In each case the paper filled this vacuum not by using Treasury estimates of what costs would be with different levels of taxation, but using figures from lobby groups.[61] The paper's typical family, the Grays, was said to have an income just over $150,000 per year. The paper indulged in a classic trick to make the hit look greater: they listed the family expenses (food, mortgage, petrol etc) on a monthly basis and the extra tax increases on an annual one.[62] (Actually the family's annualised expenses only add up to around $60,000, which suggests this family 'adrift in an ocean of debt and despair' was, after tax, clearing at least $40,000 or more in savings or discretionary spending.) Moreover, although the size of the carbon tax was unknown it was already known that the government intended to accompany it with matching income tax cuts, but there is no mention of that in the story. In addition, the Grays' biggest expense was mortgage repayments, and there was no mention of how falling interest rates should have helped them.

This was effective populist reporting, mining an always rich vein of governments ripping off innocent taxpayers. A casual reader would be unlikely to probe the provenance or validity of the statistics or think about what figures were missing. Equally, it was the type of dishonest and inaccurate reporting which would, justifiably, have angered the government.

These trends towards one-sided news presentations – not at all confined to the Murdoch press – have been compounded by Murdoch's increasing willingness to impose his own political views on judgements of newsworthiness. In 1987, a year before Murdoch endorsed the tele-evangelist Pat Robertson as Republican presidential candidate (see Chapter 7), the *Australian* embraced the 'Joh for Canberra' campaign.

Queensland National Party Premier Joh Bjelke-Petersen had won a series of election victories, routing not only the Labor Party but also the Liberals. After his victory in the 1986 election, he turned his sights on Canberra, and to leading a national conservative movement. This was a direct threat to both the Labor government and Opposition Leader John Howard. As Howard wrote, 'the *Australian* newspaper became a prominent vehicle for the propagation of the Joh cause. The editor at the time, the late Les Hollings, gave huge coverage to anything that Bjelke-Petersen said or did.'[63]

Hollings, disappointed by what he considered a lost opportunity for conservative politics under the Fraser Government and by the current electoral dominance of the Hawke Labor Government, was drawn to the Queensland Nationals. In February 1985, the paper ran a front page editorial proclaiming that 'Australia is now at the crossroads' and must choose between prosperity and unproductiveness. It agreed with Queensland Nationals that union power was 'the heart of the problem'.[64]

The *Australian* broke the Joh for Canberra story in January 1987. *Australian* columnists Des Keegan and Katharine West mounted what author Denis Cryle called a 'vendetta' against the weakness of the Fraser legacy, as they argued that there was a need for a new national conservative force. The strength of this sentiment spooked the Opposition, and they adopted much more radical programs than electoral prudence would have suggested. Eventually, as the election was getting under way, the Joh campaign collapsed. Hawke won, and many Liberals blamed the Joh campaign.

It was not only Joh's Canberra ambitions that collapsed. ABC's *Four Corners* program 'The Moonlight State', aided by some belated but welcome investigative reporting by the *Courier-Mail*, led to the Fitzgerald Inquiry, whose searing searchlight led to important reforms against police corruption. Joh's career ended in ignominy, and eventually he faced – but was controversially acquitted of – criminal charges. And Labor won its first victory in Queensland since the 1950s.[65]

It is often asserted that journalism is the first rough draft of history. Contemporary historians often see this period as one where the Hawke Government internationalised the Australian economy, especially by floating the dollar, exercised tight control over budgetary spending, had some, although limited, success in reducing inflation, reduced the number of days lost in labour disputes, all while managing to keep wage rises down to less than cost of living increases. Both sides of politics see it as a period of substantial reform. If one read the pages of the *Australian* of the period, however, especially its opinion pages, a radically different and quite misleading picture emerges.

Some aspects of the paper's campaigning style during the Joh for Canberra episode have been revived in more recent times: in particular, the use of columnists who give no credence to alternative views, and idiosyncratic and coloured judgements of newsworthiness. It is not only Labor that has found itself on the wrong side of such campaigning. In 2005, Treasurer Peter Costello, who had cut income taxes in three successive budgets, was angered by the *Australian*'s campaigning for larger tax cuts. According to Costello, 'Journalists wrote story after story on the issue and no amount of explanation could get a fair hearing', and the paper invented a 'ginger group' of backbenchers campaigning on the issue.[66]

But it was under the Rudd and Gillard Governments that the relationship developed into intense antagonism. Rudd privately called the *Australian* 'Fox News in print',[67] while Labor Minister for Communications Stephen Conroy said the *Daily Telegraph* was mounting a campaign for 'regime change'.[68] Independent MP Tony Windsor singled out News Limited at his farewell news conference for trying to dictate terms to parliament,[69] and former Greens leader Bob Brown referred to the Murdoch press and others as the 'hate media'.[70] Academics Robert Manne and David McKnight mounted scathing critiques. Even Fairfax CEO Greg Hywood referred to 'the Murdoch empire's rejection of internal dissent and insistence on groupthink'.[71]

These accusations are met with blanket rejection by senior Murdoch figures. Former News Limited CEO John Hartigan said in July 2011, 'We are the only organisation that really takes it up to the government';[72] earlier he thought that the fact that Rudd was critical of the *Australian* 'suggests to me that it is doing its job'.[73] His successor, Kim Williams, said the government was showing a glass jaw. Although hardly convincing refutations, they make a valid point: governments are far from disinterested arbiters of the press coverage they receive. But whatever the truth of specific criticisms, the key point is how much has changed. Twenty years ago, there was some optimism among journalists about trends in News Limited. One prominent Canberra press gallery member, Christine Wallace, wrote in 1994:

> The trouble with the Senate inquiry into foreign ownership of the print media is that its members assume the bad old days of proprietor impropriety and omnipotence still exist, when the truth is they have long gone ... The last time a proprietor sought

in any profound way to impose an editorial line was in 1975
when Murdoch triggered a strike … News Limited has spent the
last 20 years trying to live the episode down and restore an image
of objectivity to its flagship, the *Australian*.[74]

It would be much harder now to make such claims. The trend is
towards more opinionated and one-sided journalism, and not only
in the Murdoch press. It would be a brave employee who told
Rupert Murdoch that proprietorial power was dead. After half a
century of political involvements, his relish in using his news media
to have a political impact is undiminished.

9

Reaping the rewards
Murdoch and government action

I bet if I was going to be shot at dawn, I could get out of it.[1]

Rupert Murdoch

'I've never asked a prime minister for anything.'[2] Rupert Murdoch's testimony to the Leveson Inquiry was emphatic. 'I take a particularly strong pride in the fact that we have never pushed our commercial interests in our newspapers … I never let my commercial interests, whatever they are, enter into any consideration of elections.'[3]

Leveson was probing – and Murdoch was denying – the trading of editorial support for policy or regulatory favours, the transaction, either explicit or implicit, that many suspected was the key to Murdoch's power in Britain. The news media are unique in that their output affects the political fortunes of policy-makers directly. While media owners share with other large corporations the ability to donate money and lobby in traditional ways, they have this crucial added leverage.

Murdoch's reputation for wielding great power had been promoted by both his supporters and his opponents. Former *News of the World* journalist Paul McMullan declared that 'every political leader since Margaret Thatcher in the 1970s has had to "jump in bed with Murdoch"'.[4] Charles Douglas-Home, editor of the *Times*, said in 1984:

Rupert and Mrs Thatcher consult regularly on every important matter of policy … especially as they relate to his economic and political interests. Around here, he's often jokingly referred to as 'Mr Prime Minister'. Except that it's no longer all that much of a joke. In many respects, he is the phantom prime minister of this country.[5]

A spin doctor in the Blair Government, Lance Price, said:

I have never met Mr Murdoch, but at times when I worked at Downing Street he seemed like the 24th member of the Cabinet. His voice was rarely heard … but his presence was always felt.[6]

Similar claims have been made about Murdoch's influence in Australia, and his denial seemed more geographic than political: 'It's wrong to say I'm the most powerful man in Australia. I'm not even there.'[7] In America, Murdoch asked, 'Power? What power? I have no power. No more than any American. This myth that I have some influence up there on Capitol Hill is baloney.'[8]

In contrast to this picture of innocence and powerlessness, Bruce Page concluded that on 'most of the critical steps' in his expansion Murdoch has 'sought and received political favours' and that his success has depended on these.[9] But this is perhaps too sweeping in the other direction. Rather, two conclusions stand out:

- The 1980s were the key period where policy decisions were important to Murdoch's growth.

  Murdoch became a giant in newspaper publishing without any special help from governments, and there were no important cases of governments assisting him before the 1980s. In that decade, as he changed his citizenship, launched into TV in the US, took over the *Times* in Britain, became the dominant player in Australian newspapers, and launched the Sky TV satellite service, his relations with governments were crucial to his ability to develop as he wished.

- Since the 1990s, Murdoch's veto power has been more important than his initiating power.

  Over this long period, Murdoch has almost constantly been a controversial figure, and there have been calls for his power to be curbed – by stronger anti-monopoly measures, for example – but there are few cases of governments adopting policies that ran strongly counter to his interests. 'No government,' said Leveson, 'addressed the issue of press regulation, nor of concentration of ownership.'[10] On the other hand, he has not always succeeded in gaining legislative measures he wanted. For example, as a partner in the pay TV operator Foxtel, he has long fought the Australian anti-siphoning rules that give the free-to-air stations first choice at major sporting events, but the power of the free-to-air networks and of public opinion have protected the status quo.

Murdoch's relations with three governments – Thatcher, Hawke-Keating and Blair – have been particularly crucial, and are considered below.

Thatcher and Murdoch

As Shawcross commented, after the *Sun* swung its support to Thatcher in 1979, for the next decade and a half it 'remained astonishingly loyal to her, and that loyalty was rewarded'.[11] It was in the Murdoch-Thatcher relationship that the politics of mutual patronage reached its strongest expression, and produced the worst abuses in policy-making.

In 1959 Roy Thomson bought the *Sunday Times* and in 1966 he bought the *Times* from the Astor family. Under Thomson there was a high degree of editorial independence. The *Sunday Times* thrived both commercially and editorially, maintaining high standards of journalism and attracting the best talent, especially under the editorship of Harold Evans. However, by 1980 Thomson's ownership of Times Newspapers had 'become commercially disastrous',[12] due principally to industrial problems. Publication had been suspended for 11 months in 1978–79. The journalists, who had been paid for that entire period, then went on strike in August 1980. In the face of continuing unrest and large losses, the Thomson organisation decided to sell; if no buyer could be found, it would cease publication. It was keen to find a buyer, however, as closing the titles would result in severance payments of around £36 million.[13]

There were several potential bidders, including groups organised by the editors of the two papers. Lord Rothermere offered £20 million, but Thomson was concerned that his company intended to close the *Times* once he got control, so Murdoch's lower bid, of £12 million, prevailed.

The policy issue was whether the acquisition would be referred to the Monopolies Commission, as Murdoch already owned one national daily and one Sunday national. Any seller would prefer a purchase to be consummated without having to face an inquiry, and this was clearly Thomson's wish. Equally, any buyer would also prefer an immediate decision. Murdoch, quite reasonably, told the Secretary of State, John Biffen, that if there was an inquiry he reserved the right to renegotiate the price – the paper could well be bleeding money in the interim.[14] However, there is little reason to believe that an inquiry would have endangered the sale. It is also unlikely that Thomson would have closed the titles: he would then forfeit the purchase price, and face the large severance payments bill.

At first Biffen indicated that he would refer Murdoch's purchase to an inquiry, but then he announced that he would not. There was immediate controversy. John Smith, later leader of the Labour Party, said the acquisition would produce a concentration of newspaper power probably 'unprecedented in our history'.[15] Some Conservative backbenchers were also opposed to the lack of due process.

As Belfield and his Channel Four colleagues observed, 'Yet again, Murdoch had demonstrated his brilliance in waltzing past the regu-

lators. The key to his fancy footwork was that he was not dancing alone.'[16] Murdoch and Thatcher were 'ideological soulmates'.
Murdoch described himself as 'a great admirer' of her and on the
'same page politically',[17] and she felt she owed 'a real debt of gratitude to him'. When one *Sunday Times* journalist spoke to a Thatcher
adviser about blocking the sale, he was told to stop wasting his time
– 'You don't realize, she likes the guy.'[18] Murdoch's friend and confidant, Woodrow Wyatt, was also keen to claim credit. Twice in later
years, after he had started keeping a diary, entries referred to having
arranged 'through Margaret' that 'the deal didn't go to the Monopolies Commission which almost certainly would have blocked it'.[19]

The law required that there must be a reference unless both
papers were making a loss. In justifying his decision, Biffen said he
was satisfied that neither the *Times* nor the *Sunday Times* was a going
concern, and therefore a referral was not necessary.[20] He also presented figures which showed both papers were making a loss.[21] The
impact of industrial disputes would have given him some backing for
such calculations. However, according to Thomson's finance group
director, and most other analysts, the *Sunday Times* was profitable,
and if the two titles were taken together the company overall was
still profitable, even though the *Times* was making a substantial loss.[22]

Murdoch did have to give a series of guarantees. The most
important related to editorial independence. This would be enforced
by there being a group of national directors who would have sole
power over the appointment and dismissal of editors. Murdoch's
guarantees were widely applauded. The outgoing editor of the
Times, William Rees-Mogg, said they are 'very far reaching and there
is no reason to doubt that he will abide by them'.[23] The incom-
ing editor of the *Times*, Harold Evans, whom Murdoch had lured
across from the *Sunday Times*, and who was a journalist whose stat-
ure gave comfort to all who wanted to believe the new ownership
arrangements would work, said, 'No editor or journalist could ask
for wider guarantees of editorial independence on news and policy

than those Mr Murdoch has accepted.'[24] The guarantees seemed empty a year later, on 9 March 1982, when Murdoch demanded Evans's resignation.

Murdoch has continued to assert his observance of the editorial independence guarantees. He told the Leveson Inquiry in 2012, 'I never gave instructions to the editor of the *Times* or the *Sunday Times*',[25] and in 2007, when reassuring the owners of the *Wall St Journal* that he would observe guarantees given to them, declared, 'I have [never] given any sort of political instructions, or even guidance to one editor of the *Times* or the *Sunday Times*.'[26] He described Evans as the only *Times* editor 'we have ever asked to leave'.[27] However, only months after telling Leveson this, he dismissed another, James Harding.[28] He must also have forgotten that he forced Charles Wilson to resign in 1990.[29]

As well as the editorial dismissals, there was other Murdoch interference in both papers. This became more acute from early 1982. An obvious case was on the *Sunday Times*, when he told the editor, Frank Giles, that he wanted to appoint two new deputy editors. There was no pretence of consulting Giles, let alone getting his agreement. Giles complied and announced the new appointments, even though he knew that 'what [Murdoch] was now demanding was in complete breach of [his] undertaking'.[30]

One of the former deputy editors, Hugo Young, wrote, after he left the paper, that Murdoch did not believe in neutrality:

Indeed, rather like politicians themselves, he had difficulty comprehending it. As far as he was concerned, journalistic detachment was a mask for anti-Thatcherism.[31]

According to Evans, 'It soon became obvious that nothing less than unquestioning backing of Mrs Thatcher on every issue would satisfy Rupert.'[32] These editors' views were supported by Tom Kiernan, who recalled a New York dinner party, where the papers' criticism of Thatcher was galling to Murdoch. He:

> characterized Giles and his wife as Communists. Evans, he called
> worse. Then he went on to blast the two papers as being 'lily-
> livered' and 'straining my patience'. No one at the dinner who
> heard Murdoch's diatribe had any doubt of what was about to
> happen.[33]

The pressure to force Evans out gathered pace. On 8 February 1982:

> Murdoch provoked an atmosphere of crisis by sending a letter to
> all employees of Times Newspapers, warning them that the daily
> and Sunday would close within days rather than weeks, unless
> 600 jobs were shed.[34]

One of Evans's ongoing frustrations was that Murdoch never gave
him a budget:[35] he was told he was exceeding a budget whose content was never revealed to him. The prospect of closure and of hundreds of jobs being lost heightened the insecurity and discontent
among all employees. Evans 'was under pressure from his proprietor
above and an increasingly discontented staff below'.[36]

Soon afterwards it was revealed that – contrary to the guarantees he had given – Murdoch had transferred the titles of the
Times newspapers to News International. If Murdoch closed the
papers, he would retain the titles, and be free to reopen them later.
Former editor Rees-Mogg initiated the public outcry.[37] Evans also
denounced the move, observing that the national directors had not
been informed.[38] Once the issue became public, Murdoch transferred the titles out again.

As events moved to a climax, Murdoch offered the editorship to
Evans's deputy, Charles Douglas-Home, who accepted. However,
Evans refused to resign immediately – to show that 'editors of the
Times were not to be as casually discarded as had the 13 editors in

15 years at the *Australian*.[39] The standoff continued for some days, but then he resigned: 'I was so absolutely disgusted, dismayed and demoralized by living in a vindictive atmosphere.'[40] 'Nothing in my experience,' he wrote, 'compared to the atmosphere of intrigue, fear and spite inflicted on the paper by Murdoch's lieutenants.'[41]

The home editor of the *Times*, Fred Emery, said he was told by Murdoch, 'I give instructions to my editors all around the world; why shouldn't I in London?' When Emery reminded him of his undertakings to the Secretary of State, Murdoch replied, 'They're not worth the paper they're written on.'[42] (Two decades later, Murdoch denied to Leveson that he said this.) Evans later came to:

> agree with Murdoch that editorial guarantees are not worth the paper they are written on ... [In reality,] the national directors are incapable of monitoring the daily turmoil of a newspaper ... Arbitration is impossible on the innumerable issues which may arise in many different ways every day between editor and proprietor.[43]

There was a further case where the Thatcher Government failed to refer a Murdoch purchase to the Monopolies Commission even though the purchase gave him a third daily title. Murdoch bought the loss-making *Today* for £38 million in July 1987.[44] The daily, launched by Eddie Shah, had pioneered the use of colour and more efficient printing techniques, but had failed to make a profit. Shah first went into partnership with another prominent British businessman, Tiny Rowland, but then both became interested in selling the paper. Maxwell and Murdoch were the two interested buyers. Maxwell thought he had succeeded, and in a typical case of ego beating strategic judgement, telephoned Murdoch in the US to tell him. Murdoch realised that Maxwell in fact did not yet have crucial signatures; he moved quickly, and beat Maxwell.[45] Both seller Rowland and buyer Murdoch were keen to avoid an inquiry, and advised the government that if there was not immediate approval, the paper would close. The government agreed.[46]

The outcry was only a small fraction of the public controversy surrounding the sale of the *Times*. First, *Today*, only a few years old, lacked the *Thunderer's* iconic status. Second, Prime Minister Thatcher had much more political latitude at this time. She had just won her third election, in July 1987, and was in undisputed command of her own party and of a parliamentary majority. Third, the main alternative to Murdoch was the unscrupulous Maxwell. Fourth, the title was clearly making a loss, which meant that it was not mandatory to refer it. Finally, there was perhaps a sense of fatigue and inevitability that the Murdoch-Thatcher axis would prevail.

Nevertheless, none of this seems sufficient grounds for not referring an unprecedented acquisition of a third national daily newspaper to the Monopolies Commission. Wyatt's diaries were quite open about the political nature of the decision. In 1986, he and Murdoch had wanted a referral because, as he said to Thatcher, 'we don't want *Today* to fall into the hands of our enemy Maxwell'. In 1987, with Murdoch as the buyer, they successfully lobbied to prevent a referral.[47]

Almost a decade after the purchase of the *Times*, Thatcher allowed Murdoch to, in effect, sabotage the satellite policies her own government had adopted. In the first half of the 1980s, the government announced that it wanted to see the rapid development of satellite and was keen to achieve industrial advantages from the emerging technology.[48] But equally, it expected the capital cost of providing the satellite system to be met within the private sector.[49] The first attempts to put together a consortium to do this failed. The BBC, for example, pulled out because it could not meet the high costs, as did others who were also wary of the very large financial risks they would be incurring, with high immediate costs and at best deferred income streams. Eventually, in December 1986, the Independent Broadcasting Authority (IBA) awarded the franchise to British Satellite Broadcasting (BSB), a consortium of five media companies (not including News International, which was part of a competing tender).[50] Under the cross-media rules, each newspaper was limited to 20 per cent of the satellite broadcaster.

The government adopted 'a high cost and self-consciously "quality" approach to satellite broadcasting'. Shawcross explained: 'Under the terms of its franchise, BSB was compelled to use a new, untried and very expensive transmission system, D-MAC, which was expected to produce a better picture than the old PAL [colour encoding] system.'[51] BSB had to use a technology with more initial problems, plus a greater initial expense to potential consumers, but that would have greater long-term value. According to scholar Peter Goodwin's definitive account, 'right from the start the IBA, the government and BSB were clear that its chances of success depended on a clear run free of new competition'.[52]

In June 1988 Murdoch announced plans for Sky, a service aimed entirely at British audiences, but operating on the Luxembourg-based Astra satellite, and using the established PAL technology. This was a direct challenge to all the government's assumptions, but the government made no response.[53] As Goodwin notes, 'Murdoch also scored a marketing goal, creating an image of Sky television as the cheap and quick route into the world of satellite television.'[54] Sky launched its four-channel service in February 1989. The bulk of the programming was repeats and US material.

The directors of BSB were horrified. They 'had agreed to use an untested and expensive new technology, D-MAC, and an unlaunched satellite, Marco Polo' in return for a monopoly.[55] When they met Mrs Thatcher to voice their objections, they 'received a short lecture on the virtues of competition. She told them to stop whingeing and sent them away.'[56]

To meet the challenge, the BSB partners pledged a further £900 million in January 1990, in addition to the £423 million already committed.[57] These were unprecedented amounts in British broadcasting. Finally, BSB launched, in April 1990, 15 months after Sky, which already had 600,000 dishes in place.[58] Both sides were scrambling to buy exclusive programming rights for movies. Sky signed Fox, Orion, Touchstone and Warner Bros for an estimated £60 million, while BSB contracted with Paramount, Universal, MGM/United Artists and Columbia for £85 million.[59] Shawcross writes, 'During the summer of 1990, the Sky-BSB battle to sell dishes increased in ferocity. BSB was thought to be losing £8 million a week and Sky £2 million.'[60]

As both sides bled money, they became increasingly desperate to reach an agreement. Finally, on 2 November 1990 it was announced that Sky and BSB would merge to create BSkyB, operating on the Astra satellite and using PAL. Murdoch had alerted 'Margaret Thatcher to the merger deal a few days before it was publicly announced. The Prime Minister did not see fit to warn her Cabinet colleagues.'[61] So 'Peter Lloyd, the Broadcasting Minister, only learned about it when he read his morning newspaper.'[62]

In theory, the IBA was in control of the satellite licence, so BSB was not in a position to dispose of it, or to make the merger with Sky the way it had.[63] When news of the merger was announced, the IBA was furious.[64] But it soon felt compelled to give in to the commercial reality, especially in the absence of any strong counterindications from the government.

This was very much a shotgun marriage. The two sides detested each other. Murdoch thought BSB deserved to die.[65] For Murdoch:

the Sky team was lean, young and dedicated. By contrast, BSB
was burdened with a big, highly paid management, [who]
behaved like established fat cats.[66]

From the BSB and IBA point of view, Murdoch had, in effect, 'seized control of a British television station, BSB, and was now daring the authorities to deny it to him'. Former IBA Chairman Lord Thomson called it a 'brutal Wapping in outer space'.[67]

The Labour Party charged that the merger made a mockery of the new Broadcasting Act. Murdoch responded:

> They hate the idea of a competitive society, and it is only companies like ours that have the guts and strength to risk everything in building a competitor to the existing monopoly. That's what we are all about.[68]

He sought to portray Sky as the under-resourced but entrepreneurial outsider overcoming the establishment organisation.

The truth is almost the opposite of Murdoch's formulation. BSB received no public subsidy, but had to meet onerous publicly imposed obligations, which put it at a severe commercial disadvantage. The only justification for this was protection of its monopoly status, at least until its services were established. It had accepted the franchise on one set of conditions only to find the government had allowed that position to be completely undercut.

Allowing the merger to proceed on terms very favourable to Sky was not the last piece of assistance the Thatcher Government gave to Murdoch. Newspaper owners were limited to 20 per cent of domestic satellite broadcasters, but Sky and then BSkyB were judged not to be domestic, so Murdoch was allowed to exceed that. This helped ensure that he would always be by far the biggest shareholder. And again, with the 1988 European Broadcasting Directive, which required channels to broadcast at least 50 per cent European programming. The UK Home Office decided this did not apply to BSkyB movie channels, and so it was able to continue with its overwhelmingly US fare.[69] Lastly, Thatcher decreed that the BBC must pay £10 million a year to be transmitted on the Sky platform, although across the rest of Europe commercial broadcasters paid public broadcasters for the privilege of using their content.[70]

The British Government portrayed itself as a bystander,

allowing market forces to play out. It claimed that although BSkyB's programming operated out of London and was directed at a British audience, its satellite rights were based in Luxembourg, and therefore the government lacked direct jurisdiction. In subsequent years the Tory Government 'acted successfully to drive [European-based] UK-directed pornographic channels out of business', but such powers were never used to curb Sky or BSkyB.[71]

It is hard to exaggerate just how far the outcome differed from the satellite policies the Conservative Government had been proclaiming. BSkyB did not use or advance UK technology, or contribute to the industrial goals the government had embraced. It went back to PAL television, and so 'put high-definition television in Britain ... on hold for a decade'.[72] It was dominated by a non-UK-controlled company and it broadcast heavily non-UK programming.[73] The Thatcher Government had willingly connived in making a mockery of its own policies. In doing so, it laid the groundwork for what eventually would become a powerful monopoly, as 'the real strength of News in Britain lay in the astonishing success of BSkyB'.[74] Murdoch was speaking accurately when he told Andrew Neil, 'we owe Thatcher a lot as a company'.[75]

Hawke-Keating Labor and Murdoch

When Murdoch renounced his Australian citizenship in September 1985, he became ineligible to hold an Australian television licence. However, as he told Kiernan, he 'was sure he would figure out some way to get around' the Australian law: 'Perhaps the government would make him an "honorary citizen".'[76] Murdoch entered into a protracted period of negotiation with the Australian Broadcasting Tribunal (ABT) as he attempted to restructure arrangements so that he would remain the major shareholder and continue to reap profits from the Ten stations, but no longer 'control' the stations. His voting stock would be quarantined below the permissible 15 per cent, for example.[77] Eventually the ABT referred Murdoch's proposal to the Federal Court to rule on its legality. This long delay profited Murdoch greatly, because in the interim the Hawke Government introduced a new media policy, which sparked a scramble for media assets.

When Hawke came to power in March 1983, the media structure in Australia was one of entrenched, stable oligopoly. Four companies – Murdoch, Fairfax, Packer and the Herald and Weekly Times (HWT) – dominated. The minister, Michael Duffy, was consulting with various stakeholders for two changes in TV policy. There were proposals for aggregation of rural areas to bring competition where there was only a single commercial channel, and there were proposals about reforming the 'two station rule'. This limited any company to owning two TV stations, but it took no account of the size of the population the channels reached. So stations in, say, North Queensland, counted the same as channels in Sydney and Melbourne, which together reached 43 per cent of the TV market. At that time, Packer and Murdoch both had a Sydney-Melbourne axis. The third network, Seven, was split between Fairfax in Sydney and HWT in Melbourne.

Duffy was in favour of redefining the ownership limits so one company could own channels able to reach 43 per cent of the population, but was opposed by Hawke and Keating. The media issue became, according to media analyst Paul Chadwick, 'the most internally divisive of the Labor Government's first five years'.[78] During one tense standoff, another reform-minded minister, John Button, challenged the prime minister:

> 'Why don't you just tell us what your mates [Murdoch and Packer] want?' 'It's nothing to do with my fucking mates,' an angry Hawke is said to have replied, 'they're the only ones we've got.'[79]

The deadlock was resolved when Treasurer Paul Keating convinced the others to go with a much larger limit (initially 75 per cent), but also to introduce a ban on cross-media ownership, making it impossible to own a newspaper and a TV channel in the same market. In Keating's phrase, an owner could be a prince of print or a queen of the screen, but not both. Existing arrangements would be unaffected ('grandfathered'), but the law would apply to all future acquisitions. Banning cross-media ownership was a principle consistent with a longstanding Labor view that media ownership was too concentrated. This won assent in Cabinet, and the new policy was announced by press release the day after parliament had risen for the long summer recess.

The effect, and probably the intent, was to advantage Packer and Murdoch and to disadvantage Fairfax and HWT. Packer had no newspapers, so was not affected by the cross-media change. Eventually Murdoch would sell out of television, and so likewise would be unaffected. Fairfax and HWT's pattern of newspaper and television ownership made it very hard for either to expand. It transpired that Keating had consulted the first two but not the last two before the changes were made public. As Peter Bowers put it in the *Sydney Morning Herald*, 'Keating sees the cross-media rule as historic because it looks after Labor's long-term interests first, looks after Labor's mates second, and pays back Labor's enemies third.'[80]

Many media players thought that the changes represented the last chance to gain entry into television, and it triggered a scramble for position, with unprecedented prices. Even though the changes did not become law until the following May, there was immediate action.

In the 12 months between November 1986 and November 1987, 13 of Australia's 19 metropolitan daily newspapers changed ownership, three of them twice, and 11 of the 17 metropolitan commercial TV channels changed owners, two of them twice. None of the four companies which had dominated Australian television in November 1986 had a single channel by November 1987, and the three major players who dominated the networks in late 1987 all exited the industry within the next five years, with the Ten network going through two ownership changes.[81]

The first, biggest and most controversial single transaction was Murdoch's purchase of the Herald and Weekly Times. Murdoch described the bid he made on 3 December 1986 as the biggest newspaper takeover in the English-speaking world.[82] As it stood then, if Murdoch did not, or was not forced to, dispose of anything, the purchase would have given him more than three-quarters of the daily press, and a great number of television stations. Murdoch journalists wrote as if the deal was already a *fait accompli*, with Brian Frith in the *Australian* saying the 'Flinders Street fortress (HWT) fell in a single day', and that Murdoch's generous offer had shattered its 'long supposed impregnable takeover defence'.[83] In fact the 'mind-boggling number of cross shareholdings'[84] proved much harder and more expensive to penetrate than Murdoch had anticipated, especially as there were counter-bids from Holmes à Court and later Fairfax for parts of the group. Indeed the 'takeover battle for the Herald and Weekly Times was probably the longest, most involved and most litigious of any action in Australia'. Rather than being over in one day, it dragged on through many complications for nine weeks.[85]

From the beginning, Murdoch was confident of the government's support. He told HWT chief executive John D'Arcy at the beginning of November, 'There will be no trouble with the government.' Before then both D'Arcy and Murdoch had believed that neither the government nor the Trade Practices Commission would allow any merger that gave one publisher more than 50 per cent of the metropolitan newspapers, but now Murdoch's 'attitude was completely different, and it became apparent to me that he had a deal with' Bob Hawke.[86]

D'Arcy thought 'that Hawke and Keating had an incredible hatred of HWT and Fairfax' and affirmed journalist Geoff Kitney's observation that Hawke's reaction to Murdoch's takeover bid was 'almost joyful'.[87] Former Fairfax editor Vic Carroll wrote:

> Hawke told some senior ministers in the week before the key
> Cabinet meeting [in late 1986] that if Cabinet approved the new
> 75 per cent ownership rule for the Packer and Murdoch groups
> then his government would win the next election.[88]

Hawke called Fairfax 'the natural enemy of Labor' and HWT 'a violent, virulent anti-Labor journal'.[89] He also said the old HWT management was 'viciously anti-Labor, so if Mr Murdoch were to fire
a few salvoes at us, it couldn't be worse than what we have been
enduring'.[90] Keating told the right faction of the Labor caucus that
'Hawke was confident Packer and Murdoch were on Labor's side.'[91]

These views were widely shared among senior ALP politicians. Labor national secretary Bob McMullan told Labor MPs they
should be 'dancing in the streets'.[92] Former premier of New South
Wales Neville Wran said that he'd 'like to see Murdoch own 95 per
cent of the papers in Australia'.[93] Victorian Premier John Cain, after
'friendly and cordial' talks with Murdoch, said, 'Mr Murdoch is a
newspaperman – I have no worry about him owning the Herald and
Weekly Times.'[94]

When John Menadue expressed dismay to his close friend,
senior government minister Mick Young, Young replied, 'The
Herald and the Fairfax people – they're always against us. But you
know, sometimes Rupert is for us.'[95] Another minister put it more
pessimistically: there is no way 'we can fuck Rupert Murdoch without fucking ourselves'.[96]

Quite apart from the way that none of these politicians seemed
to see any democratic problem in this unprecedented media concentration, their pragmatism was based on problematic assumptions. Murdoch's (and Packer's) *quid* was far more obvious than
Labor's *quo*. Packer exited the industry for some years, and even
after his return it would be hard to make a case that the Nine

network showed any partiality towards Labor. He made one public statement praising the Hawke Government, but after the 1993 election, as the electoral tide was changing, he very publicly swung his support behind Howard, much to Keating's disgust.[97] Nor did the Murdoch press campaign strongly for Labor in 1987: according to Chadwick, 'Murdoch indicated to some of his journalists that he wanted election editorials to steer a middle course, although they could lean slightly to the party they thought looked the best.'[98] Given that his concentration of ownership was politically sensitive, he took the prudent course, and for the first time papers he owned editorialised in favour of different parties. In 1987, Fairfax papers were more editorially supportive of Labor than Murdoch ones.[99] From 1993 and for the next several elections, News Limited newspapers were predominantly on the Coalition side. On the other side of the ledger, one leading analyst estimated the combined selling price of the Nine and Ten networks before the government's policy change at about $800 million; after the change they commanded $1.9 billion. So in return for some temporary, tepid, qualified support, the two proprietors enjoyed a windfall of $1.1 billion.

Equally puzzling is the perception of the Murdoch and Packer groups as 'mates' and of Fairfax and the HWT as enemies.[100] In Australia, Murdoch's support for the Hawke-Keating Labor Government came only after it was elected. In 1983 the only metropolitan paper editorially endorsing Labor was the Fairfax-owned *Age*. In 1984 every metropolitan newspaper that expressed a preference, except the Hobart *Mercury*, editorialised for the re-election of the Hawke Government, so it had the support of all three major groups.[101] Some HWT papers, particularly the Melbourne *Herald*, had campaigned strongly against the government's proposals on superannuation taxation, but so had most Murdoch papers. On the basis of interviews with 223 journalists around Australia in the early 1980s, I concluded that among the three companies, journalists' accounts of political intervention and direction were very roughly in the ratio of News Ltd 10; HWT 4; Fairfax 1.[102]

While there were pieces of reporting in both Fairfax and HWT papers (and on the ABC) that angered government leaders,[103] the differences seem to have been more in attitude than content. It was the lack of direction from the top in the ABC and Fairfax that the Labor deal-makers seemed to find difficult. They thought that some of Fairfax's journalism was 'out of control and dangerous'.[104] Malcolm Fraser recognised the differences between the groups when he was seeking their support in 1975. He spoke to Murdoch, Packer and James Fairfax, 'but in the knowledge that the Fairfax papers ran differently to News Ltd – the views of the proprietor were not necessarily reflected in the copy the reporters wrote'. As for Packer and Murdoch, Fraser said, 'We did not believe the fiction that media barons do not control the policies of their papers.'[105]

Keating also clearly enjoyed being a participant, helping to shape the big moves that were remaking the Australian political landscape. He had given Murdoch and Packer, but not Fairfax, advance notice of the proposed changes. When Fairfax general manager Greg Gardiner telephoned Holmes à Court, Keating was with the latter, and – unbeknownst to Gardiner – listened in. Keating then warned Murdoch that Holmes à Court was serious, and that he [Murdoch] would have to negotiate; he thought his intervention with Murdoch was crucial in this happening.[106] Afterwards he gloated to Fairfax executives, 'I hurt you more than you hurt me.'[107]

There were three regulatory hurdles Murdoch had to clear. The first was his proposal to keep the Ten TV licence by reorganising the control structure of the channels. The second was Foreign Investment Review Board approval for foreign ownership of the HWT newspapers. The last was Trade Practices Commission approval: the level of concentration in newspaper ownership did not breach its policies. Murdoch failed the first – causing him then to sell his Channel Ten stations – and passed the other two.

173

On 20 January 1987, Murdoch's hopes had to be radically scaled back after the full bench of the Federal Court ruled that he could not own an Australian television licence because he was not an Australian citizen. One judge said that the talk of restructuring News Limited was a 'sham'.[108] This had implications not only for the disposal of the Ten network, but for News's wish to acquire HWT, as News, as a foreign company, would not be allowed to own its broadcasting assets either. A few days later the ABT indeed announced an inquiry into Murdoch's status as a foreign person. The ABT made no specific finding on the matter at this stage. In order to pre-empt potential legal difficulties, the HWT Board itself auctioned off its broadcasting assets, and they were all disposed of before the company passed into foreign hands.

The decision also brought an extraordinary response: on 22 January, News Limited issued a public statement disowning Rupert Murdoch:

> A number of statements have recently appeared in the press and elsewhere attributed to Mr K.R. Murdoch relating to News Limited and in particular its takeover bid for the Herald and Weekly Times ... The board wishes, however, to point out the following. 1. Although Mr Murdoch was formerly a director of News Ltd, he is no longer a director and he holds no office in the company. 2. Mr Murdoch has no authority to speak on behalf of or to bind News Ltd.[109]

This fiction required one to ignore recent history. On the day the bid was launched, Murdoch had been photographed with his mother, with much talk about how proud his father would have been, and commentary on him reclaiming his 'birth right'. The chair of the ABT, Deirdre O'Connor, pointed out that when Murdoch had talked about the imminent moves, he had talked of 'his' take-over of HWT and 'his' plans to sell some of its assets.[110] The charade did not last long. In the coming days and weeks, Murdoch certainly acted as if he was in charge, and no protest from the Board ever became public.

The Foreign Takeovers Act gave the treasurer power to prohibit a purchase of a corporation by foreign persons if that control was deemed contrary to the national interest. A four-member Foreign Investment Review Board (FIRB) would advise the treasurer, who would then make a public announcement of his decision, often without giving any grounds. The FIRB's advice in this case has never been made public. Treasurer Keating approved Murdoch's purchase of HWT, and so a majority of the nation's papers passed into foreign hands.

On the three other occasions during Keating's period in government when decisions involving foreign takeovers of newspapers arose, he rejected the applications. He prevented Robert Maxwell buying the *Age* and stopped a Malaysian company buying half of the afternoon paper, the *Perth Daily News*.[111] Famously, he refused to allow Conrad Black to lift his stake in Fairfax, until he saw how balanced their coverage during the 1993 election was.[112] Keating also rejected Murdoch's attempted purchase of the majority of the news agency Australian Associated Press, but approved his acquisition of AAP's share of Reuters, and also of half of Australian Newsprint Mills.[113] When the Murdoch decision was being made, leading figures tended to appeal to sentiment rather than law, to argue that Murdoch was 'really' an Australian.[114] John Singleton's advertising on Murdoch's behalf had a double-page spread headed 'Is the greatest Living Aussie a Yank?'[115]

The Trade Practices Commission (since replaced by the Australian Competition and Consumer Commission [ACCC]) had a mandate to weigh the competition impact of the takeover. The TPC said it was:

satisfied that the acquisition of HWT by News Ltd, viewed

overall, has not increased concentration of ownership of the print media in Australia. Rather has ownership become more widespread.[116]

It argued that while the Act precludes one company's domination, it does not preclude duopolies. The TPC head, Bob McComas, argued:

> There isn't any doubt in my mind that a large part of the comment was due to the person behind News rather than the acquisition itself. It is important to recognize that there was a particular feeling about the takeover which in no way related to the law.[117]

It would have been a politically hazardous course for any regulator to align itself against such powerful forces, though there were some, albeit limited, grounds for an optimistic conclusion to the taking of such a position. In no metropolitan market was the number of competitors immediately reduced. Ownership of afternoon papers – much weaker financially than morning papers – was more dispersed. None of this suffices, however, to deal with the elephant in the room: since these deals, the largest company accounted for around two-thirds of metropolitan newspaper circulation, a much bigger share than in any other democratic country.[118]

Unfortunately for the TPC, almost immediately some arrangements began to fall apart. As Frank Lowy's Northern Star company extended its TV reach, it wanted to offload the Brisbane and Adelaide papers it had bought from Murdoch. In August 1987 control of the two papers passed to local managements – who had previously worked for News Limited, whose financing was arranged by News Limited, and whose printing and distribution were negotiated with Murdoch.[119] It would be hard to argue that such arrangements constituted them as independent entities, let alone strong competition.

The newspaper casualties were quick to come: *Business Daily*, a new national business newspaper backed by HWT, did begin, as planned, in July 1987, but in the face of News Limited's hostility it closed after only six weeks.[120] In the early 1980s, Murdoch had launched a new daily in Brisbane, the *Daily Sun*, to compete with the *Courier-Mail*. Within a year of gaining control of HWT in 1987, he closed the Brisbane afternoon paper the *Telegraph*; the *Sun* switched to afternoons, and so Brisbane's newspapers were reduced from three to two.[121] Third, Holmes à Court closed his weekly *Western Mail* in December 1987, as he now owned Perth's daily newspapers.

On 9 February 1987, Murdoch, having achieved his goals in newspapers, finally bowed to legal necessity (and perhaps to his own financial needs) and sold his TV channels to Lowy. The delay had been financially rewarding. He was paid over $800 million,[122] which some estimate at more than double what he would have received if he had sold in September 1985.[123]

Cross-media ownership between newspapers and television had disappeared, but concentration within both had increased markedly. In addition, the upheavals had weakened both industries. Nevertheless, Treasurer Paul Keating was pleased with his handiwork. In 1990, he said the result was 'a beautiful position compared with what we did have'. Between 1988 and 1991, 1200 journalist jobs disappeared, the biggest loss in the industry's history, as seven of 19 metropolitan daily papers closed, and commercial TV staff declined from 7745 to 6316.[124] Meanwhile, Murdoch had, as he proclaimed, completed the biggest newspaper takeover in the English-speaking world, and achieved an unassailable position in the Australian press.

Hawke's Labor successors have had ample opportunity to regret the misdirected pragmatism of his government, which allowed one company to dominate press ownership in a way that is clearly detrimental to democracy.

Blair and Murdoch

For everyone in the British Labour Party, the savagery of the tabloids during the 1992 election was a pivotal experience. Even the political beneficiary of it all, Conservative Prime Minister John Major, described the campaign against Labour leader Neil Kinnock as 'pretty crude' and 'over the top'.[125] Alastair Campbell had no doubt 'that the systematic undermining of Labour and its leader and policies through these papers ... was a factor in Labour's inability properly to connect with the public, and [its] ultimate defeat'.[126] Blair himself resolved: 'I was absolutely determined that we should not be subject to the same onslaught.'[127] He told tabloid editor Piers Morgan that 'I had to court [Murdoch] ... It is better to be riding the tiger's back than let it rip your throat out. Look what Murdoch did to Kinnock.'[128]

Just as the experience made Blair determined to avoid any repetition, it meant others in the Labour Party were likely to be affronted by any dealings he had with Murdoch. Kinnock vented his anger one night at dinner with Campbell:

> 'You imagine what it's like having your head stuck inside a fucking light bulb' [referring to the *Sun*'s infamous front page on election day], he raged at me, 'then you tell me how I'm supposed to feel when I see you set off halfway round the world to grease him up.'[129]

Blair's approach was more attuned to strategy than to moral judgement. In government, on one occasion when Campbell was indignant over some mistreatment by the Murdoch press, Blair advised that 'he was worried my [Campbell's] sense of injustice about what they did was clouding my judgement about how to deal with them'.[130]

Blair described his early period as opposition leader, from 1994, as one of 'courting, assuaging and persuading the media'.[131] Part of what he wanted was to abandon the party's platform on media reform. He told the Leveson Inquiry that Labour made a strategic decision not to tackle the problem of media power: '[I'm] being open about the fact that, frankly, I decided as a political leader that I was going to manage that and not confront it.'[132] He felt that any policy on changing the law on the media:

> would have been an absolute confrontation. You would have had
> virtually every part of the media against you in doing it, and I felt
> that the price you would pay for that would actually push out a
> lot of the things I cared about ...[133]

Blair went beyond making a strategic decision about choosing which battles to fight, however. He sought political advantage when the Major Government moved towards some limits on media ownership which would have disadvantaged Murdoch. Responding to pressures to alleviate the previous total ban on newspapers being allowed to have a commercial TV licence,[134] Major moved towards the then fashionable view of framing ownership limits by defining a 'share of voice' across media. In 1995, his government proposed prohibiting newspaper companies with more than 20 per cent of national circulation applying for ITV licences. This would cut out the Mirror group and Murdoch.[135] McKnight notes that 'A witness to Murdoch's reaction saw him driven into a "furious rage".'[136]

Blair moved to exploit the proprietor's discontent. 'It's not a question of Murdoch being too powerful,' he commented.[137] Labour wanted the 20 per cent limit raised, so instead of being on the more regulatory side, Labour was now on the more deregulatory side. The minister, Virginia Bottomley, accused Labour of 'lurching from paranoid terror of large media groups to sycophantic devotion to them'.[138] The stance was not driven by policy merits, she claimed. Rather 'it was a carefully calculated political stratagem designed to curry favour'.[139]

Labour had Murdoch's support in 1997, and won, although as Campbell observes, 'The *Sun* backed us because they knew we were going to win. We did not win because they backed us.'[140] This set the scene for one of the more extraordinary prime minister-press proprietor relationships in British history. On the one hand, the government was at pains to please Murdoch. For example, Blair ensured that Murdoch sat next to Chinese President Jiang Zemin at a state dinner in London,[141] according him status and the chance to advance his business aspirations in China. Labour favoured the Murdoch press with interviews and leaks of important announcements,[142] and the likely reaction of Murdoch was in the forefront of government thinking when deciding policy: 'No big decision could ever be made inside No. 10 without taking account of the likely reaction of three men – Gordon Brown, John Prescott and Rupert Murdoch.'[143] This was most obvious in policy on Europe, but as former Blair staffer Lance Price observed, 'the influence of the Murdoch press on immigration and asylum policy would make a fascinating PhD thesis'.[144] Yet at the same time the government was paranoid about its dealings with Murdoch becoming public: 'In the past week both Murdoch and the new editor of the *Sun*, David Yelland, were in Number Ten for dinner – not something we've been advertising,'[145] recorded Price in his diary.

This confluence of an eagerness to please Murdoch, and a reluctance to acknowledge any relationship with him, produced an unnecessary embarrassment for the government. During a phone call, British Prime Minister Tony Blair – at Murdoch's request – asked Italian Prime Minister Romano Prodi what his attitude was to Murdoch's wish to acquire Berlusconi's Mediaset company, and Prodi replied that he would prefer an Italian company. This episode blew up into a momentary controversy after the conversation became public. When the story first surfaced in March 1998, Campbell extravagantly denounced it as 'a joke, C-R-A-P, balls'. But uncomfortable backtracking quickly followed, mainly centring on the meaning of the word 'intervene'. Blair then made public statements about his willingness to help 'any business with British interests', but as one Labour MP observed, the government's handling of the issue was a 'rather unedifying spectacle of half-truths and non-denial denials'.[146] As Piers Brendon notes, 'When revealed, this piece of lobbying embarrassed Blair as much as it delighted Murdoch [who] bragged about his access.'[147]

Did this translate into tangible policy favours? Campbell and Blair both emphasised to the Leveson Inquiry that several of their media policies ran contrary to News International's interests. For example, they increased the BBC licence fee; they blocked Murdoch's proposed takeover of Manchester United; and they expanded and strengthened the role of the regulator, Ofcom.[148] In each of these cases they were responding also to larger pressures in society and in the Labour Party. On other occasions, they clearly resisted wider currents for reform. For example, they refused to back moves in the House of Lords against predatory pricing in newspapers in February 1998,[149] when the *Times* was seeking to drive its competitors out of business using exactly this tactic. The government also opposed – in contrast to previous Labour policy and many other voices – any attempts to tighten anti-monopoly provisions in the media.

The occasion when the Labour Government ruled most directly against Murdoch's interests was over his bid to acquire Manchester United. Murdoch bid £623 million, which the club accepted in September 1998. Supporters' groups and others immediately opposed the takeover. In October, the Trade Secretary, Peter Mandelson, referred the bid to the Monopolies and Mergers Commission. Murdoch was unhappy about the referral. The following April, after a six-month investigation, the government ruled against the bid.[150] The *Sun* and the *Times* both criticised the decision, and said football would be the loser. The *Guardian* took the contrary view, with its editorial, 'Murdoch 0, Football 1'.[151]

The Commission's report was 'highly suspicious of BSkyB and United, concluding that promises offered by the two companies to help the deal go through were unlikely to be kept'.[152] Although there were and are other privately owned clubs, there were particular issues with BSkyB owning Manchester United. It would make it very difficult for any other broadcaster ever to win the rights for the English Premier League. It would give BSkyB an incentive to give preference to Manchester United over other clubs. At worst, it could be the basis for BSkyB to support a breakaway competition, à la SuperLeague in Australian rugby league.

Price gave an insight into how worried Blair was by the decision:

> He is, of course, totally preoccupied by Kosovo at the moment, but also very exercised by the decision yesterday to block Sky's bid for Manchester United. No matter what we say publicly, he's very concerned to keep Murdoch on board ... He was furious that the DTI [Department of Trade and Industry] let it be reported that the government had blocked the deal, rather than the Monopolies and Mergers Commission.[153]

Apart from observing 'no-go areas', the one area where the Blair Government adopted a policy that clearly advantaged News International was in the Communications Act of 2003, which for the first time withdrew all foreign ownership restrictions on British broadcasting, and allowed major newspaper proprietors to own the new Channel 5 terrestrial licence, but not the original commercial Channel 3 licences.[154] As Brendon puts it, 'Official denials merely convinced critics that this did not so much create a "level playing field as a landing strip for Rupert Murdoch".'[155] Neil testified before the Leveson Inquiry that Murdoch had lobbied Blair for changes in media laws that would end the ban on foreign ownership of TV licences.[156]

Leveson concluded, perhaps generously, that:

> the evidence does not support an inference of an agreement
> between Mr Murdoch and Mr Blair. Not only did Mr Blair flatly
> deny any such deal but the contemporary papers ... reveal very
> considerable thought, genuine debate and reasoned decision
> making during the development of the policy underpinning the
> 2003 Act.

Murdoch's lobbying style

The news media pride themselves on their ability to penetrate
official secrecy and maintain public accountability. It is somewhat ironic then that News Corp shows such a strong preference
for closed policy processes and a tendency to evade public commitments. Murdoch's dealings with governments and regulatory
agencies show just how much access, at the very top levels of all
governments, he and his representatives have enjoyed. They also
show his preference for closed and informal decision-making processes. As Leveson commented:

> There is a very powerful incentive and momentum precisely for
> the lobbyists of the press to guide their political relationships
> into the private sphere of friendships ... Such friendships
> not only intensify the influence of the lobbyist, they pull the
> relationship (including its lobbying dimension) out of the sphere
> of accountability.[157]

Probably Murdoch's closest relationship with a regulator was with
the Reagan-appointed chair of the US Federal Communications
Commission (FCC), Mark Fowler. Fowler's Reaganite views led
him towards radical deregulation: 'Over four years he got rid of
70 per cent of the rules and regulations that governed American

broadcasting.'[158] Beyond this Murdoch and Fowler had a close personal relationship: they were 'virtual soul mates, proponents of the free market and determined to do away with regulation at all cost ... [Murdoch described Fowler] as one of the great pioneers of the communication revolution.'[159] Fowler 'did everything he could to ease Murdoch's passage'.[160]

The FCC gave Murdoch a charmed run in the 1980s, although its most outrageous decision was of little commercial help. When Murdoch acquired six US TV stations in 1985, he also sought a waiver to keep his newspapers in New York and Chicago, despite owning TV licences in those cities. The US had had, since 1975, restrictions on cross-media ownership forbidding ownership of a TV station and a newspaper in the same city, and had never granted an exemption or even a temporary waiver to a new entrant to television. News Corp argued that it should not be forced into a 'fire sale', and so have to receive a lesser price for its papers. It even argued that selling at a lower price would be bad for media diversity. The FCC granted Murdoch an unprecedented two-year period of grace during which he could keep the newspapers. This decision seems impossible to justify. It was not an act of God that had put Murdoch in breach of the law, after all; it was his own deliberate actions. However, at least in the case of the *New York Post*, this regulatory favour essentially allowed Murdoch to keep losing money.

One recurring theme throughout Murdoch's career has been his failure to keep commitments. In 1968, Murdoch agreed not to buy any more shares in *News of the World*, but did so within months, the moment they became available.[161] When he took a stake in London Weekend TV in 1970, he had to give undertakings to the Independent Television Authority that he would not exercise executive power, but immediately did so. When reminded of this by the CEO he fired soon after, he simply replied, 'Yes, but that was before I came.'[162] He told the publisher of the *New York Post*, Dolly Schiff, in 1976 that he would retain the paper's liberal, progressive character and keep its top editorial staff.[163] In front of the Australian Broadcasting Tribunal, as he took over Channel Ten in 1979, he made a series of spectacularly inaccurate statements. He declared, 'Channel Ten will continue exactly as it is today', but two weeks after he gained the Tribunal's approval, the general manager was gone, and within two months so was the chairman.[164] He also said that although he held an American green card, it was not his desire to apply for US citizenship, and he could not imagine doing so. Six years later he did just that.[165] When asked whether he would seek to own Ten's sister station in Melbourne, he answered, 'There is no substance to that rumour, and I do not see why I should give up a very profitable station in Adelaide for a loser in Melbourne.' But three months later he did exactly that.[166]

The most controversial broken commitments – and ones which in theory were legally binding – were the guarantees of editorial independence he gave when buying the *Times*. Amazingly, the Bancroft family sought to repeat the process when selling Murdoch the *Wall St Journal*. Murdoch found the process insulting but was 'willing to sign on to an artificial set of rules he would inevitably circumvent',[167] knowing that they were 'more about other people's need for a fig leaf than about any reasonable idea of governance'.[168] Then editor Marcus Brauchli thought:

> We're all trying to put Murdoch in a straitjacket, wrap him in chains, put him inside a lead box, padlock it shut, and drop it into the East River … and five minutes later he will be standing on the bank, smiling.[169]

When it comes to complying with obligations to government, Murdoch commented to Kiernan in the early 1980s:

> One thing you must understand, Tom. You tell these bloody politicians whatever they want to hear, and once the deal is done

you don't worry about it. They're not going to chase after you later if they suddenly decide what you said wasn't what they wanted to hear. Otherwise they're made to look bad, and they can't abide that. So they just stick their heads up their asses and wait for the blow to pass.[170]

If, as former Murdoch editor David Montgomery observed, 'Rupert has contempt for the rules, contempt even for governments',[171] it is not surprising that his record is one of regulatory brinksmanship. He takes the view that a rule only applies if it can be enforced. Indeed, Murdoch's capacity to affect how regulations are enforced has probably been more important than his capacity to change policies through legislation.

10

The market for truth

A newspaper has two sides to it. It is a business like any other ...
but it is much more than a business ... it has a moral as well as
material existence and its character and influence are determined
by the balance of these forces.

C.P. Scott, the owner and editor of the *Guardian*, made this famous
statement on that paper's centenary in 1921. It opens the 1982 book
by eminent Australian author and journalist Les Carlyon on the
Norris Inquiry into Victorian newspaper ownership.[1] It is often used
by those seeking to inspire journalism towards its highest ideals, to
rise above commercial pressures.[2]

There have always been problems with Scott's formulation, primarily about who decides the 'balance' and how. What sustains the
'moral', and when and how does the 'material' enhance it or inhibit
it? Must the public simply rely on the *noblesse oblige* of journalists and
proprietors, or are there institutional forces inside newspapers that
make the achievement of the 'moral' more likely?

Perhaps most interesting is how much the balance has changed.
It is plausible to claim that the balance has swung more towards the
material in the 30 years since Carlyon's book than it did in the 60
years separating him and Scott. In the early 1980s, the notion of
editorial independence – as a bulwark against proprietors being too
commercial or too propagandistic – was still taken sufficiently seriously for it to be enshrined in the guarantees Murdoch had to make

when he bought the *Times*. Similarly, quality newspapers still talked of a separation between church (editorial) and state (advertising), believing that the two must remain independent of each other. In the decades since, corporations have become ever more intent on maximising their profits, and the internet has increased the financial pressures on newspapers.

Murdoch has never engaged in vague talk of a balance between moral and material. For him, market success is all but synonymous with democratic virtue. For him, there are not 'quality' papers and popular papers, but simply popular and unpopular papers. From 1969, when he acquired the *Sun*, his most constant target has been 'elitist' pretensions in journalism. He took to publicly criticising British journalism in general as 'dull', 'trite', 'long-winded' and 'incestuous'.[3] As late as 2007, when he was taking over the *Wall St Journal*, the refrain was similar. American newspapers 'have become monotonous'. Many are pretentious and suffer from a sort of tyranny of journalism schools so often run by failed editors.[4] In between, he pondered 'whether there is any other industry in this country which presumes so completely to give the customer what he does not want'.[5] Murdoch biographer, Tom Kiernan, felt that he 'despised the *Times* and every other paper in America that strived for journalistic quality as "snobby enterprises"'.[6] 'There's nothing wrong with talking to the masses,' Murdoch told an American TV interviewer. 'You know, William Shakespeare wrote for the masses.'[7] Steve Dunleavy, a former editor of the *New York Post*, said:

> Rupe doesn't dictate public tastes, you know. He has lots of bosses out there. Millions of them. The public tells him what they want to read and Rupe gives it to them.[8]

This initially sounds egalitarian and democratic, but for Murdoch, the constant risk was of getting 'above' the public. The London *Daily Mirror*, for example, was vulnerable because it was 'flying above the heads of [its] readers'.[9] He said that after launching the *Sun*, 'People wrote to say that they hadn't had a paper they could understand until we came along.'[10] But his view of the tabloid audience was not very flattering. When he bought the *News of the World* in 1969, he told his mother:

> Look, Mum, in Britain there are hundreds of thousands of people who are living in miserable postwar tenement places. They have nothing in the world but the Pools and, you know, this is the sort of thing that they [want].[11]

Years later, he told an American interviewer: 'You have in Britain a society that is becoming extremely decadent. You don't have the underlying puritanical history that this country's got.'[12] His private views of his American audience, expressed over a long dinner with Kiernan in 1982, were no more flattering: the *Post's* readership was 'basically a poorly educated, narrowly experienced' group, which 'craved guidance' and 'flourished on simple black and white answers'.[13]

Presumed knowledge of the audience – usually in the absence of tangible evidence – is one source of editorial authority over mere reporters. When *Sun* editor Kelvin MacKenzie was rebuking a journalist, he spelt out a somewhat alarming view of its readership:

> You just don't understand the readers, do you, eh? He's the bloke you see in the pub – a right old fascist, wants to send the wogs back, afraid of the Russians, hates the queers and weirdoes and drug dealers.[14]

So news judgements are coloured by how stories relate to the presumed readership. The *Sun* used to celebrate prominently the lucky people who won *Sun* bingo. But on one occasion, when it was won by an Asian family, the acting editor declared: 'I'm not having pictures of darkies on the front page ... That's the last thing our readers want – pictures of blacks raking it in.'[15] Also excluded were homosexuals. 'What's all this crap about poofters?' Murdoch would complain if there was a fleeting reference to homosexuality.[16] He greeted an early feature article on homosexuality with, 'Do you really think our readers are interested in poofters?'[17] It is thus not surprising that, according to Shawcross, he 'loathes the ... gay rights lobby'.[18]

Framing news to flatter the presumed audience easily slides into denigrating out-groups in line with audience prejudices. The *Sun* specialised in ethnocentrism that was amusing but also cutting. Its response to a 1984 campaign by French farmers to reduce imports of British lamb was 'Hop Off You Frogs'.[19] But the tabloids' repertoire in their attempts at such humour is limited and clichéd. In 1996 England were to play Germany in the European football championship. The three national tabloids marched in step: The *Mirror*'s headline was 'Achtung! Surrender! For you Fritz ze Euro 96 Championship is over'; the *Sun* had 'Let's blitz Fritz' and the *Star* 'Herr we Go – Bring on the Krauts'.[20] This was just 51 years after the end of World War II, a conflict in which most of the players' fathers would have been too young to fight.

It is another thing, though, to treat war as if it were a football match. When the Argentinean regime of General Galtieri seized the British colony, the Falkland Islands, in 1982, the *Sun* was in the rhetorical front line of Thatcher's determination to take it back by force. As William Shawcross reported:

> Falklands War fever gripped the *Sun* as nowhere else. *Sun* reporters gave themselves military ranks, a picture of Winston Churchill was hung up in the newsroom and, when the British military task force set sail for the South Atlantic, a new slogan was coined: 'The paper that supports our boys'.[21]

Jingoism and journalistic gimmickry reached new heights:

The first missile to hit Galtieri's gauchos will come with love
from the *Sun*. And just in case he doesn't get the message, the
weapon will have painted on the side, 'Up Yours Galtieri' ... The
copy explained that the paper was sponsoring the missile by
paying towards the ship's victory party once the war was over.[22]

Promoting the paper went hand in hand with promoting the war:
Sun readers were encouraged to send in for free 'The *Sun* says Good
Luck Lads' badges,[23] and T-shirts advertising the *Sun*, and saying
'Stick it up your Junta!'[24] The *Sun* was also keen to fight the enemy
at home, especially among its media competitors. Its editorial 'Dare
Call it Treason' underlined its first sentence: 'There are traitors in
our midst.' It then named a BBC journalist, the *Guardian* and the
Daily Mirror as treacherous.[25]

The most infamous incident occurred when the British Navy
sank the Argentine cruiser *General Belgrano*, with 320 lives lost. The
Sun headline in its first edition was 'Gotcha!', but the office had
second thoughts about such rejoicing in the loss of human lives,
and changed it for the second edition. Murdoch, however, liked the
Gotcha! headline, and told MacKenzie they should have kept it.[26]

The *Sun*'s thirst for war angered many of those it was so lavishly
praising – the servicemen and women involved. It also made life
difficult for its journalist, David Graves, who was reporting from
Buenos Aires. At one stage, he was called in by the Argentine military. 'We have been looking at your reports to London,' an admiral
said. 'They do not always appear in quite the same way in the paper
as you have written them, do they?' The admiral smiled and walked
off.[27] It may be unique in the annals of war reporting that an enemy
military censor felt sympathy for a reporter because of the way his
editors were distorting his copy.

Murdoch and MacKenzie were probably satisfied with the
paper's role. Their centre of gravity was the home audience,
and the *Sun*'s polarising performance had kept it at the centre of

attention in Britain. The war also cemented Thatcher's domestic political dominance.

Demand versus supply

In 1962, the two Sydney afternoon papers, in the face of a looming crisis as Indonesia sought to complete its decolonisation by taking Dutch West New Guinea by force, simultaneously discovered the importance of having a reporter on the spot. Murdoch's *Daily Mirror* sent Brian Hogben to the capital, Hollandia, to send back first-hand reports. As the days passed, the paper became increasingly worried that the rival *Sun* would beat it with the first story from the conflict area. Finally, the *Daily Mirror* newsroom concocted its own story. As Kiernan observed, 'Written in suitably purple ... prose, and rid-dled with jungle-warfare clichés, it told a tale, among other things, of cannibals and shrunken heads.'[28] When he heard, the furious Hogben telegraphed his home office, saying the 'nearest shrunken heads are in Sydney'.[29]

The story illustrates a more general problem in news: supply and demand do not necessarily go neatly together. *Sun* editor MacKen-zie exhorted his journalists to 'Shock and Amaze on Every Page',[30] but this takes no account of the fact that the supply of shocking and amazing material may be limited. When reality is too tame to meet the demand, the temptation is to enhance it.

One of the most infamous cases of Murdoch manufacturing supply to meet demand occurred with the serial killer 'Son of Sam' in New York in 1976–77. From July 1976 there was a series of motive-less murders of young men and women in middle-class areas; all were shot with a .44 calibre revolver late at night as they sat in the back of parked cars. In all, there were eight attacks, during which six people were killed and seven wounded.[31] At first, the *Post* had devoted little attention to the story, but 'Murdoch was determined to catch up.' He decided that 'there's only one game in town and that's Son of Sam',[32] and insisted that there had to be a new angle every day.[33]

Unfortunately, the paper 'had no real information to offer – a regular difficulty with murder stories'.[34] So what followed was not only hysterical but often simply baseless. There were several false stories, such as one about the cops letting Sam escape and another about a witness who saw him change into a wig. The paper's most fanciful invention was a story, attributed to Mafia sources, that Mafia families were out hunting the killer: 'The story was pure fantasy,' Murdoch told Kiernan with a laugh a few days later.[35] Perhaps invention was better than intrusion. Murdoch's star reporter, Steve Dunleavy, donned a doctor's smock and entered the hospital room of a wounded victim, posing as a bereavement counsellor, and so secured an exclusive interview with her parents.[36]

After the arrest of the murderer, David Berkowitz, the *Post* had a simple but effective banner, 'Caught!' The paper sold 400,000 copies more than normal that day, carrying it over the million mark.[37] But it was not finished. Several days later, it published 'How I became a Mass Killer by David Berkowitz'. It was later revealed that this was not an article by the killer, and not based on an interview with him, but was a concoction made from letters his ex-girlfriend had sold the paper, and which contained almost nothing of any relevance.[38]

Murdoch's main competitor, the New York *Daily News*, was equally culpable. Its star columnist, Jimmy Breslin, wrote some open letters to the serial killer. Giving such prominence, with the implicit promise of more to come, to a psychopath is of course grossly irresponsible. Murdoch later sought to justify his paper's behaviour by claiming that the *Post* had 'encouraged the police to get off their tails and go catch [the killer]'.[39] This is simply ludicrous: the police were already highly motivated to catch the serial killer.

A further complicating factor in the mismatch between the demand for and supply of news is that demand is not constant. In particular, in the 'market for "shock, voyeurism and scandal"', the consumer's expectations are constantly rising'.[40] Looking back four decades later, the *Sun*, although very controversial at the time, seems relatively harmless. It looked for every opportunity to have sexual content, but rarely in a nasty way. It sought to make itself the centre of attention, and to make the news, not just report it, and it was singularly unencumbered by any sense of professional obligation. What was not apparent then was that – as others sought to emulate it and as it became a prisoner of the expectations it had set for itself – it was setting up an unsustainable dynamic.

One sign of the problems this would create was the reception *Sun* journalists said they got from readers when doing soft features in the late 1980s compared with the 1970s: 'Previously it had mostly been a pleasure to ring ordinary people who had popped up in the news … But now they were detecting a new guarded note', and their requests were being turned down more often.[41]

Greater nastiness was particularly apparent in human interest stories, where the main focus often became the grotesque, especially in the 1980s, with the rise of 'Yuck journalism'. The *Sun* did a story on a horrifically burnt Falklands veteran, and instead of focusing, as the man had hoped, on his recovery from 26 skin grafts and suicidal depression, it concentrated on how he was 'hideously scarred, including misleading photos'. The rest of Fleet Street was disgusted.[42] Similarly, the mother of a 5-year-old disabled boy, who had suffered from both septicemia and meningitis, with the result that he had no sense of fear or danger, and was often involved in accidents, had arranged with a freelance journalist to publicise these problems. This was transformed by the *Sun* into a story headlined 'The Worst Brat in Britain'. One of the paper's tricks was to get the boy to sing a song he had learnt at school, which involved pulling faces. It published one of these silly faces but made no mention of the song. The mother described it as a 'hatchet job on my little boy's already sad little life'.[43]

In the frenetic competition between the tabloids in crime news, there was a constant pushing of boundaries. 'I've got a story about someone who's confessed to 17 rapes,' said MacKenzie. 'If it's a record, I want it on the front page.' On another day, he shouted, 'A story of a blind rapist. We've got our front page.'[44] Eventually MacKenzie broke an agreed taboo, and published a photo of a rape victim on the front page.[45]

The dynamic was similar in celebrity news. The *Sun* had always been preoccupied with television, and their stories had not typically been subjected to stringent tests of accuracy. As Peter Chippindale and Chris Horrie note, 'The effect of the *Sun*'s coverage was to get two soap operas running at once – the fictional on-screen lives of the characters, and the *Sun*'s parallel stories of their real lives.' This 'endemic confusion of fiction and reality' did not worry MacKenzie: 'It's all crap anyway.'[46] The coverage gradually took on a nastier edge. Sexual affairs became fodder even if no conceivable public interest was involved. 'What I want to know is who's fucking who,' Murdoch editor Wendy Henry would say.[47] The end result was the obliteration of any notion of privacy. Leveson judged:

> There is ample evidence that parts of the press have taken the
> view that actors, footballers, writers, pop stars – anyone in whom
> the public might take an interest – are fair game, public property
> with little, if any, entitlement to any sort of private life or respect
> for dignity, whether or not there is a true public interest in
> knowing how they spend their lives. Their families, including
> their children, are pursued and important personal moments are
> destroyed.[48]

This absence of boundaries was accompanied by an increasing emphasis on 'trashing [the] reputations' of those covered, and an emotional tone where 'anger and vindictiveness [were] the default settings'.[49]

Taste versus truth

In the early years of Murdoch owning the *New York Post*, its two most famous headlines were 'Headless Body in Topless Bar' and 'No One is Safe from Son of Sam'.[50] There is a crucial difference between these two headlines. The first was true; the second was not. The increase in the risk of any New Yorker being murdered during the Son of Sam episode was all but zero, because there was a pattern to his victims that excluded most people.

There are many confused debates about popular, 'tabloid' journalism. Some centre on issues of taste, preferences for some types of news – such as sport, crime, 'human interest' and celebrity – over the main topics of more upmarket journalism, such as political, international and business news. Some centre on styles of presentation, with tabloid journalism marked by large headlines, more pictures, and shorter stories.

But there is no reason for tabloid newspapers to be less accurate than 'quality' papers, or held to a lesser standard of truth. Perhaps the most common issue comes from the search for sensation, the wish to make the story more dramatic than reality. In the early years, Murdoch was unhappy with the *New York Post*: he felt it was insufficiently dramatic. He brought his own people into senior positions, overlapping their authority with that of the existing editors. In January 1977, murderer Gary Gilmore became the first person to be executed in the US for nine years. There was a peaceful candlelight vigil outside the prison, but the Murdoch editor had a headline with the protesters 'storming' the prison.[51] When the editor, Paul Sann, insisted that the inaccurate headline be dropped, it 'left no doubt in Murdoch's mind of what he already suspected – that the incumbent staff would resist his every move'.[52] It is symptomatic that Murdoch saw it as a test of will and authority, and was seemingly uninterested in the merits of the headline's accuracy.

Just as the mismatch between demand and supply can lead to problematic news coverage, so inaccuracies are more likely when there is no market punishment for them: when the errors will be invisible to the audience, or when they confirm audience expectations, or when the sources are unlikely to complain. International news has thus often been more error prone than domestic reporting. Kiernan was witness to the *New York Post*'s coverage of Israeli invasions of Lebanon in the summer of 1982. He claimed:

> Throughout that period, the paper was without a single reporter on the scene, yet its stories were laced with unattributed 'eyewitness' descriptions of Arab atrocities and Israeli heroics, many of them invented in its New York city newsroom.

Meanwhile, the paper's conservative columnists regularly attacked what they took to be the anti-Israeli coverage of the US TV networks.[53] In 1986, after the Chernobyl nuclear disaster in the Soviet Union, it reported, without any basis, that there were 'Mass graves for 15,000 N-Victims'.[54] It never admitted that this was a wild exaggeration.

In 2011, the *Sun* carried a story on its front page headlined 'Swan Bake', accusing asylum seekers of eating the queen's swans. The story proved to be baseless, and the paper later carried a half-hearted retraction – on page 41.[55] At the other end of the social scale, but similarly often lacking a direct public voice, *Sun* editor MacKenzie told reporters on stories about the royals: 'Don't worry if it's not true – so long as there's not too much of a fuss about it afterwards.'[56] A later *Sun* editor, David Yelland, had a front page exclusive, headlined 'Queen has rubber duck in her bath … and it wears a crown' with photos of both the queen and a rubber duck.[57]

The *Sun* under MacKenzie made many errors, but he believed in:

never correcting anything unless he absolutely had to. His attitude was that if something wrong got in the paper it was 'hard fucking luck'. He'd bollock the person who made the mistake, but he never believed in owning up to mistakes in public, saying critics would attack anyway, so why give them ammunition?[58]

However, he made two errors that proved very expensive. The first came after the Hillsborough disaster, the worst stadium-related fatal incident in British history. In April 1989, at an FA cup match between Liverpool and Nottingham, after a crush of spectators against fences, 96 people were killed and over 700 injured. It was an outdated venue, and crowd control procedures were archaic. To the horror of the reporter who wrote the story,[59] the paper had a bald headline – 'The Truth' – above claims that accused some fans of picking the pockets of victims, and urinating on 'brave cops'. It claimed that some drunken Liverpool fans had 'viciously attacked rescue workers'. Most of the claims were shown to be false. The paper's sales in Liverpool dropped by 40 per cent, and remained lower than elsewhere for more than a decade afterwards.

The other financially disastrous story stemmed directly from MacKenzie's 'appalled fascination' with homosexuality.[60] On 25 February 1987, the *Sun* had a headline story 'Elton in Vice Boys Scandal/Star's lust for bondage'. This was the start of an 18-month saga that ended in complete ignominy for the paper. In recent years, MacKenzie has said that this was the only time in his 13 years as editor he checked a story, and it turned out to be wrong. He told the Leveson Inquiry: 'I never did it again. Basically my view was that if it sounded right it was probably right and therefore we should lob it in.'[61]

This is a cute line, but fundamentally misleading. Other *Sun* journalists recalled that MacKenzie was feeling desperate for a sensational story, and became determined to publish the story, which wrongly claimed that rock star Elton John had paid for sex with underage 'rent boys'. Nearly everyone who saw the story could see its basis was far too slight – the uncorroborated word of a male prostitute who had been paid for the story. The legal department objected, and when their advice was ignored took the very unusual step of putting that advice in writing. But it was still ignored.[62]

When Elton John saw the story, he was determined to sue because the story wasn't true. His friends advised otherwise. Mick Jagger, for example, said it was 'not worth fighting because they'll try to rake up so much muck'.[63] Elton did sue, and the paper did rake up as much muck as it could.

The second day's headline was 'Elton's kinky kinks/Elton's drug capers'. This resulted in a second writ. On the third day the *Sun* had 'You're a liar Elton', with a strap over 'the story they're all suing over', and its competitor, the *Daily Mirror*, reported that Elton was in New York on the day the 'rent boy' testified they had been together.

The paper was becoming desperate. It started a massive trawl through the singer's past, and pursued him wherever he went. The pop star testified that he was 'mega-depressed' by all the *Sun*'s attention. The paper entered into an arrangement with a Scottish man, who provided them with a series of affidavits (he was paid £1750 for each) of rent boys saying they had had sex with Elton, until the paper realised it was being ripped off and the affidavits were sheer invention.

The *Sun*'s last error came on 28 September 1987, when it splashed with 'Mystery of Elton's Silent Dogs', a story that claimed Elton had had his vicious Rottweiler dogs silenced by a horrific operation and they were now silent assassins.[64] It was easily refuted – Elton did not have Rottweilers and his dogs were manifestly loud barkers. Elton's lawyer issued writ number 17. Six weeks later, the *Daily Mirror* tracked down the original 'rent boy', whom the *Sun* had put into hiding, and he admitted it had all been 'a pack of lies'.

A year later, in December 1988, the inevitable finally happened. On the day the court hearing was to begin, the paper published a front page headline: 'Sorry Elton!' It was the first libel apology to lead the paper, and also explicitly admitted that the singer would receive £1 million, double the previous highest settlement. The paper had lost massively in every way. It had been exposed as having published a baseless story, and then compounding this with prolonged bullying and persecution of the person it had wronged. The root of the problem was not only sloppiness and arrogance, but the editor's apparent inability to understand that a gay singer might actually be popular with the paper's readers.[65]

Murdoch's most famous mistake, however, was a profitable one. His name will forever be linked with contemporary journalism's greatest monument to gullibility – the publication of the 'Hitler diaries'. The German magazine *Stern*, which had a respectable journalistic reputation, had paid $3.1 million for material allegedly written by the Führer.[66] Even though there had never been any hint that Hitler kept a diary, the magazine believed the volumes were authentic, and started an auction for English language rights. Several organisations were interested, but they had to take the diaries on trust, as *Stern* refused access to the originals. Murdoch became involved in an atmosphere marked by competitiveness and urgency, and won the bidding contest.

Some journalists at the *Sunday Times* were very worried, because the paper had been taken in by fake Mussolini diaries in 1966. Investigative reporter Phillip Knightley, remembering that incident, wrote a memo which concluded 'that secrecy and speed work for the con man'.[67] It was a warning that disappeared amid the mounting excitement of what the paper thought would be a world scoop. On the News International Board was one of Britain's leading historians on World War II, Hugh Trevor-Roper, Lord Dacre. He read some excerpts and initially thought they were genuine.

On the Saturday evening when the presses were about to roll with the first excerpts, the journalists involved were having a celebratory drink in editor Frank Giles's office, feeling satisfied and excited at the splash they were about to make, when Giles spoke to Trevor-Roper, who told the horrified editor that he now had substantial doubts about the material's authenticity. Giles phoned Murdoch, who in the most famous moment in the saga, ordered, 'Fuck Dacre. Publish!'

The instruction has been cited to show Murdoch's disregard for truth, but at that moment he had almost no choice. The real faults had come earlier. *Stern* itself was the victim of one of its journalists, a con man who was in partnership with a forger, but the secrecy and limits it imposed on the bidders made proper testing impossible.

Harold Evans, by then the former *Times* editor, put the blame squarely at the top: 'Once Murdoch himself became involved in the excitement of negotiation and of sensational scoops, all serious journalistic standards were swept aside.'[68] However, the unhealthy hierarchy within News International, which produced a willingness among key participants to deflect responsibility upwards, was equally important. When journalists expressed suspicion, editor Giles reassured them that 'the proprietor has no doubts'.[69] This lack of responsibility, or perhaps reluctance to bring unwelcome news to the proprietor, was also at the heart of the very late warning from Trevor-Roper. He had told the *Times* editor, Charles Douglas Home, of his doubts on the Saturday morning, but – amazingly – Douglas Home told no one else, and allowed his *Sunday Times* colleagues to continue on their road to professional disaster.[70]

After publication, *Stern* at last released copies for examination, and the German Federal Archive declared that all seven of the volumes they inspected were forgeries: 'Chemical analysis had shown that the paper, the binding, the glue and the thread were all of post-war manufacture.'[71]

The journalists felt humiliated. Murdoch was sanguine. Evans noted, 'When he was told that the diaries were fake, he reassured the worried editorial men at Times Newspapers who feared for their credibility: "After all," Murdoch said, "we are in the entertainment business."'[72] The Hitler diaries episode increased the circulation of the paper by 60,000,[73] and the revealing of them as forgeries of course meant Murdoch did not have to pay. He did not have the intense feeling of shame the journalists did. In Bruce Page's words, 'a bet had simply gone wrong'.[74]

One trivial falsehood that appears in every Murdoch newspaper is an astrology column. When the *Australian* began he insisted that there be one, and syndicated it from the UK, apparently the different constellations in the northern and southern hemispheres making no difference to the forecasts.[75] When he took over *TV Guide* magazine it hired an astrologer who was given the job of charting the likely fortunes of new shows.[76] At one stage, the *Sun*'s astrologer was found to have been recycling predictions, and was sacked by the editor, MacKenzie, who was said to have begun the letter of dismissal, 'As you will no doubt have foreseen ...'[77] Murdoch editors take their astrology columns seriously. One of the few times in a research interview where I had trouble keeping a straight face was with Peter Wylie, Murdoch's very able and energetic editor of the Sydney *Daily Mirror* in the early 1980s. Wylie was totally preoccupied with beating the *Sun*, and he was going through a very long catalogue of ways in which the *Mirror* was superior, when he said, 'We have better stars than the *Sun*.' Puzzled, I asked what he meant: sports stars, TV stars? 'Stars stars,' he replied. 'The *Sun* has one astrology column and we have three!'[78] No doubt Murdoch was just trying to add to reader appeal, but some have claimed that he was himself superstitious and, like many gamblers, looked for omens. In the 1970s, the London *Sun* editor, Larry Lamb, used to 'lean on the paper's astrologer to doctor the Pisces entry to assure [Murdoch] that he would have a good day, and urge him to be full of good will'.[79]

Rather more seriously, Murdoch publications have not had a good record in covering scientific disputes. At the moment there is much contention over their coverage of climate change, but there were also problems with earlier disputes. Murdoch has been a long-term friend of the tobacco industry. He served on the board of Philip Morris,[80] and leading members of that company have served on the News Corp board. An internal Philip Morris document named Murdoch as a media proprietor sympathetic to their position, said that 'Murdoch's papers rarely publish anti-smoking articles these days', described them as 'our natural allies', and planned to build 'similar relationships to those we now have with Murdoch's News Limited with other newspaper proprietors'.[81] When New York City banned smoking in bars in 2001, the *Post* fulminated against 'Nicotine Nazis' and claimed that mayor Michael Bloomberg was an elitist zealot who would like to 'ban smoldering incense at St Paul's Cathedral'.[82]

On the issue of HIV/AIDS, Murdoch's two most famous tabloids made diametrically opposed errors. In 1989, the London *Sun* had a headline story 'Straight Sex cannot give you AIDs – Official'. This was accompanied by an editorial that said 'forget the idea that ordinary heterosexual people can contract AIDS. They can't ... Anything else is just homosexual propaganda.' It quoted *Sun* doctor Vernon Coleman as claiming that the AIDS scare was 'the biggest hoax of the century'.[83] In 1985, it had publicised someone it said was a 'psychologist' saying that homosexuals should be exterminated to stop the spread of AIDS.[84] Meanwhile, *New York Post* editor Steve Dunleavy briefed a reporter to do a story that AIDS could be spread by kissing. When the reporter protested that it was not proven, Dunleavy replied: 'Let's not be too technical, mate – it's a good yarn.'[85]

But poor coverage was not confined to Murdoch's tabloids. In the early 1990s, Andrew Neil's *Sunday Times* ran what Bruce Page described as a 'crackpot assault' on the 'AIDS establishment'.[86] The paper gave publicity to dissident Berkeley academic Alan Duesberg, who argued that HIV was not associated with AIDS, and that AIDS, in the sense of a pandemic, did not exist. Under a headline

'The emperor's clothes', came the claim that 'AIDS was sustaining a vested interest of great power'.[87] In an October 1993 article titled 'the plague that never was' it gave publicity to a French couple in Africa who used to believe in AIDS, but had concluded that 'it is something that has been invented'.[88] When the paper's coverage was criticised, for example in an editorial in *Nature* magazine, its response was to sound themes that would become even more familiar in the climate change debate. It said it was challenging 'orthodoxy' and standing up to the medical and scientific 'establishments', and accused critics of representing 'vested interests' and of 'censorship'.[89]

Friends and enemies

When he was a rising Labor MP in 1998, Mark Latham had lunch with three Sydney *Daily Telegraph* senior staff members: Col Allan, Malcolm Farr and Piers Akerman. According to Latham's diary:

> The lunch conversation is a long way from policy debate. Running the *Tele* is about good food, good wine and good hatchet jobs. These blokes have scores of public figures they hate, and the purpose of the paper is to do them in.[90]

Later, when he became Labor leader, Latham became one of the public figures the paper was keen to 'do in'. On Saturday, 19 June 2004 the paper's front page headline was 'The Dismissal: how Mark Latham's temper ended a proud 115 year cricketing tradition'. The story referred to an incident 25 years earlier, when Latham was 18 and playing cricket for Sydney University. After an umpire gave him out LBW, Latham had given the umpire 'the bird', and been suspended by the club for one week. According to the *Telegraph*, this was the first ever suspension in the club's 115-year history. Latham commented:

> [I]f you were standing in the bar of the uni pavilion in 1979 and said to someone, 'you know, Latho's blue with the umpire today, that will be front page news in 25 years' time', they would have locked you up in the madhouse.[91]

This dividing of the world into friends and enemies seems to be widespread in News Corp publications. A former editor of the *New York Post* said that Paul Newman, a popular movie star who often expressed liberal political views, was their Public Enemy Number One. 'He topped our permanent, ineradicable hate list.' The *Post* simply banned Newman from its pages: 'The exception was bad news. Otherwise no Newman. We banned him from the TV listings.'[92] British Labour MP Tom Watson, who had supported Gordon Brown and publicly said Tony Blair should set a date for retiring, was told at the Labour Party conference by a *Sun* political correspondent, 'My editor [Rebekah Wade (now Brooks)] will pursue you for the rest of your life. She will never forgive you for what you did to her Tony.'[93]

Sometimes the original reason for such enmity was commercial. One of News Limited's worst moves in Australia was its attempt to circumvent the existing rugby league competition and set up a rival SuperLeague. Eventually the two competing leagues came together, but in making it one competition again, some clubs were omitted, most notably the South Sydney Rabbitohs. Popular Australian TV personality Andrew Denton was a passionate Rabbitohs supporter and thus supported the fight against News Limited's exclusion of the club from the competition. On ABC TV Denton said, 'I wish I could take Lachlan Murdoch [and] … Ken Cowley by their smug little jowls … [and explain to them that] tradition in sport is a very, very powerful thing.' Bruce Guthrie discovered this after he ran a feature on Denton in the *Australian* magazine, which he was editing. An assistant whispered to him, 'You know that Denton is *persona non grata* around here.' Three weeks later, according to Guthrie, the

Australian's editor, Chris Mitchell, reported that Lachlan Murdoch had just rung from New York, 'very pissed off' that Denton had received favourable publicity.[94]

Guthrie also discovered that some individuals were protected at News. Many years earlier, when he was Beecher's deputy editor at the Melbourne *Herald*, the paper's gossip columnist had gently chided *New Idea* boss and Murdoch executive Dulcie Boling for her icy demeanour. He received a faxed rebuke from Rupert in New York within a matter of hours: 'If you think this sort of garbage sells newspapers, you are sadly mistaken.'[95] Similarly, when, in a commercial case involving anti-competitive practices, Justice Sackville criticised News Limited solicitor Ian Philip, Australian News Ltd CEO John Hartigan rang Guthrie, seeking to minimise the way it would be reported.[96]

Individuals can move from one category to the other. Possibly one of the reasons for News Limited firing Guthrie from the editorship of the *Herald-Sun*, despite the fact that by almost all measures he was succeeding at the paper, was that he had run a story about Victorian Police Commissioner Christine Nixon taking a free flight with Qantas. Nixon was a good friend of Murdoch's sister and News Limited Board member Janet Calvert-Jones.[97] Guthrie was told the story had gone too far; soon after that the company tried to dismiss him. After Guthrie made these concerns public – when he brought his case for unfair dismissal – the paper started attacking Nixon much more strongly, particularly over her handling of the tragic Victorian bushfires in early 2010. She continued to be a target during the Royal Commission inquiring into official responses to those massive fires. In her memoirs, Nixon criticised the paper's coverage of her; around the time the book was to be published the paper again carried several negative stories about her. Amusingly, the publisher, Melbourne University Press's Louise Adler, revealed that she had her 'own insight into the tactics of tabloid journalism': someone at a *Herald-Sun* news conference inadvertently left his phone on after speaking to her, and she heard a discussion about putting MUP higher up in the story. The resulting story on page 4 was headlined 'Uni in Nixon book row'.[98]

It is only News Corp enemies, not its friends, whose past lives are pursued for damaging material. In 2011 the independent Tasmanian MP Andrew Wilkie was pursuing an issue close to his heart: legislation to limit the damaging impact of poker machines on problem gamblers and their families. According to *Crikey* journalist Stephen Mayne, the pokies industry had 'just signed contracts to spend millions of dollars on paid advertising demonizing pokies reform'.[99] During the controversy, the *Herald-Sun* splashed with a story about Wilkie's behaviour during officer training at Duntroon 28 years earlier.

At least this was a story about Wilkie's own actions. Relatives and associates of unfavoured leaders can also find themselves in a negative news spotlight. As discussed in Chapter 6, the *New York Post* ran a banner and front page headline claiming that the long dead father of 1984 Democratic vice-presidential candidate Geraldine Ferraro had 40 years earlier been arrested for illegal gambling, although the charge was not proceeded with and no conviction was recorded.[100]

The search through people's closets for skeletons is not always successful, though. When left-wing politician Ken Livingstone, 'Red Ken', became mayor of London in 1981, *Sun* editor Kelvin MacKenzie sent journalists looking for material to discredit him, but all they came back with was that he kept newts. 'All you can find is fucking newts!' MacKenzie raged at them.[101] When the paper was pursuing another of its targets, the left-wing homosexual Labour candidate Peter Tatchell, again reporters came back empty-handed, only to be admonished by one of the editorial staff, 'When will you lot get it through your heads that Kelvin's not interested in whether things are true or not. What you've got to do is give him what he wants.'[102]

In 1998, in another story about relatives of enemies, the *New York Post* wrote a front-page story about Chelsea Clinton's visit to a university counsellor after a failed romance.[103] After News International turned against Conservative Prime Minister John Major, the love life of his son was deemed newsworthy. Once, according to Major's testimony to the Leveson Inquiry, the *News of the World*, trying to get information on his son's relationship with his girlfriend, misrepresented themselves as a hospital needing to carry out an emergency operation, but first having to find out if she was pregnant. Then a motorcyclist 'had been instructed to follow my son "day and night" in the hope of providing a story'. Major's son became concerned that the person following him may have been a terrorist, and pulled into a police station, where the pursuer had to confess to the police that he was from the *News of the World*.[104]

In contrast to the invasion of the privacy of unfavoured leaders' children, even the principals of the favoured side may be protected. The *News of the World* had a story in the lead-up to the 1997 election about shadow foreign minister Robin Cook having an affair, but as Murdoch was then on Labour's side, it was not used.[105] When Murdoch met Reagan in person, he 'was surprised by the president's age and frailty'. Murdoch attended a lunch, with several other guests, where 'Reagan actually fell asleep during the meal.' Murdoch described the experience as 'awful',[106] but clearly it was not something that Murdoch readers needed to know.

Murdoch publications often seem to enjoy conflict for its own sake, keen not just to attack others, but also to make themselves the centre of attention. For Kiernan:

> a favourite tactic of Murdochian journalism is to attack rival newspapers in print for the very sins – factual distortion and invention – that Murdoch's papers are regularly accused of committing. The tactic is partly a circulation ploy based on the theory that there is nothing the reading public enjoys more than a nasty word-brawl between competing newspapers. But it has another purpose, too, which is that 'the best defence is a good offense'.[107]

The combative nature of Murdoch's publications in Australia is clearest in the responses of the *Australian* and its editor, Chris Mitchell, to criticism. Journalist Jonathan Holmes commented on 'the *Australian*'s habit of launching vitriolic personal attacks, which can sometimes last years, against anyone bold enough to criticize it'.[108] During one conflict, Mitchell threatened to 'use every journalistic and legal measure available' against Victoria's Office of Police Integrity because of a clash over the paper's coverage of a police raid.[109] In another, the paper editorialised, 'it is now clear that senior members of the media … have embarked on a concerted campaign to delegitimize tough reporting and this newspaper'.[110] Journalist Elisabeth Wynhausen, who was sacked by Mitchell in 2009, thought:

> He was a tireless strategist whose best and worst instincts were
> filtered through the same tendency to turn almost any subject
> into an excuse for an argument with a bunch of imagined
> enemies. He treated the paper like the spoils of war, routinely
> using its pages to campaign against people who had ever dared to
> take him on.[111]

Whether or not this is an accurate characterisation of Mitchell, it is almost a job description for Murdoch editors.

Rewards and punishments

The key aspect in defining a workplace culture is what gets rewarded and what gets punished. Murdoch discovered the perils of placing the moral over the material early in his career, and it led to his first firing of an editor; it was of Rohan Rivett, his friend and mentor, who had put the Adelaide *News* back on a sound basis both journalistically and commercially.

Rivett had started to question the way the police had secured a murder conviction against an Indigenous man, Max Stuart.[112] This grew into a campaign that pitted the paper against not only the police, but also the South Australian legal establishment and the government of the long-serving South Australian premier, Thomas Playford. It led to a Royal Commission, which concluded that justice had been done, and to a very unusual prosecution of the newspaper – for criminal libel – which could have resulted in Murdoch and Rivett going to jail. The decisions which had led to the criminal libel case had been Murdoch's, made when Rivett was on holiday.

It was a very anxious period for both of them. Soon after the case was over, Murdoch, in a brief letter, terminated Rivett's editorship. Over the years, Murdoch has given several specious reasons for this decision.[113] He has always denied that the Stuart case was behind the sacking,[114] but Shawcross's explanation is probably close to the mark:

> Murdoch had had enough of advocacy journalism. He was expanding his empire and was more interested in cash than in confrontation, in profits than in political positions. He wanted editors who were safe rather than scintillating, whom he could rely upon however far away he might be.[115]

Rivett's successor, Ron Boland, stayed as editor for almost two decades, and achieved the type of paper Murdoch was hoping for. On the other hand, the paper was, according to John Lisners, risk averse. Lisners spent some weeks in 1968 putting together a campaigning story about the large number of fatalities discovered among workers inhaling asbestos dust; it included extensive research made available to him from Adelaide University. However, 'Boland refused to print the story to avoid offending major advertisers.'[116]

Although the reputation of Murdoch's newspapers emphasises their outrageousness, especially in monopoly and semi-monopoly situations, they are often very particular about what fights they pick.

As we saw above, Paul Sann's editorship of the *New York Post*

became doomed when he made a stand for accuracy in reporting the vigil outside an execution. When Matt Driscoll, a sports
reporter, was rebuked by *News of the World* editor Andy Coulson for
having only taken a shorthand note rather than taping an interview,
and he replied that he would accept the warning, but didn't feel
he had done anything wrong, Coulson responded that 'In my view
your actions on this matter merited dismissal.' Eventually Driscoll
won a huge payout for unfair dismissal, but before the final verdict,
News International fought the case hard, three times appealing the
verdict.[117] So taking a short-hand note rather than making a tape,
and then not wholeheartedly accepting the editor's reprimand, were
thought grounds for dismissal, and the sacked employee's claims
were vigorously and expensively contested.

In contrast, the paper had run a story on Max Mosley – a former
president of the international federation governing Formula 1 and
other motor racing events, a millionaire, and the son of Britain's
most famous Nazi, Oswald Mosley. Max Mosley was photographed
in a sadomasochistic orgy with five prostitutes. The paper reported
it under the headline 'F1 boss in sick Nazi orgy with 5 hookers'.
Mosley sued for breach of privacy, and the trial exposed the paper's
methods. It had paid one of the prostitutes, and offered her more
money if she did an interview, which consisted of agreeing to a
script already written by a reporter, and which was later changed
without her knowledge. It told two others it would name them in
print if they did not co-operate. It used the word 'Nazi' to describe
the event, and thus linked it to the Holocaust, because one participant, who was in fact German, spoke some German. The paper 'lost
the case, refused to apologise and claimed publicly that it deserved
a journalism award for the story'.[118] Though the judge criticised the
'erratic and changeable' testimony of the paper's principal reporter,
Neville Thurlbeck, and said his emails to potential interviewees
were tantamount to blackmail, no action was taken against him.[119]

During the phone hacking scandal, scholar Brian Cathcart

observed that even with cases involving adverse legal findings and large financial penalties:

> there was no introspection … afterwards. The damages were paid, and the books were closed, and they moved on, a state of affairs almost guaranteed to deliver more mistakes and failures.[120]

Justice Leveson similarly observed that despite defamation actions and complaints upheld by the Press Complaints Commission, 'the inquiry has been given no evidence of disciplinary action having been taken in response to those breaches of the PCC code'.[121]

Guthrie pointed to the lack of consequences for mistakes in Australian News Limited papers. The Sydney *Sunday Telegraph* and Melbourne *Sunday Herald-Sun* ran front-page photos purporting to be of a semi-naked Pauline Hanson, the right-wing populist politician. News allegedly had paid $15,000 for the pictures. Not that publication would have been justified if the photos had been genuine, but the papers looked very bad when they turned out to be fakes. 'Despite the immensity of the error,' said Guthrie, 'no one had paid with their job.'[122]

Similarly, Guthrie thought that 'Mitchell had done a good job at the *Courier-Mail* during his seven years there'[123] but had made 'one very serious mis-step'. Australia's best-known historian, Manning Clark, had died in 1991. He had become a hate figure for many on the right. A Cold War conspiracist, Peter Kelly, became convinced that Clark had been awarded an Order of Lenin by the Soviet Union. Mitchell assigned journalist Wayne Smith to work with Kelly, and in August 1996 published eight pages of commentary and background to accompany the lead story 'By Order of Lenin'.[124] The story quoted one KGB expert saying that such a secret award indicated that Clark was not only an extremely significant agent of influence, but possibly also a very important agent.

The *Courier-Mail's* case 'quickly began to collapse'. Apart from the fact that they thought Clark had left-wing views, their only actual piece of evidence was that a couple of people said they had seen Clark wearing the award at a function at the Soviet embassy. Wearing such an award in public would have been bad tradecraft if Clark had been a secret agent. However, it seemed that he might have been wearing a ceremonial ribbon he received when he gave a lecture in the Soviet Union in 1970. The Soviet archives were open by this time, but no archival evidence has ever been produced. The Australian Press Council, after a complaint by 15 eminent public figures, found that the paper was not justified in publishing its key assertion and the conclusions flowing from it.[125] The paper's appeal was dismissed, but it refused to publish a retraction. Mitchell was unrepentant: he called Clark 'a David Irving of the Left',[126] a reference to the famous Nazi apologist. As Guthrie noted, 'the episode didn't derail Mitchell's progress through News Limited. As I would later learn, such mistakes rarely do.'[127] In 2002 Mitchell became editor of the *Australian*, a position he still occupies.

Perhaps there are more likely to be internal consequences if there are external consequences, but even that relationship – between market rewards and punishments and professional performance – is at best erratic. Indeed some observers of the contemporary media think that market rewards run counter to professional standards. For former prime minister Sir John Major, 'across Fleet Street, sensational and exclusive stories sold extra copies – straight reporting did not. Accuracy suffered.'[128] For Tony Blair's spin doctor, Alastair Campbell, 'Speed now comes ahead of accuracy, impact comes ahead of fairness, and in parts of the press anything goes.'[129] Some practitioners think along similar lines – a senior producer on the Fox TV network's *A Current Affair* thought that what made the program 'different was that it never tried to be fair'.[130]

Such changes are beyond the control of any individual. Murdoch has been but one of many drivers. Moreover, there is great variation between Murdoch's titles in different markets and countries and periods. However, the contemporary balance between the material and the moral is very different from anything C.P. Scott envisaged.

11

The Republic of Fox

I challenge anybody to show me an example of bias on Fox News
Channel.

Rupert Murdoch, 2001[1]

Fox News was Murdoch's last great win against the odds. It has
been for him a triumph, a fusion of political mission with commercial success. After a press conference in early 1996 announcing
the launch of Fox News, its CEO, Roger Ailes, said to Murdoch,
'They're laughing at us.' Murdoch replied, 'They always laugh in
the beginning. That never bothers me.'[2] It was far from clear that
there was a market for a further cable news channel. CNN, then
20 years old, had, after a shaky start, become profitable and the
well-established leader. It was about to be joined by MSNBC, an
all-news channel run by one of the three major networks.[3] As it
turned out, Fox News was breaking even by the time of the 2000
election, much earlier than expected.[4] In 2002 it overtook CNN as
the highest rating cable news channel,[5] a position it has held for
most of the time since. By 2010, 'Fox News reaped an estimated
profit of $816 million – nearly a fifth of Murdoch's global haul',
rivalling that of News Corp's entire film division, including 20th
Century Fox.[6] Murdoch laughed last, and longest.

Murdoch's triumph is shared by Ailes, the only CEO Fox News
has ever had, and it is the crowning achievement of Ailes' long career
in politics and television. The success of Fox has made him rich; he

earns $23 million a year.[7] According to Michael Wolff, when Murdoch and Ailes decided to start Fox News, Ailes insisted that he should have sole control of the new network, that 'Murdoch, the great meddler, would not interfere.'[8] Fox's commercial success has strengthened Ailes's claims to independence.

Ailes's first job after graduating in 1962 was as a 'gofer' on the Mike Douglas TV chat show. He was a 'TV wunderkind', with an 'uncanny feel for stagecraft' and how to give viewer appeal to conversational performances on live television. By the time he was 25 he had become executive producer.[9] He impressed one of the guests, Richard Nixon, with his straight talking about how Nixon needed to embrace TV if he wished to become president.

Soon afterwards he joined the Nixon campaign. Tim Dickinson notes:

> It was while working for Nixon that Ailes first experimented
> with blurring the distinction between journalism and politics ...
> To bypass journalists [whom he thought hostile to Republicans]
> Ailes made Nixon the star of his own traveling roadshow – a
> series of contrived newslike events that the campaign paid to
> broadcast in local markets across the country.[10]

Ailes called this the 'man in the arena concept'.[11] Nixon fielded friendly questions in front of live audiences.[12] The format played to Nixon's strengths and avoided his televisual weaknesses, allowing him to feed off the interaction with the audience while limiting the scope for journalists to interrogate him. Ailes's political mistake was to co-operate with a young journalist, Joe McGuiness, whose book *The Selling of the President*, became a bestseller. Ailes admitted talking to McGuiness; Nixon was angry; and Ailes's work for the White House ended.

He then threw himself into a variety of projects, including one which was an uncanny prefiguring of Fox News. In 1972, a wealthy right-wing Republican, Joseph Coors, started a conservative TV news operation. Its marketing slogans included 'traditional network news is slanted to the liberal left [and] not objective', whereas 'we play it straight down the middle' and 'tell both sides'.[13] Its idea of straight down the middle can be seen in a memo to staff that 'Martin Luther King was an avowed communist revolutionary', and so it was not 'necessary for us to cover him ... just because the other networks do'.[14] It suffered almost non-stop internal drama – at one stage most of its journalists were purged, and it went through three news directors; Ailes became its fourth. The Coors people trusted Ailes because of 'his affiliation with the Republicans', and because he was 'not a newsman'.[15] The channel lasted only a few years.

Ailes's most successful and most infamous campaign as a political consultant was the election of President George H.W. Bush in 1988. Although in the end Bush won comfortably, before the campaign it was felt he faced two major obstacles: majority opinion tended to favour the Democrats on a range of issues, and Bush 'needed to overcome his "wimp" image'.[16] The campaign marked an escalation in professionalism, ruthlessness and negativity that became a reference point for all future campaigns. The Democratic candidate, Michael Dukakis, had been Governor of Massachusetts and was considered a political liberal. The Republicans had several clever advertising themes – a Do Not Swim in Boston Harbor ad, to attack his environmental credentials; Dukakis looking goofy while travelling in a tank, to attack his defence credentials.

The most controversial, however, zeroed in on law and order. During Dukakis's governorship, one prisoner, an African-American called Willie Horton, had escaped while on weekend leave and had raped a white woman and terrorised her husband.[17] Ailes's partner in the campaign, Lee Atwater, said, 'We are going to make it look like Willie Horton is Michael Dukakis's running mate.'[18] A front group was set up and made a graphic ad featuring Horton. Then the official Bush campaign ad, without mentioning

Horton by name, ran an advertisement featuring revolving doors with prisoners, many of them African-American, slowly moving in and out, while a voiceover said Dukakis had vetoed the death penalty and given leave to first-degree murderers not eligible for parole. The ads made law and order a more prominent issue, and the percentage agreeing that Bush was 'tough enough' on crime rose from 23 per cent in July to 61 per cent in October.[19]

Atwater said of Ailes, admiringly, that he had two speeds: attack and destroy.[20] However, despite the dramatic success of the 1988 campaign, Ailes had sown the seeds of his own destruction as a political operative. When he got involved in later campaigns, Democrats made Ailes himself the issue, calling him 'Mudslinger in Chief'.[21] Even Republican colleagues expressed their reservations: 'If I were in a knife fight, I would want Roger on my side, but that doesn't mean I have to like a lot of the stuff he is doing.'[22] His next prominent political campaigns, although marked by his character-istic aggression and negativity, failed to deliver victory, and his last, at a special election in 1991, saw his Republican candidate begin with a 45 point lead, and end up losing. In December that year, he announced he was giving up politics.[23]

His next major career step was to become director of CNBC, NBC's business channel. He was very successful there, also starting a new channel, titled America's Talking. His strategy was personal-ity-centred:

> One of the biggest mistakes producers make today is that they think they are living in a totally topic-driven world. But what's 'The Oprah Winfrey Show' without Oprah?'[24]

However, NBC axed the America's Talking channel to make room for a new news network, created with Microsoft, called MSNBC. Ailes decided he had lost out in an internal power struggle, and rang Rupert Murdoch.[25]

The birth of Fox News

The union of Murdoch and Ailes was the perfect partnership for Fox News. They shared their conservatism, their extensive contacts in American right-wing politics, their disdain for mainstream journalism and their combative competitiveness. Murdoch brought his capital, his financial courage and his sense of business strategy. Ailes brought energy and decisiveness, and deep expertise in both television and propaganda.

Murdoch had, for some years, wanted to establish his own news channel, one, he said, that would reflect 'American ideals'.[26] In 1992, Murdoch said, 'I honestly cannot distinguish one [TV news] program from another … It's like every news director in the marketplace graduated from the same dumb journalism class.'[27] Murdoch declared in 1996, 'We think it's about time CNN was challenged, especially as it tends to drift further and further to the left. We think it's time for a truly objective news channel.'[28] He asserted that there was a 'growing disconnect' between those who made the news and those who watched it. A recent poll had found 40 per cent of Americans, but only 5 per cent of journalists, considered themselves conservative. 'In that gap, there is opportunity,' thought Murdoch.[29] According to Ailes, 'Rupert Murdoch and I and, by the way, the vast majority of the American people, believe that most of the news tilts to the left.'[30]

They came together at a propitious moment. The cable industry had grown and developed, and there was now a demand for more specialised channels. In the 18 months to the end of 1995, 15 new cable channels were launched.[31] According to Nielsen Media Research, the proportion of TV households with cable television grew from 17 per cent in 1977 to 67 per cent in 1996. For the first time in television, there was hardware chasing software, rather than the reverse.

Moreover, talk radio had shown the way. The Reagan administration had abolished the Fairness Doctrine, which had required radio broadcasters to attempt to be impartial and balanced. It was probably unworkable in an increasingly complex and pluralistic political, not to say litigious, environment. Its disappearance released talk radio from all inhibitions, and 'was a gift to ... stations in search of a new identity and audience'.[32] Soon the phrase 'shock jock' was born. Talk radio became almost entirely Republican-supporting. One study by a left-wing think tank judged that among the radio stations most listened to, 91 per cent of total weekday radio programming was conservative and 9 per cent progressive.[33]

The brightest star in this new conservative firmament was Rush Limbaugh. When the Republicans won a majority in the 1994 House of Representatives election, the Republican leaders called Limbaugh 'the majority maker' and named him an honorary member of the freshman class of the 104th Congress. One said that after House leader Newt Gingrich, 'Rush was the single most important person in securing a Republican majority.'[34]

Ailes's early recipe for success with the Fox News Channel 'was to take conservative talk radio and move it onto cable television'.[35] He scoured the tabloid TV shows for talent;[36] his model for Fox programming was in many ways closer to the America Talks network he had pioneered at NBC than to a news network like CNN. For 40 years, Ailes had been producing 'compelling, winning television', whether for political clients or for Murdoch.[37] He hired his old mentor on the *Mike Douglas Show*, Chet Collier, as a senior vice-president. Like Ailes, Collier was first and foremost an entertainer, and looked with 'amused detachment' at those he called 'newsies'. His aim was to present the news 'with the most excitement', and to get the best possible people 'because people watch television because of the individuals they see on the screen'.[38]

One of the first shows planned was an 'aggressive, opinionated news program' fronted by TV host and commentator Bill O'Reilly.[39] As David Brock and Ari Rabin-Havt note, 'O'Reilly's acerbic style was an unknown quantity. Instead of conducting standard interviews, he was willing to throw red meat at his audience. And it worked.'[40] He became the network's star, and much of its early popularity was based on his appeal.[41]

The result, in Wolff's view, was that:

> Fox is self-consciously down-market, rude, loud, opinionated. This not only defines a lower-end, secondary news market, but does it in a way that's much cheaper than how the other guy does it ... Fox News is original. It has taken the News Corp. formula of the on-the-cheap and the third rate and turned it into a culture-changing, paradigm-altering, often jaw-dropping spectacle. About this, Murdoch is proud.[42]

Ailes coined two snappy and wildly successful slogans for the new channel: 'Fox News. Fair and Balanced' and 'We report. You decide.' They have provoked derision — how can the network which is 'the most biased name in news'[43] call itself fair and balanced? However, they should be seen not as descriptions of content or even of aspirations; they represent a branding strategy the aim of which is to imply that everyone else is unfair and biased. There has always been a conservative constituency that is suspicious of the news media. A member of *Time* magazine's letters department told sociologist Herbert Gans in the 1970s that the pattern of complaints had not changed since the 1950s: 'Even when *Time* was conservative (under Henry Luce), most of the letters came from conservatives, and, for them, no one can ever be conservative enough.'[44] The size of this constituency and the intensity of its feelings varies over time, but it often includes older people resentful of, or at least anxious about, the pace of change. Calling the news media biased is one way of avoiding troubling complexities and controversies.

Moreover, niche audiences were becoming financially viable. News Corp's chief operating officer, Peter Chernin, told a company conference in 1998 that sometimes intense media coverage of major sporting or cultural events makes them even bigger, bringing global audiences. But at the other end of the spectrum, technology has also made niche audiences much more the norm. So what happens to the middle? For Chernin:

> The answer is that choice and fragmentation are killing the middle, which lacks the grabbing power of the big event or the custom tailoring of the niche. The general interest magazine – dead. The variety show – dead. The all-purpose department store – dead.[45]

Chernin argued that bland programming was 'death warmed over'. News's programming must 'seize the edge', must 'leap out with brand identity'.[46]

This deftly catches the Fox News strategy. The audience is almost exclusively white (just 1.4 per cent are African-Americans). The typical viewer of one of its main programs, that of Sean Hannity, was pro-business (86%), Christian conservative (78%), a Tea Party backer (75%) with no college degree (66%), aged over 50 (65%), who supports the National Rifle Association (73%), doesn't back gay rights (78%) and thinks government does too much (84%). A colleague commented, Hannity's 'got a niche audience and he's programmed to it beautifully. He feeds them exactly what they want to hear.'[47] A former Fox correspondent said it was common to hear Fox producers whisper, 'We have to feed the core.'[48]

Earlier major innovations in the business of US journalism were largely politically centrist and brought professional advances as well as commercial success. The rise of Associated Press – and then of news agency journalism – in the 19th century brought a news service that allowed newspapers to gain news from outside their local area. This meant they had a variety of clients, with different political outlooks, who wanted agency news to be safe and reliable. The agencies' growth brought an emphasis on strong leads, brevity, 'hard' sourcing (where all claims were attributed to a definite source) and the forms of news presentation that came to be associated with 'objectivity'.[49] The 'penny press' and 'yellow press' that developed in the late 19th century brought a stronger orientation towards the audience, and the cultivation of a new urban working-class audience. While it was sensationalist, often irresponsibly so, it brought new life to reporting, enlarging the scope of public information; in some cases this led to 'muckraking' – socially progressive investigations of corruption. Around the same time, the *New York Times* and others were developing serious reporting – priding themselves on being independent of any parties, and covering the news without fear or favour. In the 1920s and 1930s *Time* magazine arrived. While its politics were skewed very much to the right under its owner, Henry Luce, it pioneered interpretive journalism, which eventually also enriched the journalistic mix. Finally, from the early 1960s on, the three US TV networks brought TV news reporting of national affairs, with a strong emphasis on balancing sources and partisan neutrality, to a larger audience. In each case, the market leaders provided exemplars of professional standards, which their competitors respected and emulated.

Fox News may or may not be an innovation as important as these, but unlike them it has been calculatingly sectarian in its appeal, and retrograde in its professional standards. CNN pioneered the multi-channel environment, allowing people to access news whenever they wanted, not just when networks scheduled it. Fox has seen that a fragmented audience allows market success to follow from a much lower market share – which means that a more opinionated, less centrist news appeal can still be profitable. It is part of a trend in journalism where the ferocity of opinions rather than the strength of evidence, and partisanship rather than impartiality, are rewarded with market success.

The growth of Fox News

Fox News began on 7 October 1996, just under a month before President Bill Clinton's re-election. It kept up a relentless drumbeat against [his] administration. A reporter who joined the network from ABC left in horror after a producer approached him, rubbing her hands together and saying 'let's have something on Whitewater [some real estate deals in Arkansas around which some Republicans were trying to weave a scandal] today'.[50]

'Fox News found its perfect story in President Clinton's affair with a White House intern, Monica Lewinsky.'[51] Talk radio had started to 'go crazy' with the story, but the main TV networks were not initially devoting great coverage to it. Fox decided they would 'grab this pent-up anger' on talk radio and 'put it on television'. It was a story that viewers 'just couldn't take their eyes off'.[52] Ailes mined it relentlessly. He brought Matt Drudge, the conservative blogger who had initially reported the scandal, aboard as a host, and the network floated rumours that there was 'a second intern who was sexually involved with the President'.[53]

As Kerwin Swint says, 'Nothing galvanized this core audience group more than Fox's coverage after the September 11 attacks.'[54] Fox introduced a ticker across the bottom of the screen, and the other cable news channels quickly followed. It added the US flag to the Fox News logo. 'From then on, the flag became our trademark,' said one executive.[55] Presenters wore US flags on their lapels. More problematically, Geraldo Rivera, a Fox News correspondent, 'armed himself with a pistol and proclaimed that he would be honoured to kill Osama bin Laden'.[56] This ostentatious patriotism was a marketing strategy.

The failure of the war in Iraq did not seem to dent the Fox audience's enthusiasm for the network, but as Bush's domestic troubles mounted, ratings slipped. Hurricane Katrina, which hit New Orleans in August 2005, marked a turning point in the Bush presidency. During the following year, Fox's audience decreased by more than 30 per cent.[57]

As the Democrat surge continued in the lead-up to 2008, Fox was increasingly out of step with the public mood. Ailes personally got into trouble during the lead-up to the primaries, making a weak joke based on the similarity of Obama and Osama: 'It is true that Barack Obama is on the move. I don't know if it is true that President Bush called [Pakistani President] Musharraf and said "Why can't we catch this guy?"'[58] The other Democrats then withdrew from a planned debate on Fox, a decision which prompted Bill O'Reilly to call them Nazis.

As it became clear that Obama was likely to win, Murdoch, ever willing to catch a populist wave and be on the winning side, was tempted to back him. But once Ailes learned that the *New York Post* was thinking of endorsing Obama he confronted Murdoch and threatened to quit.[59] Murdoch relented. Fox mounted various character attacks on Obama but had no impact on his political momentum.

With Obama's victory, the country was in transition, and so was Fox News. But Ailes had the audacity not to be hopeful. From the beginning he was planning a strategy of unrelenting opposition: 'By the time Obama defeated McCain, Ailes had hired former Bush aide Karl Rove and Mike Huckabee and went on to assemble a whole lineup of prospective 2012 contenders: Palin, Gingrich, Santorum, and John Bolton.'[60] Apart from his 'candidate-hiring binge',[61] Ailes's most important move was to hire Glenn Beck.[62] Beck was hired to solve the five o'clock problem. As journalist Gabriel Sherman writes:

[His] debut was the day before Obama's inauguration. Within a month, Beck became a phenomenon. He doubled the time slot's viewership, providing a powerful boost that carried into the prime-time hours.[63]

He not only drew viewers; he also created controversies across the media that drew attention to Fox. The hiring of Beck was also testimony to how politically embattled Ailes felt. At their meeting to discuss the deal, Ailes said to him, 'I see this as the Alamo ... If I just had somebody who was willing to sit on the other side of the camera until the last shot is fired, we'd be fine.'[64]

A week after the November election, two months before Obama assumed control, Sean Hannity said:

> This is really the Obama recession in this sense: the people that have money are looking at this, [saying,] 'Look, if he is true to his word, you know what? I'm getting out now.'[65]

Days before Obama's inauguration, Rush Limbaugh declared:

> I hope he fails.

On Day 2 of Obama's presidency, Hannity declared:

> [H]e is not going to succeed ... Socialism has failed.

On Day 3 Fox News contributor Laura Ingraham declared:

> [O]ur country is less safe today.

On Day 4 Beck said Obama had:

> declared the end to the war on terror.

By Day 11 he had concluded that the country was on a march towards socialism; Hannity said it was the end of capitalism. On Day 17 Bret Baier unsurprisingly observed that 'some are wondering if the honeymoon is already over'.[66]

It is little wonder that *Media Matters for America* concluded that by 'early 2009, we noticed a marked increase in politically motivated misinformation coming from Fox News'.[67] But by resisting rather than embracing the dominant political mood, Ailes was soon able to build ratings again. Fox News mobilised against Obama's planned health reform. 'Fox gave the Tea Party the oxygen to prosper,' one admiring conservative said.[68]

This period – in the fortunes of both Fox and the Republicans – was crowned by the 2010 Congressional elections. The Republicans won 63 seats in the House of Representatives, the largest gain by any party since 1948, to become the majority party.[69] As *Washington Post* columnist Dana Milbank noted:

> At Rupert Murdoch's cable network, the entity that birthed and nurtured the Tea Party movement, Election Day was the culmination of two years of hard work to bring down Barack Obama – and it was time for an on-air celebration of a job well done.[70]

Milbank also quotes Sarah Palin exulting, 'That's an earthquake. It's a darn big deal.'[71] After the election, Fox News hosted a televised victory party, full of celebrating Republican candidates and party officials.[72]

Expectations were high that this momentum would continue into the 2012 election season, but problems came for both Fox and the Republicans. By this time, Fox had deals with all the potential Republican presidential candidates not then in elected office – except Mitt Romney.[73] However, while the candidates had been united against the Democrats in 2010, now they were competing against each other. Increasing tensions between high-profile hirings – notably Sarah Palin and Karl Rove – became more disruptive.

Moreover, the star of the first two years of the Obama presidency – Glenn Beck – was becoming an embarrassment. In July

2009, Beck called Obama a racist, with a 'deep-seated hatred for white people'.[74] It was the beginning of a theme that Fox nurtured – it was always on the lookout for racism against whites. 'You know what this president is doing right now?' asked Beck. 'He is addicting this country to heroin – the heroin that is government slavery.'[75] Beck actively campaigned for the Tea Party, and made himself the centre of attention. In August 2010 he held a 'Restoring Honor' rally in Washington. Brock and Rabin-Havt write that, 'The event was supposed to be part of Beck's "100-year plan" to stop the "ticking time bomb" that progressives had set in motion a century earlier to create a "socialist utopia".'[76]

A list of Beck's '10 worst quotes' in 2010 included:

God will wash this nation with blood if he has to;

Putting the common good first leads to death camps;

Women are psychos;

We have been sold a lie that the poor in America are suffering;

Charles Darwin is the father of the Holocaust.

He likened himself to the Israeli Nazi-hunters, and vowed, 'to the day I die, I am going to be a progressive-hunter'.[77] This is clearly a graduation from mere vitriol up into insanity. His show was leaking viewers – almost a million – and the network had had to manage a boycott by more than 300 sponsors. Beck was no longer a plus.[78] In April 2011, Fox and Beck announced that Beck was leaving.[79] This was part of what Ailes called a 'course correction'.[80]

Nevertheless right up to (and well into) election night, Fox was expecting Obama's defeat. Indeed its presenters seemed to be going through a grieving process as the results came in – Ed Henry, 'stone-faced from Obama headquarters as it erupts in jubilation', reported, 'The crowd here is near pandemonium now, despite the fact that unemployment is hovering near 8 per cent.'[81]

The result was a blow not only to the Republicans, but at least in the short term also to Fox. According to Reed Richardson, Fox's viewership at the time of Obama's second inauguration in 2013 was only half what it had been at his first.[82] Generally, however, it remains comfortably ahead of MSNBC and CNN, with an average night-time viewing figure of just under two million.[83]

Command and control

At a Fox News party after the network overtook CNN in the ratings, in 2002, a television set was mounted high on the wall – first the MSNBC logo came on and was greeted by boos; then the CNN logo prompted much more booing. Then the third slide appeared – the face of Roger Ailes – and 'the Foxistas went wild' with prolonged loud cheering.[84] According to star presenter Bill O'Reilly, 'Roger Ailes is the general. And the general sets the tone of the army. Our army is very George Patton-esque. We charge. We roll.'[85] For talk radio star Rush Limbaugh:

> One man has established a culture for 1700 people who believe in it, who follow it, who execute it. Roger Ailes cannot do everything. Roger Ailes is not on the air ... and yet everybody who [is] is a reflection of him.[86]

What his admirers praise, his critics deplore.

There has never been a television operation in the English-speaking democracies with a more centralised and hierarchical control of opinion. The process began with a political filter placed on the selection of staff. When Murdoch was asked in the 1990s whether it would be a problem that Fox would have to rely on the liberal journalists from the existing networks, he replied, 'I don't think we employ those sorts of people. Roger Ailes keeps a very close watch on that.'[87] And he did. One of Ailes's first acts was to ask each of the 40 existing journalists at the Fox TV network 'if they were liberal or not'; he was going to try to get rid of the liberals.[88] In 1996, Andrew Kirtzman, a respected New York City cable news reporter, was interviewed for a job with Fox, and they asked what his political affiliation was. When he refused to tell them, 'all employment discussion ended'.[89]

In the early years there were occasional problems until the pattern was firmly established. One producer resigned after being ordered to change a story to play down statistics showing a lack of social progress among African-Americans. Several former employees complained of management sticking their fingers into the writing and editing of stories. One said, 'I've worked at a lot of news organisations and never found that kind of manipulation.'[90] An early directive was to 'seek out stories that cater to angry, middle-aged white men who listen to talk radio and yell at their television'.[91]

Fox News may be unique in that every morning it distributes an executive memo 'addressing what stories will be covered and, often, suggesting how they should be covered'. Former producer Charlie Reina thought this the root of its bias.[92] For many years, these memos were written by John Moody, a senior assistant to Ailes. Many memos have been leaked over the years, and they give a direct insight into the politically loaded approach to story selection and treatment.

The memos reveal the approach to reporting the Iraq War. It was, perhaps, best captured by a memo quoted in the film *Outfoxed*: 'Remember when you're writing about this, it's all good. Don't write about the number of dead ... Keep it positive. Emphasise all the good we're doing.'[93] After the exposure of atrocities by members of the US military against Iraqi prisoners at Abu Ghraib, Moody wrote: 'It is important that we keep the Abu Ghraib situation in perspective.' Apart from ensuring proper 'perspective', Moody was keen that viewers not develop misplaced sympathies or worries about violence and suffering: 'It won't be long before some people decry the use of "excessive force". We won't be among that group'; 'Do not fall into the easy trap of mourning the loss of US lives and asking out loud why we are there'; and as the coalition forces prepared to attack Fallujah, 'let's not get lost in breast-beating about the sadness of the loss of life. They had a chance'; 'Whatever happens, it is richly deserved.'[94] In November 2006, Moody wrote:

> the [congressional] elections and Rumsfeld's resignation were
> a major event, but not the end of the world. The war on terror
> goes on without interruption ... and let's be on the lookout for
> any statements from the Iraqi insurgents, who must be thrilled at
> the prospect of a Dem-controlled Congress.[95]

The memos were just as directive about how to cover US domestic politics. They showed the orchestrated use of the term 'flip-flopping' to describe John Kerry during the 2004 election, a line that dovetailed neatly with the attacks coming out of the White House. In fact, Fox News was working directly with the Bush administration.[96] Similarly, in coverage of Obama's health reform proposals, Fox journalists were told to use the term 'government option' (favoured by the opponents of reform) rather than 'public option' (used by the administration).[97] Its commentators had no qualms about using the phrase 'death panels', coined by Sarah Palin.

The network still practises news management by memo. After the shootings at Sandy Hook Elementary School in Connecticut left 20 children and six adults murdered, Rupert Murdoch took to Twitter and urged strong action by President Obama on gun control. At Fox News, however, producers were instructed that 'this network is not going there'. One Fox News source said, 'We were expressly forbidden from discussing gun control.'[98]

If, despite all this, a slip occurred, correction was swift and clear to all. A young producer covering Palin's campaign in 2008 accurately described how McCain's staff were preventing reporters from asking Palin any questions. Ailes immediately barred the producer from making any more on-air appearances.[99]

Beyond formal memos, Ailes, like Murdoch, makes his general views known in strong, indeed crude, statements. Howard Kurtz offered two examples he observed:

> The talk turns to terrorism. Ailes is angry about an AP report that 29 worshippers were killed by a suicide bomber in Baghdad's largest Sunni mosque during prayers. 'How do we know they were worshipping?' he demands. I think the AP is so far over the hill, they've become left wing, anti-war. Gotta watch their copy.[100]

> Fox was developing a series on Regulation Nation. Ailes said 'regulations are totally out of control'. Bureaucrats hire PhDs to 'sit in the basement and draw up regulations to try to ruin your life'.[101]

As is also apparent from these examples, Ailes has very strong preconceptions which run a long way ahead of supporting evidence. Ken Auletta reported on Ailes working 'himself into a lather' over what he saw as a weak CBS interview by Dan Rather with President Chirac in the lead-up to the Iraq War. Ailes thought the interview was 'anti-American'. He was angered by the questions he thought Rather should have asked but didn't, such as 'How about the seven million Muslims down the street that are going to blow up the Eiffel Tower? Does that bother you?'[102] Insofar as this makes sense at all, it seems to imply that invading Iraq will help protect France against the Muslims who live in that country. Ailes's stereotypical thinking was on display one day in the Fox offices when he observed a dark-skinned man in what he perceived to be Muslim garb. Ailes put the whole of Fox News into lockdown. 'This guy could be bombing me,' he shouted. The suspected terrorist turned out to be a janitor. But the incident demonstrated Ailes's fears about his personal safety (he has a personal security contingent) and his particular paranoia about people who are Muslim.[103]

He is quick to leap to conclusions about Democrats as well. In 1994, before Fox News began, Ailes was producing Rush Limbaugh's weekly television program. At the time, there was considerable speculation in right-wing circles, following the suicide in a park of Vince Foster, who had been suffering from depression. Foster was a Clinton appointee, brought to Washington from Arkansas. Limbaugh claimed that Foster had actually been murdered in an apartment owned by Hillary Clinton and his body then taken to a park. Ailes supported this exclusive, saying he didn't have any evidence because 'These people [the Clintons] are very good at hiding or destroying evidence.'[104] So Limbaugh and Ailes, wrongly, indeed baselessly, accused the Clintons of being complicit in a murder. It is remarkable that neither of their careers suffered from these irresponsible false accusations. It clearly presents problems of quality control when someone so prone to leaping to wrong conclusions is the unchallengeable arbiter of 'fair and balanced'.

The politics of polarisation

The Tet offensive, launched by the communist forces on the lunar new year, 30 January 1968, is often cited as the turning point of the Vietnam War, even though that war continued for another seven years. The US had had combat troops there since 1965, and by early 1968 had around half a million troops in the country. Nevertheless the scale and ferocity of the Communist attacks shocked them. Four weeks in, on 27 February, as the fighting continued, Walter Cronkite, the news anchor of CBS, after much anguish, delivered a broadcast which was pessimistic about future victory.

When President Lyndon Johnson watched the broadcast, he told his press secretary that if he had lost Walter Cronkite, he had lost Mr Average Citizen.[105] It fed directly into his decision not to seek re-election.

Cronkite's statement generated great controversy, but what is most interesting from today's perspective is that it is impossible to imagine any US president making a similar statement about any media figure today. It is impossible to imagine President Obama saying, 'If I've lost Bill O'Reilly [or, more interestingly, Jon Stewart] I've lost Mr Average Citizen.' No one has, or could have, the political authority Cronkite once did. The audience is more fragmented; the public is more polarised.

This sort of authority came from 'the era of the captive mass public, from the 1950s through the '70s – when people had access to only a few TV channels'.[106] In the 1970s, the audience for the three networks' news programs was 46 million, or 75% of people watching TV at the time.[107] As writer Paul Starr notes, 'For a time, this seemed to be the permanent structure of the news and national politics in the age of electronic media. In retrospect, it was the peaking of the unified national public.'[108] By 2005, their total audience was down to 30 million, or around one-third of TV viewers.[109] By 2013, it had further declined, to 22 million.[110] While some other sources of news – notably cable – have grown, the net impact has been a sharp decline in total news consumption. By 2008, the number of Americans who say they don't get the news from any medium on an average day was 19 per cent, and among 18 to 24-year-olds it was 34 per cent.[111]

Attitudes have changed as much as audience sizes. Several polls suggest declining confidence in the news media. For example, the proportion agreeing that stories are often inaccurate has all but doubled, from 34 per cent in 1985 to 66 per cent in 2011.[112] A Pew study found that positive ratings of news organisations' believability declined from 71 per cent in 2002 to 56 per cent in 2012.

That series of Pew studies also showed a growing polarisation in judgements. In 2002, 76 per cent of Republicans and 67 per cent of Democrats thought Fox News was believable. By 2012, both figures had declined, but the fall was much sharper among Democrats: 67 per cent of Republicans, but only 37 per cent of Democrats, thought Fox was believable.

But the polarisation in judgements has grown for all news media, especially as Republicans have become more distrusting of most other news organisations. So in 2002 there was a 12 per cent gap on CNN (Democrats 84: Republicans 72), but by 2012 that had grown to 36 (Democrats 76: Republicans 40). For the *New York Times*, the 2004 figure already showed a substantial 20 per cent gap (D 70%: R 50%) but by 2012 it had grown to 28 per cent (D 65%: R 37%).[113] So in 2012, almost twice the proportion of Republicans found Fox News believable than found the *New York Times* believable.

The other best US data set on trust in TV news comes from Public Policy Polling, which began doing an annual survey in 2010. The only TV news which more of the public trusted than distrusted was PBS.[114] Apart from this, there were stark partisan differences: 'Democrats trust everything except Fox, and Republicans don't trust anything other than Fox.'[115] For Fox, among Democrats the net rating is −44 (22–66 per cent trust/distrust), while among Republicans it is +55 (70–15). On CNN, for example, the net rating among Democrats is +36 (57–21), but among Republicans it is −49 (17–66), with the other non-Fox networks having broadly similar profiles.

The polarisation in the public is matched by attitudes among political activists. 'Watch Fox News! Watch Fox News!' chanted Republican delegates at CNN's floor set during the Republicans' 2004 convention.[116] In contrast, in 2011, as Fox reporters began live feeds of a protest by public sector employees in Wisconsin, the crowd started chanting 'Fox News lies' and 'Tell the truth.'[117]

The growing partisan trust division for different news sources, and especially the Republican distrust of the main TV network news services, indicates that they have finally caught up with the views put forward by Ailes and Murdoch over a much longer period. 'I really believed there was no fairness or balance' elsewhere in the media, Ailes said in 2011.[118] He used to refer to CNN as the Clinton News Network,[119] although that was better than CBS, which he called the Communist Broadcasting System.[120] During the Republican primaries, Ailes criticised the 'mainstream media' for calling Romney a weak frontrunner:

> 'Weak' is a word the mainstream press will give to all Republicans always, as a precursor to killing them off ... It saddens me. America used to be able to get straight journalism.[121]

It is not clear when he thinks America got this 'straight journalism', as in the 1960s he already thought it was anti-Republican. Nevertheless he is insistent that the situation is getting worse: 'The hardest part of my job now is to maintain any kind of journalistic standards, because they're being weakened all over the country by newspapers and magazines.'[122]

Sometimes these criticisms of the liberal media are just a game for Ailes:

> The *New York Times* used to be the paper with all the news fit to put into the bottom of your dog kennel ... Now when the owners leave, the dogs are calling up and canceling their subscriptions ... It's a dying asset.[123]

There was no humour intended, however, when in a speech at Ohio University he described *New York Times* reporters as 'a bunch of lying scum'.[124] He also said that 'one thing that qualifies me to run a journalism organization is the fact that I don't have a journalism degree', and advised journalism students to 'change your major'.[125] He also described National Public Radio as Nazis, as noted earlier, but publicly apologised for this after complaints from Jewish organisations.[126]

It is common for competitors to disparage each other. What is unusual with Murdoch and Ailes is that they seem to hold everyone else in the industry in contempt, to dislike the whole profession they are involved in:

> What surprises colleagues is that Ailes appears actually to disdain journalism; Ailes says that he detests what he thinks of as 'elite' journalists with 'a pick up their ass' who treat journalism as 'a from-the-Mount profession'. Some senior executives at Fox express private puzzlement that Ailes seems, in the words of one, to 'hate journalists so much ... I've never seen him use the word "journalism" and smile at the same time'.[127]

The polarisation in attitudes to the media has been driven particularly by declining trust among Republicans towards the main news services. It is paralleled by the increasing polarisation in political rhetoric, again principally driven by the conservative side:

> There is no 'after the Cold War' for me. So far from having ended, my cold war has increased in intensity, as sector after sector of American life has been ruthlessly corrupted by the liberal ethos ... We have, I do believe, reached a turning point in American democracy. Now that the other Cold War is over, the real cold war has begun.

This 1993 statement by Irving Kristol, dubbed the godfather of neoconservatism, encapsulates the rhetorical escalation.[128] We saw above the statement by Glenn Beck that he was – on the model of Israeli Nazi-hunters – fearlessly declaring that he would be a progressive-hunter until he dies. On his Fox News program in the 18 months after Obama's inauguration, Beck made 202 mentions of Nazis or Nazism, 147 mentions of Hitler and 193 mentions of 'fascism' or 'fascist', and 'most of these were directed in some form at Obama'.[129] For the most prominent voice in talk radio, Rush Limbaugh, 'Democrats are the enemy.'[130] He has also said, 'I don't know how a real man – I mean, a real man – could even be a liberal, much less vote for one.'[131] In 2004 he said that Democratic candidate Kerry's base voters 'hate God [and] they hate people of religion'.[132] 'There is a culture of death with liberalism,' said Limbaugh in 2007. 'They own that as well as they own defeat in Iraq.'[133]

Later came the creation of the Tea Party, which took its name from the Boston Tea Party of 1773, a significant event in the lead-up to the American War of Independence. The Tea Party calls on 'American patriots' to 'take back' their country. Sometimes Tea Party members pump fists and yell 'USA, USA'. Their talk of patriotism rather obscures the fact that their targets are other Americans. When the struggle is viewed as being between patriots and non-patriots, it is a short step to picturing opponents as enemies.

So groups such as liberals and progressives, who fall well within the democratic consensus and have always been a central part of American political history, observing democratic processes, are now equated with violent, totalitarian extremists. And democratically elected government members from an opposing political party are equated with foreign colonialists. Politics is always subject to rhetorical inflation, but the way the lines are drawn now is a narrowing of pluralism and a denial of legitimacy to competing groups.

Fox News has both crystallised and amplified these political currents. It has been a driver towards more rancorous and polarised political discourse, and towards a journalism less disciplined by evidence, especially complex and politically inconvenient evidence. It is better seen as part of the right-wing noise machine[134] than as a normal news service. For Kathleen Hall Jamieson and Joseph Capella, it is one of the three parts of a right-wing 'echo chamber': Fox, conservative talk radio, especially Rush Limbaugh, and the intellectual fibre of the op-ed pages of the *Wall St Journal*, which all reinforce each other.[135]

One of Fox's tools is spectacular misrepresentation, an ability to conjure a threat or an outrage from seemingly straightforward statements. When Obama said to 'Joe the plumber', in Ohio during the 2012 campaign, that we should 'spread the wealth around', Fox News framed it as Obama advocating socialism. After the election, Washington editor Bill Sammon said it was 'a premise that privately I found rather far-fetched', but at the time internal memos showed that focusing on it was part of the Fox strategy.[136] When President Obama told the Turkish Parliament that 'the United States is not ... at war with Islam', Hannity accused him of 'seemingly apologizing for our engagement in the war on terror'.[137] When the president proposed creating a civilian humanitarian force, Beck said it was 'about building some kind of thugocracy', and that 'this is what Hitler did with the SS'.[138] Democratic congressional leader Nancy Pelosi criticised attempts to disrupt public meetings and said that 'drowning out opposing views [was] simply un-American'. One Fox commentator said she had said that anyone who speaks out is un-American; a second said that Pelosi said that opposing her view is un-American; a third claimed that she was calling hard-working Americans 'Nazis' and 'brownshirts' and 'un-American'.[139] When Obama, again in the 2012 campaign, talked of how business thrived when government helped by providing good infrastructure and a well-educated workforce, he was said to have insulted business owners.[140]

A second tool is its promotion of its own agendas, and especially of the 'culture wars'. Culture wars are appealing to the media because they provide easy copy with few demands on gathering and verifying evidence. From a conservative viewpoint, they help to reframe issues in a simple way. The concept of elite, for example, is now dissociated from the wealthy and attached to those who embrace liberal social values;[141] the issue is now thus not about economic inequality, but about conflicting values. 'Culture wars' provide fodder to maintain a sense of outrage, which is especially easy when it is the audience's values that appear to be under attack. One annual target is the 'war on Christmas'. In December 2010 Fox reported that an elementary school in Florida had banned 'traditional Christmas colours'. Several programs covered the story, but no one called the school district – the entire story was a lie; all the bluster and outrage had no basis.[142] In December 2012, *The O'Reilly Factor* devoted more than three times as much airtime to the 'war on Christmas' than it did to actual wars in Iraq, Afghanistan, Syria, Libya and Gaza.[143]

Reframing political controversies in a way that favours one's own side is a common strategy in all democracies. One of the techniques Fox News often uses to avoid debating issues is to label opponents instead. When allegations were raised about mistreatment of prisoners at Guantanamo, Britt Hume, then the Washington editor for Fox, commented:

> I think that these kinds of problems and accusations and so forth
> grow out of a community that stretches from the American left
> through much of Europe to enemies across the world from which
> terrorism springs, who want the world to believe that America is
> what's wrong with the world.[144]

The same process has been applied to immediate policy debates. For E.J. Dionne of the *Washington Post*, the genius of American conservatives has been to change the terms of political debate:

> Sensible regulation was cast as a dangerous quest for government
> control. Modest measures to alleviate poverty became schemes
> to lock the poor into 'dependency'. Advocates of social insurance
> were condemned as socialists. Government was said to be
> under the sway of a distant 'them', even though in a democracy,
> government is the realm of 'us'. And attempts to achieve a

bit more economic equality were pronounced as assaults on liberty.[145]

During the first 18 months of the Obama presidency, Beck not only made the hundreds of references to Nazi themes cited above; he also made 802 references to socialism.

Such deployment of each side's rhetorical arsenal – done with varying degrees of honesty – is part of democratic manoeuvring. Less legitimate has been the way Fox and some Republicans have promoted the idea that Obama is in some sense inherently unfit to be president, in a determined attempt to turn the exotic elements of Obama's background into something alien. 'What if [Obama] is so outside our comprehension that only if you understand Kenyan, anti-colonial behavior can you begin to piece it together?' asked prominent Republican Newt Gingrich.[146] Another Republican, Mike Huckabee, was forced to backpedal after suggesting that Obama grew up in Kenya.[147] In 2008, Fox promoted a series of allegations about Obama – 'he of the terrorist fist bump and uncertain ancestry and socialist leanings'.[148] One was the claim that Obama had 'spent at least four years in a so-called Madrassa, or Muslim seminary, in Indonesia'. Fox ran with the story, and asked viewers their reaction, and, in one of their typical ploys to cover a lack of evidence, said there were questions Obama had to answer. Fox News presenter Steve Doocy baldly asserted that Obama was 'raised as a Muslim'.[149] In contrast, a CNN reporter visited the school Obama had attended in Jakarta, and simply reported that it was not a madrassa.[150]

The most persistent false claim was that Obama was not born in the US, and so not eligible to be president. Such a claim involved not only a complex conspiracy, but conspirators with amazing prescience. In 2011, TV personality and momentary pretender to the Republican candidacy Donald Trump revived 'birtherism'. In March and April, Fox devoted 52 segments to the subject; in 44 of these, the false charges went completely unchallenged.[151] In the prevailing atmosphere, allegations of conspiracy were easily made. When unemployment dropped slightly, during the campaign, from 8.1 per cent to 7.8 per cent, Jack Welch and some other conservatives immediately labelled the figures 'unbelievable'.[152] As the 2012 polls turned against Romney, some posited a conspiracy in which pollsters and the media were deliberately oversampling Democrats to inflate numbers for Obama and so discourage Republicans from voting.[153] Some conservative commentators believed that Romney would be ahead in 'unskewed polls' ('Everything – except the polls – points to a Romney landslide,' said Rush Limbaugh), and right up to election day, some on Fox were predicting that landslide.[154]

The impact of all this on viewers' knowledge and attitudes is difficult to ascertain. The legendary Democrat senator Daniel Patrick Moynihan once said that every man is entitled to his own opinions but not to his own facts. One 2003 study found that while misperceptions about the Iraq War were widely held, they were higher among Fox News viewers than those who got their news from other sources. While 48 per cent of those surveyed thought the US had found clear evidence that Saddam Hussein was working closely with Al Qaeda, 67 per cent of Fox viewers believed this. While 22 per cent overall thought that the US had found Weapons of Mass Destruction in Iraq, 33 per cent of Fox News viewers thought this.[155] Following the 2010 congressional election, the University of Maryland released a study that showed that Fox News viewers were 31 percentage points more likely than non-Fox viewers to agree that 'it is not clear that Obama was born in the United States'; and 30 points more likely to agree that 'most scientists do not agree that climate change is occurring'. A 2012 survey by Fairleigh Dickinson University found that those whose only news consumption is Fox News were less likely to be able to answer knowledge questions about domestic and international politics correctly than those who had no news exposure at all. On domestic affairs, for example, respondents overall averaged 1.6 correct answers out of five questions. Those who had 'no news exposure' answered 1.22 correctly, while those who 'only watched Fox News' answered 1.04 correctly; these differences are statistically significant.[156]

Fox has responded to all such academic findings with its usual combativeness. A Fox executive reacted to the 2010 study by attacking the University of Maryland's rankings on various measures.[157] In 2012, an anonymous Fox spokesperson similarly dismissed the Fairleigh Dickinson University findings by attacking the university's rankings among American universities.[158] A Pew Project for Excellence in Journalism study in 2005 showed that when covering the Iraq War, 73 per cent of Fox stories included opinion from anchors and reporters; on MSNBC the figure was 29 per cent and on CNN it was just 2 per cent. Ailes dismissed the Pew Foundation as a 'liberal lobbying organization'.[159]

Playing Republican politics

For most of Ailes's tenure, 'the roles of network chief and GOP kingmaker have been in perfect synergy'.[160] Fox ratings have risen and fallen partly in line with Republican fortunes. For the first decade and a bit of its existence it was best seen as just part of the right-wing noise machine, its coverage distorted in a conservative direction. The guest list of the network's flagship program, *Special Report*, had Republicans outnumbering Democrats 8:1.[161] Double standards abounded: the past guilty secrets of opponents, but not allies, were pursued relentlessly; the dubious relatives and associates of opponents, but not allies, were denounced. Heads of agencies in the Bush administration were simply referred to by their title, but under Obama their counterparts were 'czars'. Interviews with President Bush were conducted respectfully, even deferentially. In contrast, when Bill O'Reilly interviewed Obama, he interrupted the president 48 times.[162] Some misreporting was just due to incompetence. For example, in one Fox graphic, the real unemployment rate for 2009 was given as 7.8 per cent, but for 2012 as 14.7 per cent. The first figure is the official unemployment rate, which for that month in 2012 was 8.1 per cent.[163] *Media Matters for America* regularly features Fox's misleading graphics. The scale of the incompetence is sometimes puzzling, and the errors always seem to be in the same ideological direction.[164]

However, according to Brock and Rabin-Havt, by mid-2009 it became clear that Fox was changing: 'No longer was it simply a conservative news network. It had morphed into a political campaign.'[165] It increasingly stepped outside what had been the accepted limits of news media political activity. It waged a relentless assault on Obama's health care reforms. The most damaging impact came from the idea that health care reform would create 'death panels' with the power to decide who receives treatment and who is left to die.[166] One commentator, David Bromwich, felt that:

> Looking back, one feels it was an astonishing negligence for
> the Obama White House to embark on a campaign for national
> health care without a solid strategy for fighting the tenacious
> opposition it could expect at the hands of Fox radio and TV.
> Month by month the jeering hosts ate away Obama's popularity
> and cast doubt on his plans.[167]

The network openly proclaimed its stance. One headline boasted: 'Fox Nation Victory! Congress delays health care rationing bill'.[168]

Then it started promoting Tea Party events. In the lead-up to the Iraq War, it had ignored or attacked anti-war rallies, which sometimes numbered in the tens of thousands. Now it 'rewarded [Tea Party] meetings attended by as few as a dozen people with hours of air time and live satellite feeds'.[169] It not only found these events extraordinarily newsworthy, but it started to exhort people to attend, and its own employees participated. It aired 'at least 107 commercials for its coverage of the April 15 Tea Parties'.[170] Fox Business anchor Cody Willard yelled at one rally: 'When are we going to wake up and start fighting the fascism that seems to be permeating this country?'[171]

Then the network took an unprecedented step: it started playing a role in fundraising for Republican candidates.[172] It became common for Republican candidates to ask viewers for funds.[173] Sharron Angle, a Republican candidate, asked a million Fox viewers to each send her $25 for her campaign.[174] (Hannity praised one of her advertisements, which claimed that Democratic Senator Harry Reid had 'voted to use taxpayer dollars to pay for Viagra for convicted child molesters and sex offenders'.)[175] During an interview, Glenn Beck asked Tea Party candidate Michele Bachman, 'How can I help you raise money? ... We should have a fund raiser for you, Michele.'[176] Brock and Rabin-Havt found that altogether, 'Over the course of the 2010 election cycle, more than 30 Fox News employees endorsed, raised funds for, or campaigned for over 300 Republican candidates and organisations.'[177]

Much of the financing of election campaigns in the US is done through Political Action Committees (PACs) rather than directly to candidates and parties. Thus on a candidate's declaration, the PAC is listed as donor rather than the people who gave money to the PAC. Two regular Fox contributors, Karl Rove and Dick Morris, ran their own PACs, and sometimes they sought to raise money for them on Fox.[178] Both also sometimes discussed electoral races in which their PACs had a large stake, without disclosing that.[179] No other network did this.

Fox was increasingly oblivious to the professional constraints and obligations most other news organisations follow. But Ailes and Murdoch went even further. Not content with reporting events, they sought to shape them. Ailes was unimpressed by the range of likely Republican candidates, and approached Chris Christie, governor of New Jersey, to run for president.[180] However, he refused.[181]

Ailes and Murdoch then approached General David Petraeus, still commander in Afghanistan and on the way to becoming head of the CIA. According to a tape obtained by investigative reporter Bob Woodward, Fox correspondent K.T. McFarland, before beginning an interview, told Petraeus: 'The big boss is bankrolling it. Roger's going to run it. And the rest of us are going to be your in-house.' (Ailes also had a staff member ask Petraeus if there was anything Fox was doing right or wrong or should do differently.)

According to Woodward's partner in Watergate reporting, Carl Bernstein:

> Murdoch's goal seems to have been nothing less than using his media empire – notably Fox News – to stealthily recruit, bankroll and support the presidential candidacy of General David Petraeus in the 2012 election.[182]

Bernstein cannot understand:

> the ho-hum response to the story by the American press and the country's political establishment, whether out of fear of Murdoch, Ailes and Fox – or, perhaps, lack of surprise at Murdoch's, Ailes' and Fox's contempt for decent journalistic values or a transparent electoral process.[183]

For Simon Maloy of *Media Matters for America*, 'it's a perverse sort of dynamic in which the president of a news organization is shielded from revelations of unethical behaviour by his long-established record of unethical behaviour'.[184]

It is clear that the senior controllers of Fox News seek to shape political outcomes, not just report or analyse them. Although there is rarely authoritative evidence for the political impacts of media, it is plausible that in many ways Fox News has directly assisted the conservative side against progressives – Republicans against

Democrats. It has heightened the conservatives' capacity to mobilise outrage and oppose social reforms. It has made it more difficult for governments to tackle health care issues or global warming, for example. It has probably made it easier for Republicans to mobilise their base, thus helping them to win in the mid-term 2010 congressional elections.

But there is a need to examine the paradoxical and unintended impacts of media partisanship as well. In some ways Fox News is now more of a problem for the Republicans than for the Democrats. Most of its viewers are already Republicans, so its main impact is inside the Republican Party: it has strengthened the Tea Party and other extreme views, and so made it more difficult for moderate Republicans within the party.

'There would not have been a Tea Party without Fox,' said Sal Russo, one of its founding leaders.[185] But the Tea Party, and Fox News, which acted as its midwife, have been a decidedly mixed blessing for Republicans. Jamieson and Capella's 'echo chamber' has made a target of RINOs (Republicans in Name Only) and so helped to change the balance inside the party. While after their successes in the 2010 congressional elections they proclaimed themselves the wave of the future, in 2012 they provided many embarrassments. Perhaps the worst were Todd Akin (with his memorable phrase 'legitimate rape') and Richard Mourdock ('pregnancy resulting from rape is God's will'), who both lost their seats. For the Dutch academic Cas Muddle, the lesson to be learned is that 'there is no Tea Party without extreme social conservatism, but there is no GOP national majority with extreme social conservatism'.[186]

Many analysts think that the dominance of conservative voices has made it difficult for the Republicans to be anything but intransigent in Washington politics.[187] Two leading congressional scholars in the US, Thomas Mann and Norman Ornstein, have called the current GOP:

an insurgent outlier in American politics ... It is ideologically
extreme; scornful of compromise ... and dismissive of the
legitimacy of its political opposition.[188]

For some, the Republican Party 'has been infected by a faction that
is more of a psychological protest than a practical, governing alternative'.[189]

The Fox network played a central role – as did the party's conservative base – in shaping the primaries in 2012:

No other network head was so actively sought out by candidates
for advice on their campaigns.[190]

The network chief [functioned] as a kind of proxy kingmaker
within the [Republican] party, frequently meeting with
Republican politicians to offer strategic advice.[191]

You can't run for the Republican nomination without talking to
Roger. Every single candidate has consulted with Roger.[192]

But in the process, David Frum thinks, 'Conservatism has evolved
from a political philosophy into a market segment.'[193]

In 2008, Sarah Palin was credited with electrifying the Republican convention and the party's base; to others she seemed less qualified for national leadership than any major party candidate in living
memory. She boasted that 'everything I need to know, I learned on
the basketball court',[194] but what she knew did not include the difference between North and South Korea or the fact that America
did not go to war in Iraq because Saddam Hussein had attacked the
US on September 11.[195] But, as journalist Roger Cohen comments,
after Palin has come a 'deluge of dysfunctional presidential candidates. ... Palin is no longer an anomaly ... Experience, knowledge,
accomplishment – these no longer may matter.'[196]

Ailes turned 'the GOP race into a political X-Factor',[197] with much of the action happening on his network. However, partly because of the lack of strong candidates, it was one of the more bizarre primary seasons of recent times. As Cohen notes, there was a procession of presidential hopefuls. Michele Bachman and Mike Huckabee disappeared fairly early. Then came Texas Governor Rick Perry, who entered the race, immediately became a front runner, then collapsed after poor debate performances. He was followed by Herman Cain, who was very prominent on Fox News in the second half of 2011:[198] 'For a while, he was a front-runner. He had a nonsensical tax plan, zero knowledge of foreign affairs, and had never held elective office.'[199] All these early candidates attempted to appeal, via Fox News, to the far right of the party. Two other high-profile figures – Sarah Palin and Donald Trump – flirted with the same constituency, but then declared they would not run. Candidates who lasted longer, such as Rick Santorum and Newt Gingrich, fought a series of damaging and unedifying primary struggles, which pushed 'Romney to make very right-wing promises on issues like immigration, which would haunt him during the actual campaign.'[200]

The influence of Murdoch and Ailes did not finish with Romney's nomination. Murdoch was openly unenthusiastic about Romney, whom he thought lacked heart and stomach. The two occasions when Romney visited the 'editorial board of the *Journal*, Mr Murdoch did not work very hard to conceal his lack of excitement'. Someone at the meetings commented, 'there was zero enthusiasm, no engagement'.[201] Murdoch and the *Wall St Journal* were, however, very keen on the nomination of Paul Ryan as the vice presidential candidate: he was an 'almost perfect choice' tweeted Murdoch about the deficit hawk, who wanted to radically cut government spending. A *Wall St Journal* editorial dismissed 'every Beltway bedwetter' who warned that Ryan would be too risky.[202]

How much did all this help Obama to win? After all the suspense, and the predictions of a Romney victory or of a cliffhanger,

Obama won by a comfortable and decisive margin. In the popular vote, he beat Romney by 3.2 million votes, 51–48 per cent, and he won the electoral college by 332 to 206 votes.

Although it is more common than not for incumbent presidents to win re-election – there are many factors assisting their cause – given the state of the US economy the result was far from inevitable. Obama won with unemployment around 8 per cent, the highest for a president winning re-election since FDR in 1936:

> Pew Research Center polling found that 46% of Americans say they're worse off since late 2007 and only 31% say they're better off; the rest see no change.[203]

> By 2009, the US male median wage had dropped 28 per cent in real terms since 1970. Since 2007, median household income has fallen by almost 10 per cent.[204]

Although Obama inherited the financial crisis, the sluggish and uneven recovery since has meant that many have blamed Obama rather than Bush for today's economic problems. Economic management is tricky in the US because of the combination of a long-term structural deficit with the need for immediate economic stimulus. Many blame Obama for failing to reach consensus with the Republicans in Congress to solve the problems surrounding the US deficit and the way it has ballooned in recent years. Obama's soaring rhetoric of 2008 was ground down by this gridlock. Such economic discontents and political problems are hardly a recipe for easy re-election. Possibly, trends in the Republican Party, aided and abetted by Fox News, are part of the explanation for his victory.

After the election, there were the usual recriminations on the losing side, with many blaming Romney as a weak candidate. But some post-mortems were unusual. Some prominent conservatives charged that major players had allowed their pursuit of personal wealth and ego to take precedence over political goals. As Eric Boehlert reported:

> The nasty 'racket' accusation highlights what's happened as Republicans have handed over more and more of their branding and marketing to media personalities whose ultimate barometers of success (ratings and personal income) differ from those who run political parties (getting candidates elected to office).[205]

And as Brock and Rabin-Havt put it:

> Fox gives political exiles and marginal political figures the opportunity to compete without the party machinery.[206]

After Huckabee disappeared from the Republican race, for example, he got his own show. As scholar Nicole Hemmer notes:

> Yet far from being an oddity, Huckabee's twin tracks – candidate and commentator – have become a standard feature of Republican Party politics. These days, a revolving door exists between conservative media and Republican candidates.[207]

The problem is that the two spheres involve different skills and have different measures of success. Extremism and conflict make for bad politics but great TV. [208] As media analyst Andrew Beaujon notes, Fox News and the talk radio shock jocks across the country win whether or not conservatives are in power; these purveyors of political entertainment thrive under a Democratic president, perhaps even more than under their preferred candidates.[209] David Frum concluded, 'Republicans originally thought that Fox worked for us and now we're discovering we work for Fox.'[210]

A fair and balanced future?

An episode of *The Simpsons* made fun of Fox News. A Fox-style roll-ing ticker across the bottom of the screen had a series of head-lines: 'Pointless news crawls up 37 per cent ... Do Democrats cause cancer? ... Rupert Murdoch: Terrific dancer ... Study: 92 per cent of Democrats are gay ... JFK posthumously joins Republican Party ... Oil slicks found to keep seals young, supple.' According to the creator of *The Simpsons*, Matt Groening, Ailes threatened to sue Fox Entertainment, which makes *The Simpsons*. Groening said he thought Murdoch would not be impressed with one arm of Fox suing another.[211] Ailes denied threatening to sue.

Being satirised in a leading television program is perhaps an ironic indicator of cultural impact. But one group rumoured not to be amused by Fox were members of the circle around Murdoch. In what appeared to be a calculated public criticism, in early 2010, Matthew Freud, Murdoch's son-in-law, vehemently criticised Fox News to the *New York Times*:

> I am by no means alone within the family or the company in
> being ashamed and sickened by Roger Ailes's horrendous and
> sustained disregard of the journalistic standards that News Corp,
> its founder, and every other global media business aspires to.[212]

A spokesman for Murdoch replied that his son-in-law had been speaking for himself, and that Murdoch was 'proud of Roger Ailes and Fox News'.[213]

The possibility that Murdoch is unhappy with Ailes and Fox gained some credence from Wolff's biography. Not only is Ailes said to be 'the one person in News Corp whom Murdoch will not cross',[214] but 'it should not be underestimated how much Murdoch does not want himself or News Corp, in his or its legacy, forever yoked to Ailes and Fox News'.[215] Later, in the magazine *GQ*, Wolff made the startling revelation that one of the reasons he was invited in 2007 to write a biography of Murdoch, with his full cooperation, was to be a 'weapon in the increasing war against Ailes'. He also revealed that in return for all the access to Murdoch he wanted, he had to make 'a devil's bargain not to talk to Ailes'.[216]

It is impossible from the outside to know the extent of the 'war' inside News Corp against Ailes. In November 2010, a time when Fox was riding high (and when Murdoch thought that Obama would lose to any strong Republican candidate), Murdoch gave an interview to veteran Australian journalist Max Suich. He didn't hide 'his pleasure at the controversy surrounding Fox News' and it was clear 'how much Murdoch enjoys conflict and competition for its own sake, and the consequent fun of deploying his power and influence to make mischief for competitors and enemies'. Asked if he was worried about attacks on Fox News for bias, Murdoch replied: 'Nooo ... people love Fox News.'[217]

Murdoch's public statements have never wavered from this stance. Indeed he has expressed frustration that BSkyB's Sky News was 'not more like Fox News ... He concluded that the only reason that Sky News was not more like Fox News was that "nobody at Sky listens to me".'[218] Many others would rate Sky more highly than Fox: it is the 'only Newscorp organ to gain a reputation for objectivity: its staff privately attribute their success to the [British] regulatory system's protection'.[219] It covered the Iraq War, for example, in a much more balanced way than Fox News. This brought no gratitude from its proprietor. According to a *Guardian* editorial: 'The billionaire (Murdoch) is reported to consider Sky's output as having a "liberal bias" and being a version of "BBC Lite".'[220]

If there was a war, Ailes won. Murdoch 'yoked' himself to Ailes for four more years, when he extended his contract in October 2012.[221]

Nevertheless, the medium-term fortunes of Fox News are far from certain. It is owned by an octogenarian, and run with an iron fist by a septuagenarian who is the only CEO it has ever had. The average age of its viewers is 65 and of its on-air presenters is 57.[222] The era of a steadily expanding pay TV market is over. While 90 per cent of US TV households paid for a subscription service in 2012, the number subscribing has started to decline, and is expected to keep on doing so as internet TV becomes more common.[223]

But Fox News has particular problems, beyond those of the cable industry in general. It has already been engaged in controversies that would have sunk a normal news organisation. Its owner, head of a huge corporation, with a lifetime spent in political controversy, is able to absorb pressures in a way few other business executives could. Its chief executive, similarly with decades of partisan political involvement and strong networks among right-wing politicians, plus the prestige that comes from developing the network from nothing, has accumulated authority as well as a thick skin. It is hard to imagine that their successors will have the political will, or the sangfroid, to carry such a problematic and crisis-prone genre into a successful future.

12

Those who live by scandal

It is a scandal rich in ironies – a scandal sheet brought down by scandal; journalists always quick to accuse others of hypocrisy having their own lies exposed; newspapers which demand transparency of others caught in a cover-up; newspaper executives who routinely condoned the invasion of others' privacy indignant when their own actions are scrutinised; and members of an institution whose democratic rationale is to hold the powerful to account shown to have themselves become an unaccountable power which was detrimental rather than beneficial to democracy.

This chapter outlines the public development of the *News of the World* phone hacking scandal; the next puts it in the context of the organisational culture of News Corp.

The dogs that didn't bark – containment 2007–11

One of the most astonishing aspects of the scandal is how long it took to develop. News International's success in containing it for so long – even though by early 2011 its strategy was coming under ever-increasing strain – is a testament to its power and to the reluctance of key institutions in British society to confront it.

News Corp's involvement in phone tapping first came into the public domain in August 2006, when *News of the World* Royal reporter Clive Goodman and private investigator Glenn Mulcaire were arrested. The arrests related to two stories in late 2005 which made the trivial revelations that Prince William had hurt his knee and had borrowed some audiovisual equipment. The prince's entourage was convinced the paper had obtained the information illegally, and a subsequent Scotland Yard investigation uncovered the phone tapping.

Goodman and Mulcaire pleaded guilty and apologised. In January 2007, both were sentenced to jail. The paper's editor, Andy Coulson, resigned, taking formal responsibility while denying any knowledge of their actions and asserting the company line that it was all the work of a single rogue reporter and no one else knew anything. In June, Coulson, whose journalistic career had begun in show business reporting, and whose previous main contribution to political journalism had been to ask Tony Blair whether he and wife Cherie were members of the 'mile high' club,[1] went to work for Conservative leader David Cameron as chief spin doctor.

News International's 'single rogue reporter' defence should not have survived at all. The court proceedings themselves showed it was not true. Counts 16 to 20 against Mulcaire, to which he pleaded guilty, recorded the names of five other people whose phones he had tapped – and none of them had anything to do with royalty. In the judge's summing up of these five counts he noted that Mulcaire 'had not dealt with Goodman but with others at News International'.[2]

In early 2007, Manchester-based solicitor Mark Lewis wrote to the five non-Royal hacking victims named. Only Gordon Taylor, chief executive of the Professional Footballers' Association, wanted to pursue a civil claim for invasion of privacy. During the negotiations it became clear to Lewis just how keen News was to keep the matter out of court. In January 2008, Scotland Yard eventually gave the legal team some of the material they had collected from Mulcaire, and the team immediately realised that it was 'dynamite'. It included what became called the 'For Neville' email: the transcripts of 35 voicemail messages involving Taylor. Lewis raised his demand from what was then an ambit claim of £200,000 to £1 million. In June 2008 News agreed to pay Taylor £700,000 including legal fees, an unprecedented amount for such a claim. Soon after, the corporation also agreed to pay two associates of Taylor sums totalling around £300,000. A key part of what seemed a wildly generous settlement was that it be kept confidential.

This secrecy held until July 2009, when, after months of work, the *Guardian* investigative reporter Nick Davies revealed that News International had made these payments to Taylor and his two associates. The story also said that phone hacking was rife at *News of the World*. Within hours, the Assistant Commissioner of the London Metropolitan Police, John Yates, announced that there was no reason for any further inquiry. News International stridently denied the story: 'all of these irresponsible and unsubstantiated allegations against the *News of the World* ... and its journalists are false'.[3] Rebekah Brooks, head of News International, said, 'The *Guardian* coverage has, we believe, substantially and likely deliberately misled the British public.'[4] In August, the new editor of the *News of the World*, Colin Myler, announced that internal inquiries had uncovered no further evidence of phone hacking at the paper. In November, the Press Complaints Commission found no evidence against the Sunday paper and indeed concluded that the *Guardian* report 'did not quite live up to the dramatic billing'.

For *Guardian* editor Alan Rusbridger:

the most interesting period in the story ... was the 18 month period following the *Guardian's* original revelation of the Gordon Taylor settlement [in 2009] ... it was interesting precisely because nothing happened ... fascinating in what it said about Britain, [and] the settlement so many people in public life had made, over two generations or more, with Rupert Murdoch.[5]

Despite the continued denials and lack of public action, the

Guardian story had one important consequence. Another of the five named, Max Clifford, got in touch with lawyer Charlotte Harris and mounted his own law suit. In March 2010, he and News International settled. On 9 March the headline story in the *Guardian* reported 'Max Clifford drops *News of the World* phone hacking action in £1m deal'. The settlement was meant to be secret, but Clifford himself went public, charging that the *News of the World* lawyers had leaked the news. However, as Watson and Hickman note, 'Despite disclosing the payment of yet more hush money, the *Guardian's* story was not followed up by any other national newspaper.'[6]

In April, the *Guardian*, based on Freedom of Information material, had another Nick Davies exclusive. So far only a small number of hacking victims had been named in court, and Assistant Commissioner John Yates said there were provable offences against only a handful of people. But Davies' story revealed that Mulcaire's notes, which had been in police custody since 2006, contained 4332 names and 2978 phone numbers. (In February Davies had disclosed in the *Guardian* that three mobile phone companies had discovered that more than 100 of their customers had had their inboxes accessed by Mulcaire.) News of the settlements and about the scale of the hacking was starting to prompt more litigants to come forward. In spring 2010, another of the five named in the trial, sports agent Sky Andrew, began legal action, and others, including actor Sienna Miller and MP Chris Bryant, were making inquiries about how they were covered in Mulcaire's notes.

In February 2010, the *Guardian* published a Davies story which, although one of the figures could not be named because of a trial in progress, was still astounding. It revealed that Coulson, as editor of *News of the World*, had immediately rehired a private detective once he had been released from jail, and that that private detective was now on trial for murder. There was zero reaction. Rusbridger said, 'This was quite a moment for me. It did seem to me that there was an almost wilful blindness in British police, press, regulatory and political circles to acknowledge what was becoming increasingly difficult to ignore.[7]

Rusbridger arranged for all three party leaders – Brown, Cameron and Clegg – to be briefed about what the *Guardian* had found. He had also become so desperate at the lack of other news media following up the *Guardian's* investigative reporting that he contacted Bill Keller, the editor of the *New York Times*. The *Times* sent three reporters to England, and they spent some months working on the story. On 1 September 2010 they published a series of articles that confirmed the *Guardian's* claims, and included material from some other *News of the World* journalists prepared to speak publicly about what had gone on. The *Times* stories were again met with blanket denials at News, and the issue still had little public traction.

As Leveson observed:

> The next steps required the persistence of civil litigants who secured significant admissions, and, in particular, Sienna Miller, who pursued the litigation both systematically and thoroughly; as a result, far greater wrongdoing was exposed than had hitherto been uncovered.[8]

On 15 December 2010, her lawyer, Mark Thomson, revealed the name of the journalist who had commissioned Mulcaire's intercepts. In early January 2011, *News of the World* suspended the paper's news editor, Ian Edmondson. In May, News admitted liability for the entirety of Sienna Miller's claim; in a statement read in open court it admitted invasion of her privacy and a campaign of harassment of over 12 months.[9] She had charged that *News of the World* had published 11 articles about her and her then boyfriend, Jude Law, based on phone hacking.

As the civil cases mounted, attitudes changed inside the police and prosecution authorities. The police began Operation Weeting, under Deputy Assistant Commissioner Sue Akers: 45 officers were assigned to it. In March 2011, the murder charge against Jonathan Rees, the private detective with a criminal record whom Coulson had rehired, collapsed. It was for the 1987 murder of his partner, Daniel Morgan. The case had gained notoriety because of the laxity of the police investigation and the corruption thus revealed. The end of the trial allowed the *Guardian* to publish Nick Davies' story: 'Jonathan Rees: private investigator who ran an empire of tabloid corruption'. So by June 2011 News International's defences were increasingly vulnerable, but still no one foresaw the storm to come.

The July 2011 explosion

The *Guardian's* revelation on 5 July that murder victim Milly Dowler's mobile phone had been tapped created a furore that grew into an unstoppable scandal which has engulfed News International ever since. This action was so grotesquely cynical, so telling about the tabloid's sense of entitlement, and so devoid of any legitimate public purpose, let alone normal human compassion, that it became the focus of sustained outrage. Politicians of all parties and other news media rushed to catch up with public anger.

The following day, 6 July, police made an equally terrible disclosure: Glenn Mulcaire had also targeted the parents of two small girls horrifically murdered in Soham in 2002. Police had known this since February, when it was revealed to them by Charlotte Harris, one of the main solicitors in the civil cases. Harris had gone to police headquarters to inspect the transcripts regarding two of her clients, footballer Lee Chapman and his wife, actor Leslie Ash, and noticed that she happened to have the same name as the father of one of the murdered girls. Harris saw Mulcaire's handwritten note of 'Soham', made the connection and alerted Akers.[10] The police announcement heightened the impact of the previous day's disclosures.

A stream of sponsors announced that they were withdrawing their advertising from *News of the World*. Nevertheless it was a shock when on Thursday (7 July), James Murdoch emailed staff to announce that the following Sunday's edition would be the last for the 168-year-old paper, which was still profitable, and still Britain's biggest-selling title. Rebekah Brooks explained to staff that the paper had become a 'toxic brand' with advertisers. Some staff may have been partly mollified by the heavy hint that the paper would eventually be replaced by the launch of the *Sun on Sunday* (which happened in March 2012). In the final edition of *News of the World*, there were no advertisements, and News International announced that all the money from sales was going to charity. A senior executive said he had to beg to find charities that would accept the money.

On the Thursday, Andy Coulson was arrested. Opposition Leader Ed Miliband and Prime Minister David Cameron issued strong statements, although Cameron was subjected to awkward questioning about his relationship with News and what type of investigation he would launch. On 13 July, an inquiry was announced. It was to be conducted by Lord Leveson, to have wide-ranging terms of reference, and to have powers to compel witnesses. The broad remit of the inquiry and the all-party support was partly due to the strong campaigning by the interest group HackedOff, which had kept in close touch with the hacking victims, including the Dowler family.[11]

The timing of the scandal's eruption was particularly bad for News, because it had just secured in-principle approval from Culture Secretary Jeremy Hunt for the single biggest takeover in its history, extending its ownership of BSkyB from 39 per cent to 100 per cent.[12] During the time allowed for public consultation, the Milly Dowler story was published. The takeover became the main focus of political anger.[13] More than 300,000 people signed a petition opposing it. Soon the government was also backing away. Hunt, who had said since February that the scandal was irrelevant to the bid, now reversed his stance.

On 13 July Miliband moved a motion in parliament requesting Rupert Murdoch and News International to withdraw their bid for BSkyB, in the public interest. The Liberal Democrats agreed, and then so did the Conservatives – in the face of their own government's previous approval: 'The motion was agreed to without a vote.'[14] News International withdrew the bid.

News Corp swung into a public show of remorse, although it started shakily. Rupert Murdoch arrived on Sunday, 10 July, clearly out of touch with the public mood in Britain. When filmed by journalists on his way out to dinner with James Murdoch and Rebekah Brooks, he was asked what his priority was. 'This one,' he replied, pointing to Brooks. Murdoch's commitment was not sufficient to save Brooks, who resigned the following Friday, and was arrested on Sunday, 17 July. Les Hinton, the previous head of News International, now in New York as head of Murdoch's Dow Jones, resigned at the same time.

That day, News International ran full-page ads in the national newspapers apologising, and in another act of public contrition Rupert and James went to visit the Dowlers to personally apologise. The following Tuesday, 19 July, they appeared before a parliamentary committee – 'the most humble day of my life,' said Rupert – but the total abjectness of the apologies was matched by the equally total denial of responsibility.

On the Sunday before, the *Sunday Times* had revealed that the head of the London Metropolitan Police Force, Sir Paul Stephenson, had received thousands of dollars' worth of free hospitality at a health spa, and he resigned later that day. The following day, 18 July, the Assistant Commissioner, John Yates, also resigned.

Cameron, who had departed on a tour of Africa, cut it short in order to address the growing scandal. Eventually he spent 163 minutes in parliament fielding 136 questions from MPs,[15] a virtuoso performance which in some ways signalled the end of this climactic period, marked as it had been by dramatic disclosures, arrests, forced resignations, the closure of a newspaper, and the withdrawal of a bid for BSkyB. This was the moment at which closeness to Murdoch suddenly switched from political asset to political liability.

Sustaining attention

Although the drama and publicity peaks of July inevitably dissipated, the scandal was then sustained by several other sources. The civil cases – which had been so important in breaking down News International's defences – continued to proliferate. News was keen to settle them quickly, with the least damaging publicity, and in January consented to the assessment of aggravated damages. So on a single day, 19 January 2012, it settled 37 cases, with former deputy prime minister John Prescott, for example, receiving £40,000 and Jude Law £130,000. On 9 February another batch of cases was settled.[16] By April 2012, when Rupert Murdoch testified before the Leveson Inquiry, 72 cases had been settled,[17] although more were still pending: the company estimated in May 2012 that it could face up to 520 further claims.[18] These cases did not produce any startling revelations, but the parade of celebrities and others and their anger at News brought a steady stream of headlines, and together underlined yet further the scale of the company's wrongdoing.

In addition, there was a continuing stream of criminal charges, especially against News International employees. Operation Weeting, which had been established in January 2011 to investigate phone hacking, was later supplemented by Operation Elveden, set up to investigate payments to public officials, and Operation Tuletta, set up to investigate allegations of computer hacking. By late 2012, around 90 people had been arrested in connection with these operations,[19] with the prospect of criminal trials in the future. It is not yet clear whether all these will go to trial, nor whether there will be still others charged, as investigations continue.

Another source of news was the House of Commons' Culture,

Media and Sport Committee, which had played an important early role. Its peak attention came on 19 July, when it had required Rupert and James to testify. They had at first refused.[20] The headlines that day were hijacked by a 'comedian' who tried to put a plate of shaving cream in Rupert's face but was impressively intercepted by his alert wife, Wendi.[21] Although the Murdochs suffered no great damage from the day, neither were their public appearances a great success, with Rupert often appearing somewhat doddery and out of touch, and James described as 'half Harry Potter, half Hannibal Lecter'.[22] But their defences set up two longer-term problems. A crucial moment came when Tom Watson asked James, 'When you signed off the Taylor payment, did you see or were you made aware of the "For Neville" email, the transcript of the hacked voicemail messages?' James Murdoch answered unequivocally: 'No, I was not aware of that at the time.'[23] Within days, lawyer Tom Crone and former *News of the World* editor Colin Myler had contradicted James's account. The second problem came with their claim that the law firm Harbottle and Lewis had done an extensive review and failed to find wrongdoing.

In mid-August the committee made two more important revelations. It published the letter sent by Clive Goodman from prison appealing against his dismissal, because, it said, the actions which had landed him in prison had been carried out with the full knowledge of senior editors. The letter included the claim that:

> Tom Crone and the editor [Andy Coulson] promised me on
> many occasions that I could come back to a job at the newspaper
> if I did not implicate the paper or any of its staff in my mitigation
> plea.[24]

The law firm Harbottle and Lewis, after being freed from its obligation of client confidentiality by News, said that it had had only a very limited and focused brief: namely, to determine whether or not

Goodman was entitled to a valid claim for unfair dismissal. It concluded he was not, but noted that News International had paid him £250,000 – unnecessarily, in their legal view. The law firm found it 'hard to credit' James Murdoch's claim that News International rested on its work as part of its defence, and said it was 'inaccurate and misleading' to suggest that the law firm had had a wider investigatory brief.[25] It also noted that some of the most crucial emails it had obtained in 2007 now appeared to be missing from those submitted to the police by News, and stated again that News's public claims about the law firm's findings had gone far beyond what the firm had actually found.

The parliamentary committee had become less prominent, as the Leveson Inquiry assumed centre stage, but it finished with a climax. In its report on 1 May 2012, the majority concluded that Rupert Murdoch was not a fit person to exercise stewardship of a major international company.[26] This critical conclusion made headlines around the world. News Corp seized on the fact that the main finding against Rupert was not unanimous, but passed along party lines. The Conservatives voted against it, partly, some said, because that conclusion went beyond their terms of reference. But tellingly for Murdoch, their coalition partner, the Liberal Democrats, voted with Labour, to produce a majority against him. The fact that all Labour MPs would vote for such a strong conclusion shows just how far Murdoch's political fortunes had diminished.

There were many damning parts of the report which all parties agreed on. MPs concluded nine to one that it was 'simply astonishing' that Rupert and James did not realise the one-rogue-reporter line was untrue until December 2010.[27] James Murdoch was deemed to have shown wilful ignorance of the extent of phone hacking, and three senior News International employees – Hinton, Myler and Crone – were all found to have misled the committee in 2009, when News International still had hopes that the scandal could be contained.

By far the most important source of continuing attention to the scandal, however, was the Leveson Inquiry. On 13 July 2011, as noted, Prime Minister David Cameron commissioned Lord Justice Leveson to conduct an inquiry, in two parts. The first part included making recommendations for a new and more effective regulatory regime that would support the integrity and freedom of the press. The second part was to inquire into the extent of unlawful and improper conduct within News International, and in the institutions it was dealing with, including the police and politicians.

As the inquiry noted in its Executive Summary, 'in nearly nine months of oral hearings, 337 witnesses gave evidence in person' and the statements of nearly 300 others were read into evidence: 'It has become the most public and the most concentrated look at the press that this country has seen.'[28] The victims of phone hacking were given a public voice, and a range of politicians and – more unusually – leading figures in the news media were cross-examined under oath. Leveson had to avoid all matters that might impinge on the impending criminal trials, which means that some of the most interesting questions have not yet been publicly pursued, and the second part of his inquiry has been indefinitely delayed.

The hearings began in November 2011, and were roughly divided into three modules. The first, on the behaviour of the press in relation to the public, had several witnesses who had been victims of distorted or intrusive press reporting. Thus on the first day, the parents of Milly Dowler, and film star Hugh Grant, appeared.

Module Two, on the relationships between the press and the police, began in February 2012, and included interviews with many who had been involved in investigating phone taps, as well as a more general probing of the relations between individual officers and tabloid journalists and the expensive hospitality they lavished on each other.

In late April several editors and proprietors – whose relevance spanned all modules – appeared, climaxing with James Murdoch on 24 April and Rupert on the following two days. Rupert gave a good performance on the first day, but on the second 'his recollection seemed noticeably absent when discussing his own wrong-doing, but entirely there if someone else was at fault'.[29] Rupert used 'cannot remember' or some similar phrase 30 times, fewer than James (41) or David Cameron (59).[30] Such a simple amnesia scoreboard is misleading, however: James Murdoch and Cameron often could not remember details, while Rupert said he could not remember whole meetings with people or whether he had ever met particular people.

Module Three, on the press and politicians, began in early May. Three former prime ministers – Gordon Brown, Tony Blair and John Major – appeared, as did members of the present and former governments, and other important players, such as Blair's chief spin doctor, Alastair Campbell. Rebekah Brooks and Andy Coulson were quizzed about their relationships with politicians. Later, Culture Secretary Jeremy Hunt was questioned about his dealings with News International on the BSkyB bid. This module climaxed with David Cameron appearing for a whole day in mid-June. The last round of public hearings, much less spectacular than the first three, involved proposals for more effective regulation.

A new stage began when the first part of the Leveson Inquiry's results – four volumes totalling 2000 pages – was published in November 2012. Its key proposal was to replace the Press Complaints Commission with a body that had statutory force, could impose fines as well as demand publication of corrections, and would be independent of both government and publishers. Prime Minister Cameron had earlier promised to follow the recommendations unless they were 'bonkers', and had said the key test would be whether the victims of unethical press coverage, such as the Dowlers and others,[31] were satisfied with the result. But within hours of the report's public release he rejected its key recommendations, incurring the wrath of exactly those people. His response also led immediately to political debate, with the Liberal Democrats and Labour endorsing the recommendations.

Before and after – contrasting responses

For three and a half years until July 2011, the most notable aspect of the responses of most politicians, police and media to the allegations was their passivity, which revealed the strength of the previous relationships. However, once the scandal gained unstoppable momentum, the power of this earlier web of self-interest, patronage and fear collapsed. The contrast was stark.

Labour MP Tom Watson, who played such an important role in uncovering the scandal, said that in the summer of 2009:

> every single MP I know thought the campaign [to expose phone hacking] was bordering on insane. No one wanted to know. It was simply career suicide to challenge the powerful people that ran News International.[32]

All three major party leaders told Leveson – rather euphemistically – that politicians had become 'too close' to the press.[33] Lord Mandelson put it more honestly: 'We were cowed.'[34]

Historian Timothy Garton Ash called it:

> a fear that dared not speak its name; a self-deceiving cowardice that cloaked itself in silence, euphemism and excuse. Inwardly, politicians, spin doctors, PR men, public figures and, it now emerges, even senior police officers, said to themselves: don't take on Murdoch. Never go up against the tabloids.

The threat that the tabloids would go after you 'was always there'.[35] But in July 2011, 'startlingly, a wave of openness spread over politics'.[36]

Even though Murdoch had turned so strongly against the Labour government, in opposition the party was still keen to woo him back. One of new Opposition Leader Ed Miliband's early appointments was of a former News journalist, Tom Baldwin, as his spin doctor. Baldwin sent an email to Labour MPs instructing them to go easy on the scandal, and in particular not to link it to the impending takeover decision on BSkyB. Before July 2011, Miliband had told confidants that he had no choice but to ignore the scandal, because the alternative would be 'three years of hell' at the hands of the Murdoch press.[37] On 5 July 2011 Miliband and his team had what they dubbed their 'sod it' meeting,[38] and decided that the political calculus had changed decisively. After that, Labour became a consistent voice of criticism and supporter of reform.

The Conservatives, and especially Prime Minister David Cameron, were in a much more vulnerable position. Before the scandal erupted in July 2011, they had consistently dismissed the charges as Labour propaganda. In September 2010, for example, London mayor Boris Johnson denounced them as 'codswallop', and a 'politically motivated put up job by the Labour Party',[39] and a staff member had advised the police not to fall for the 'political media hysteria'.[40]

There were charges that key Conservatives were too close to News International. Documents tabled to the Leveson Inquiry showed that Cameron's ministers met with News Corp executives more often than with any other media organisation: 107 meetings in just over a year. Some ministers were particularly close. Education Secretary Michael Gove's wife worked for the *Times*, as had he previously. Between 2005 and 2009 he had received at least £60,000 a year for articles he wrote for the *Times*, and an unspecified advance from HarperCollins for a biography of 18th century politician Viscount Bolingbroke. The Foreign Secretary, William Hague, in opposition had received £195,000 a year for a column in *News of the World*, and around £300,000 from HarperCollins for biographies of William Pitt the Younger and William Wilberforce.[41]

Cameron himself was particularly vulnerable for three reasons. The first involved charges of misjudgement: in hiring Andy Coulson in 2007 and, after he won the 2010 election, in appointing him as the government's Director of Communications.[42] The 2007 hiring was designed to overcome Cameron's apparent problem with the tabloids in general and Murdoch in particular – at first Cameron seemed too much of a toff and too moderate to appeal to the Murdoch tabloids.

Murdoch's papers indeed began to warm to Cameron after he hired Coulson; also, Cameron was increasingly eager to please. In 2009, while the Conservatives were still in opposition, and following the papers' disapproval of Cameron's shadow home secretary Dominic Grieve for being too soft on crime, Grieve was moved to another portfolio.[43] Cameron soon adopted a much tougher stance on social issues, embracing the *Sun*'s rhetoric of 'Broken Britain'.[44] After an increasingly ardent courtship, the Murdoch press strongly supported the Conservatives in the lead-up to the 2010 election.

Cameron's argument was that Coulson deserved a second chance, having taken formal responsibility for, but not having himself being involved in, the Goodman-Mulcaire Royal phone hacking. But other embarrassments kept appearing. One was an unusually large payout, £800,000, to former *News of the World* sports reporter Matt Driscoll for being bullied while working under Coulson. Later it was revealed that – at least technically – Coulson had broken House of Commons rules by not declaring that he was still receiving considerable income from News International through his severance settlement.[45] Before appointing Coulson as Director of Communications in 2010, Cameron and other senior figures had been privately warned by the *Guardian* about Coulson's links with Jonathan Rees, the ex-criminal and private investigator. There had been five police inquiries into the 1987 murder of Rees's partner Daniel Morgan,[46] and eventually this all became public, to the government's embarrassment.[47] Whether out of loyalty or over-confidence, Cameron ignored the warnings. Coulson resigned from his position in January 2011.

Cameron's second problem involved 'his appearance of coziness' with Murdoch's News International executives.[48] His social circle included Rebekah Brooks and her husband, Charlie, and Elisabeth Murdoch and her husband Matthew Freud. Peter Oborne described this 'Chipping Norton set' as 'a group of louche, affluent, power-hungry and amoral Londoners'. As is often the case with scandals, the exposure of backstage behaviour[49] brought its own embarrassments, namely the tabling of texts between Cameron and Brooks. Brooks texted Cameron at the 2009 Conservative Party Conference: 'I am so rooting for you tomorrow not just as a proud friend but because, professionally, we're definitely in this together! Speech of your life! Yes he Cam!'[50] And the world learnt that Cameron used to sign LOL, until Brooks told him it meant Laugh Out Loud rather than Lots of Love. There was also a humorous sequel. At the height of the scandal in July, Cameron had talked of cleaning out the stables.[51] Later it was disclosed that the Metropolitan Police had lent a retired police horse to Brooks,[52] and Cameron had ridden it, with some linking the 'Horsegate' episode back to Cameron's stables declaration.

It all looked very un-prime ministerial. But the third and most important problem for Cameron was that his government had just approved Murdoch's bid to increase his ownership of the very profitable satellite broadcaster BSkyB from 39 per cent to 100 per cent. This was potentially a major moment in redrawing the British media map. BSkyB had annual revenues of £6.8 billion, not far below the combined revenues of the BBC, ITV, Channel 4 and Channel 5.[53] On 30 June the Cameron Government announced its intention to wave through the takeover, which would become final on 8 July, following a brief public 'consultation period'. Success looked assured. But then came the *Guardian* story, on 5 July.

The BSkyB decision 'was firing the scandal'[54] and provided a tangible target for the public anger. The bid had always been politically fraught. It was not coincidental that Murdoch launched it immediately after Cameron's election. The first minister to have carriage of the decision, Liberal Democrat Vince Cable, was dramatically removed from that responsibility after it was leaked that he had said to two people he thought were constituents, but who were, in fact, journalists, that he had declared war on Murdoch.[55] The prime minister handed responsibility to Jeremy Hunt, whose earlier public statements had seemed friendly to the bid, to the point where critics had dubbed him the Minister for Murdoch.

Hunt had consistently maintained that any criminal charges against Murdoch's *News of the World* were irrelevant to the BSkyB decision, but the intensity of the scandal swept away such niceties; moreover, it shone a searching new light on the process of approval. It was revealed, for example, that Hunt had had a meeting with James Murdoch, with no public servants present and no minutes taken, and then another with the BSkyB chief executive, despite the public service warning him that media regulation issues were likely to arise as a result of holding such a meeting.[56] When James Murdoch testified, the Leveson Inquiry published 163 pages of emails which News International had given them on interactions between the company and Hunt's office. An immediate casualty was an unfortunate Hunt staff member, Adam Smith, who was required to resign for allegedly exceeding his authority in dealings with News, although as the News International lobbyist Fred Michel – who was texting Smith an average of five times every working day during the crucial period[57] – stated, 'His [Hunt's] advisers were there to assist and advise Jeremy Hunt and it was my understanding that when they told me something, it was always on behalf of the minister and after having conferred with him.'[58]

Hunt's ministerial role in the decision was meant to be – in the British political lexicon – 'quasi-judicial'. But his actions showed how politically charged the process was. In November 2010 he had sent an urgent memo to the prime minister saying James Murdoch was 'pretty furious' that Cable had referred the bid to Ofcom, the official regulator: Cable had merely followed due process.[59] After the phone hacking scandal blew up in July 2011, according to News International lobbyist Michel, Hunt 'asked me to advise him privately in the coming weeks and guide his and No. 10's positioning'.[60] The emails from Michel show that he was thoroughly informed of every move the government was about to make. He told Brooks in early June that Hunt would approve the takeover late that month, and that Hunt believed that 'phone hacking has nothing to do with media plurality issues'.[61] In December 2010, after the merger cleared a regulatory hurdle in the EU, Hunt texted James Murdoch, 'Congrats on Brussels. Just Ofcom to go!'[62] The barrister assisting, Robert Jay, put it to Rupert Murdoch at the Leveson Inquiry that Hunt had acted as a cheerleader for the bid, rather than as an impartial arbiter.[63] Rupert denied this, and Hunt maintained that he had acted 'scrupulously fairly'.[64] Cameron resisted opposition demands that Hunt resign, and after a heated debate the government defeated a House of Commons motion to hold an inquiry into his behaviour.[65] Eventually Cameron moved Hunt out of the firing line, by promoting him to health minister.[66]

Perhaps more surprising than the failure of the politicians was the equally abject failure of the police – 'pathetic', judged lawyer Charlotte Harris;[67] 'meek and mild' rather than a 'fearless, impartial investigator' thought Watson and Hickman;[68] and one MP thought the efforts of senior officer Andy Hayman were more Clouseau than Columbo.[69] John Whittingdale, a Labour MP, verbalised what many suspected, that:

> the only reason ... that the hacking enquiry was not fully pursued was that it was a story that the police did not wish to uncover. They did not want to spoil their relationships with News International.[70]

Leveson judged that the decision to limit the 2006 prosecution was 'entirely justifiable'.[71] Several reasons can be used to support that decision – to spare the prince/s the experience of being cross-examined in court, to set up a straightforward case with a very high prospect of success, and because it was necessary to prioritise scarce police resources, especially given London's recent experience of terrorism. The police failures began immediately, though. They pledged to notify all those whose phones Mulcaire had hacked, but inexplicably failed to do so. The material they had collected from Mulcaire, which was later revealed to be 11,000 pages, sat stored in garbage bags for the next several years.

Leveson saw no reason to challenge the integrity of the police, including senior officers, but he noted that they were responsible for 'poor decisions, poorly executed'.[72] The response to the first *Guardian* article, in July 2009 – on the Gordon Taylor financial settlement – had set the tone. Assistant Commissioner John Yates took only hours to dismiss the *Guardian* report, and falsely claimed that the individuals affected had all been notified; as noted, he also did not undertake any review of the Mulcaire evidence.[73] The Leveson Inquiry found that Yates 'not only failed to require a more measured review'; 'he positively refused to allow it to happen'.[74] 'Mr Yates was right to conclude that the *Guardian* had not revealed anything that would be new to the police, but that was precisely the point'[75] – the police already had the material, but had not examined it.

One of those originally involved in 2006, Andy Hayman, had left the force – in two years as Commissioner he had run up £19,000 on his Scotland Yard credit card[76] – and in response to *Guardian* reports he wrote an article for the *Times*, claiming that the original investigation had 'left no stone unturned' and that if there had been the 'slightest hint others were involved ... they would have been investigated'. So a decision not to pursue because of other priorities had now become an exhaustive investigation. Leveson was properly critical of these 'extraordinary assertions'.[77] He judged that the police response to this first *Guardian* article set up 'a defensive mindset' which affected all that followed.[78] Defence quickly turned to counter-aggression. After the *New York Times*, in September 2010, quoted former show business reporter Sean Hoare confirming phone hacking, Yates instructed that Hoare be interviewed under caution, meaning that anything he said could be used in court: 'It looked as if Yates's first moves ... had been [designed] to scare off other whistleblowers.'[79]

The police's public responses were consistently dismissive. For example, Yates on several occasions said there was no evidence that Mulcaire had tapped Deputy Prime Minister John Prescott's phone,[80] but it turned out he had never looked, and that Prescott's phone had indeed been hacked. The police were also very slow to respond to requests. MP Chris Bryant, for example, had to wait eight months to find out if he figured in the files,[81] and Charlotte Harris found that 'the police would only provide documents under court order and when you did get the documents they would be redacted in a random way'.[82] Senior police officers also sought to dissuade the *Guardian* from pursuing the story.[83]

The phone hacking scandal highlighted the close links – mutual hospitality plus mutual patronage – between the London police and News International. The Murdoch tabloids and the police had a shared interest in promoting law and order stories. Of the 45 press officers in Scotland Yard, 10 were former News International journalists. There seemed to be a revolving door of appointments and consultancies, and lucrative post-retirement publishing options. Throughout, senior Scotland Yard figures continued to socialise with senior editorial figures in News International, the organisation whose misdeeds they were meant to be investigating. At this stage, there was still no public knowledge of the extensive bribery by News of police officers.

Prompted by the Crown Prosecution Service, police attitudes changed decisively in late 2010, with the establishment of

Operation Weeting. Now the police had a determination born not just of the crimes themselves, but of the way they had allowed themselves to be played for fools. The head of Operation Weeting, Deputy Assistant Commissioner Sue Akers, testified that, 'I think it is everybody's analysis that (public) confidence has been damaged in the Metropolitan Police. If we do not get this right, it will continue to be damaged.'

The third initially passive group was the rest of the media, apart from the *Guardian*. A study by Judith Townend and Daniel Bennett found that from 2006 to the end of 2010 the *Guardian* published 237 articles on hacking. The tally for the *Mail* and *Mail on Sunday* was just 38, and for the *Mirror* and *Sunday Mirror* a mere 11 – that is, less than three a year.[84] In January 2011, as public interest in the scandal was mounting, Rupert Murdoch visited London. The following morning the nine national newspapers devoted a total of 12,585 words to Murdoch and the scandal, with the *Guardian* at the top (4703) and the *Sun* at the bottom (41).[85]

Guardian editor Alan Rusbridger was perplexed by the media's lack of interest. The Tuesday following the *Guardian* article in July 2009, Rusbridger and Davies had appeared before the Commons Select Committee on Culture, Media and Sport. Davies flourished hard copies of the 'For Neville' emails. Experienced reporter Andrew Sparrow blogged: 'Wow! I've been covering Commons committees for 15 years and I've never heard such a dramatic opening statement.' But there was barely any coverage in the next day's papers.[86] In February 2010, that parliamentary inquiry concluded that it was 'inconceivable' that knowledge of the *News of the World*'s phone hacking was limited to Goodman and Mulcaire, and strongly criticised that paper's witnesses for their collective amnesia. There was very brief and limited coverage of the Committee's report, with the main theme being that Coulson had been 'cleared'. None of the major media felt the need to publicise the findings at length.[87]

Similarly, when a tribunal found that *News of the World* sports reporter Matt Driscoll had suffered from bullying by Andy Coulson, and was awarded an 'astonishing' £800,000, only the *Guardian* found it newsworthy. As Rusbridger notes, 'The nearer Cameron edged to the door of 10 Downing Street, the less appetite there was to run anything negative about Coulson.'[88]

The reasons for the press lacking its normal sense of newsworthiness can only be speculated on. It may have been a general dog doesn't eat dog attitude, or perhaps other tabloids knew their own news-gathering methods had been less than pure. One reason for believing mutual protection may have been a motive had been dramatically illustrated by Operation Motorman, begun in 2003. Here the UK Information Commissioner looked at the files of one private detective, Steve Whittamore, and found that 305 journalists and most national newspapers had used his services in tracing confidential personal information. The targets included eight England footballers and the head of the intelligence agency MI6. His biggest client was the *Daily Mail*, which had paid him £143,150 in connection with 1728 requests.[89] Despite the scale of a single detective's illicit activities, and the disclosure of this information black market, coverage of the Operation Motorman report in the major news media was strangely muted.

Later press responses were equally revealing. In contrast to their usual approach to law and order issues, they lobbied strongly against harsher punishments for data protection offences.[90] Leveson found 'the extent to which Mr Whittamore's services continued to be used by some titles after his conviction' revealing.[91] He also observed that 'none of these revelations led to any newspaper conducting an investigation either into its own practices or into those of other titles';[92] neither did they lead to any 'in-depth look to examine who had been paid for what and why or to review compliance requirements'.[93]

The cover-up

At News Corp's annual meeting in New York on 15 October 2010, Rupert Murdoch told investors:

> We have very strict rules. There was an incident more than five years ago. The person who bought a bugged phone conversation was immediately fired and in fact he subsequently went to jail. There have been two parliamentary inquiries, which have found no further evidence of anything at all. If anything was to come to light, we challenge people to give us evidence, and no one has been able to.[94]

Even then many of these claims were clearly wrong; by the 2011 meeting they were indefensible. Instead he told that meeting: 'We could not be taking this more seriously or listening more intently to criticisms.' Then he limited contributions from the investors present to a maximum of one minute,[95] having already made shareholders register for a ticket four days before the meeting, the most unfriendly environment that shareholder activist Stephen Mayne had ever seen at an AGM.[96] The following year repentance was no longer on the agenda. Just before the 2012 meeting, Murdoch tweeted: 'Signs pretty peaceful, but any shareholders with complaints should take profits and sell.' The whole AGM was wound up 'in a slick hour and 21 minutes'.[97]

Through the early years of the scandal, News International denials could not have been more emphatic. There was an unqualified and total dismissal of any and all claims of possible wrongdoing. Harold Evans thought there was 'a pattern to the Murdoch sagas. What is denied most furiously turns out to be irrefutably true.'[98] Just as revealing is the lack of any internal soul-searching, or even curiosity, about what might have occurred. To deny, to cover up was the automatic response. Brian Cathcart observed, 'It is striking that not a single hint has emerged in all these years to suggest that there was internal debate about this choice.'[99]

Public declarations of cooperation were coupled with private obstruction. Justice Leveson observed that 'most responsible corporate entities would be appalled that employees were or could be involved in the commission of crime in order to further their business. Not so at the *News of the World*.'[100] From the beginning, in 2006, when police sought to execute a warrant to search Clive Goodman's desk and computer in connection with the phone hacking, 'they were confronted and driven off by staff at the newspaper', and their attempt was 'substantially thwarted'. After a 'tense standoff', many officers were prevented from entering the building. No subsequent search was attempted as police believed any relevant evidence would have been destroyed.[101]

In late 2009, a management memo headed 'Opportunity' recommended that 'subject to compliance with legal and regulatory requirements', they should delete emails 'that could be unhelpful in the context of future litigation in which NI [News International] is a defendant'.[102] The barrister representing the phone hacking victims, in his concluding address to the Leveson Inquiry, talked of News's cover-up, including the destruction of millions of emails, saying that these occurred at strategic moments as public revelations threatened, while News publicly professed cooperation.[103] Rupert Murdoch told the Leveson Inquiry that the new *News of the World* editor, Colin Myler, brought in to replace Andy Coulson, was appointed to 'find out what the hell was going on', but Myler immediately rebutted this, saying he was given no such brief, and that his role was simply to edit the paper.[104]

Similarly, News International had brought in the legal firm Harbottle and Lewis for the strictly circumscribed purpose of answering Clive Goodman's appeal against his dismissal. The lawyers decided in the company's favour on that score, but were subsequently angered by News International's referring to their advice when making much broader claims relating to phone hacking in general. As noted earlier, the firm finally achieved a waiver of client confidentiality, allowing them to make this clear. As Leveson says about the hiring of Harbottle and Lewis:

> It is revealing that the [News] concern was to identify material that would cause the company further embarrassment or damage their prospects in an Employment Tribunal rather than ascertain whether the allegations made by Mr Goodman [about phone hacking being widespread and approved at the paper] were true.[105]

Harbottle and Lewis had discovered evidence of News International bribes to police, totalling more than £100,000. This knowledge had first been given to News International management in 2007. When someone asked for a copy of their report again – in March 2011 – the company gave it to Lord Macdonald, previously a Director of Public Prosecutions, now in private practice, who immediately recommended that it should be handed to the police. Finally, three months later, on 20 June, the company gave police the evidence it had first received four years earlier.[106] Perhaps it had hoped the BSkyB approval would be finalised before any action was taken.

A week after Clive Goodman was sentenced to prison, Les Hinton sacked him. Goodman then wrote a letter of appeal which 'in 360 precise words' threatened 'to explode the company's defence: he was claiming phone hacking had been carried out routinely, with management's full knowledge'.[107] In response, News International lifted Goodman's severance pay considerably, to almost £250,000. Goodman's letter did not prevent Hinton from later telling the parliamentary committee that 'there was never any evidence given to me that suggested that the conduct of Clive Goodman spread beyond him'.[108]

The strength and totality of News International denials (*News of* the *World* managing editor Stuart Kuttner, for example, maintained, 'It happened once at the *News of the World* … The reporter was fired')[109] make strange reading given subsequent revelations, and especially in light of the large sums of money involved. News International had earned the nickname 'Shoestring International'[110] because of its stinginess, and yet here were very large sums of money flowing out. As former *Sun* editor David Yelland said in December 2010, it was inconceivable that the editor did not know that Mulcaire was on a contract that paid him over £100,000 a year.[111] However, Rebekah Brooks told the parliamentary committee that the first time she had heard Mulcaire's name was in 2006, after the arrests.[112] Similarly, as Akers testified to Leveson, 'there appears to have been a culture at the *Sun* of illegal payments, and systems have been created to facilitate such payments while hiding the identity of the official receiving the money'. However, senior editors, for instance, want to know, especially on problematic or sensitive stories, how the reporter knows it is true.

Apart from such large cash flows requiring institutional processes, there was anecdotal evidence of occasions on which editors had referred to such activities. Most famously Rebekah Wade (later Brooks): in March 2003, 'a supremely confident and striking figure' appeared before the House of Commons committee, and looking 'unabashed and unperturbed (declared) "we have paid the police for information in the past"'.[113] Piers Morgan, in his published diary, wrote, 'Rebekah excelled herself by virtually admitting she's been illegally paying police for information. I called her to thank her for dropping the tabloid baton.'[114] Dominic Mohan, now editor of the *Sun*, had once jokingly thanked Vodafone for its lax security.[115]

While it is clear that senior editorial management knew what was happening, it is less clear what James and Rupert Murdoch knew and when. Asserting Rupert's ignorance runs against the Murdoch mythology, which has him in close command of all his operations, a 'detail man' who 'speaks with his top media executives several times a day'.[116] When the *Guardian* reported the payout to Gordon Taylor, Rupert, then in the United States, denied it to a media conference: 'If that had happened, I would have known about it.' James said that Rupert had not been advised of the payment.[117] This seems strange, given the importance of the matter. What is doubly strange is that even after Rupert made a public statement that was wrong, no one bothered to enlighten him.

James's knowledge was much more directly in dispute. Crone and Myler were adamant that he had known about the 'For Neville' chain of emails. Both sides agree on the lead-up events: Myler and Crone wanted a meeting because they had to settle with Gordon Taylor, because, as Myler said in his email of 7 June 2008, in which he requested a meeting with James, of 'Taylor's vindictiveness' and because the email chain that Taylor and his solicitors had was 'as bad as we feared'.[118] Crone said, 'We went to see Mr Murdoch and it was explained to him what this document was and what it meant.'[119]

While the primary concern when investigating cover-ups is the honesty and frankness of the responses, how the respondents draw the lines of guilt and innocence is certainly also an issue. The Murdochs may find that this returns to haunt them. Before the parliamentary committee James and Crone and Myler just claimed discrepant memories. But at the Leveson Inquiry, James and Rupert hardened the line of difference into deliberate deception. James claimed that News International executives had withheld the information about phone hacking from him because they feared he would 'cut out the cancer'.[120] The email chain that Myler sent James on 7 June 2008 showed that evidence of widespread phone hacking was the reason they had to pay Taylor such a large sum. To be credible, James's assertion means that Crone and Myler knew he wouldn't read what they had sent him. Nor can they be blamed for James failing to ask any questions about why such an unprecedented payout was necessary. Not surprisingly, Leveson preferred Crone and Myler's evidence in this regard.[121] Rupert also blamed Myler for the internal cover-up about phone hacking and seemed to place primary blame on Crone:

> someone [who] took charge of a cover-up which we were
> victim to [sic] ... the person I'm thinking of was a friend of the
> journalists and a drinking pal and a clever lawyer ... and he
> forbade people to go and report to Mrs Brooks or to James.[122]

In this version, Crone deliberately misled his superiors. Crone, who worked as News International's lawyer for more than two decades, immediately issued a statement saying that Rupert's claim was a 'shameful lie'.

Myler and Crone were in a difficult position. They had upheld the company line for several years. Watson and Hickman observed that at the parliamentary committee, 'Myler and Crone's tactics soon emerged: confusion, obfuscation and spectacular memory loss.'[123] Both had at various times publicly committed themselves to the single rogue reporter defence, although Crone later recanted, saying he always knew it was wrong, and that it would 'one day probably come back to bite the company'.[124] Myler made several unequivocal statements: for example, he told the parliamentary committee in 2009, 'I have never worked or been associated with a newspaper that has been so forensically examined.'[125]

Another source of alienation, and hence a possible stimulus to defection, is the very different amounts of money people had received via redundancy and severance arrangements. Watson and Hickman report that both former news editor Ian Edmondson and chief reporter Neville Thurlbeck, of the 'For Neville' email fame, have said they are suing *News of the World* for wrongful dismissal. 'There is much I could have said publicly to the detriment of News International but so far have chosen not to,' said Thurlbeck, furious that he had been sacked without a payoff after working there for 21 years.[126] News International's payment of £10.8 million to Rebekah Brooks[127] has no doubt set the bar very high for the others.

Scale and consequences

One of the most breathtaking aspects of the scandal was its sheer scale. The extensiveness of the surveillance operations is most immediately evident in the use of private detectives. *News of the World* employed at least four.

The best-known was Glenn Mulcaire, who had an £102,000 a year contract with the paper, supplemented by extra cash payments for particular jobs, and was paid at least £850,000 over eight years. Mulcaire's notes, which were seized by the police in 2006, and then sat unexamined for years, totalled 11,000 pages. He probably tapped the phones of over 1000 people, and caught conversations involving around 5000 people.[128] In Robert Jay's opening statement on 14 November 2011, he said Mulcaire's notes showed 2266 'taskings' by the paper, of which 95 per cent came from four journalists, and that his work for the paper probably continued until 2009.[129]

While Mulcaire worked almost exclusively for News International newspapers, the second private investigator, whose work was first revealed in Operation Motorman, Stephen Whittamore, worked for many titles; the *Daily Mail* was his largest contract. Most of his work seemed to be penetrating data security – finding telephone numbers, addresses, car registrations and so on – and an unknown amount of it was illegal. The total amount paid by newspapers for these items of information may have been as high as £500,000, which 'gives an indication that the supply of personal information was, for those involved, a lucrative business'.[130]

The third, and perhaps most notorious, private detective used by *News of the World* was Jonathan Rees, whose service for the paper was interrupted by a seven-year prison sentence for conspiring to pervert the course of justice. Upon his release in 2005, he was immediately re-engaged by the paper, for £150,000 a year.[131] Neither that conviction nor the fact that he was on several occasions implicated in investigations into the 1987 murder of his partner dimmed the paper's enthusiasm for his services. It is interesting that the paper was paying him 50 per cent more than Mulcaire's retainer, but it is less clear what services he was providing. Watson and Hickman speculate that it may have been that Rees delivered information on criminal investigations using corrupt associates in the police force.

The fourth one was Derek Webb and his firm Silent Shadow. While 'Mr Whittamore's *métier* was to obtain personal data', Mr Webb 'was an expert in surveillance', and some of Mulcaire's data may have been used to assist Webb's surveillance tasks.[132] He revealed on 7 November 2011 that *News of the World* had ordered him to follow more than 100 high-profile individuals over eight years, running right up to the paper's closure in July. Webb said, 'I don't feel ashamed. I know to a certain extent people's lives have been ruined … but if I wasn't doing it, somebody else would have been.'[133] Angered that the paper hadn't treated him as generously in severance pay as other freelance contributors, Webb threatened to act as a witness against News International in court cases that concerned his activities.[134]

The scale of these activities makes it clear that 'large parts of the press had been engaged in a widespread trade in private and confidential information, apparently with little regard to the public interest', and that newspapers 'felt they had a right to know whatever they wanted to know about whoever crossed their paths, no matter how vulnerable and powerless those people were'.[135] The determination with which they carried out their task is illustrated by the fact that David Beckham had 13 sim cards for his mobile telephones and Mulcaire had penetrated all of them. It was not only celebrities and their associates who were targeted, but victims of crime and others caught up in the news. It seems that at least five Cabinet ministers in the Labour government had had their phones tapped, while the details of the head of the intelligence service MI6 were in Whittamore's files, and Mulcaire's files included information about several people who had been placed under witness protection. Former

Prime Minister Gordon Brown's bank accounts had been illegally accessed. David Sherborne, counsel to the Inquiry for 50 victims of phone hacking, was not exaggerating when he said that over the last nine months, the public had witnessed the unravelling of 'possibly the most outrageous and largest criminal malpractice this country's press has ever known'.[136]

In terms of custodial sentences, the most important criminal charges relate to the payment of bribes to police officers and public servants. As of late 2012, 21 *Sun* journalists had been arrested in relation to bribery charges, including Coulson and Brooks.[137] Operation Elveden, relating to bribery of officials, had resulted in 52 arrests – 25 of those were journalists.[138]

Before the Leveson Inquiry began, one line of defence by News International did not question the accuracy of the claims, but sought to deflect them as not deserving the attention they were receiving. As the police had said, pursuing phone hacking was less important than working against terrorism, or solving more serious crimes. Roger Alton, executive editor of the *Times* said, 'For me it's roughly on a par with parking in a resident's parking bay in terms of interest.'[139] When the scandal was at its height, on 20 July 2011, the *Sun* had a story about a UNICEF official urging the media to focus on the drought in Africa, headlined 'UN: forget hacking, kids are starving'.[140] This indicated a welcome discovery of the importance of global poverty by the *Sun*, and perhaps Murdoch. Earlier, when a senior journalist had wanted to write a story about the Third World, then editor Kelvin MacKenzie leant over his desk, and 'speaking slowly to emphasise each word' told him, 'Get this through your fucking head. Nobody gives a fuck about the Third World.'[141] Woodrow Wyatt claims that he once suggested that in penance for the *Sun* having leaked the Queen's Christmas message Murdoch should give £200,000 to Princess Anne's favourite charity, Save the Children, and that Murdoch replied, 'What, all those Africans?'[142]

For a few, invasion of privacy continued to be a minor offence or even a public service. The most notorious was the unrepentant former *News of the World* journalist Paul McMullan, who proclaimed to the Leveson Inquiry:

> In 21 years of invading people's privacy, I've never actually come across anyone who's been doing any good. The only people I think need privacy are people who do bad things ... Privacy is particularly good for paedos ... privacy is evil ...[143]

In contrast, Alan Rusbridger commented on 'how sickened people feel when their privacy is invaded'. Victims of phone hacking 'tell you how deeply repulsive it was to think of a stranger listening into private communications with loved ones or family', and he cited former *Sun* editor MacKenzie saying how violated he had felt when shown transcripts of his own intercepted phone messages.[144] Not only did these stories serve no conceivable public interest, but any stories which resulted were typically hurtful and demeaning to those written about.

But their impact reached beyond the content of stories, to these people's personal relationships. The testimony of many witnesses confirmed the psychological impact of feeling that they had no private life at all. Sienna Miller couldn't understand why photographers and reporters always knew where she would be, and she felt 'constantly very scared and intensely paranoid', that 'every area of my life was under constant surveillance':[145]

> I remember one occasion when I sat my family and friends down in a room and I accused them of leaking stories to the press as a story had come out that only they had known about. Looking back, it makes me extremely angry that I was forced into being so suspicious of people that I love and care for, and that I had to suffer such feelings of betrayal, especially by those who had done nothing wrong.[146]

The author of the Harry Potter books, J.K. Rowling, became a focus of surveillance simply because of her huge success. In an effort to gain access, a reporter put a note in her young daughter's school bag. As Rowling said, 'It's very difficult to say how angry I felt that my 5-year-old daughter's school was no longer a place of, you know, complete security from journalists.'[147]

Sometimes the surveillance – usually by persons unknown, for purposes only guessed at – had a sense of menace. Labour MP and former minister Tom Watson would change his route home in case someone might be in pursuit, and still obsessively memorises the number plates of unfamiliar vehicles parked outside his house: 'That's what it does to you when you're at the receiving end of the Murdoch fear machine – the threats, bullying, covert surveillance, hacking, aggressive reporting and personal abuse make you permanently wary.'[148]

The stake-outs and harassment have an impact on the targets irrespective of what gets published. Tinglan Hong achieved newsworthiness as the mother of Hugh Grant's baby, and then she and her baby were besieged in their home by photographers and reporters. When her 61-year-old mother took photos of one photographer, he accelerated his car towards her, forcing her to jump out of the way.[149]

These outrageous assaults on privacy were on people who were in – or connected to people who were in – the public eye because of their own activities. The most obviously outrageous acts of surveillance were on people who became newsworthy as victims of crime, or, for example, as relatives of soldiers or victims of terrorism. Here the invasion of privacy, in Leveson's words:

> has caused real hardship and, on occasion, wreaked havoc with the lives of innocent people whose rights and liberties have been disdained. This is not just the famous but ordinary members of the public, caught up in events (many of them truly tragic) far

larger than they could cope with but made much, much worse by press behaviour that, at times, can only be described as outrageous.[150]

It is hard to argue that such offences are not worthy of the intense attention they eventually received. The bribery charges potentially carry greater punishment, but former *Sun* heavyweights, such as political editor Trevor Kavanagh and editor Kelvin MacKenzie, defended them as being in the public interest. MacKenzie believed that 'tip fees' served a public purpose,[151] and equated the police officers receiving bribes with whistleblowers. For MacKenzie the arrests were 'the real scandal'.[152] Deputy Assistant Commissioner Akers told the Leveson Inquiry that one *Sun* journalist had been given £150,000 to distribute to sources, a bit more than the Christmas bottle of whiskey that MacKenzie was likening it to. She also judged that most of the resulting stories involved 'salacious gossip rather than anything that could be remotely regarded as in the public interest'.[153]

The consequences for the 90 people facing criminal charges, several of which potentially involve custodial sentences, are yet to be seen. The wider consequences for the Murdoch empire are even harder to discern. Michael Wolff's dramatic claim in February 2012 that 'an extraordinary corporate death is taking place'[154] may turn out to be true in some respects. Nevertheless, News Corp as a major corporation with interests in television, satellite television, films, pay TV channels and newspapers will surely survive, embodied in one or two or more corporate entities.

There are more questions about its governance arrangements, and the continuing role of Rupert and his children. If Murdoch were a holder of public office, there is little doubt he would have already been forced to resign. But no such democratic process can force him out, as he still controls by far the biggest bloc of voting shares in News Corp. Nevertheless he is not immune from shareholder sentiment. In 2012, the Anglican Church in Australia sold its holdings in News Corp in response to the phone hacking scandal,[155] and the prominent superannuation fund, First Super, also sold out, citing concerns about the company's poor governance and bloated executive salaries.[156] In July 2012, a letter calling on Murdoch to resign was signed by 18 major shareholders, including Connecticut's state pension fund and the UK's Legal and General.[157] Also, there were strong protest votes against James and Lachlan being on the board of News Corp at the October 2011 AGM, with a majority of independent shareholders voting against them.[158]

Because of the scandal, the Murdoch model of governance – a docile board, acquiescent management in thrall to the 'genius' of their CEO, a vision of hereditary succession, and a 'whatever it takes' ethic – is coming under continuing challenge.

13

The roots of scandal

Sometimes the accounts of the internal workings of British tabloids challenge credulity as much as do the stories they publish.

A *News of the World* journalist, Charles Begley, was ordered by his editor, Rebekah Wade (later Brooks), to officially change his name to Harry Potter and dress up as the fictional wizard at news conferences. In Watson and Hickman's words:

> A few hours after the September 11 attacks on the Twin Towers, Begley was rebuked for not wearing his robes and being 'in character' ... Begley went home and later rang in sick with stress.

He stayed home for the next few days, undecided about his future. News editor Greg Miskiw rang him and Begley told him of his disillusion. In a conversation which Begley taped, Miskiw sought to convince him to return with the apparently persuasive line – 'Charles, this is what we do – we go out and destroy other people's lives.'[1]

Even when the key facts are agreed on, scandals remain a political battleground. There are disputes over procedures, over proposed penalties and over proposed policy reforms to prevent future abuses. There are also conflicts over explanations and interpretations. Were the offences aberrations, the work of a few rotten apples (or a single rogue reporter), or did they reflect institutionalised corruption? Unsurprisingly, Murdoch himself claimed, in relation to the phone hacking scandals, that 'the problems were isolated to one part of the company'.[2] He emphasised the relative insignificance of *News of the World* in the total scale of the empire: 'News employs 52,000 people across four continents and generates annual revenues of US$S33 billion.'[3]

In many ways, the phone hacking scandals were a product of the particular subculture of the British tabloids, of that peculiar world where an editor, just after the 9/11 tragedies, could demand a journalist act as Harry Potter. In other ways, though, they are an outgrowth of wider forces in News Corp's structure and culture. As one of Murdoch's most successful editors, Andrew Neil, put it:

> You create a climate in which people think it's alright to do certain things. And I would argue that Rupert Murdoch with his take-no-prisoners attitude to journalism – the end will justify the means, do whatever it takes – created the kind of newsroom climate in which hacking and other things were done with impunity on an industrial scale.[4]

This chapter examines the roots of scandal both in the particular milieu of the Murdoch British tabloids and in the more general organisational ethos created by Murdoch.

The power of one

Michael Wolff said of News Corp: 'No other public company of its size [has ever been] such a singular reflection of one man.'[5] In Murdoch's view, that has been a key to his success: 'You can't build a strong corporation with a lot of committees and a board that has to be consulted at every turn. You have to be able to make decisions on your own.'[6]

Murdoch had this attitude right from the beginning. He became a director of News Limited in October 1953, and, according to one of the other directors, Sir Norman Young, 'by the end of 1954, [the 23-year-old's] ascendancy over the News Board was complete'.[7] By

1959 it was clear that Rupert was 'determined to run the company without any prior consultation with other Directors'. He would tell them what he had done after the event and 'expect them to endorse his decisions'.[8] In Young's judgement he had already shown great ability as a business manager, but equally had shown that he 'was not prepared to work in committee style', and had 'a touch of arrogance'. He wanted 'good henchmen who would obey his orders on major issues without question'.[9]

Ever since, News Corp boards have been notable for their subservience. Peter Gladwin, a long-serving London editor, for example, said he 'was made a director simply to agree with whatever Rupert wanted'.[10] In Michael Wolff's opinion, 'The board – all men, partly because Murdoch believes that women talk too much – may not be the most docile in corporate America, but it is certainly among the most reverential',[11] and as David Carr notes, 'Being a board member of News Corp is not a bad gig; it pays over $200,000 a year and requires lifting nothing heavier than a rubber stamp.'[12]

The directors' passivity became more of an issue in recent years. With the commercially problematic purchase of the *Wall St Journal* and the phone hacking scandals, the directors have been criticised for lack of proper oversight. On the move to buy the *Wall St Journal*, for example, 'As was typical, none [of the directors] objected ... and the following Tuesday the board unanimously approved the offer.'[13] In 2011, a group of News Corp shareholders comprising prominent US banks and investment funds brought a law suit accusing the board of allowing Murdoch to use News Corp as his 'own personal fiefdom'.[14]

News Corp considers nine of its 16 directors independent, yet several of these nine 'owe their careers to' Murdoch, or have 'made millions of dollars making him richer'.[15] The monitoring group Governance Metrics International (GMI) gave News Corp its lowest rating of F, placing it in the bottom 5 per cent of the 5400 corporations it examined, for ESG (Environment, Social and Governance) ratings.[16] (GMI showed more courage than the Australian institution, AMP Capital. It compiled an extensive post-scandal report on News as part of a report on corporate governance which was sent to clients. However, 'a nervous public relations department' removed all reference to News two days before the report was made public.)[17]

Murdoch's domination of his managers and employees is at least as great as of his boards of directors. Bruce Guthrie found that 'in five years at News, I had learned that most senior executives don't do anything without first asking themselves: "What would Rupert think about this?"'[18] Former London *Sun* editor David Yelland said much the same thing in an interview:

> All Murdoch editors … end up agreeing with everything Rupert says but you don't admit to yourself that you're being influenced. Most Murdoch editors wake up in the morning, switch on the radio, hear that something has happened and think: what would Rupert think about this? It's like a mantra inside your head, it's like a prism. You look at the world through Rupert's eyes.[19]

When Alastair Campbell accompanied Tony Blair to Queensland's Hayman Island, and watched Murdoch's speech at the Leveson Inquiry, he found it:

> fascinating, but a bit chilling, to watch all these grown men, and some women, hanging on every word, and knowing that an inflection here or there would influence them one way or the other.[20]

Later, after a meeting with *Sun* senior journalists, who were very right-wing, he was reassured that despite their own proclivities they 'would do what they were told' by Murdoch, and found them 'all a bit Moonie-fied'.[21]

Andrew Neil, who worked for Murdoch for more than a decade, put it most dramatically:

> When you work for Rupert Murdoch you do not work for a
> company chairman or chief executive: you work for a Sun King
> … All life revolves around the Sun King: all authority comes
> from him. He is the only one to whom allegiance must be owed
> and he expects his remit to run everywhere, his word to be
> final.[22]

A Sun King has a highly personal management style, marked by the weakness of formal processes and formal structures. Murdoch detested lengthy meetings and formal strategy sessions. Rather, thought *Wall St Journal* reporter Sarah Ellison, he 'ran News Corp like a small club'.[23] As Bruce Dover notes:

> If you were asked to draw an organisational chart of News Corp,
> it would have Murdoch on top and under him a single straight
> line to everyone else.[24]

As one senior News Ltd insider told Paul Barry in 2012: 'It's a family company. No one thinks they don't work for Rupert.'[25] Whatever their formal position of the moment, they know that this is their fundamental role. Bruce Rothwell – who orchestrated Murdoch's coverage of Australian politics in 1975 – described himself as 'Rupert's handyman'.[26] His 'compliant lieutenants' call one another 'henchmen'.[27]

One means by which Murdoch maintains this centralised control is by moving people around frequently. After a visit from Murdoch there is always considerable 'job shuffling'.[28] Such mobility spread 'the Murdoch values', which included the mantra that no one is indispensable. By uprooting employees from their previous social supports and attachments, they became more dependent on him.

A strategy of managerial instability is often accompanied by destabilisation of those who fall out of favour, and prudent employ-ees know to avoid this. After Guthrie mounted his suit for wrong-ful dismissal, former Herald and Weekly Times colleagues rarely contacted him, and when they did 'it was usually ... from a public telephone box'. When HWT management heard that one colleague who had left the company talked to Guthrie about the paper in unflattering terms, they initially ordered him to refund his payout; they retreated when he employed a lawyer.[29]

According to Harry Evans's account, Murdoch would fire mock pistol shots into the back of the editor of the *Sunday Times*, Frank Giles, through his office window. Once, 'he told Evans with a side-long grin: "I'm just going over to terrorise Frank."'[30] After his own forced resignation, Evans reflected that 'Nothing in my experience compared to the atmosphere of intrigue, fear and spite inflicted on the paper by Murdoch's lieutenants.'[31]

Eric Beecher's career with Murdoch had some parallels with Evans's. When Murdoch had taken over his father's old paper, the afternoon Melbourne *Herald*, in 1987, he lured Beecher away from the editorship of the Fairfax *Sydney Morning Herald* to become its editor-in-chief and editor,[32] saying how he wanted to restore the paper's quality, and praising his new editor's ability. Beecher hired several good staff from Fairfax, so Murdoch was also benefiting from destabilising a competitor.[33]

The paper's circulation did not rise in the way Murdoch had wanted, and Beecher soon found himself out of favour. On a visit to Melbourne, Murdoch reviewed that day's paper with Beecher and Guthrie:

> We had, said Murdoch, created a paper that was intellectual when he wanted only intelligent, and literary when he only wanted well written ... After about 20 minutes, our bollocking was complete. Murdoch had never raised his voice, and was unfailingly polite. But he had flattened us ... It was obvious

what had just happened … Sure enough, we were gone by the following March.[34]

When he first took the job, Beecher thought that Murdoch had changed, but he later discovered that he hadn't.[35] The basic problem, he thought, was that 'Rupert has contempt for those who work for him, and total contempt for those whom he can bend.'[36]

Given the contemporary view of Murdoch's management style as 'calculated terror',[37] it is important to remember that originally many Australian journalists found him a breath of fresh air. In contrast to the stuffiness of the Fairfaxes, the conformity of HWT management and the aggressive bullying of the Packers, Murdoch, affectionately known as the 'boy publisher', had a much more egalitarian and friendly style. David Bowman, later to become a strong critic, recalled that on his first Christmas in Sydney, in 1961, when he knew no one, Rupert invited him to share Christmas dinner with the Murdoch family; he did the same for other employees in a similar situation.[38] When Rod Lever, an executive from Murdoch's early years in Australia, stayed at Cavan, Murdoch's farm, he was astounded one morning when Rupert cooked breakfast and brought it in to him and his wife in their bedroom.[39]

He was particularly good at creating a sense of adventure and teamwork. Murdoch would be there, in his shirt-sleeves, helping launch whatever new against-the-odds venture it was. Moreover, some people then moved with Murdoch to new challenges. Some went from Adelaide to work on his Perth Sunday paper, and then some went on to Canberra or Sydney:

Out of his Adelaide and Perth newspaper cadres Murdoch had formed a small, loyal circle of editorial cohorts who understood and agreed with his inflammatory journalistic style, and whom he could trust to carry it out under his constant goading and supervision.[40]

Later, some moved from one country to another: in accounts from the employees they were displacing, 'Australian' often became synonymous with 'barbarian'.

Murdoch's expansion offered opportunities for his cadres, and many in middle management felt they were also a part of the News success story. As Guthrie put it, 'Sitting at that lunch [in 1987], it was hard not to think for a moment at least that you were at the epicentre of modern media', and could bask in Murdoch's 'reflected glory'.[41] But this sense of loyalty and belonging has a downside. For Wolff, Murdoch 'tends to hire people who are grateful for the chance, who feel they're getting more from life because of him than they would have without him'.[42] Some of these 'lifers' (as Wolff calls them), who have had no significant professional experience except working for Murdoch,[43] are strongly loyal. Guthrie recounted how Rocky Miller, who had been with the company for almost half a century, including eight years as editor of the Sydney *Sunday Telegraph*, was to introduce Murdoch at a Cancún gathering of News Corp executives. Miller became emotional: 'Just before you come up here, Rupert, I want to say one thing, though: you're my fucking hero.' He repeated, 'No, no, you are my fucking hero' before Murdoch gently took the microphone from him.[44]

While good for control, Murdoch's strategies have their costs in organisational quality and functioning. Neil commented that:

> During the 11 years I was editor, Rupert fired or eased out every
> chief executive of real talent or independent mind-set. As a
> result, there is no historic memory at the top … This reflects
> Rupert's general disdain for individuals. He has never expressed
> regret about those he has axed and has repeatedly said that every
> individual can be replaced.[45]

Wolff, in particular, has judged that 'News Corp has been, for most of its history, distinguished by its self-effacing, if not weak, executives',[46] and that Murdoch's 'little band [is] not ready for prime time'.[47] Whether or not this judgement is too sweeping, Murdoch himself has said, 'There may be more brilliant people wandering outside sometimes, [but] you have to favour the people that are prepared and ready to give themselves to you.'[48]

But rating deference above competence can have a substantial cost. Perhaps the outstanding case was when Murdoch fired Adrian Deamer as editor of the *Australian* in 1971. Murdoch's original choice as editor, Maxwell Newton, had failed, and he filled the post-Newton vacuum with Walter Kommer, but Kommer was more inclined to the business side, and asked Deamer to take over as editor.[49] This was an inspired move. Deamer's tenure at the *Australian* is among the most successful editorships, both professionally and commercially, in Australian journalism. Circulation grew substantially, while David Bowman, then at the *Sydney Morning Herald*, recalled how frequently *Herald* 'news conferences began with a sad admission that the *Australian* had found the dimensions in the day's news that everyone else had missed'.[50]

Having rescued a paper that seemed doomed to close did not earn Deamer Murdoch's gratitude, however. Instead he was full of criticisms: Deamer's fatal fault was that he was not sufficiently acquiescent. Murdoch finally said, 'You're not producing the sort of paper I want.' Deamer replied, 'Rupert, I don't think you know what sort of paper you want. So until you do I'll go on producing the paper I want.'[51]

Deamer later said that:

the gist of Murdoch's complaint was that the paper had become too intellectual and too political: 'It was anti-Australian, it preferred black people to white people, it wanted to flood the country with Asians. He complained it took up every "bleeding heart" cause that was fashionable among the long-haired left. It was not interested in the development and progress of Australia.

It criticised the political leaders he supported. It was dull, it was a knocking paper, and it stood for everything he opposed and opposed everything he stood for.'"[52]

According to Shawcross:

[Murdoch] began to worry that he could not depend on Deamer. He was too strong, too independent. As his empire grew, Murdoch felt increasingly that he needed men on whom he could rely ... And thus, over time, he came more and more to appoint rather colorless editors who would not disturb the outposts of empire.[53]

The *Australian* was Murdoch's most visionary gamble, but in firing Deamer for being insufficiently deferential, he inflicted almost terminal damage upon it.

The dismissal of Deamer demonstrated that however egalitarian and friendly Murdoch's personal style often was, it did not betoken any willingness to share power. Rather his approach was uncompromisingly hierarchical. 'When one of my editors tries to prevent me from exercising my rightful domain over a paper, he's gone,'[54] he told Kiernan. When *New York Post* journalists went on strike the year after he bought the paper, he was furious. Their letter to him protested about 'insidious' editorial bias in story selection, and their fear that the *Post* 'is gaining the reputation of being a sheet where facts don't matter'.[55] In a meeting, one senior journalist said to him:

It's our paper too. 'Oh no, it's not,' Murdoch snarled. 'When you pay the losses you can say it's your paper too. It's my newspaper. You just work here and don't you forget it.'[56]

Murdoch's view of the contrasting rights and needs of capital and labour is almost feudal. An employee, no matter how good, cannot rise into the ranks of the owners. Barry Diller, who was already wealthy when he started to work for Murdoch, who had been the architect of News Corp's acquisition of Fox Studio and the launch of the Fox Network, and who had turned both into strong enterprises, which he ran with relatively little interference from Murdoch (although sufficient to irritate Diller)[57] was by 1991 increasingly determined to become a principal, not just an employee. He asked Murdoch if he could become a principal in a real sense, but Murdoch replied that there was only one principal in his company.

According to Neil, 'the semi-autonomous nature of Diller's Fox empire – almost a state within a state – had infuriated Rupert for some time'.[58] Murdoch and Diller, acknowledging the insuperable nature of their conflict, worked out the terms of Diller's departure: a financial settlement of approximately $34 million. Shawcross notes, 'Murdoch was delighted that he would now have Fox to himself.'[59] Later that year other senior executives left, as Murdoch exercised more day-to-day control.[60]

The great irony in this episode is that Diller's experience with Murdoch mirrored that of Sir Keith Murdoch with the owners of the Herald and Weekly Times two generations earlier. In the view of the Murdoch family, Keith built the fortune of HWT, but they never allowed him to acquire a proper share of it. Now Murdoch was doing to Diller exactly what the Murdoch family resented about HWT and Sir Keith.

Neil also felt that Murdoch was prone to jealousy of any employee who built too much of an independent reputation. 'Do not underestimate how much Rupert resents you becoming a public figure in your own right,' one of Murdoch's closest associates warned Neil in 1994.[61] Several years earlier a senior Murdoch manager, Bruce Matthews, when Neil's relationship with his employer was going very well, warned him: 'Don't fall in love with Rupert. He turns on lovers and chops them off.' Neil's view was that 'Rupert does not allow himself to make lasting friendships.' Gus Fischer, another senior News International executive, said 'he cannot afford friends. He has built his empire by using people then discarding them when they have passed their sell-by date.'[62]

A hierarchical and conforming culture

Murdoch asserted his dominance using this combination of concentrated control and a willingness to wield power ruthlessly. Richard Lever, the beneficiary of breakfast in bed at Rupert's farm, was also witness to Murdoch's rituals of domination. He recalled conferences with editors at which Murdoch would go through the pages of a newspaper uttering 'Bullshit' and 'Crap', or 'I've told you over and over and over again not to run this sort of rubbish but you never listen to me. No one ever listens to me.' These conferences, thought Lever, 'were generally a theatrical performance which a psychologist would say demonstrated a desire to dominate. He wanted to rattle people, keep them off balance.'[63]

Neil Chenoweth has similarly commented:

The voice was alternately seductive, endlessly persuasive, or frigidly dismissive. Murdoch was the master of the little politeness, the long silence, the questioning pause, the icy rage. He could inspire remarkable loyalty as well as enormous bitterness.[64]

Perhaps strangely, the people who probably most frequently bore the brunt of Murdoch's bullying were the editors of the *Sun* who contributed so much to building his fortune – Larry Lamb and Kelvin MacKenzie. MacKenzie:

endured almost daily 'bollockings' from the man he always referred to as 'the boss' – a steady stream of transatlantic vituperation and four-letter words was his regular diet for over

12 years, even though he ran a paper which netted his proprietor £70–90m a year. 'He treats the tabloid editors like dirt,' [confirmed] John Dux, who was managing director at Wapping in the early nineties.[65]

There was an element of the bully in this: Rupert ranted at Kelvin and others because he knew he could get away with it – they were prepared to put up with it.[66] MacKenzie once said that if the boss told him to print the paper in Sanskrit he would readily do so.[67]

In public, Murdoch always spoke well of the man he occasionally referred to in private as 'the young Hitler'. He told one interviewer: 'MacKenzie is what he is. He's out there screaming, and he's good. Somehow it works.'[68]

But in private sometimes, Murdoch's calls were the most terrifying of all: 'You're losing your touch, Kelvin. (Pause) Your paper is pathetic. (Pause) You're losing your touch, Kelvin.' Then the phone would go down. After a call like this, life in the office would be hell for everyone.[69]

Although there are substantial cultural differences between the various Murdoch papers in various countries, Murdoch clearly values editors in the MacKenzie mould, such as Col Allan. Nicknamed 'Col Pot' in Sydney, Murdoch moved him to the *New York Post*:

Lack of restraint and decorum is also [Col] Allan's newsroom management style. Not only is he a legendary screamer – the morning news meeting is a daily and by now ritualistic drama of reporters and editors having the shit screamed out of them – he's a deeply disorganised one.[70]

The Leveson Inquiry produced considerable evidence of a very hierarchical workplace where the editor's word was law, and management practices less than enlightened. Ian Edmondson, news editor at *News of the World*, described 'an environment where anyone in the newsroom had to comply with an instruction from the editor'.[71] The National Union of Journalists' submission cited an anonymous journalist who said, 'the *News of the World* was an incredibly tough and unforgiving workplace', and described seeing three or four members of staff collapse in the office at least in part from stress.[72] This view was supported by others such as Sean Hoare (a 'culture of intimidation and bullying'), the defender of phone hacking Paul McMullan ('ruthless') and Matt Driscoll ('anyone on the floor who complained too much [about the techniques] would find themselves pushed out').[73]

Nor is this just a recent phenomenon. Peter Chippindale and Chris Horrie's account of the *Sun* in the 1980s under MacKenzie said that some journalists were told to their face that they had no future in the place, and were then given impossible jobs, huge workloads, and personally insulted. MacKenzie would 'come up to their desks, put his face close to theirs and say, "You still here then, eh? Haven't you gone yet, eh?"'[74] But the result was that when MacKenzie made probably his most commercially disastrous decision, in the coverage of the Hillsborough tragedy (see Chapter 10), his 'dominance was so total there was nobody left in the organisation who could rein him in, except Murdoch'.[75] This hierarchical culture, plus the lack of internal checks and balances, and the valuing of outcome over process, made it hard for dissent to be voiced even as the papers adopted increasingly scandalous practices.

Hubris

After its re-election in 1992, the Major Government was humiliatingly forced to withdraw from the European exchange rate mechanism. The prime minister called *Sun* editor MacKenzie to tell him and to ask how the tabloid planned to cover the story. MacKenzie replied: 'Well, John, let me put it this way: I've got a large bucket of shit lying on my desk, and tomorrow morning I'm going to pour it all over your head.'[76] Clearly the editor of the largest-selling newspaper felt no need to show excessive deference to the elected leader of the country.

As the Murdoch empire grew, its members felt increasingly empowered in their dealings with others. Murdoch has always encouraged a journalism that seeks to place itself at the centre of events: 'Both Fox News and the *New York Post* took a manic delight in their influence.'[77] Paul McMullan gave a sense of the satisfaction that came with apparent influence: 'In a bizarre way, I felt slightly proud that I'd written something that created a riot and got a paediatrician beaten up, or whatever was the case.'[78] He was referring to an infamous episode where the *News of the World*, under Wade, decided to name and shame paedophiles. This was discontinued after some ugly incidents, including one where a paediatrician (confused by a reader with paedophile) was beaten up.

Matt Driscoll observed the same sense of power during his years at News International:

> As a result of this aggressive and grotesque arrogance, those
> in charge – the proprietors and the editors – came to believe
> that they could do and say whatever they wanted and remain
> untouchable ... they felt that they were almost beyond the
> reach of the law ...[and] could leave their morals and their
> respect for ethics at the door when they clocked in each
> morning. The next front page was all that mattered, however it
> was obtained.[79]

Perhaps that tendency was heightened by the backgrounds and rapid rise of those with editorial authority. The change in news priorities inevitably brought a shift in the types of people who achieved internal success. Those covering celebrities often became celebrities themselves, and editors of the *Sun*'s Bizarre column, such as Andy Coulson, Piers Morgan and Dominic Mohan, frequently appeared in pictures with the stars they were reporting on.[80] More seriously, as show business became 'ever more important in shifting copies', journalists from that area were promoted into positions of editorial responsibility:

> In their late twenties and early thirties, [Piers Morgan, Rebekah Wade and Andy Coulson] were pitched into a lucrative, adrenaline-charged whirl, the backseat of chauffeur-driven limousines and – to their delight and surprise – the dining chairs of Downing Street.[81]

They had proved themselves by their energy and enterprise, and frequently also by their ruthlessness and inventiveness, and while their experience with soap operas might seem to equip them for political coverage, it had not prepared them for its real-world consequences. Moreover, the speed of their success and their ambition easily led to arrogance. So, during the disappearance of Milly Dowler, *News of the World*, on the basis of a wrong number on the victim's telephone, thought it knew better than the police what was happening, and wouldn't be convinced otherwise.[82]

Equally, during the first long period of the scandal, when the *Guardian*'s investigative reporting was not evoking any response, Rebekah Brooks remained confident. In public she charged that the *Guardian* was probably deliberately misleading the British public; in private she told colleagues that the story was going to end with *Guardian* editor Alan Rusbridger 'on his knees, begging for mercy'.[83]

The most remarkable example of the hubris at the top of News International came before the 2010 election. The *Independent* had produced a series of innocuous ads, saying 'Rupert Murdoch won't decide this election. You will.' James Murdoch and Rebekah Brooks took umbrage. They arrived unannounced at the newspaper, and James yelled at the editor, Simon Kelner – 'What are you fucking playing at?' Kelner took them into his office, and they left 20 minutes later. Journalists were shocked at the 'bizarre' scene.[84]

My company right or wrong

News Corp has always been 'a company with a chip on its shoulder',[85] aggressively counter-attacking and maligning its critics. This mentality stems directly from Murdoch himself, who has always nursed vendettas and – perhaps more puzzlingly for someone born into such privilege – has always had a strong sense of resentment. Neil Chenoweth thinks that Murdoch has 'a deep wellspring of anger … looking for a target'. He quotes the former head of *New York* magazine and for a time a Murdoch friend Clay Felker, who felt that Murdoch 'feels the world is out to get him'.[86]

According to Kiernan, who was close to Murdoch for over 10 years, 'he is quick to duck blame' when accused of questionable or untoward things. Instead he usually engages in 'an often obscenity-filled diatribe' against 'his absent adversary of the moment'. Typically this focuses not on the point at issue, but 'on the alleged wrongs, stupidities, and character defects of the other person', and is often accompanied by 'promises of retribution'.[87] Such retribution was directed at well-known New York columnist Pete Hamill when he criticised the *Post*'s coverage in 1977. Murdoch retaliated by running excerpts from an unflattering story Hamill had written about Jackie Kennedy many years earlier, knowing that in 1977 Hamill was engaged in a romance with the former First Lady. It was 'self-indulgent on my part', Murdoch told a journalist, 'but I don't apologise for it. People have got to learn.'[88]

Journalism's key ethic is to increase transparency. It is a view publicly endorsed by Murdoch, who testified to the Leveson Inquiry that 'I don't think [politicians are] entitled to the same privacy as the ordinary men in the street. If we're going to have a transparent society, a transparent democracy, let's have everything out in the open.'[89] However, the standard response of News Corp is to cloak its own actions in secrecy. Not only was this its initial response during the phone hacking scandal,[90] but during 2003, when Roy Greenslade was seeking to investigate the unanimity among the Murdoch press on the issue of the Iraq War, no Murdoch editors responded to his calls and emails, producing the paradoxical situation that 'journalists [were] more tight-lipped than soldiers'.[91]

An amusing case of the company's attempts at secrecy came after September 2009, when *New York Post* associate editor, Sandra Guzman, was fired. She claimed that her work environment had changed irreparably the previous February when she criticised a strange cartoon that some said likened President Obama to a chimpanzee. The cartoon prompted a public outcry about racism, and Murdoch made a formal apology. After her dismissal, she filed a complaint alleging harassment, and including many embarrassing claims, including that the Washington Bureau head had told her that their aim was to destroy Obama's presidency. She also maintained that editor Col Allan and others encouraged an internal culture that was sexist, offensive and domineering, and that various decisions were driven by racial prejudice.[92] As part of the larger action, she sought to find out what Murdoch and Allan had said to each other about the public apology for the cartoon.[93] Allan made the novel claim that such conversations should be covered by 'editorial privilege', but the court did not accept this new doctrine.[94]

Confronted by criticism, Murdoch's response is often not to debate its merits, but to recast the issue as 'us versus them'. Throughout the phone hacking scandal, there was the standard Murdoch/News Corp ascription of ulterior motives to all external critics. In a November 2010 speech to British editors, *News of the World* managing editor, Bill Akass, defended his brand of tabloid journalism against the 'snobbish elite', saying that their complaints were 'a kind of proxy for sneering at the working class'. A month earlier, when the *New York Times* had reported its investigation of the phone hacking scandal, he 'sent an indignant letter arguing that the paper had attacked Murdoch's publication because of the *Times'* rivalry with the *Wall St Journal*'.[95] The *Wall St Journal* urged its readers to 'see through the commercial and ideological motives of our competitor-critics'.[96] Murdoch told the parliamentary committee:

> A lot of people had different agendas, I think, in trying to build this hysteria ... All our competitors in this country formally announced a consortium to try and stop us [in the BSkyB bid]. They caught us with dirty hands and they built the hysteria around it.[97]

Behind the public statements had come much more strenuous private efforts. As late as 5 July 2011, when Ed Miliband took what Watson and Hickman judged to be the biggest risk of his political career, and called for Brooks to examine her conscience and consider her position, while calling the phone hacking truly immoral, 'senior Murdoch journalists were furious'. Tom Newton Dunn, the *Sun's* political editor, said: 'We do take it personally and we're going to make it personal to you. We won't forget.'[98] The phrase 'would not be forgotten' had also been used by News International representatives to journalists inquiring about the scandal, and to Chris Bryant when he raised the issue in July 2010 in the House of Commons.[99] When Alastair Campbell did a series of interviews following the *Guardian* story of July 2009, he 'received a series of what [he said could] only be termed threatening text and phone messages from both Rebekah and the office of James Murdoch'.[100]

Politicians were also targeted. In May 2012, Neville Thurlbeck, by then disillusioned with his former employer, said that *News of the World* reporters had spied around the clock on members of the House of Commons' Culture, Media and Sport Committee: 'The objective was to find as much embarrassing sleaze on as many members as possible in order to blackmail them into backing off from its highly forensic inquiry into phone hacking.' It was a plan hatched by News International executives – 'It wasn't journalism. It was corporate espionage.'[101] An earlier member of the committee, Plaid Cymru MP Adam Price, said that after Brooks had refused to appear in early 2010, 'the committee's members had been warned that if they had called Brooks their private lives would be raked over'.[102]

The chief parliamentary critic of phone hacking, Labour MP Tom Watson, was placed under surveillance by *News of the World* journalist Mazher Mahmood (famous as the 'fake sheikh' in some of the paper's 'stings') in the hope of finding him having an affair.[103] After Watson threatened to sue the *Sun* for libel over a series of articles:

> [My] neighbour caught people rummaging through my bins and rustling through papers in my garage. He got one of them in a headlock and demanded to know what he was doing, and the person told him he was working for the *Sun*.[104]

An equally crude approach was taken towards solicitors Mark Lewis and Charlotte Harris, who were working on the civil cases for phone hacking victims. They were placed under surveillance during two periods, with the aim of discrediting them and so damaging their ability to pursue the cases. In early 2010, the News solicitors, Crone and Pike, arranged for this surveillance, wrongly believing them to be having an affair. Pike told Leveson he would do the same again in the same circumstances.[105] They also checked the birth certificates of Harris's two sons to see who was listed as their father.[106]

Perhaps the most brazen and tellingly tribal of all the News International surveillance episodes was of police officer David Cook and his wife Jacqui Hames, a former police officer who now presented the BBC's Crimewatch program. Cook appeared on the program making a public appeal for information in 2002 when they were reinvestigating the 1987 murder of Daniel Morgan, the business partner of Jonathan Rees, who often acted as a private detective for the *News of the World*. The next day Scotland Yard warned Cook that it had picked up intelligence that Rees's current partner, Sid Fillery, had been in touch with Rees's main contact at *News of the World*, who had agreed 'to sort Cook out'. Mulcaire then put them under surveillance. Cook and Hames found vans parked outside their house; both were leased to News International. At a press social event at Scotland Yard in January 2003, Cook and his superior officer approached *News of the World* editor, Rebekah Wade, about the surveillance. Wade replied that the paper was trying to discover whether Hames and Cook were having an affair (they were married). Scotland Yard took no further action either. Hames said the surveillance 'left me distressed, anxious and needing counselling and contributed to the breakdown of my marriage'. She told the Leveson Inquiry she believed that *News of the World* had put her and her husband under surveillance because 'suspects in the Daniel Morgan murder inquiry were using their association with a powerful and well-resourced newspaper to intimidate us and try to ... subvert the investigation'.[107]

These cases are testimony to News International's ruthlessness. But equally they show its *modus operandi* – the best way to refute criticism is to discredit the critic; the substance of what they have said can be ignored if, for example, you can charge that they are having an extra-marital affair. It gives credence to actor Steve Coogan's dramatic comparison of the company to a 'protection racket'. It employs the prospect of negative coverage, he charged, 'as a weapon against those who get in [its] way. ... Be nasty to us ... and you will feel our wrath.'[108] For Wolff:

the fundamental currency of the company has always been reward and punishment. Both the *New York Post* and Fox News maintain enemy lists.

Threats pervade the company's basic view of the world. 'We have stuff on him,' Murdoch would mutter about various individuals who I mentioned during my interviews with him. 'We have pictures.'[109]

Leveson commented that:

a general defensive approach has led to some newspapers resorting to high volume, extremely personal attacks on those who challenge them ... There is a cultural tendency within parts of the press vigorously to resist or dismiss complainants almost as a matter of course. Securing an apology, a correction or other appropriate redress, even when there can be no argument, becomes drawn out and difficult.[110]

One amusing example of just how reluctant Murdoch journalists are to admit error came with the testimony of the *Sun* showbiz correspondent Gordon Smart. In 2009, Chris Atkins made a feature documentary *Starsuckers*, part of which involved feeding fake celebrity stories to the daily tabloids, some of which were published without having been checked. The *Sun* had published two stories concocted by Atkins. One claimed that Guy Ritchie had given himself a black eye while juggling cutlery. But at the inquiry Smart contended, 'Well, I would disagree that they weren't true.' For some time, against all the evidence, he claimed that the two stories, even though they had been made up by the *Starsuckers* team, were factually true, and that he had checked them. Eventually Leveson intervened, 'It would be quite a remarkable coincidence if Mr Atkins invented a story that sounds bizarre and it happened to be true.'[111]

The Leveson Inquiry was unusual in that Murdoch himself was subjected to public cross-examination under oath. Even here he showed his reluctance to acknowledge wrongdoing. Some aspects were predictable: his refusal to give any credit to the *Guardian* for its investigative reporting of the scandal, for example. Similarly, his *ad hominem* dismissal of critics came to the fore when he was asked to respond to the quotation from David Yelland (earlier in this chapter) about Murdoch editors taking on Murdoch's views. He said it was 'nonsense', and should be taken 'in the context of Mr Yelland's very strange autobiography, when he said he was drunk all the time he was at the *Sun*, which we didn't notice'.[112] When it was put to him that in a legal case, the Mosley prostitutes case, Justice Eady had used the word 'blackmail' in relation to a *News of the World* journalist, Murdoch said he didn't know about it, but then seemed to dismiss the incident by saying, 'It's a common thing in life, way beyond journalism, for people to say, "I'll scratch your back if you scratch my back."'[113] When Murdoch was asked about a tribunal finding that Andy Coulson had presided over a culture of bullying, he replied he had never heard of it, and shrugged it off with the comment, 'They always strike me as a very happy crowd.'[114] When further questioned over one journalist's testimony of a bullying culture at the paper, he responded by asking why the complainant hadn't resigned if she had not liked working for his newspaper, which prompted Justice Leveson to intervene: 'I think the problem with that might be that she needs a job.'[115]

An ethics-free zone

Bruce Guthrie discovered that raising questions about ethics was not a wise career move at News Corp. Guthrie, as an associate editor of the Melbourne *Herald*, attended 'a confab in Aspen, Colorado, of [Murdoch's] best and brightest' in June 1988. The news editor of the London *Sun*, Tom Petrie, gave an exuberant presentation on how:

> we don't report the news; we make it ... His presentation was wildly entertaining with its stories of chequebook journalism,

general skullduggery and, ultimately, 'heavy lifting' of rival papers' stories if they were unable to match them. For anyone who took journalism seriously, it was appalling.[116]

At the end, Guthrie asked from the floor, 'Do you have any ethical framework at all at the London *Sun*?' Eric Beecher told Guthrie that Murdoch turned red with anger at the question. Amid the resulting hubbub, Murdoch weighed in directly with, 'I would have thought it's news if the captain of the England cricket team is taking bar-maids up to his room the night before a Test match', referring to a recent *Sun* story.[117] When the session finished, Guthrie saw Mur-doch and his Australian head Ken Cowley in conversation, and Cowley later told him Murdoch said, 'I see we have a Fairfax wanker in our midst.' The following year, after Beecher's departure, Cowley offered Guthrie the editorship of the about to be launched *Sunday Herald*, and foreshadowed a visit to New York, saying, 'It would be good for you to get together with Rupert again because you upset him a bit with that question of yours at Aspen.'[118]

More typical was the response of former *Sun* editor, Kelvin Mac-Kenzie, to the Leveson Inquiry: ethical questions 'were not issues I bothered with. I do hope that this inquiry is not seeking to impose them on print journalists – that would be bloody funny to watch.'[119] He is also alleged to have joked, 'Ethics? as far as I'm concerned that's that place to the east of London where people wear white socks.'[120]

Reading some of the dealings in the Murdoch and other English tabloids, one passes through a looking glass in which none of the normal rules of human decency apply. Kate McCann, mother of a girl who was abducted while the family was on holiday in Portugal, had to endure not only the deep grief of that but also the English tabloid feeding frenzy when the Portuguese police decided for a period that the missing girl's family were persons of interest in the investigation. The police had taken – and then returned – Kate

McCann's diary, in which she kept her personal thoughts and feelings, which she had shown to no one, not even her husband. The *News of the World*, under Colin Myler, obtained McCann's diary, and then without her permission or knowledge published long extracts. She spoke later of the sense of violation she felt as she read her private thoughts and feelings in the tabloid.[121]

Another *News of the World* reporter, Paul McMullan, swindled the source of a story about Robert de Niro sharing a bubblebath with two girls. 'One of [the girls] was foolish [enough] to tell me all about it and give me all the pictures without signing a contract.' The normal fee for such a spread would have been 'ten grand' … [But] we didn't pay her. She was on my back for ages.' However, McMullan got a '750 quid bonus for ripping off the source of the story'.[122]

Former tabloid reporter Richard Peppiatt wrote:

> I cannot remember a single discussion over content that included
> empathetic consideration on the subject of the coverage …
> Consider the *Sun's* front page fascination with 'Britain's Youngest
> Dad' in the spring of 2009. For weeks a boy of 13 and a girl of
> 15 were subjected to the full glare of a tabloid feeding frenzy,
> frothing comment passed on their upbringing, education and
> morality. Was the welfare of these vulnerable teens … given
> consideration?[123]

He told the Leveson Inquiry that he 'would have been laughed out the door' of his newspaper if he had tried to use the Press Complaints Commission editors' code to raise an ethical issue.[124]

The escalation of the dark arts

As Roy Greenslade came to understand at the beginning of his career:

> We [journalists] operated to our own rules ... Living inside the
> journalistic bubble, especially at a time of even greater official
> secrecy and bureaucratic opacity than exists today, inured us to
> criticism.[125]

So, in the belief that they were serving the greater good, adopting
dubious means was justified. Within their own subculture, informal
norms evolved, and although these often ran counter to the official
rules in the wider society, there were recognised limits.

However, suspect means were celebrated even when they were
not serving a democratic purpose: 'The great and the good of popular journalism ... liked nothing better than to tell stories of ethically
suspect escapades.'[126] Murdoch's most celebrated reporter, Steve
Dunleavy, started as a journalist on the Sydney *Daily Mirror*:

> The Sydney competition was so fierce that reporters would do
> anything to get a story – literally anything. I lost count of the
> number of times I posed as a cop, a public servant or a funeral
> director.[127]

According to Australian journalistic folklore, he once punctured the
tyres of his father's car in order to beat him sending photos back
from a story in the Blue Mountains. Dunleavy's defence is that he
knew the car belonged to the rival *Sun* newspaper, but didn't know
his father was at the scene.[128] Murdoch assigned his star reporter to
boost the *New York Post*'s coverage of Son of Sam. When Dunleavy
gained access to one victim's family in a hospital ward – dressed as a
doctor and pretending to be a bereavement counsellor – this clearly
met with Murdoch's approval: he 'chuckled' that it was this kind of
thing that 'gives the young reporters confidence'.[129]

Similarly, according to Chippindale and Horrie's well-informed
account of life at the London *Sun*, MacKenzie liked to be surrounded by 'made men', journalists:

who had proved themselves by pulling off some outrageous
stunt at the expense of the opposition … Hacks refusing to
get involved in this sort of behavior [such as stealing from a
competitor] were suspect – falling into the category of those who
were not fully with him, and could therefore be presumed to be
against him.[130]

Sharon Marshall, in her book *Tabloid Girl*, declared her tribal loyalty:

I'm not proud of everything we did, but I loved the tabloid
journalists I worked with. Every single, double-crossing, devious,
scheming, ruthless, messed up, brilliantly evil one of them.[131]

The problem with informal systems is that they allow private competitive advantage to be equated with larger public purpose. One
consequence of this is that the norms of acceptability do not remain
stable. As the stakes become higher, or as rule-breakers become
more brazen, there are fewer and fewer constraints. Thus, for example, Watson and Hickman note that:

[from] the mid-1990s onwards, the *News of the World* newsroom
… was extreme, even by Murdoch standards. Exhorted by him
to smash its closest competitors, the *People* and the *Sunday Mirror*,
its management fostered an ultra-competitive atmosphere.
Reporter was set against reporter and executive against executive
… Fearful about the consequences of carrying out their orders,
reporters sometimes illicitly taped the briefings they received
from news editors.[132]

So, as Greenslade observed, the phone hacking scandal was not
an isolated incident or an aberration, but the 'culmination of a his-
torical process stretching back many years'.[133] Equally, although
ethically suspect shortcuts may be as old as reporting itself, their

scale and prevalence escalated in response to competitive pressures and personal ambitions. When Jeremy Tunstall did his pioneering survey research on the specialist reporters in Britain in the late 1960s, he found that payments by journalists to sources were largely circumscribed. Of the nine specialist areas of reporting he covered, payments were common only in the fields of crime and football. Payments were small, mainly for tips, and only rarely to police officers or football players themselves. They were most frequently made by the popular papers. Elsewhere there were emphatic denials that paying sources was ever a means of obtaining information.[134] By the early 1990s, however, when Tunstall did another round of interviews with newspaper journalists,[135] he was struck by how much more prevalent talk of payments to sources was.

Others have sought to trace trends in, for example, the number and size of payments to paparazzi. According to Watson and Hickman:

> In the early 2000s, demand soared for stories delving into the private lives of actors, pop stars and TV presenters. Paparazzi pictures which would have fetched £5000 in 2000 made £100,000 in 2005.[136]

The police told Hugh Grant that:

> the paparazzi were increasingly recruited 'from the criminal classes' – who would 'show no mercy, no ethics', because the bounty on some of these pictures is very high.[137]

Publicity agents who mediated between the media and their clients for a fee were another growing industry. In Australia, leading figures have been Harry M. Miller and Max Markson. In Britain, the dominant figure was Max Clifford, who later became a victim of phone hacking. Clifford had been supplying stories to the press for

30 years. He noted that as the competition got fiercer and circulations started to slide, 'the methods became more and more creative'.[138] Even in political coverage, as Nicholas Jones notes, 'the cheque book reigned supreme and the going rate was escalating as a result of the opportunism of the publicist Max Clifford, who dominated the market in kiss-and-tell disclosures'.[139] One of the largest deals involved the *News of the World* paying Rebecca Loos £300,000 in April 2004 for a story on 'Beckham's Secret Affair'.[140] The first time Coulson's *News of the World* won newspaper of the year, 'there was a lot of criticism that the stories were Max Clifford jobs'.[141] But after the paper did a nasty story on one of his clients, Clifford cut his ties with it.

The breaking of rules became more calculated. For example, under Piers Morgan, *News of the World* 'bribed staff on the rival *Sunday Mirror* and the *People* to obtain their news lists', and tried to steal their exclusives:

> On 15 October 1994, [Morgan] sent his cunning new features
> editor, Rebekah Wade, to hide in a toilet dressed as a cleaner
> so she could run back to the *News of the World* from Wapping's
> print works with a copy of [their sister publication] the *Sunday*
> *Times's* serialisation of Jonathan Dimbleby's new book on Prince
> Charles.[142]

Morgan made decisions about breaking copyright solely on a financial basis, not on a legal or moral one. So he stole a copyrighted interview with rugby player Will Carling and his wife. The *Mail on Sunday* explicitly warned him not to, but he 'laughed at the warnings from the *Mail*'. He made the calculation – '£50,000 maximum damages – well worth a front page and two spreads inside.'[143]

So the step from paying moles at competing newspapers or for scripts of *East Enders* in advance[144] to bribing public officials and police officers was more easily made. In 1998 MacKenzie had said,

'If a policeman receives a tip fee for revealing a break-in that should have been reported anyway, that's fine.'[145] In 2003 Rebekah Wade admitted to the House of Commons committee that the tabloid had been paying police officers for stories:

> It was a perfunctory response from a media executive who saw no moral dilemma nor problem with the idea of paying and therefore potentially corrupting a police officer.[146]

Journalism has always encountered closed doors and yet found its way to publicly important information. There has always been some professional admiration for those who, through cultivating sources or other means, served the public's right to know. Sometimes investigative journalism has engaged in breaches of ethics in the cause of the public interest. However, Richard Thomas, of the British Government's Information Office, declared that he hadn't 'seen a whiff of public interest' in the breaches of privacy laws he was investigating.[147] Indeed, many of these stories increased rather than reduced the sum of human suffering. Moreover, unethical means of gathering information, which in matters of great public importance might have been a course of last resort, became instead a means of first resort on matters of no public interest, or in general fishing expeditions. What was illegal and, indeed, abhorrent to most of the public had become the norm inside the tabloid journalistic bubble.

The pirate king and his crew

Murdoch's Chief Operating Officer, Peter Chernin, told a company meeting in 1998, alluding to Nike advertisements featuring basketball star Michael Jordan:

> You know those 'Be Like Mike' commercials? ...We have to be

like Rupert. We have to institutionalise the imagination, nerve and vision he represents.[148]

It is an interesting question how long Rupert Murdoch, as an employee, would last working for Rupert Murdoch. Two senior employees, for a time Murdoch favourites, made employment-ending miscalculations when seeking to be like Rupert.

Stephen Chao, a 36-year-old Harvard MBA, had reached the top of Fox Television in nine years.[149] His success at Fox, including several programs that pushed the boundaries of taste, such as the recently launched *Studs*, had given him prestige inside News Corp. He rejoiced in a reputation for outrageousness: for example, he decorated his office 'with [make-believe] stained diapers and excrement'.[150] At a company gathering in Aspen in June 1992, he was to debate others, including Vice-President Cheney's wife Lynne, about the 'threat to democratic capitalism posed by modern culture'. Chao livened up his talk by having a male stripper nearby taking his clothes off as Chao spoke. Mrs Cheney turned her back. Murdoch was not amused. He sacked Chao that day, and told the gathering, 'It's a terrible thing to see a brilliant young career self-destruct. And it's a bitter loss. But the point is that there are limits.'[151]

Another executive who had a rapid rise but then a rapid departure was Judith Regan: 'Murdoch, who met her in early 1993, took to her right away – and hired her, not least of all, to annoy the people at HarperCollins.'[152] Her imprint, ReganBooks, quickly established itself, earning up to one quarter of HarperCollins's annual revenue, with her mix of titles showing tabloid tastes mixed with right-wing authors.[153] 'She was the perfect demonstration that inside News Corp, if you have Murdoch's nod, you have vast powers of your own.'[154]

She pioneered a new genre, 'fictional biography', in which, for example, it was planned that baseball legend Mickey Mantle would have an affair with Marilyn Monroe. This created some controversy, but much bigger was to come when it became public that she was planning to publish a 'fictional' book by O.J. Simpson about the murder of his wife, to be titled *If I Did It*.[155] The senior levels of News Corp decided not to publish the book, which led to sharp internal conflicts, during which Regan was dismissed. While her departure was as rapid as Chao's, the aftermath was much messier. Both sides made charge and counter-charge. She was accused of making comments about the 'Jewish cabal' at the company,[156] and she counter-charged that Roger Ailes had wanted her to lie in a court case to protect Rudy Giuliani – mayor of New York, Republican presidential hopeful, and close to Murdoch and Ailes. Eventually she secured an out-of-court settlement of US$10.75 million.[157]

Both Chao and Regan thrived by testing boundaries but eventually overstepped, causing Murdoch great embarrassment. On the other hand, Murdoch has often stood by employees who either breach social mores or who are caught in unethical behaviour. Wolff calls these 'Rupert's reprobates'.[158] The alcohol consumption of *New York Post* columnist Steve Dunleavy became legendary, but did not bother Murdoch. Eric Breindel had a career as editor and executive with News Corp, and his hawkish views and strong right-wing connections in Washington helped to make him 'a favourite of Murdoch's' in spite of a background that included a 1983 bust for buying heroin.[159]

Perhaps the most spectacular single incident came in late 2005. Then *Sun* editor, Rebekah Wade, aged 37, and Murdoch had attended a party at the home of Elisabeth Murdoch and her husband, Matthew Freud. After leaving the party she got into a drunken brawl with her husband, Ross Kemp, an actor who played a tough guy in a TV soapie. At 4am, Kemp called the police, terrified of his wife. The police arrested her and she spent eight hours in a cell sleeping it off, while Murdoch waited for her in the office. The other tabloids had fun with the story, especially given that Wade's *Sun* had been campaigning against domestic violence at the time.[160]

Less amusing was when Fox News star Bill O'Reilly was accused of 'brutal sexual stalking and bullying'. The lawsuit, supported by phone transcripts, was settled out of court. Murdoch stood by O'Reilly, who kept his starring role at the network.[161]

Richard Johnson, the editor of the *New York Post* 'Page Six' gossip page, was exposed as accepting bribes and having other ethical shortcomings, as a result of law suits mounted by two disgruntled former journalists, both of whom had been dismissed for ethical derelictions. In their suits for wrongful dismissal, they claimed that editor Col Allan 'was regularly provided with liquor and sex' at a particular strip club. In a clever PR ploy, News Corp used Page Six to air the ex-employees' allegations, admitting some (that Allan did frequent the club) while denying others (saying that his behavior was 'above reproach'). Allan was convinced he would be fired but he survived.[162] Johnson also remained in his job. Indeed, Wolff felt that in some sense it 'actually [seemed] to confirm Johnson's status for Murdoch as an old-time, walk-on-the-wild-side, dangerous, rule-bucking, proudly cynical newspaperman'.[163]

Murdoch is often forgiving to those who have personal weaknesses or commit offences. Apart from any other considerations, those who survive probably become even more psychologically indebted to him. The danger, however, is that an organisational culture condoning unethical practices develops. A dramatic case of this comes not from journalism, but from what one would imagine would be the sedate world of supermarket advertising.

News America Marketing, owned by News Corp, the 'obscure but profitable in-store and newspaper insert marketing business', 'has paid out about $655 million to make embarrassing charges of corporate espionage and anticompetitive behaviour go away'.[164] The cheapest, but perhaps most interesting, involved a small company, Floorgraphics. This was 'a classic American start-up', begun in 1996 to pioneer the idea of decal ads on supermarket floors.[165] It grew quickly. The founders, the Rebh brothers, met the head of

News America Marketing, Paul Carlucci, in 1999, and according to their account in court, he told them that if they wandered into his territory he would destroy them: 'I work for a man who wants it all and doesn't understand anybody telling him he can't have it all.' Years later, investigating what they thought was an underhand campaign against them, the Rebh brothers discovered that News America had hacked into their computer 11 times between October 2003 and January 2004. News America admitted this, but blamed it on a rogue individual whom they could not identify.[166] Floorgraphics mounted a legal case, and eventually News settled for $29.5 million; days later News bought the company.[167] In another case, at the beginning of 2011, News America 'paid out $125 million to Insignia Systems to settle allegations of anticompetitive behavior and violations of antitrust laws'. Its most costly payout was to Valassic Communications in 2010 – $500 million. This settlement was agreed just before the case was due to go to court.[168]

Carlucci used to show the sales staff the scene from the movie *The Untouchables* where Al Capone beats a man to death with a baseball bat. According to testimony by a former employee, Robert Emmel, he told employees uncomfortable with the company's philosophy – 'bed-wetting liberals' – that he could arrange to have them 'outplaced from the company'.[169] Murdoch promoted him in 2005, adding publisher of the *New York Post* to his role as CEO of News America Marketing.[170]

Emmel worked for News America Marketing for seven years, from 1999 to 2006, but, increasingly troubled by some of its practices, he turned whistleblower in his last year there, and became a witness in the Floorgraphics case. He alleged that News America Marketing was engaging in 'criminal conduct against competitors' and using 'deceptive and illegal business practices' to defraud its retailer customers out of money owed. After dismissing him, News filed a lawsuit against him. The court found in Emmel's favour on all counts but one, and even that conviction was overturned by a court of appeal. Originally Emmel's legal costs were paid by plaintiffs in other cases, but this stopped when those cases were settled:

> News Corp has devoted the efforts of up to 29 lawyers to pursuing Emmel personally, at a cost estimated at more than $2 million. Emmel, by contrast, has relied on two lawyers ... working for no pay since January 2009.[171]

A claim by News to cover its legal fees for the breach of contract element of the lawsuit forced Emmel into bankruptcy. Then News demanded further investigations to make sure the bankruptcy was in order. According to Emmel's lawyer, News America has engaged in 'Rambo litigation tactics. They have a scorched earth policy, and it's taken a huge toll on [Emmel].'[172] News Limited in Australia has lobbied in favour of whistleblower protection for public servants,[173] but when it came to a whistleblower in its own company, News Corp opted for the legal equivalent of Al Capone's baseball bat.

❝ ❞

The phone hacking and bribery scandal engulfing News Corp and some of its executives and employees is the biggest media-related scandal in the history of English-speaking democracies. Yet there are still some who minimise its gravity. Former *Sun* editor Mac-Kenzie thought the Leveson Inquiry 'should decide there is nothing wrong with the press'.[174] In public, Murdoch himself has been correct and contrite about the abuses. But in a meeting with *Sun* journalists, secretly taped by three of them,[175] he deplored how they had been 'picked on' by the 'old right-wing establishment' and 'even worse, the left-wing get-even crowd'.[176] Then he denounced the 'incompetent', 'disgraceful' cops for 'the biggest inquiry ever, over next to nothing'.[177] Whatever his personal resentments, however, the scandal will forever colour how Murdoch is remembered and how his career is interpreted. This wilful blindness about the immorality of what was done is one of the roots of the scandal.

It was not inevitable that these scandals occurred in News Corp, but neither is it simply an unfortunate coincidence. These outrages were not the product of a few rogue individuals so much as of a rogue corporation. Of course the great majority of News Corp's 50,000+ employees – and the overwhelming majority of its journalists – are as repelled as the rest of the population by the abuses that have been revealed. However, the scandals were the product of a corporation where power is, perhaps uniquely, concentrated, and where a conforming hierarchical culture makes it difficult for instructions to be questioned or challenged. This is a corporation impatient with any ethical impediments to achieving the results it wants, and which greets external criticism with blanket denial and, often, aggression. And as Murdoch has said, 'For better or worse, [News Corp] is a reflection of my thinking, my character, my values.'[178]

There are still many ready to pay homage. Australian Prime Minister Tony Abbott, on the eve of his election, praised Murdoch fulsomely:

> I've got a lot of time for Rupert Murdoch because, whether
> you like his papers or don't like his papers, he's one of the most
> influential Australians of all time. Aussies should support our
> hometown heroes, and that's what I think, in his own way, Rupert
> Murdoch is.[179]

Murdoch's businesses teetered on the brink of disaster a few times, and included important errors that are sometimes glossed over, but the growth of his career, from a small Adelaide company to a global giant, is still one of the most fascinating corporate careers ever. After the corporate split of 2013, Twenty-First Century Fox is as well placed to meet the challenges of the internet age as any other established media company. It is much less clear how the new News

Corp, which includes the newspaper and publishing side, will fare.

Business success is not the only measure of Murdoch's impact, however. The scandal is evidence that media power corrupts as much as any other power. It is an ingrained habit of mind for us to think of the press as a protector of democracy rather than a threat to it. It is just as much a part of making democracy work better to make media power accountable as it is to make government power accountable. For American journalist Carl Bernstein, 'no other story eluded' the American press as much as that 'of Murdoch's destructive march across our democratic landscape'.[180] Murdoch is the largest employer of journalists in the English-speaking democracies but in many ways lacks sympathy for their professional ideals of impartiality and independent disclosure. He has been more intent on being a political player, and has often wielded power impressively to help his favoured politicians and his own commercial interests. His power, though, has more often diminished rather than benefited the quality of our democratic life.

Notes

Abbreviations

AAP	Australian Associated Press	DT	*Daily Telegraph* (Sydney)
ABC	Australian Broadcasting Corporation	G	*Guardian*
		I	*Independent*
AFR	*Australian Financial Review*	MMFA	*Media Matters for America*
Aust	*Australian*	NYRB	*New York Review of Books*
BBC	British Broadcasting Corporation	NYT	*New York Times*
		WP	*Washington Post*

1 The passing of the Murdoch era?

1. Young p. 146
2. www.ft.com/intl/companies/ft500
3. Shawcross 1997, p. 398
4. Page 2004, p. 329
5. Leapman p. 222
6. Kiernan p. 123
7. Howard p. 378
8. Belfiel et al. p. 1
9. Leapman p. 107
10. Greenslade 2004, p. 587; Brendon 2012, p. 62
11. Belfield et al., p. 34
12. Kiernan p. ix
13. Greenslade 2011
14. Leveson Executive Summary p. 3
15. Leveson p. 510
16. Leveson Executive Summary p. 3
17. Watson & Hickman p. xvii
18. Fallows p. 88
19. McKnight p. 6
20. Curtis 1998, p. 359
21. McKnight p. 118
22. Hawke 1994
23. Howard 2010
24. Price 2012
25. Leveson transcript Murdoch 26-4-2012
26. Sparrow G 15-6-2012
27. Leveson p. 34
28. Belfield et al. p. 132
29. Leapman p. 124
30. Munster p. 193–4
31. Leapman p. 150
32. Curtis 2000, p. 359
33. Munster p. 186
34. Tiffen 1984, p. 164
35. Kiernan p. 64
36. Munster 1985
37. Ellison 2010
38. Glover 2012; Travis 2012; Wallis 2012
39. O'Carroll 2012
40. Ellison p. xxvii
41. Shafer 2008
42. Curtis 1998, pp. 200–03
43. Leapman p. 202
44. Belfield et al. p. 48
45. Kiernan p. 153
46. Gillette *Businessweek* 18-4-2013
47. Chozick *NYT* 22-4-2013
48. Dyer *Crikey* 23-4-2013
49. *Economist* 14-7-2011
50. Myers *Poynter* 28-6-2012
51. Wolff G 28-6-2012
52. Dyer *Crikey* 29-6-2012
53. Beaujon *Poynter* 28-6-2012
54. Greenslade G 2-7-2012
55. Ghosh & Baker *AFR* 24-12-2012
56. Chenoweth *AFR* 30-6-2012
57. Kruger *Age* 18-5-2013

2 Building the empire

1. Hawke 1994, p. 210
2. Younger 2003, p. 344
3. Chenoweth 2002, p. 24

4. Chenoweth 2002, p. 26; Younger p. 348
5. Kiernan p. 47
6. Kennedy pp. 288–9
7. Goot 1979, p. 6
8. Munster p. 60
9. Munster p. 67
10. Hall 1976, p. 43
11. Hall 1976, pp. 44–5
12. Griffen-Foley 1999, pp. 280–1
13. Kiernan p. 81
14. Page 2004
15. Page 2004; Cryle 2008
16. Munster p. 74; Shawcross 1997 p. 59
17. Munster 1985
18. Barry 1993
19. Kiernan p. 139
20. Tiffen 1994
21. Belfield et al. pp. 55–64
22. Chenoweth 2002, p. 44
23. Leapman p. 42
24. Leapman p. 44
25. Kiernan p. 97
26. Munster p. 131
27. Greenslade 2004, p. 213
28. Wolff 2008, p. 124
29. Greenslade 2004, p. 214
30. Greenslade 2004, pp. 157, 215f
31. Kiernan pp. 120, 122
32. Greenslade 2004, p. 250
33. Greenslade 2004, p. 357; Seymour-Ure 1991, pp. 28–9
34. Tunstall 1996, p. 41
35. Halliday 2012
36. Kiernan p. 144
37. Wolff 2008, p. 16
38. Wolff 2008, p. 19
39. Tuccille 1989, p. 46; Kiernan pp. 147–8
40. Tuccille 1989, p. 49
41. Munster p. 160
42. Kiernan p. 194
43. Leapman p. 95
44. Bowman p. 175; Shawcross 1997, p. 98
45. Kiernan p. 303
46. Kiernan p. vii
47. Tuccille 1989, pp. 56, 190
48. McKnight p. 93
49. Shawcross 1997, p. 212
50. Tuccille p. 194
51. McKnight p. 147
52. Wolff 2008, p. 209
53. Kruger *Age* 18-5-2013
54. Tuccille p. 162
55. Walker 1982
56. Leapman pp. 182–3
57. Leapman p. 189
58. Shawcross 1997, p. 132
59. Read 1992
60. Lawrenson & Barber 1985, p. 18; Belfield et al. p. 284f; Greenslade 2004, pp. 376–7
61. Tuccille p. 121
62. Kiernan p. 243
63. Greenslade 2004, p. 470
64. Greenslade 2004, p. 472
65. Crainer p. 12
66. Greenslade 2004, p. 475
67. Chippindale & Horrie p. 205
68. Neil p. 140
69. Neil p. 154
70. Neil p. 185
71. Marjoribanks p. 123
72. Neil p. 186
73. Greenslade 2004, p. 477
74. Leveson Report 2012, p. 101
75. *Herald* 22-11-1979
76. Belfield et al. p. 137
77. Chenoweth 2002, p. 66
78. Chenoweth 2002, pp. 66–7
79. Chenoweth 2002, pp. 80–6
80. Kiernan p. 270
81. Tuccille p. 90
82. Chenoweth 2002, p. 42
83. Munster pp. 256–7; Kiernan pp. 276–9
84. Tuccille pp. 132–3; Wolff p. 186
85. Kiernan p. 272
86. Tuccille p. 142
87. Tuccille pp. 142–3
88. Kiernan p. 304
89. Kiernan p. 133
90. Leapman pp. 60–1
91. Kiernan pp. 134–5
92. Munster p. 142
93. Tuccille pp. 141–4

94. La Monica p. 55
95. Hay *AFR* 15-7-1994
96. Kimmel 2004
97. Tuccille p. 174
98. Tuccille pp. 170–1
99. Belfield et al. pp. 276–7
100. Kiernan p. 298
101. Tuccille p. 223
102. Tuccille p. 198; Belfield et al. p. 232
103. Chenoweth 2002, p. 87
104. Chenoweth 2002, p. 70
105. Belfield et al. p. 291
106. McIlwraith *AFR* 21-12-1990; Hack p. 288
107. Chenoweth 2002, pp. 69–70; Shawcross 1997, p. xx
108. Chenoweth 2002, p. 71
109. Fidler *AFR* 16-4-1991
110. Chenoweth 2002, pp. 71-74
111. Belfield et al. p. 307
112. Peers *AFR* 25-11-1991
113. Chenoweth 2002, p. 120
114. Belfield et al. p. 3
115. Greenslade 2004, p. 559
116. Chenoweth 2002, p. 146
117. Belfield et al. p. 167
118. Chenoweth 2004, p. 94
119. Belfield et al. p. 184
120. Chenoweth 2002, p. 98
121. Chenoweth 2002, p. 98
122. Chenoweth 2002, p. 99
123. Belfield et al. p. 217
124. Rohm pp. 92–7; Wolff 2008, p. 310
125. Chenoweth 2012
126. Shawcross 1997, p. 402
127. Chenoweth *AFR* 30-8-1999
128. Tiffen 2007
129. Belfield et al. p. 326; Dover pp. 6, 26
130. Shawcross 1997, p. 403
131. Shawcross 1997, p. 404
132. Hyland *AFR* 8-3-2005
133. Dover p. 182
134. 'STAR (Greater China)' Wikipedia
135. Crainer p. 15
136. Robichaux p. 183
137. Rohm p. 46
138. Swint p. 172; Robichaux p. 186;
     Chenoweth 2002, p. 147–50
139. Robichaux p. 94
140. Robichaux p. 127
141. Blumenthal & Goodenough pp. 129ff
142. Robichaux p. 265
143. Hack p. 390
144. Rohm p. x
145. Rohm p. 257
146. Rohm p. 234
147. Chenoweth 2002, pp. xi–xii
148. Sorkin & Schiesel *NYT* 29-10-2001
149. Labaton *NYT* 11-10-2002
150. La Monica pp. 130–3
151. La Monica p. 72
152. Kirk & Edgecliffe-Johnson *FT* 22-7-2011
153. Kirk & Edgecliffe-Johnson *FT* 22-7-2011
154. Potter *AFR* 5-5-2011
155. Holgate *AFR* 11-5-2012; Chozick *AFR* 24-1-2012
156. Dover pp. 271–2
157. Dover p. 299
158. Wolff p. 38
159. Sykes *AFR* 27-10-2004
160. Wolff p. 39
161. Wolff pp. 119–20
162. Chessell *AFR* 20-6-2012
163. *BBC News* 11-8-2011
164. Watson & Hickman p. 64
165. Dyer *Crikey* 9-8-2012; Chenoweth *AFR* 25-2-2009; Chessell 2011b
166. Crainer pp. 97–8
167. Maney pp. 173, 177, 179
168. Beaujon 4-3-2013

3 Midas of the media

1. Kiernan p. 21
2. Shawcross 1997, p. 40
3. Kiernan p. 51
4. Greenslade 2004, p. 216
5. Munster p. 3
6. Brendon 2012, p. 30
7. Greenslade 2004, p. 337
8. Leapman p.57
9. Leapman p. 57
10. Wolff 2008, p. 132
11. Shawcross 1997, p. 79

12. Page 2003, p. 83
13. Chippindale & Horrie p. 24
14. Chippindale & Horrie p. 41
15. Chippindale & Horrie p. 29
16. Greenslade 2004, p. 250
17. Greenslade 2004, p. 250
18. Rooney 2000, p. 103
19. Brendon 2012, p. 30
20. Chippindale & Horrie p. 32
21. Menadue p. 95
22. Chippindale & Horrie p. 16
23. Lisners p. 92
24. Leapman p. 59
25. Wolff 2008, p. 133; Chippindale & Horrie p. 12
26. Brendon 2012, p. 31
27. Chippindale & Horrie p. 40
28. Greenslade 2004, p. 251
29. Wolff 2008, p. 205
30. Leapman p. 121
31. Belfield et al. p. 247
32. Perez-Pena *NYT* 8-5-2008
33. Wolff 2008, p. 200
34. Bowman p. 100
35. Leapman p. 213
36. Brendon 2012, p. 27
37. Shawcross 1997, p. 304
38. Auletta 2003, p. 275
39. Watson & Hickman p. 13
40. MacKenzie 2005, p. 73
41. Guthrie p. 11
42. Guthrie p. 12
43. Wolff 2008, p. 306
44. Chenoweth 2002, pp. 232–3
45. Conn G 15-6-2012
46. Wolff 2008, p. 305
47. La Monica p. 55
48. Crainer p. 42
49. Andrews p. 240
50. Chenoweth 2002, p. 234
51. Wolff 2008, p. 304
52. Collins *AFR* 14-2-2002
53. Chenoweth 2002, p. 235
54. Real p. 352
55. Real p. 340
56. Andrews p. 240
57. Wolff 2008, p. 186
58. Young 1991, p. 143
59. La Monica pp. 123–4
60. Chenoweth 2002, p. 231
61. Chenoweth *AFR* 7-7-2001
62. Kiernan p. 50
63. Greenslade 2004, p. 219
64. Tuccille p. 58
65. Leapman p. 126
66. Crainer p. 2
67. Wolff 2008, pp. 16, 34
68. Wolff 2008, pp. 130, 126
69. Wolff 2008, p. 298
70. Leapman p. 14
71. Ellison p. 63
72. Dover p. 127
73. Wolff 2008, p. 151
74. Wolff 2008, p. 390
75. Wolff 2008, p. 180
76. Crainer p. 9
77. Wolff 2008, p. 148
78. Wolff 2008, pp. 155, 157
79. Wolff 2008, p. 143
80. Dover p. 40
81. Wolff 2008, p. 187
82. La Monica p. 49
83. Crainer p. 134
84. Dover p. 12
85. Kimmel p. 151
86. Kennedy p. 287; Tuccille p. 42
87. Brendon 2012, p. 45
88. Thomas & Litman 1991
89. Brendon 2012, p. 38
90. Crainer p. 66
91. Chenoweth 2002, p. 93
92. Dover p. 3
93. Leapman p. 240
94. Tuccille p. 118
95. Wolff 2008, p. 115
96. Wolff 2008, p. 5
97. Crainer p. 93
98. Chenoweth 2002, p. 204
99. Kiernan p. 219
100. Leapman p. 247
101. Tuccille 1989, p. 92
102. Fallows 2003, p. 85
103. Leapman p. 127
104. Munster p. 188
105. Munster p. 188
106. Bowden *Atlantic* July/August 2008
107. Ellison 2010, p. xviii
108. Greenslade 2004, p. 590

109. Chenoweth 2002, p. 279
110. Greenslade 2004, pp. 558–62
111. Dover p. 122
112. Ahmed & Thompson *AFR* 14-10-2010
113. Riddell *AFR* 1-11-2010
114. Chenoweth 2002, pp. 147–50
115. Chenoweth 2002, p. 203
116. Robichaux p. 102
117. Robichaux p. 94
118. Robichaux pp. 86, 182
119. Robichaux pp. 93, 111
120. Wolff 2008, p. 375
121. Osborne *Daily Telegraph* (UK) 22-1-2010; Dyer *Crikey* 22-1-2010
122. Deans & Tryhorn *G* 8-2-2010
123. Ricketson *Age* 30-7-2008

4 Midas's lost touch

1. Wolff 2008, p. 351
2. Chenoweth *AFR* 3-5-2012
3. Lachapelle et al. *Bloomberg News* 18-7-2011
4. Kiernan p. 94
5. Wolff 2008, p. 151
6. Mayne *Crikey* 18-1-2011
7. Crainer p. 115
8. Wolff 2008, p. 8
9. Dover p. 18
10. Dover p. 22
11. Dover p. 21
12. Dover p. 53
13. Dover pp. 31–2
14. Dover p. 178
15. Rohm p. 261
16. Dover pp. 62ff
17. Dover p. 291
18. Dover p. 224
19. Dover p. 161
20. Dover p. 171
21. Dover p. 165
22. Dover pp. 44, 243
23. Dover p. 243
24. Dover p. 244
25. Dover p. 257
26. Dover pp. 261–2
27. Dover p. 253
28. Dover p. 181
29. Dover p. 179
30. Wolff 2008, p. 329
31. Dover p. 70
32. Crainer p. viii; Rohm p. 245
33. Hack p. 378
34. Rohm p. 235
35. Dover p. 188
36. Dover pp. 194–5
37. Rohm pp. 244–5
38. Crainer p. 95
39. Luft *G* 17-11-2008
40. Crooke *Crikey* 8-11-2011
41. Rohm p. 257
42. Rohm p. 108
43. Aylmer *AFR* 12-11-2005
44. La Monica p. 166
45. La Monica pp. 6–7
46. La Monica p. 163
47. *BBC News* Business 11-8-2011; Shoebridge *AFR* 30-6-2011
48. Chenoweth *AFR* 5-2-2011
49. Wolff *AFR* 7-1-2013
50. Kohler *Crikey* 9-4-2010
51. Ellison p. 24
52. *Economist* 21-7-2011
53. Chenoweth 2002, p. 107
54. Sloan *CNN Money* 24-2-2011
55. Rushton *AFR* 25-8-2012; Watson & Hickman p. 162
56. Sweney *G* 5-9-2012
57. Chessell *AFR* 30-6-2012
58. Chenoweth *AFR* 16-9-2004
59. Chenoweth *AFR* 13-4-2004
60. Chenoweth *AFR* 26-8-2005
61. Chenoweth *AFR* 18-2-2011
62. Chenoweth *AFR* 3-11-1993
63. Guy *AFR* 22-10-2007
64. Aylmer *AFR* 13-11-2004
65. Wolff 2008, p. 39
66. Toohey *AFR* 8-10-2005
67. Kohler *The Age* 13-8-2005
68. Chenoweth *AFR* 1-8-2005
69. Chenoweth *AFR* 31-1-2004
70. La Monica pp. 140–1
71. Chenoweth *AFR* 13-8-2005
72. La Monica p. 142
73. Chenoweth *AFR* 27-1-2004
74. Wolff 2008, p. 119
75. Wolff 2008, p. 120
76. www.statista.com/statistics/195726/

revenue-of-directv-since-2006/
77. McKnight pp. 31, 39, 136, 149, 191ff
78. McKnight p. 26
79. La Monica p. 23
80. McKnight p. 34
81. Tuccille p. 6
82. Chenoweth 2002, p. 144
83. Wolff 2008, p. 209; Chenoweth *AFR* 5-2-2011
84. Wolff 2008, p. 208
85. Leveson 2012, p. 107
86. Wolff 2008, p. 57
87. Ellison p. 107
88. MacMillan *Reuters* 6-2-2009
89. Ellison pp. 108, 72
90. Wolff 2008, p. 120
91. Wolff 2008, p. 392
92. Brendon 2012, p. 57

5 From Lenin to Palin

1. Chenoweth 2002, p. 21
2. Shawcross 1997, p. 78
3. Kiernan pp. 22–7
4. McKnight pp. 52, 47
5. Kiernan p. 79
6. Kiernan p. 132
7. McKnight p. 70
8. Cryle 2008, pp. 185–6; Munster p. 88
9. *Australian* 30-4-1965
10. Cryle p. 190
11. Cryle p. 206
12. Cryle p. 218; Freudenberg pp. 327ff
13. Greenslade 2004, p. 457
14. Kiernan pp. 167–8
15. McKnight p. 119
16. McKnight pp. 132–6
17. Neil p. 166
18. Neil p. 166
19. Crainer p. 117
20. McKnight p. 119
21. Wolff 2008, p. 2
22. Crainer p. 119
23. Wolff 2008, p. 122
24. McKnight p. 128
25. Welch *Age* 2-1-2012
26. Griffiths *Reuters* 21-4-2012
27. Griffiths *Reuters* 21-4-2012
28. Mayne *Crikey* 6-2-2012
29. Mayne *Crikey* 6-2-2012
30. *Hollywood Reporter* 10-1-2013
31. *Hollywood Reporter* 10-1-2013
32. Macmillan *SMH* 14-10-2012
33. Macmillan *SMH* 14-10-2012
34. *Hollywood Reporter* 10-1-2013
35. AAP *Daily Telegraph* 31-1-2012
36. Wheatcroft *NYRB blog* 14-3-2012
37. *Hollywood Reporter* 10-1-2013
38. Ellis *The Global Mail* 17-10-2012
39. Simpson *SMH* 29-3-2012
40. Simpson *SMH* 29-3-2012
41. Fickies *The Daily Beast* 18-11-2012
42. Murphy *Christian Science Monitor* 18-11-2012
43. *Hollywood Reporter* 10-1-2013
44. Beinart *The Daily Beast* 18-12-2012
45. Brendon 2012, pp. 33, 35
46. Brendon 2012, p. 35; Chippindale & Horrie p. 72
47. Evans 1983, p. 288
48. Shawcross 1997, p. 141
49. Belfield et al. p. 43
50. Munster p. 203
51. Neil p. 169
52. Cryle pp. 217–18
53. McKnight p. 77
54. Neil p. 168
55. McKnight p. 91
56. McKnight p. 90
57. Wolff 2008, p. 271
58. Brendon 2012, p. 41
59. McKnight pp. 190, 207, 210; Greenslade 2004
60. Wolff 2008, pp. 271, 309, 259
61. Kiernan pp. 27–8
62. Menadue p. 89

6 The enthusiastic player

1. Menadue p. 90
2. Chenoweth *AFR* 12-4-2003
3. Crainer p. 119
4. Kennedy p. 294
5. Munster pp. 2–3
6. Brendon 2012, p. 39
7. McKnight p. 80
8. Curtis 2000, p. 177

9. Wolff 2008, p. 269
10. Stephens 1982, p. 44
11. Hack p. 133
12. Hack p. 133
13. Rich *New York* 31-7-2011
14. Kennedy p. 295
15. Kiernan p. 209
16. Dunstan 1981, p. 61
17. Munster p. 64
18. Souter 1981, p. 380
19. Calwell 1972, p. 93
20. Munster p. 71
21. McKnight p. 57
22. Munster pp. 82–3
23. McKnight p. 58
24. Ramsey pp. 338ff
25. Page 2003, pp. 116–19
26. Oakes & Solomon p. 275
27. Munster p. 99
28. Menadue pp. 110–11
29. Freudenberg 1977, p. 236
30. Page 2003, p. 160
31. Menadue pp. 113–14
32. Munster pp. 104–5
33. Kiernan p. 168
34. Dorling *Age* 20-5-2013
35. McKnight p. 65
36. Hocking pp. 46–7
37. Hocking pp. 47–8
38. Kiernan p. 142
39. Griffen-Foley 2003, p. 188
40. Menadue p. 108
41. Munster p. 95; Menadue p. 109
42. Menadue p. 109
43. Munster p. 101
44. Menadue p. 112
45. Hocking p. 187
46. Leapman pp. 50–3
47. Wolff 2008, p. 127
48. Auletta PBS documentary
49. Horne p. 64
50. Munster p. 111
51. Leapman p. 67
52. Kiernan p. 174
53. Lloyd p. 291
54. Kiernan p. 172
55. Munster p. 110
56. Leapman p. 70
57. Munster p. 108

58. Chadwick p. 217
59. Cohen *WP* 18-7-2011
60. Bagehot *Economist* 22-11-2003
61. Wolff 2008, p. 396
62. Kiernan p. 140; Wolff 2008, p. 267
63. Australian Electoral Commission
64. Leapman p. 141
65. Tuccille pp. 7, 42
66. Goot 1978; Tiffen 1994, p. 333
67. Kelly 1995, p. 244
68. McAllister et al. pp. 277–8
69. Goot 1983, pp. 206, 205
70. Tiffen 1989, p. 150
71. Ramsey p. 80

7 The passionate player

1. Munster pp. 136–7
2. Munster p. 147
3. Munster p. 148
4. McKenzie & Silver 1968
5. Chippindale & Horrie pp. 48–51
6. Greenslade 2004, p. 252
7. Chippindale & Horrie p. 60
8. McKnight p. 169
9. Greenslade 2004, p. 543
10. Chippindale & Horrie p. 140
11. Curtis 1998, p. 359
12. Page 2003, p. 358
13. Page 2003, p. 373
14. Young 1989, p. 454
15. Young 1989, p. 432
16. Page 2003, p. 377
17. Page 2003, p. 378
18. Kiernan p. 319
19. Young 1989, p. 437
20. Page 2003, p. 382
21. Kiernan p. 320
22. Kiernan pp. 285–7
23. Page 2003, p. 387
24. Belfield et al. p. 105
25. Page 2003, pp. 390–1
26. Tempest *G* 12-1-2006
27. Greenslade 2004, p. 550
28. Chippindale & Horrie p. 359
29. Greenslade 2004, pp. 548–9
30. Greenslade 2004, pp. 606–611
31. Curtis 1999, p. 3
32. Greenslade 2004, p. 612
33. Greenslade 2004, pp. 616–8;

Tumber 2004
34. Kiernan p. 144
35. Schudson 1993, p. 104
36. Bernstein & Woodward WP 9-6-2013
37. Wolff 2008, p. 266
38. Wolff 2008, p. 267
39. McKnight p. 68
40. Kiernan p. 145
41. McKnight p. 76
42. Kiernan p. 260
43. Belfield et al. p. 85
44. McKnight & Hobbs p. 846
45. Neil p. 172
46. Young 1989, p. 350
47. Kiernan p. 287
48. McKnight p. 78
49. McKnight pp. 73–5
50. Kiernan p. 288
51. McKnight p. 82
52. Ellison p. 23
53. McKnight p. 42
54. Ellison p. 173
55. Chenoweth 2002, pp. 209–211; McKnight p. 144; Wikipedia 'Pat Robertson controversies'
56. McKnight p. 144
57. Curtis 2000, p. 36
58. McKnight pp. 145, 190–197
59. Shawcross 1997, p. 141
60. McKnight p. 106
61. Wolff 2008, p. 250
62. Ellison p. 116
63. Ellison p. 139
64. Tunstall 1996, pp. 240, 247
65. McNair 2000, pp. 141–2; Tunstall 1996
66. McNair p. 142

8 The dominant player

1. Brendon 2012, p. 55
2. Adley G 14-5-2012
3. Watson & Hickman p. 78
4. Massie Foreign Policy 13-7-2011; O'Carroll G 17-5-2012
5. Leveson 2012, p. 1188
6. Hack pp. 375–6
7. Ramsey p. 353
8. Williams AFR 7-10-2012
9. Littlemore 2003
10. Lewis AFR 4-12-1999
11. Chenoweth AFR 14-7-2006
12. Grattan 2006
13. McKnight p. 178
14. Tunstall 1996, p. 253
15. Greenslade 2004
16. Leveson p. 105
17. Greenslade G 7-3-2005
18. Leveson transcript 25-4-2012
19. Ramsey p. 357
20. Neighbour p. 24
21. Daily Telegraph editorial 5-8-2013
22. Tiffen 2007
23. Shawcross Time 3-11-1999
24. Murdoch 2008
25. Greenslade 2004, p. 620
26. Price 2005, p. 86
27. McSmith 2005
28. McKnight pp. 176, 182
29. Greenslade 2004, p. 662
30. McKnight & McNair 2012, p. 7
31. Manne 2005, p. 76
32. Lusetich Australian 10-4-2003
33. McKnight pp. 36-7
34. McKnight & McNair p. 12
35. McKnight p. 198
36. McKnight p. 199
37. McKnight p. 202
38. Manne 2011, p. 18
39. McKnight p. 189
40. Auletta 2003, p. 260
41. McKnight p. 200
42. Wolff 2008, p. 213
43. McKnight & McNair p. 9
44. McKnight p. 202
45. McKnight & McNair p. 12
46. McKnight & McNair p. 16
47. Manne 2005, p. 86
48. Manne 2011, p. 23
49. Manne 2005, p. 82
50. Manne 2011, p. 18
51. McKnight p. 203
52. Manne 2011, p. 22
53. Sheridan Australian 26-4-2003
54. Wheatcroft NYRB Blog 21-3-2012
55. Schultz 1998, p. 25
56. Leveson 2012, p. 1196
57. The Sun 28-8-2009

58. Roshco p. 23
59. Wright *Age* 15-7-2011
60. Keane *Crikey* 11-5-2011
61. Holmes *ABC Media Watch*, May 2011
62. Carswell *DT* 11-5-2011
63. Howard p. 157
64. Cryle p. 313
65. Tiffen 1999
66. Costello with Coleman p. 281
67. Hartcher *Age* 21-11-2009
68. Thompson *ABC News* 18-7-2011
69. Crook *Crikey* 26-6-2013
70. Thompson and staff *ABC News* 20-7-2011
71. Hywood *SMH* 29-7-2013
72. Barker *Inside Story* 18-7-2011
73. Hartcher *SMH* 21-11-2009
74. Wallace *AFR* 10-6-1994

9 Reaping the rewards

1. Shawcross 1997, p. 62–3
2. Leveson transcript 25-4-2012
3. Leveson transcript 25-4-2012
4. Watson & Hickman p. 172
5. Kiernan p. 311
6. Price G 1-7-2006
7. Leapman p. 239
8. Hack p. 329
9. Page 2003, p. 1
10. Leveson p. 1432
11. Shawcross 1997, p. 113
12. Leveson p. 1233
13. Shawcross 1997, p. 124
14. Leveson transcript 25-4-2012
15. Leveson 2012, p. 1241
16. Belfield et al. p. 81
17. Leveson 2012, p. 1121
18. Belfield et al. p. 81
19. Leveson 2012, p. 1243
20. Page 2003, p. 271
21. Shawcross 1997, p. 129
22. Page 2003, p. 262
23. Brendon 1982, p. 247
24. Page 2003, p. 273
25. Leveson transcript 25-4-2012
26. Ellison p. xxvii
27. Leveson transcript 25-4-2012
28. Greenslade G 13-12-2012;
    O'Carroll G 12-12-2012
29. Shawcross 1997, p. 341
30. Giles pp. 215–6
31. Belfield et al. p. 85
32. Evans 2009, p. 437
33. Kiernan p. 241
34. Munster p. 235
35. Page 2003, p. 314
36. Leapman p. 224
37. Leapman p. 226
38. Kiernan p. 244
39. Evans 1983, p. 395
40. Sabbagh & O'Carroll G 17-5-2012
41. Evans 2009, p. 440
42. Evans 1983, p. 401
43. Evans 1983, pp. 441, 402
44. Belfield et al. p. 37
45. Shawcross 1997, p. 254
46. Greenslade 2004, p. 482
47. Page 2003, p. 269
48. Goodwin pp. 46–7
49. Goodwin p. 44
50. Goodwin p. 48
51. Shawcross 1997, p. 301
52. Goodwin p. 48
53. Goodwin p. 51
54. Goodwin p. 51
55. Belfield et al. p. 186
56. Belfield et al. p. 189
57. Shawcross 1997, p. 342
58. Goodwin p. 51
59. Shawcross 1997, p. 303
60. Shawcross 1997, p. 344
61. Goodwin p. 52
62. Belfield et al. p. 211
63. Goodwin p. 51
64. Belfield et al. p. 212
65. Shawcross 1997, p. 354
66. Shawcross 1997, p. 343
67. Shawcross 1997, p. 355
68. Shawcross 1997, p. 355
69. Goodwin p. 52
70. Toynbee G 3-1-2012
71. Goodwin p. 52
72. Chenoweth 2002, p. 343
73. Goodwin p. 53
74. Shawcross 1997, p. 401
75. Neil p. 248
76. Kiernan p. 301

77. Shawcross 1997, p. 241
78. Chadwick p. 11
79. Barry 1993, pp. 322–3
80. Bowman p. 24
81. Tiffen 1994, pp. 330–5
82. Bowman p. 21
83. D'Arcy p. 94
84. D'Arcy p. 40
85. D'Arcy p. 125
86. D'Arcy pp. 1–2
87. D'Arcy pp. 97–8
88. Carroll 1990, p. 68
89. Chadwick p. 36
90. Shawcross 1997, p. 244
91. Chadwick p. 23
92. Chadwick p. 36
93. Bowman p. 26
94. Chadwick p. 47
95. Page 2003, p. 408
96. Brendon 2012, p. 25
97. Tiffen 1995, pp. 29–31
98. Chadwick p. 204
99. Chadwick p. 206; Lee Report pp. 258–9
100. Hywood AFR 13-12-1985
101. Lee Report pp. 258–9
102. Tiffen 1987
103. Tiffen 1995, p. 25
104. Carroll 1990, p. 61
105. Fraser & Simons, pp. 291–2
106. Belfield et al. p. 143
107. Carroll p. 93
108. Belfield et al. p. 154
109. 'Announcement by the Board of Directors of News Limited' 22-1-1987
110. Australian Broadcasting Tribunal 27-1-1987, pp. 5–6
111. Chadwick p. 98
112. Senate Select Committee 1994
113. Given 2002, p. 253
114. Chadwick p. 97
115. Chadwick p. 95
116. Chadwick p. 92
117. Belfield et al. p. 141
118. Noam, Eli (ed.) 2013 forthcoming
119. Belfield et al. p. 160
120. Chadwick p. 176
121. Chadwick p. 188
122. Chadwick p. 117
123. Walsh SMH 23-4-1987
124. Tiffen 1994, pp. 335–6
125. Leveson 2012, p. 1134
126. Leveson 2012, p. 1135
127. Leveson 2012, p. 1137
128. Watson & Hickman p. 7
129. Campbell p. 79
130. Campbell p. 369
131. Leveson 2012, p. 1139
132. Lister I 28-5-2012
133. Leveson 2012, p. 1137
134. Goodwin p. 143
135. Goodwin p. 148
136. McKnight p. 172
137. McKnight p. 174
138. Goodwin p. 152
139. Barnett 2012, p. 352
140. O'Carroll G 14-5-2012
141. Dover p. 178
142. Watson & Hickman p. 7
143. Price G 1-7-2006
144. Price G 1-7-2006
145. Price 2005, p. 13
146. Chenoweth 2002, pp. 271–3; Leveson Murdoch witness statement p. 25; Leveson transcripts 25-4-2012
147. Brendon 2012, p. 55
148. Leveson 2012, pp. 1146–7
149. Watson & Hickman p. 7
150. Larsen & Grice I 10-4-1999; Gibson & Watt G 10-4-1999
151. 'Murdoch 0, Football 1' G 10-4-1999
152. Larsen & Grice I 10-4-1999
153. Price 2005, p. 95
154. Barnett 2012, p. 353
155. Brendon 2012, p. 56
156. Barry Crikey 12-7-2012
157. Leveson Report p. 1450
158. Belfield et al. p. 115
159. Rohm p. 30
160. Shawcross 1997, p. 216
161. Wolff 2008, p. 125
162. Page 2003, pp. 126–7; Munster pp. 139–41
163. Kiernan p. 189
164. Kiernan p. 237

165. Page 2003, pp. 343–4
166. Leapman p. 128; Munster p. 189
167. Ellison p. 206
168. Wolff 2008, p. 233
169. Ellison p. 145
170. Kiernan, p. 238
171. McKnight p. 4

10 The market for truth

1. Carlyon p. 1
2. Schultz 1994
3. Kiernan p. 122
4. Ellison p. 186
5. Belfield et al. p. 254
6. Kiernan p. 254
7. Shawcross 1997,p. 193
8. Tuccille p. 29
9. Leapman p. 77
10. Shawcross 1997, p. 82
11. Bowman p. 88
12. Shawcross 1997, p. 279
13. Kiernan pp. 254–5
14. Chippindale & Horrie p. 148
15. Chippindale & Horrie p. 179
16. Page 2003, p. 153
17. Page 2003, p. 135
18. Shawcross 1997, p. 421
19. Greenslade 2004, p. 422
20. Greenslade 2004, p. 657
21. Shawcross 1997, p. 151
22. Chippindale & Horrie p. 116
23. Chippindale & Horrie p. 114
24. Chippindale & Horrie p. 115
25. Munster p. 245
26. Chippindale & Horrie pp. 118–9; Munster p. 333
27. Chippindale & Horrie p. 121
28. Kiernan p. 68
29. Leapman p. 30
30. Chippindale & Horrie p. 332
31. Leapman p. 105
32. Leapman p. 106
33. Shawcross 1997, p. 102
34. Page 2003, p. 218
35. Kiernan p. 202
36. Page 2003, p. 217
37. Shawcross 1997, p. 102
38. Page 2003, p. 221
39. Kiernan p. 204
40. Davies *Open Democracy* 7-7-2011
41. Chippindale & Horrie p. 178
42. Chippindale & Horrie pp. 166–7
43. Chippindale & Horrie pp. 321–2
44. Chippindale & Horrie p. 179
45. Chippindale & Horrie p. 302
46. Chippindale & Horrie pp. 149, 152
47. Chippindale & Horrie p. 150
48. Leveson Executive Summary p. 10
49. Marsh 2012
50. Page 2003, p. 215
51. Leapman p. 92
52. Kiernan p. 200
53. Kiernan p. 262
54. Kiernan p. 263
55. Lewis 2011
56. Chippindale & Horrie p. 106
57. Yelland *Mail Online* 27-3-2010
58. Chippindale & Horrie p. 181
59. Greenslade G 7-9-2007
60. Chippindale & Horrie p. 255
61. Bloomberg *Age* 10-1-2012
62. Chippindale & Horrie p. 260
63. Brendon 2012, p. 31
64. Chippindale & Horrie p. 269
65. Chippindale & Horrie p. 268
66. Munster pp. 248–9
67. Knightley p. 143
68. Evans 1983, p. 403
69. Kiernan p. 247
70. Kiernan p. 247
71. Giles p. 241
72. Evans 1983, p. 404
73. Giles p. 242
74. Page 2003, p. 77
75. Brendon 2012, p. 22
76. Belfield et al. p. 252
77. Chippindale & Horrie p. 170
78. Tiffen 1989
79. Chippindale & Horrie p. 46
80. Chenoweth 2002, p. 199
81. Brookes *Mother Jones* 24-8-1998
82. Gutstein *rabble.ca* 26-7-2011
83. Chippindale & Horrie p. 325; *Sun* 17-11-1989
84. Chippindale & Horrie p. 181
85. Page 2003, p. 206
86. Page 2003, p. 472
87. Page 2003, pp. 454–5

88. McKnight p. 122
89. McKnight pp. 44, 123
90. Latham 2005, p. 91
91. Latham 2005, p. 299
92. McKnight p. 84
93. Watson & Hickman p. 10
94. Guthrie p. 224
95. Guthrie p. 225
96. Guthrie p. 244
97. Guthrie p. 14
98. Crook *Crikey* 3-8-2011
99. Mayne *Crikey* 18-4-2011
100. Kiernan p. 290
101. Chippindale & Horrie p. 131
102. Chippindale & Horrie pp. 136–7
103. Chenoweth 2002, p. 318
104. Leveson p. 1130
105. McKnight p. 177
106. Shawcross 1997, p. 155
107. Kiernan p. 161
108. Holmes *The Drum* 21-12-2012
109. Dodd, Andrew *Crikey* 22-6-2011
110. *Australian* editorial 14-9-2010
111. Neighbour p. 20
112. Inglis 2002
113. Page 2003, pp. 102ff
114. Young 1991, p. 151
115. Shawcross 1997, p. 51
116. Lisners p. XII
117. Watson & Hickman pp. 26, 191
118. Cathcart pp. 42–3
119. Leveson Report p. 502; Cathcart pp. 42–3
120. Cathcart p. 45
121. Leveson Report p. 503
122. Guthrie pp. 279–82
123. Guthrie p. 215
124. Macintyre & Clark p. 68
125. Australian Press Council Adjudication No. 890 (November 1996)
126. McIntyre & Clark p. 71
127. Guthrie p. 215
128. Leveson Report p. 471
129. Mair 2012, p. 51
130. Shawcross 1997, p. 288

11 The Republic of Fox

1. Ackerman 2001
2. Swint p. 155
3. Brock & Rabin-Havt p. 51
4. Auletta 2003, p. 257
5. Auletta 2003, p. 251
6. Dickinson
7. Kurtz 2011
8. Wolff *GQ Magazine* 5-1-2012
9. Dickinson 2011
10. Dickinson 2011
11. Auletta 2003, p. 265
12. Swint pp. 24–5
13. Swint p. 59
14. Brock & Rabin-Havt p. 29
15. Brock & Rabin-Havt p. 31
16. Auletta 2003, p. 265
17. Swint p. 91
18. Swint p. 38
19. Swint pp. 91-3
20. Brock & Rabin-Havt p. 32
21. Swint p. 99
22. Swint p. 101
23. Swint pp. 108–9
24. Swint p. 113
25. Auletta 2003, p. 253
26. Hack p. 300
27. McKnight p. 154
28. Hack p. 342
29. Hack p. 344
30. Swint p. 156
31. Swint p. 114
32. Jamieson & Capella p. 45
33. Swint p. 137
34. Jamieson & Capella p. xiv
35. Brock & Rabin-Havt p. 36
36. Swint p. 166
37. Swint p. 164
38. Swint p. 164
39. Swint p. 165
40. Brock & Rabin-Havt pp. 52–3
41. Hack p. 386
42. Wolff 2008, pp. 282, 346
43. Ackerman p. 1
44. Gans p. 229
45. Day *Aust* 10-4-2003
46. Day *Aust* 10-4-2003
47. Dickinson 2011
48. Auletta 2003, p. 258
49. Schudson 1978
50. Dickinson 2011

51. Auletta 2003, p. 256
52. Auletta 2003, p. 257
53. Dickinson 2011
54. Swint p. 168
55. Brock & Rabin-Havt p. 57
56. Auletta 2003, p. 258
57. Sherman p. 23
58. Swint p. 209
59. Sherman p. 23
60. Sherman p. 24
61. Sherman p. 87
62. Brock & Rabin-Havt p. 41
63. Sherman p. 24
64. Brock & Rabin-Havt p. 83
65. Brock & Rabin-Havt p. 80
66. Brock & Rabin-Havt pp. 92–3
67. Brock & Rabin-Havt p. 11
68. Sherman p. 23
69. Brock & Rabin-Havt p. 241
70. Milbank *WP* 3-11-2010
71. Milbank *WP* 3-11-2010
72. Brock & Rabin-Havt p. 243
73. Brock & Rabin-Havt p. 243
74. Brock & Rabin-Havt p. 143
75. Brock & Rabin-Havt p. 98
76. Brock & Rabin-Havt p. 220
77. *Crikey* 14-1-2011
78. Brock & Rabin-Havt p. 252
79. Sherman p. 22
80. Kurtz 2011
81. Oremus *Slate* 7-11-2012
82. Richardson p. 12
83. Holcomb et al.
84. Dickinson 2011
85. Dickinson 2011
86. Brock & Rabin-Havt p. 38
87. McKnight p. 157
88. McKnight p. 159
89. Ackerman 2001
90. Ackerman 2001
91. *SourceWatch*
92. *SourceWatch*
93. *Outfoxed* video
94. *Media Matters for America* 14-07-2004
95. Swint p. 68
96. Dickinson 2011
97. Brock & Rabin-Havt pp. 86–7
98. Sherman *NY* 17-12-2012
99. Sherman 2011, p. 24
100. Kurtz 2011
101. Kurtz 2011
102. Auletta 2003, p. 273
103. Dickinson 2011
104. Swint p. 120
105. Halberstam p. 716
106. Starr 2010
107. Vaughn 2007
108. Starr 2010
109. Vaughn 2007
110. Knox *Newser* 30-4-2013
111. Starr 2010
112. Silverman *Poynter* 19-4-2012
113. Pew Research Center 16-8-2012
114. Public Policy Polling
115. Public Policy Polling
116. McKnight p. 21
117. Brock & Rabin-Havt p. 286
118. Moore *Yahoo News* 5-10-2011
119. Swint p. 176
120. Dickinson 2011
121. Kurtz 2011
122. Auletta 2003, p. 279
123. Swint p. 187
124. Kurtz *Daily Beast* 22-5-2012
125. Moos *Poynter* 22-5-2012
126. Adams G 18-11-2010
127. Auletta 2003, p. 277
128. McKnight p. 141
129. Milbank *WP* 18-7-2010
130. Jamieson & Capella p. 184
131. Bromwich *NYRB* 25-11-2010
132. Jamieson & Capella p. 101
133. Jamieson & Capella p. 65
134. Brock 2004
135. Jamieson & Capella
136. Brock & Rabin-Havt pp. 4–5
137. Brock & Rabin-Havt p. 100
138. Brock & Rabin-Havt p. 145
139. Brock & Rabin-Havt p. 126
140. Johnson *MM* 26-7-2012
141. Jamieson & Capella p. 64
142. Brock & Rabin-Havt p. 165
143. Dimiero et al. *MM* 19-12-2012
144. Swint p. 161
145. Dionne *WP* 26-4-2010
146. Frum *NY* 2011
147. Brock & Rabin-Havt p. 252
148. Sherman 2011 p. 22

149. Dickinson 2011
150. Brock & Rabin-Havt pp. 65–6
151. Brock & Rabin-Havt p. 253
152. Rugaber & Mayerowitz *Portland Press Herald* 6-10-2012
153. Maloy MMFA 26-9-2012
154. Boehlert *Media Matters* 7-11-2012
155. Kull pp. 13,14
156. Beaujon *Poynter* 23-5-2012
157. Brock & Rabin-Havt pp. 13-4
158. Beaujon *Poynter* 25-5-2012
159. Swint p. 220
160. Sherman p. 22
161. *SourceWatch*
162. *Crikey* 10-2-2011
163. Pleat *MM* 11-9-2012
164. Groch-Begley & Shere *MM* 1-10-2012
165. Brock & Rabin-Havt p. 285
166. Brock & Rabin-Havt p. 117
167. Bromwich *NYRB* 25-11-2010
168. Brock & Rabin-Havt p. 122
169. Brock & Rabin-Havt pp. 106–7
170. Brock & Rabin-Havt p. 110
171. Brock & Rabin-Havt p. 111
172. Brock & Rabin-Havt p. 285
173. Brock & Rabin-Havt p. 199
174. Brock & Rabin-Havt p. 228
175. Brock & Rabin-Havt p. 228
176. Brock & Rabin-Havt p. 215
177. Brock & Rabin-Havt p. 213
178. Brock & Rabin-Havt p. 216
179. Hananoki 2012
180. Sherman p. 23
181. Brock & Rabin-Havt p. 255
182. Bernstein *WP* 20-12-2012
183. Bernstein *WP* 20-12-2012
184. Maloy MMFA 4-12-2012
185. Sherman p. 25
186. Muddle *Open Democracy* 9-11-2012
187. Keller, Bill *NYT* 12-8-2012
188. Dionne *WP* 24-12-2012
189. Lieven *Open Democracy* 15-10-2012
190. Brock & Rabin-Havt p. 281
191. Richardson p. 11
192. Sherman 2011
193. Frum *NY* 20-11-11
194. Lilla *NYRB* 12-1-2012
195. Cohen *WP* 13-3-2012
196. Cohen *WP* 13-3-2012
197. Kurtz *Daily Beast* 25-9-11
198. Brock & Rabin-Havt p. 282
199. Brock & Rabin-Havt p. 282
200. Muddle *Open Democracy* 9-11-12
201. Peters *NYT* 5-7-2012
202. Kurtz *Daily Beast* 22-5-2012
203. Samuelson *WP* 7-9-2012
204. Lieven *Open Democracy* 15-10-2012
205. Boehlert 11-12-2012
206. Brock & Rabin-Havt p. 278
207. Hemmer *The Conversation* 23-4-2012
208. Frum *NY* 20-11-2011
209. Beaujon *Poynter* 8-11-2012
210. *Media Matters for America* 23-3-10
211. *SourceWatch*
212. Chavets *Vanity Fair* 5-3-2013
213. Chavets *Vanity Fair* 5-3-2013
214. Wolff 2008, p. 346
215. Wolff 2008, p. 347
216. Wolff 2012
217. Suich *AFR* 5-11-10
218. La Monica p. 87
219. Page *Open Democracy* 23-4-2012; Jones 2003
220. *Guardian* editorial 8-5-06
221. Moos *Poynter* 22-5-2012
222. Richardson p. 12
223. Nielsen 'Cross-Platform Report Q3 2011' Reports and Insights

12 Those who live by scandal

1. Gilligan 2011
2. Leveson 2012, p. 308
3. Watson & Hickman p. 85
4. 'Phone-hacking denials: what Murdoch executives said' *Guardian* 16-8-2011
5. Rusbridger p. 154
6. Watson & Hickman p. 114
7. Rusbridger 2012, p. 156
8. Leveson, Executive Summary p. 8
9. Leveson 2012, p. 510
10. Tiffen *The Conversation* 22-11-2012
11. Cathcart 2012a, p. 103
12. Deans & Sweeney *G* 30-6-2011
13. Watson & Hickman p. 217
14. UK Parliament 13-7-2011
15. Gerson *WP* 22-7-2011

16. Watson & Hickman pp. 306–7
17. Leveson 2012, p. 510
18. O'Carroll G 1-6-2012
19. Leveson Executive Summary p. 3
20. Myers *Poynter* 14-7-2011
21. Watson & Hickman p. 4
22. Watson & Hickman p. 241
23. Watson & Hickman p. 5
24. Watson & Hickman p. 55
25. Davies G 16-8-2011
26. Sabbagh & Halliday G 1-5-2012
27. Sabbagh G 1-5-2012
28. Leveson Executive Summary p. 3
29. Hopkins p. 14
30. Mair 2012a p. 48
31. Sabbagh G 27-11-2012; Mulholland G 7-10-2012
32. Bennett & Townend p. 176
33. Leveson Executive Summary p. 24
34. Leveson Executive Summary p. 26
35. Ash G 14-7-2011
36. Watson & Hickman p. 210
37. Oborne *Spectator* 7-7-2011; Watson & Hickman p. 162
38. Barnett *Open Democracy* 17-7-2011
39. Hill G 15-9-2010
40. Watson & Hickman p. 176
41. Watson & Hickman pp. 258–9
42. Cohen 2011
43. Editorial G 19-1-2009
44. Watson & Hickman pp. 63-4
45. Peston *BBC News Business* 22-8-2011; Curtis & Robinson G 24-8-2011
46. Leveson 2012, p. 27
47. Watson & Hickman pp. 107, 121
48. Gerson *WP* 22-7-2011
49. Tiffen 1999, p. 80ff
50. Mair 2012b, p. 51
51. Massie *Foreign Policy* 13-7-2011
52. Beaujon *Poynter* 29-2-2012
53. Barnett 2013, p. 357
54. Watson & Hickman p. 217
55. Sparrow G 6-5-2012
56. Watson & Hickman p. 144
57. Plunkett & O'Carroll G 31-5-2012
58. Wintour & Sabbagh G 24-4-2012
59. Weir *Open Democracy* 27-5-2012
60. Sabbagh & Wintour G 11-5-2012
61. Sabbagh & Wintour G 11-5-2012
62. Plunkett & O'Carroll G 31-5-2012
63. Leveson transcripts 26-4-2012
64. Plunkett & O'Carroll G 31-5-2012
65. Wintour G 30-4-2012
66. Burns *NYT* 4-9-2012
67. Tiffen *The Conversation* 22-11-2012
68. Watson & Hickman p. 313
69. McGurran *BBC News* 13-7-2011
70. Lisners p. 143
71. Leveson Executive Summary p. 19
72. Leveson Executive Summary p. 18
73. Watson & Hickman pp. 84–5, 165
74. Leveson 2012, p. 361
75. Leveson 2012, p. 367
76. Watson & Hickman p. 86
77. Leveson 2012, p. 374
78. Leveson Executive Summary p. 19
79. Watson & Hickman p. 133
80. Leveson 2012, p. 369; Watson & Hickman p. 308
81. Watson & Hickman pp. 88–9
82. Watson & Hickman p. 113
83. Watson & Hickman pp. 102, 235; Rusbridger 2012
84. Cathcart 2012a, p. 26
85. Arango *NYT* 19-2-2011
86. Rusbridger 2012, p. 155
87. Hind *Open Democracy* 18-7-2011; Bennett & Townend p. 171; Watson & Hickman p. 105
88. Rusbridger 2012, p. 155
89. Cathcart 2012a, pp. 30–1; Watson & Hickman p. 30; Oborne *Spectator* 7-7-2011
90. Watson & Hickman p. 40
91. Leveson 2012, p. 269
92. Leveson Executive Summary p. 7
93. Leveson Executive Summary p. 9
94. Watson & Hickman p. 138
95. Watson & Hickman p. 238
96. Mayne *Crikey* 21-10-2011
97. West *SMH* 17-10-2012
98. Mair 2012b, p. 52
99. Cathcart 2012a, p. 25
100. Leveson Executive Summary p. 7
101. Leveson Executive Summary pp. 7, 8; Leveson Report pp. 288, 305–6
102. Watson & Hickman p. 124, see also

pp. 133, 150.
103. Barry *Crikey* 26-7-2012
104. Leveson 2012, p. 338
105. Leveson 2012, p. 341
106. Watson & Hickman pp. 170, 185
107. Watson & Hickman p. 56
108. Watson & Hickman p. 98
109. 'Phone-hacking denials: what Murdoch executives said' G 16-8-2011
110. Brendon 2012, p. 32
111. Mair 2012a, p. 221
112. Lisners p. 61
113. Lyall & Becker *NYT* 7-7-2011
114. Watson & Hickman p. 8
115. Watson & Hickman p. 285
116. Ignatius *WP* 14-7-2011
117. Watson & Hickman pp. 83, 243
118. Watson & Hickman p. 72
119. Watson & Hickman pp. 276–7
120. Kissane *SMH* 25-4-2012
121. Leveson 2012, pp. 347–8
122. Leveson transcript 25-4-2012
123. Watson & Hickman p. 90
124. Watson & Hickman p. 302
125. Cathcart 2012a, p. 24
126. Watson & Hickman p. 280
127. Sabbagh & O'Carroll G 12-12-2012
128. Cathcart 2012a, pp. 33, 12
129. Watson & Hickman pp. 289–90
130. Leveson 2012, p. 266
131. Cathcart 2012a, p. 33; Watson & Hickman pp. 108–12
132. Leveson 2012, pp. 512, 413
133. Watson & Hickman pp. 284–5
134. Doward & Jiminez G 19-11-2011
135. Leveson Executive Summary p. 7; Cathcart 2012 p. 34
136. Jones 2012, p. 132
137. Barry *Crikey* 21-11-2012
138. Leveson 2012, p. 433
139. Watson & Hickman p. 173
140. Watson & Hickman p. 262
141. Chippindale & Horrie p. 223
142. Curtis 2000, p. 176
143. Leveson 2012, p. 505
144. Rusbridger 2012, p. 158
145. Watson & Hickman p. 294
146. Cathcart 2012a, p. 16
147. Catchart 2012a, p. 61
148. Watson & Hickman p. xviii
149. Marsh p. 103
150. Leveson Executive Summary p. 4
151. Jones, Paul pp. 127–8
152. MacKenzie *Daily Mail Online* 20-2-2012
153. Jones, Paul pp. 128–9
154. Watson & Hickman p. 317
155. *ABC News* 8-8-2012
156. Crook *Crikey* 10-1-2013
157. Rushe G 19-7-2012
158. Mayne *Crikey* 25-10-2011; Mayne *Crikey* 1-3-2012

13 Murdoch's road to scandal

1. Watson & Hickman p. 19
2. Flint & James *LA Times* 9-8-2011
3. Chessell *Aust* 23-7-2011
4. Watson & Hickman p. 315
5. Wolff 2008, p. 402
6. Crainer p. 98
7. Young 1991 p. 146
8. Young 1991, p. 149
9. Young 1991, p. 150
10. Lisners p. xiv
11. Wolff 2008, p. 141
12. Carr *NYT* 6-5-2012
13. Ellison p. 85
14. Pilkington G 13-9-2011
15. Peters *NYT* 9-8-2011
16. GMI Ratings October 2011
17. Grigg *AFR* 5-10-2011
18. Guthrie p. 7
19. Leveson transcripts 26-4-2012
20. Campbell p. 76
21. Campbell p. 111
22. Neil p. 160
23. Ellison p. 178
24. Dover p. 136
25. Barry *Crikey* 22-6-2012
26. Kiernan p. 140
27. Wolff 2008, p. 6
28. Guthrie p. 6
29. Guthrie pp. 284–5
30. Brendon 2012, p. 35
31. Evans 2009, p. 440
32. Guthrie p. 41
33. Shawcross 1997, p. 246

34. Guthrie p. 9
35. Shawcross 1997, p. 297
36. Shawcross 1997, pp. 296–7
37. Neil p. 183
38. Bowman p. 93
39. McKnight p. 57
40. Kiernan p. 66
41. Guthrie p. 81
42. Wolff 2008, p. 18
43. Wolff 2008, p. 246
44. Guthrie pp. 221–2
45. Neil p. 192
46. Wolff 2008, p. 42
47. Wolff 2008, p. 18
48. Guthrie p. 49
49. Page 2003, p. 154
50. Page 2003, p. 155
51. Page 2003, p. 157
52. Leapman p. 39
53. Shawcross 1997, p. 84
54. Kiernan p. 78
55. Leapman p. 110
56. Leapman p. 110
57. Belfield et al. p. 131
58. Neil p. 416
59. Shawcross 1997, p. 389
60. Belfield et al. p. 130
61. Neil p. 412
62. Neil p. 182
63. McKnight p. 57
64. Chenoweth 2002, p. 321
65. Neil p. 175
66. Neil p. 176
67. Page 2003, p. 367
68. Greenslade 2004, p. 501
69. Chippindale & Horrie p. 329
70. Wolff 2008, p. 212
71. Leveson 2012, p. 501
72. Leveson 2012, p. 498
73. Watson & Hickman pp. 130, 198; Leveson 2012, p. 526
74. Chippindale & Horrie p. 206
75. Chippindale & Horrie p. 283
76. Massie 2011
77. Wolff 2008, p. 7
78. Leveson 2012, p. 496
79. Watson & Hickman p. 304
80. McConville & Smith p. 302
81. Watson & Hickman p. 14
82. Leveson 2012, p. 546; Cathcart 2012a, pp. 14–5
83. Rusbridger 2011
84. Muir & Martinson G 22-4-2010
85. Ignatius WP 14-7-2011
86. Chenoweth 2002, p. 41
87. Kiernan p. 161
88. Kiernan p. 222
89. Leveson transcripts 25-4-2012
90. Leveson 2012, p. 306
91. Page 2003, p. 480
92. Stein Huffington Post 25-11-2011
93. Greenslade G 4-7-2012
94. Stoeffel Observer.com 4-7-2012
95. Ignatius WP 14-7-2011
96. Bennett & Townend p. 178
97. Watson & Hickman p. 244
98. Watson & Hickman p. 194
99. Watson & Hickman pp. 175, 163
100. Watson & Hickman p. 95
101. Leveson 2012, p. 517; Watson & Hickman p. 94
102. Watson & Hickman pp. 103–4
103. Leigh & Davies G 22-5-2012
104. Lyall & Becker NYT 7-7-2011
105. Leveson 2012, p. 516
106. Watson & Hickman pp. 118–9; Leveson 2012, p. 516; Tiffen The Conversation 22-11-2012
107. Cathcart 2012a, p. 66; Watson & Hickman pp. 110–2
108. Robinson G 18-11-2011
109. Wolff Adweek 8-8-2011
110. Leveson Executive Summary p. 11
111. Atkins p. 28ff
112. Leveson transcripts 26-4-2012
113. Leveson transcripts 26-4-2012; Leveson 2012, p. 521
114. Leveson 2012, pp. 498–9
115. Harcup p. 278
116. Guthrie p. 89
117. Chippindale & Horrie p. 246
118. Guthrie pp. 87–9, 97
119. Turner p. 346
120. Chippindale & Horrie p. 350
121. Cathcart 2012a, p. 36
122. Watson & Hickman p. 16
123. Peppiatt p. 22
124. Harcup p. 279

125. Greenslade 2012a, p. 419
126. Greenslade 2012a, p. 419
127. Shawcross 1997, p. 54
128. Arango *NYT* 29-9-2008
129. Page 2003, p. 217
130. Chippindale & Horrie p. 94
131. Watson & Hickman p. 301
132. Watson & Hickman p. 13
133. Greenslade 2012a, p. 417
134. Tunstall 1971, pp. 168–71
135. Tunstall 1996
136. Watson & Hickman p. 22
137. Watson & Hickman p. 293
138. Jones 2012, p. 131
139. Jones 2012, p. 127
140. Watson & Hickman p. 23
141. Robinson *G* 19-2-2006
142. Watson & Hickman p. 15
143. Cathcart 2012a, p. 40
144. Chippindale & Horrie p. 152
145. Jones 2012, p. 127
146. McConville & Smith p. 300
147. Leveson 2012, p. 263
148. Rohm p. 61
149. McKnight p. 142
150. Hack p. 302
151. Shawcross 1997, p. 395
152. Wolff 2008, p. 215
153. McKnight & Hobbs p. 844
154. Wolff 2008, p. 215
155. Crainer pp. 231–3
156. McKnight & Hobbs p. 844
157. Rich *New York* 31-7-2011
158. Wolff 2008, p. 210
159. McKnight p. 92
160. Wolff 2008, p. 210
161. Wolff 2008, p. 211
162. Wolff 2008, pp. 198–9
163. Wolff 2008, p. 211
164. Carr *NYT* 17-7-2011
165. Benjamin & Calabresi *Time* 15-8-2011
166. Benjamin & Calabresi *Time* 15-8-2011
167. Carr *NYT* 17-7-2011
168. Carr *NYT* 17-7-2011
169. Carr *NYT* 17-7-2011
170. Reuters 2-9-2011
171. Carr *NYT* 17-7-2-11
172. Pilkington *G* 17-8-2011
173. Knott *Crikey* 1-5-2013
174. Barry *Crikey* 13-10-2011
175. Chenoweth *AFR* 13-7-2013
176. Jukes *The Beast* 4-7-2013
177. Greenslade *G* 4-7-2013
178. Shawcross 1997, p. 398
179. *ninemsn* 6-9-2013
180. Bernstein *G* 20-12-2012

References

AAP 'Rupert Murdoch tells Twitter fans Google is piracy leader' *DT* 31-1-2012

ABC 'Church of England dumps News Corp shares' *ABC News* 8-8-2012

Ackerman, Seth 'The most biased name in news' FAIR (Fairness and Accuracy in Reporting) July/August 2001

Adams, Richard 'Fox News chief Roger Ailes apologises after describing NPR as "Nazis"' *G* 18-11-2012

Adley, Esther 'Alastair Campbell back at the Leveson inquiry – and with great clunking balls' *G* 14-5-2012

Ahmed, Nabila and Thompson, Sarah 'Another day, another fight for Murdoch' *AFR* 14-10-2010

Andrews, David L. 'Sport and the transnationalising media corporation' *Journal of Media Economics*, 16(4), 2003

Arango, Tim 'A "Tabloid Guy" calls it a night after 41 years with Murdoch' *NYT* 29-9-2008

—— 'The Murdoch in Waiting' *NYT* 19-2-2011

Ash, Timothy Garton 'Britain should seize this chance to break the culture of fear at its heart' *G* 14-7-2011

Atkins, Chris 'How the tabloids obfuscated and misled in the face of Starsuckers evidence' in Richard Lance Keeble and John Mair (eds) *The Phone Hacking Scandal. Journalism on Trial* (Bury St Edmonds, Arima, 2012)

Auletta, Ken *Backstory. Inside the Business of News* (NY, Penguin, 2003)

—— 'Who's afraid of Rupert Murdoch?' (PBS documentary, *Frontline*, 2005)

—— 'What Murdoch faces now' *New Yorker* 17-7-2011

Australian Broadcasting Tribunal. Inquiry into Foreign Control of the Herald and Weekly Times Limited. Brief for Counsel Assisting. 27-1-1987

Australian editorial Yes, we will keep reporting' 14-9-2010

Australian editorial 30-4-1965

Australian Electoral Commission 'House of Representatives – Two Party Preferred Results 1949 – Present'

Australian Press Council *Adjudication No.* 890 November 1996

Aylmer, Sean 'Bidders aren't the only ones feeling toxic about' *AFR* 13-11-2004

—— 'Murdoch talks up web, cuts forecasts' *AFR* 12-11-2005

Bagehot 'Peer today, gone tomorrow' *The Economist* 22 November 2003

Barker, Geoffrey 'Is this News Limited's defence?' *Inside Story* 18-7-2011

Barnett, Anthony 'After Murdoch' *Open Democracy* 17-7-2011

Barnett, Steven 'It's ownership, stupid: why plurality lies at the heart of media policy reform – and how to achieve it' in Richard Lance Keeble and John Mair (eds) *The Phone Hacking Scandal. Journalism on Trial* (2012)

Barry, Paul *The Rise and Rise of Kerry Packer* (Sydney, Bantam Books, 1993)

—— "'Arse-kicking' pollies cause media woes", says ex-Sun ed' *Crikey* 13-10-2011

—— 'The Power Index: biz bosses, Rupert Murdoch at #4' *Crikey* 22-6-2012

—— 'Murdoch and ex-editor trade blows' *Crikey* 12-7-2012

References

—— 'So whodunit? The great phone hacking cover up' *Crikey* 26-7-2012

—— 'Charges against Brooks, Coulson show Murdoch can't escape' *Crikey* 21-11-2012

BBC News 'News Corp profits fall on sale of MySpace website' Business 11-8-2011

Beaujon, Andrew 'Morning media roundup: How to borrow a horse from Scotland Yard' *Poynter* 29-2-2012

—— 'Survey: NPR's listeners best-informed, Fox viewers worst-informed' *Poynter* 23-5-2012

—— 'Anonymous Fox spokesperson bravely talks trash about school behind news habits survey' *Poynter* 25-5-2012

—— 'News Corp. announces split, "will wow the world"' *Poynter* 28-6-2012

—— 'Did conservative media fail its audience election night?' *Poynter* 8-11-2012

—— 'Buffett, Newhouses, Murdoch on Forbes list of billionaires' *Poynter* 4-3-2013

Beinart, Peter 'Rupert Murdoch's tweet about the "Jewish Owned Press" is dumb and offensive' *The Daily Beast* 18-12-2012

Belfield, Robert, Hird, Christopher and Kelly, Sharon *Murdoch. The Great Escape* (London, Macdonald & Co., 1991)

Benjamin, Mark and Calabresi, Massimo 'News Corp's US hacking problem' *Time* 15-8-2011

Bennett, Daniel and Townend, Judith 'Press "Omerta": How newspapers' failure to report the phone hacking scandal exposed the limitations of media accountability' in Richard Lance Keeble and John Mair (eds) *The Phone Hacking Scandal. Journalism on Trial* (2012)

Bernstein, Carl 'Murdoch's Watergate?' *Newsweek* 9-7-2011

—— 'Why the US media ignored Murdoch's brazen attempt to hijack the presidency' *G* 20-12-2012

Bernstein, Carl and Woodward, Bob '40 years after Watergate, Nixon was far worse than we thought' *WP* 9-6-2013

Bloomberg 'Murdoch "angry" over Elton John settlement' *Age* 10-1-2012

Blumenthal, Howard J. and Goodenough, Oliver R. *This Business of Television* (3rd edn, NY, Billboard Books, 2006)

Boehlert, Eric The Romney "landslide" that wasn't' *Media Matters for America (MMFA)* 7-11-2012

—— 'Is conservative media one big "racket"?' *MMFA* 11-12-2012

Bowden, Mark 'Mr Murdoch goes to war' *Atlantic* July/August 2008

Bowman, David *The Captive Press* (Melbourne, Penguin, 1988)

Brendon, Piers *The Life and Death of the Press Barons* (London, Secker & Warburg, 1982)

—— *Eminent Elizabethans* (London, Jonathan Cape, 2012)

Brock, David *The Republican Noise Machine. Right-wing Media and How it Corrupts Democracy* (NY, Random House, 2004)

Brock, David, Rabin-Havt, Ari and MMFA *The Fox Effect. How Roger Ailes turned a network into a propaganda machine* (New York, Random House, 2012)

Bromwich, David 'The rebel germ' *NYRB* 25-11-2010

Brookes, Julian 'Tobacco and Rupe' *Mother Jones* 24-8-1998

Burns, John F. 'British Premier reshuffles Cabinet, promoting official linked to Murdoch case' *NYT* 4-9-2012

Calwell, A.A. *Be Just and Fear Not* (Melbourne, Lloyd O'Neil Pty Ltd, 1972)

Campbell, Alastair *The Blair Years. Extracts from the Alastair Campbell Diaries* (London, Hutchinson, 2007)

Carlyon, Les *Paper Chase. The Press under Examination* (Melbourne, Herald & Weekly

Times, 1982)

Carr, David 'Troubles that money can't dispel' *NYT* 17-7-2011

—— 'The cozy compliance of the News Corp board' *NYT* 6-5-2012

Carroll, V.J. *The Man who Couldn't Wait. Warwick Fairfax's Folly and the Bankers who Backed Him* (Melbourne, William Heinemann Australia, 1990)

Carswell, Andrew 'New rich adrift in ocean of debt and despair/Federal budget: Special edition' *DT* 11-5-2011

Cathcart, Brian 'The press, the Leveson Inquiry and the Hacked Off campaign' in Richard Lance Keeble and John Mair (eds) *The Phone Hacking Scandal. Journalism on Trial* (2012a)

—— *Everybody's Hacked Off. Why we don't have the press we deserve and what to do about it* (London, Penguin, 2012)

Chadwick, Paul *Media Mates: Carving up Australia's Media* (Melbourne, Sun Books, 1989)

Chavets, Zev 'Exclusive excerpt: Roger Ailes off camera' *Vanity Fair* 5-3-2013

Chenoweth, Neil 'The story behind News' super shares' *AFR* 3-11-1993

—— 'Murdoch's millennium gamble: a titanic tussle for eyeballs' *AFR* 30-8-1999

—— 'Rabbitohs teach News a lesson in losing' *AFR* 7-7-2001

—— *Virtual Murdoch. Reality Wars on the Information Highway* (London, Vintage, 2002)

—— 'How I won the war' *AFR* 12-4-2003

—— 'Malone, Murdoch's new best friend' *AFR* 27-1-2004

—— 'The man the Murdoch children fear' *AFR* 31-1-2004

—— 'QPL buy-out pitched $500m above rivals' *AFR* 13-4-2004

—— 'Lot of stuff wrapped up in News' *AFR* 16-9-2004

—— 'Murdoch, Malone play corporate cat and mouse' *AFR* 1-8-2005

—— 'Murdoch may be losing grip on News' *AFR* 13-8-2005

—— 'Murdoch family reaps a cool $97m from News' *AFR* 26-8-2005

—— 'There's a new game in town' *AFR* 14-7-2006

—— 'There's always the son' *AFR* 25-2-2009

—— 'A second coming, again' *AFR* 5-2-2011

—— 'Mystery over Murdoch family payout' *AFR* 18-2-2011

—— 'Control is embedded in Murdoch's DNA' *AFR* 3-5-2012

—— 'Abandon ship' *AFR* 30-6-2012

—— 'The stalking of Rupert Murdoch' *AFR* 13-7-2013

Chessell, James 'Shocked market contemplates the future of News' *Australian* 23-7-2011

—— 'Rupert Murdoch reaffirms his faith in newspapers' *Australian* 12-8-2011

—— 'Foxtel's clear reception' *AFR* 20-6-2012

—— 'Failed News deal points to future' *AFR* 30-6-2012

Chippindale, Peter and Horrie, Chris *Stick it up your Punter! The Rise and Fall of the Sun* (London, Mandarin, 1990)

Chozick, Amy 'Star rises for News' Mr Fixit' *AFR* 24-1-2012

—— 'News Corp in $139 million settlement with shareholders' *NYT* 22-4-2013

Cohen, Richard 'Just desserts for "Citizen Murdoch"' *WP* 18-7-2011

—— 'Sarah Palin's foolishness ruined US politics' *WP* 13-3-2012

Cohen, Roger 'The Cameron collapse' *NYT* 19-7-2011

Collins, Luke 'Murdoch's vision fades to a blur' *AFR* 14-2-2002

Conn, David 'How football had kept the Murdoch empire afloat' *G* 15-6-2012

Cook, John 'What happened to climate change? Fox News and the US elections' *The Conversation* 1-10-2012

References

Costello, Peter with Coleman, Peter *The Costello Memoirs* (Melbourne, Melbourne University Press [MUP], 2008)

Crainer, Stuart *Business. The Rupert Murdoch Way. Ten Secrets of the World's Greatest Deal Maker* (Oxford, Capstone Publishing Company, 2002)

Crikey 'How many times did Bill O'Reilly interrupt Obama? *Crikey* 10-2-2011

Crikey Comment 14-1-2011

Crook, Andrew 'Forget news media diversity, the internet has tightened News' squirrel grip' *Crikey* 8-11-2011

—— 'Nixon book launch: Adler eavesdrops on a revealing Hun news conference' *Crikey* 3-8-2011

—— 'Super fund takes Rupert's advice, sells out of News Corp' *Crikey* 10-1-2013

Cryle, Denis *Murdoch's Flagship. The First Twenty-five Years of the Australian Newspaper* (Melbourne, MUP, 2008)

Curtis, Polly and Robinson, James 'Andy Coulson "broke" Commons pass rules by failing to declare NI payments' G 24-8-2011

Curtis, Sarah (ed.) *The Journals of Woodrow Wyatt Vol. One* (London, Macmillan, 1998)

—— *The Journals of Woodrow Wyatt Vol. Two* (London, Pan, 1999)

—— *The Journals of Woodrow Wyatt Vol. Three* (London, Macmillan, 2000)

D'Alpuget, Blanche *Robert J. Hawke: A Biography* (Melbourne, Schwartz, 1982)

D'Arcy, John *Media Mayhem. Playing with the Big Boys in Media* (Melbourne, Brolga Publishing, 2005)

Daley, Gemma and Chessell, James 'Media law reforms to hit News Corp' AFR 25-2-2013

Davies, Nick 'Phone hacking: News of the World reporter's letter reveals cover-up' G 16-8-2011

Davies, William 'Hack-gate: the latest cultural contradiction of British conservatism?' *Open Democracy* 7-7-2011

Day, Mark 'Bias all part of Fox's battle plan' *Australian* 10-4-2003

Deans, Jason and Tryhorn, Chris 'BSkyB to sell 10% stake in ITV' G 8-2-2010

Deans, Jason and Sweeney, Mark 'News Corp's BSkyB bid: Jeremy Hunt gives green light for takeover' G 30-6-2011

Dickinson, Tim 'How Roger Ailes built the Fox News fear factory' *Rolling Stone* 9-6-2011

Dimiero, Ben, Gertz, Matt and Savillo, Rob 'Bill O'Reilly covers the "War on Christmas" more than actual wars, again' MMFA 19-12-2012

Dionne, E.J. 'The right court fight' WP 26-4-2010

—— 'Paul Ryan and the triumph of theory' WP 13-8-2012

—— 'It's our system on the cliff' WP 24-12-2012

Dodd, Vikram 'News International "deliberately" blocked investigation' G 20-7-2011

Dorling, Philip 'Whitlam radical, Fraser arrogant, Hawke moderate: secret cables reveal Murdoch insights' *Age* 20-5-2013

Dover, Bruce *Rupert's Adventure in China. How Murdoch Lost a Fortune and Found a Wife* (Melbourne, Viking, 2008)

Doward, Jamie and Suarez Jiminez, Silvia 'News of the World private detective vows to expose tabloid stalker culture' G 19-11-2011

Dunstan, Don *Felicia, the political memoirs of Don Dunstan* (Melbourne, Macmillan, 1981)

Dyer, Glenn 'Court rules against Murdochs: stake in ITV is pie in the sky' *Crikey* 22-1-2010

—— 'News split: print losses not tolerated anywhere, says Murdoch', *Crikey* 29-6-2012

—— 'News takes axe to assets with $2.9b cut in value' *Crikey* 9-8-2012

—— 'News Corp settles' *Crikey* 23-4-2013

Economist 'How to lose friends and alienate people' 14-7-2011

Economist 'Britain's phone-hacking scandal: wider still and wider' 21-7-2011

Ellis, Eric 'Calling a scumbag a scumbag: Rupert Murdoch's revealing twitter habit' *The Global Mail* 17-10-2012

Ellison, Sarah *War at the Wall Street Journal. How Rupert Murdoch Bought an American Icon* (Melbourne, Text Publishing, 2010)

Evans, Harold *Good Times, Bad Times* (London, Weidenfeld & Nicolson, 1983)

—— *My Paper Chase. True Stories of Vanished Times. An autobiography* (London, Little Brown, 2009)

Fallows, James 'The age of Murdoch' *Atlantic* September 2003

Fickies, Jonathan 'Rupert Murdoch's most offensive tweets' *Daily Beast* 18-11-2012

Fidler, Stephen 'Murdoch rescued from the brink' *AFR* 16-4-1991

Fitzsimmons, Jill and Fong, Jocelyn 'The *Wall Street Journal*: dismissing environmental threats since 1976' *MMFA* 2-8-2012

Flint, Joe and James, Meg 'Rupert Murdoch's LA dinner featured steak – but not hacking' *LA Times* 9-8-2011

Fraser, Malcolm and Simons, Margaret *Malcolm Fraser. The Political Memoirs* (Melbourne, Miegunyah Press, 2010)

Freudenberg, Graham *A Certain Grandeur. Gough Whitlam in Politics* (Melbourne, Sun Books, 1977)

Frum, David 'When did the GOP lose touch with reality?' *New York* 20-11-2011

Gans, Herbert *Deciding What's News. A Study of CBS Evening News, NBC Nightly News, Newsweek and Time* (New York, Pantheon Books, 1979)

Gerson, Michael 'The Murdoch mess complicates life for David Cameron' *WP* 22-7-2011

Ghosh, Sayanti and Baker, Liana B. 'News Corp publishing wing deep in red' *AFR* 24-12-2012

Gibson, Janine and Watt, Nicholas 'BSkyB bid for United blocked' *G* 10-4-1999

Giles, Frank *Sundry Times* (London, John Murray, 1986)

Gillette, Felix 'Rupert Murdoch, News Corp dodge phone-hacking ruin' *Bloomberg Businessweek* 18-4-2013

Gilligan, Andrew 'Scandal could sink Cameron' *Age* 20-7-2011

Given, Jock *Turning off the Television. Broadcasting's Uncertain Future* (Sydney, UNSW Press, 2003)

Glover, Stephen 'Thatcher, Murdoch and the meeting that was erased from history' *I* 19-3-2012

Goodwin, Peter *Television under the Tories. Broadcasting Policy 1979–1997* (London, BFI Publishing, 1998)

Goot, Murray 'The media and the campaign' in Howard R. Penniman (ed.) *Australia at the Polls. The National Elections of 1980 and 1983* (Sydney, Allen & Unwin, 1983)

—— *Newspaper Circulation in Australia 1932–1977* (Melbourne, La Trobe University Media Centre Papers, 1978)

Governance Metrics International 'GMI Ratings' Risk List: News Corp' *GMIRatings* October 2011

Greenslade, Roy 'Their master's voice' *G* 17-2-2003

—— *Press Gang. How Newspapers make Profits from Propaganda* (London, Pan Books, 2004)

—— 'Why the *Sun* is anti-Labour again' *G* 7-3-2005

References

—— 'Sun reporter was "aghast" at MacKenzie's Hillsborough headline' Greenslade blog, *G* 7-9-2007

—— 'How Murdoch's philosophy created a climate of misbehaviour' *G* 18-7-2011

—— 'News Corporation split – it's GoodCo versus BadCo' *G* 2-7-2012

—— 'What did Murdoch say to *New York Post* editor about "racist" cartoon?' *G* 4-7-2012

—— 'James Harding gets a terrific send-off as staff signal their support for him' *G* 13-12-2012

—— 'Hacking's Disreputable History' in Richard Lance Keeble and John Mair (eds) *The Phone Hacking Scandal. Journalism on Trial* (2012)

—— 'Rupert Murdoch revealed – tape exposes the media mogul's real opinions' *G* 4-7-2013

Greenwald, Robert *Outfoxed: Murdoch's War on Journalism* (Brave New Films, MoveOn. org, 2004)

Griffen-Foley *The House of Packer. The Making of a Media Empire* (Sydney, Allen & Unwin, 1999)

—— *Party Games. Australian Politicians and the Media from War to Dismissal* (Melbourne, Text Publishing, 2003)

Griffiths, Peter 'Murdoch mocks UK government as arrives for ethics inquiry' *Reuters* 21-4-2012

Grigg, Angus 'No News good news for AMP' *AFR* 5-10-2011

Groch-Begley, Hannah and Shere, David 'A history of dishonest Fox charts' *MMFA* 1-10-2012

Guardian 'Phone-hacking denials: what Murdoch executives said' 16-8-2011

Guardian editorial 'Murdoch 0, Football 1' 10-4-1999

—— 'Sky News boss to leave' 8-5-2006

—— 'This is Andy Coulson's reshuffle' 19-1-2009

Guthrie, Bruce *Man Bites Murdoch. Four decades in Print, Six Days in Court* (Melbourne, MUP, 2011)

Gutstein, Donald 'Murdoch's ties to Big Tobacco' *rabble.ca* 26-7-2011

Guy, Robert 'Murdoch struggles with rebellious investors' *AFR* 22-10-2007

Hack, Richard *Clash of the Titans. How the Unbridled Ambition of Ted Turner and Rupert Murdoch has created global empires that control what we read and watch* (Beverley Hills CA, New Millenium Press, 2003)

Halberstam, David *The Powers that Be* (New York, Dell, 1979)

Hall, Susan *Supertoy: 20 Years of Australian Television* (Melbourne, Sun Books, 1976)

Halliday, Josh '*Guardian, Daily Mail* and *Daily Express* circulations rise month on month' *G* 8-12-2012

Hananoki, Eric 'Report: 30+ Fox News hosts and contributors who are campaigning for Republicans' *MMFA* 1-11-2012

—— 'Roger Ailes' hypocrisy on "dividing people into groups"' *MMFA* 11-2-2013

Harcup, Tony 'The "conscience clause": coming soon to a newsroom near you?' in Richard Lance Keeble and John Mair (eds) *The Phone Hacking Scandal. Journalism on Trial* (2012)

Hawke, Bob *The Hawke Memoirs* (Melbourne, William Heinemann Australia, 1994)

Hay, David 'Murdoch claims it is fourth network' *AFR* 15-7-1994

Hemmer, Nicole 'Obama is a Muslim Black Panther! Republican candidates and the conservative media' *The Conversation* 23-4-2012

Herman, Edward S. and Chomsky, Noam *Manufacturing Consent: the political economy of the mass media* (London, Vintage, 1994)

Hill, Dave 'Boris Johnson dismisses concerns over *News of the World* phone hacking as "codswallop"' G 15-9-2010

Hind, Dan 'The BBC investigates' *Open Democracy* 18-7-2011

Hocking, Jenny *Gough Whitlam: His time. The Biography Vol. II* (Melbourne, Miegunyah Press, 2012)

Holcomb, Jesse, Mitchell, Amy and Rosenstiel, Tom 'Cable: by the numbers' *The State of the News Media 2012* (An Annual Report, The Pew Research Center's Project for Excellence in Journalism)

Holgate, Ben 'News profit jumps 47pc in March quarter' *AFR* 11-5-2012

Hollywood Reporter 'Rupert Murdoch's 12 best tweets of 2012' 10-1-2013

Holmes, Jonathan 'Beware the unsourced figure' *Media Watch*, ABC 16-5-2011

—— 'Trivial pursuit: when the *Australian* gets personal' *The Drum* 21-12-2012

—— 'The unwritten rule of the drop' *MediaWatch*, ABC 15-4-2013

Hopkins, Huw L. 'The rotten apple drops, bounces, rolls, settles and grows, and its seeds spread far and wide: an updated hackgate timeline' in Richard Lance Keeble and John Mair (eds) *The Phone Hacking Scandal. Journalism on Trial* (2012)

Horne, Donald *Death of the Lucky Country* (Melbourne, Penguin, 1976)

House of Representatives Select Committee on the Print Media *News and Fair Facts. The Australian Print Media Industry* (AGPS, Canberra, March 1992) (The Lee Report)

Howard, John *Lazarus Rising. A personal and political autobiography* (Sydney, HarperCollins, 2010)

Hyland, Anne 'Murdoch to raise his Star in the East' *AFR* 8-3-2005

Hywood, Greg '"Mates" and others: Hawke's view of the media groups' *AFR* 13-12-1985

Ignatius, David 'The world according to Rupert Murdoch' *WP* 14-7-2011

Inglis, K.S. *The Stuart Case* (2nd edn, Melbourne, Black Inc., 2002)

Jamieson, Kathleen Hall and Capella, Joseph N. *Echo Chamber. Rush Limbaugh and the Conservative Media Establishment* (New York, Oxford University Press [OUP], 2008)

Johnson, Melody 'Fox "doubling down" on deceptively edited comments' *MMFA* 25-7-2012

Jones, Nicholas 'Good political theatre Mr Jay, a shame about the questions: Why the Leveson public hearings were a missed opportunity' in Richard Lance Keeble and John Mair (eds) *The Phone Hacking Scandal. Journalism on Trial* (2012)

Jones, Paul 'Regulating for freedom: media lessons from Australia' *Open Democracy* 18-9-2003

Jukes, Peter 'Rupert Murdoch admits "mistakes" and "panic" in leaked tape' *Daily Beast* 4-7-2013

Kain, Erik 'The Republican Party needs to ditch Fox News if it wants to win' *Mother Jones* 7-1-2012

Keane, Bernard 'A partisan paper now wants to silence dissenters' *Crikey* 29-11-2010

—— 'War on the middle class? More a war on our kids' *Crikey* 11-5-2011

Keller, Bill 'The Romney package' *NYT* 12-8-2012

Kelly, Paul *November 1975. The Inside Story of Australia's Greatest Political Crisis* (Sydney, Allen & Unwin, 1995)

Kennedy, Trevor *Top Guns* (Melbourne, Sun Books, 1988)

Kiernan, Thomas *Citizen Murdoch* (New York, Dodd, Mead & Company, 1986)

Kimmel, Daniel M. *The Fourth Network. How Fox Broke the Rules and Reinvented Television*

References

(Chicago, Ivan R. Dee, 2004)

Kirk, Stuart and Edgecliffe-Johnson, Andrew 'From headlines to bottom line' *FT* 22-7-2011

Kissane, Karen 'James Murdoch kept in dark over phone hacking because he would "cut out cancer"' *SMH* 25-4-2012

Knightley, Phillip *A Hack's Progress* (London, Jonathan Cape, 1997)

Knott, Matthew 'Media giants unite to blow the whistle on source protection' *Crikey* 1-5-2013

Knox, Merrill 'Evening news ratings' *Newser* 30-4-2013

Kohler, Alan 'Murdoch's poison pill leaves a bad taste' *Age* 13-8-2005

—— 'Rupert's wrong: distribution, not content, is king' *Crikey* 9-4-2010

Kruger, Colin 'Break-up could breathe new life into News' *Age* 18-5-2013

Kull, Steven 'Misperceptions, the media and the Iraq war' The PIP/Knowledge Networks Poll (Program on International Policy Attitudes, University of Maryland, 2003)

Kurtz, Howard 'Roger's reality show' *Daily Beast* 25-9-2011

—— 'Ailes regrets "scum" attack on *NYT*' *Daily Beast* 22-5-2012

—— 'Rupert Murdoch gets his man as Mitt Romney picks Paul Ryan' *Daily Beast* 12-8-2012

La Monica, Paul R. *Inside Rupert's Brain* (London, Portfolio, 2009)

Labaton, Stephen 'FCC blocks EchoStar deal with DirecTV' *NYT* 11-10-2002

Lachapelle, Tara, Kucera, Danielle and Sherman, Alex 'News Corp. at 50% discount shows diminishing Murdoch: real M&A' *Bloomberg News* 18-7-2011

Larsen, Peter Thai and Grice, Andrew 'Murdoch's Man Utd bid blocked' *I* 10-4-1999

Latham, Mark *The Latham Diaries* (Melbourne, MUP, 2005)

Lawrenson, John and Barber, Lionel *The Price of Truth. The Story of the Reuters Millions* (London, Sphere Books, 1985)

Leapman, Michael *Barefaced Cheek. The apotheosis of Rupert Murdoch* (London, Hodder & Stoughton, 1983)

Leigh, David and Davies, Nick '*News of the World*'s "fake sheikh" had Tom Watson followed, emails show' *G* 22-5-2012

Leveson Inquiry *The Report* (www.leveson.org.uk) 29-11-2012

—— *Executive Summary* (www.leveson.org.uk) 29-11-2012

—— Transcripts (www.levesoninquiry.org.uk/hearings) 2011–12

Lewis, Justin 'A different kind of plurality: securing diverse media' *Open Democracy* 16-7-2011

Lewis, Steve 'What a difference a mogul makes' *AFR* 4-12-1999

Lieven, Anatol 'The future of democracy in America' *Open Democracy* 15-10-2012

Lilla, Mark 'Republicans for revolution' *NYRB* 12-1-2012

Lisners, John *The Rise and Fall of the Murdoch Empire* (London, John Blake, 2012)

Lister, Sam et al. 'No pact with Rupert Murdoch, says Tony Blair' *I* 28-5-2012

Littlemore, Stuart 'Doing favours: the Murdoch *Telegraph*, Tony Abbott and Pauline Hanson' (The Bruce Allen Memorial Lecture, Macquarie University, 29-9-2003)

Lloyd, Clem *Profession Journalist. A History of the Australian Journalists' Association* (Sydney, Hale & Iremonger, 1985)

Luft, Oliver 'Rupert Murdoch: the internet won't destroy newspapers' *G* 17-11-2008

Lusetich, Robert 'Battle stations for the hearts and minds of middle America' *Australian* 10-4-2003

Lyall, Sarah and Becker, Jo 'A tenacious rise to the top in the brutal men's world of tabloids' *NYT* 7-7-2011

Macintyre, Stuart and Clark, Anna *The History Wars* (Melbourne, MUP, 2003)

MacKenzie, Kelvin 'Why Dacre's worth his million' *British Journalism Review* 16(1), 2005

—— 'Arrests are the real scandal' *Daily Mail Online* 20-2-2012

Macmillan, Arthur 'Biden attacked in Murdoch's twitter storm' *SMH* 14-10-2012

MacMillan, Robert 'Update 1 – Dow Jones costs News Corp $2.8 bn in writedown' *Reuters* 6-2-2009

Mair, John 'A peep into the tabloid world – courtesy of Leveson' in Richard Lance Keeble and John Mair (eds) *The Phone Hacking Scandal. Journalism on Trial* (2012)

—— 'TOWIE: the only way is ethics (not)' in Richard Lance Keeble and John Mair (eds) *The Phone Hacking Scandal. Journalism on Trial* (2012)

Maloy, Simon 'Conservative media embrace poll trutherism in face of Romney Decline' *MMFA* 26-9-2012

—— 'Roger Ailes and Fox News' lack of accountability' *MMFA* 4-12-2012

Maney, Kevin *Megamedia Shakeout. The Inside Story of the Leaders and the Losers in the Exploding Communications Industry* (New York, John Wiley & Sons, Inc., 1995)

Manne, Robert 'Murdoch and the War on Iraq' in Robert Manne (ed.) *Do Not Disturb. Is the media failing Australia* (Melbourne, Black Inc., 2005)

—— 'Bad news: Murdoch's *Australian* and the shaping of the nation' *Quarterly Essay* 43, 2011

Marjoribanks, Timothy *News Corporation, Technology and the Workplace. Global strategies, Local Change* (Cambridge, Cambridge University Press [CUP], 2000)

Marsh, Kevin ' ... but what comes after?' in Richard Lance Keeble and John Mair (eds) *The Phone Hacking Scandal. Journalism on Trial* (2012)

Massie, Alex 'Revenge of the MPs' *Foreign Policy* 13-7-2011

Mayne, Stephen 'After under-performing decade, is it time for Rupert to go? *Crikey* 18-1-2011

—— 'Rupert, Hitler, 1983, beat ups ... doesn't all this sound familiar?' *Crikey* 18-4-2011

—— 'The most dramatic News Corp AGM since Maxwell came to town' *Crikey* 21-10-2011

—— 'Record protests as News Corp shareholders get rankings dead right' *Crikey* 25-10-2011

—— 'How about a Rupert tweet on Sir Rod's surprise gong?' *Crikey* 6-2-2012

—— 'James Murdoch's resignation means nothing' *Crikey* 1-3-2012

McAllister, Ian, Mackerras, Malcolm and Brown Boldiston, Carolyn *Australian Political Facts* (2nd edn, Melbourne, Longman Cheshire, 1990)

McConville, Ben and Smith, Kate 'Crossing the thin blue line' in Richard Lance Keeble and John Mair (eds) *The Phone Hacking Scandal. Journalism on Trial* (2012)

McGurran, Deborah 'Hacking inquiry "more Clouseau than Columbo" jibe' *BBC News* 13-7-2011

McIlwraith, Ian 'TV report rocks News shares' *AFR* 21-12-1990

McKenzie, Robert Trelford and Silver, Allan *Angels in marble: Working class Conservatives in urban England* (London, Heinemann, 1968)

McKnight, David *Rupert Murdoch. An Investigation of Political Power* (Sydney, Allen & Unwin, 2012)

McKnight, David and McNair, Brian 'The empire goes to war: News Corporation and Iraq' *Australian Journalism Review* 34(2), 2012

References

McKnight, David and Hobbs, Mitchell '"You're all a bunch of pinkos": Rupert Murdoch and the politics of HarperCollins' *Media, Culture and Society*, 33, 2011

McNair, Brian *Journalism and Democracy. An Evaluation of the Political Public Sphere* (London, Routledge, 2000)

McSmith, Andy 'What Tony said to Rupert – and why it says volumes about his friends and enemies' *Independent on Sunday* 18-9-2005

Media Matters for America 23-3-2010

—— '33 internal Fox editorial memos reviewed by MMFA reveal Fox News Channel's inner workings' (mediamatters.org) 14-7-2004

Menadue, John *Things you Learn Along the Way* (Melbourne, David Lovell Publishing, 1999)

Milbank, Dana 'The Tea Party makes trouble with a capital T' *WP* 18-7-2010

—— 'On Fox News, election 2010 is cause for cheer' *WP* 3-11-2010

Moore, Frazier 'Roger Ailes looks back on 15 years of Fox News' *Yahoo News* 5-10-2011

Moos, Julie 'Roger Ailes criticizes *New York Times*, AP during Ohio University talk' *Poynter* 22-5-2012

—— 'Report: Roger Ailes signs 4 year deal to run Fox News and more' *Poynter* 19-10-2012

Muddle, Cas 'America's election and the Tea Party' *Open Democracy* 9-11-2012

Muir, Hugh and Martinson, Jane 'James Murdoch at the *Independent*: "like a scene out of Dodge City"' G 22-4-2010

Mulholland, Helene 'David Cameron tells hacking victims he still has an open mind over Leveson' G 7-10-2012

Munster, George *A Paper Prince* (Melbourne, Viking, 1985)

Murdoch, Rupert *A Golden Age of Freedom* Boyer Lectures (Sydney, ABC, 2008)

Murphy, Dan 'Rupert Murdoch's Jewish problem. And his Egyptian one' *Christian Science Monitor* 18-11-2012

Myers, Steve 'Rupert, James Murdoch refuse to testify for phone-hacking inquiry next week' *Poynter* 14-7-2011

—— 'Murdoch: split of News Corp into two companies unrelated to phone hacking scandal' *Poynter* 28-6-2012

Neighbour, Sally 'The United States of Chris Mitchell: The power of a Murdoch man' *The Monthly*, August 2011

Neil, Andrew *Full Disclosure* (London, Macmillan, 1996)

News Limited Board 'Announcement by the Board of Directors of News Limited' 22-1-1987

Nielsen 'Cross-Platform Report Q3 2011' *Reports and Insights*

ninemsn 'I've got a lot of time for Rupert: Abbott' (news.ninemsn.com.au) 6-9-2013

Noam, Eli (ed.) *Media Concentration* (Oxford, OUP, 2014, forthcoming)

Oakes, Laurie and Solomon, David *The Making of an Australian Prime Minister* (Melbourne, Cheshire, 1973)

Oborne, Peter 'What the papers won't say' *Spectator* 7-7-2011

O'Carroll, Lisa 'Jeremy Hunt criticized for failure to oversee adviser' G 14-5-2012

—— 'NI denies Murdoch had "selective amnesia" about Thatcher meeting' G 14-5-2012

—— 'Leveson inquiry: make political lying a criminal offence, says Peter Oborne' G 17-5-2012

—— 'Phone hacking: News International could face more than 500 claims' G 1-6-2012

—— 'Rupert Murdoch hits out at Andrew Neil over lobbying of Tony Blair' G 11-7-2012

—— '*Times* editor James Harding resigns' G 12-12-2012

Oremus, Will 'The five stages of Fox News grief' *Slate* 7-11-2012

Osborne, Alistair 'Sky's ITV gamble may cost it £500m – but was it worth it?' *Daily Telegraph* (UK) 22-1-2010

Page, Bruce *The Murdoch Archipelago* (London, Simon & Schuster, 2003)

—— 'The end of the Murdoch Archipelago' *Open Democracy* 23-4-2012

Peers, Martin 'News' annual pay-out $US1bn for nine years' *AFR* 25-11-1991

Peppiatt, Richard 'The story factory: infotainment and the tabloid newsroom' in Richard Lance Keeble and John Mair (eds) *The Phone Hacking Scandal. Journalism on Trial* (2012)

Perez-Pena, Richard 'TV Guide, having just been bought, is bracing to be sold' *NYT* 8-5-2008

Peston, Robert 'Coulson got hundreds of thousands of pounds from News Intl' *BBC News Business* 22-8-2011

Peters, Jeremy 'For Murdoch, a board meeting with friendly faces' *NYT* 9-8-2011

—— 'Shots by Murdoch at Romney play out to conservative core' *NYT* 5-7-2012

Pew Research Center 'Further decline in credibility ratings for most news organisations' (Pew Research Center for the People and the Press, 16-8-2012)

Pilkington, Ed 'A life unraveled … whistleblower who incurred wrath of the Murdoch empire' G 17-8-2011

—— 'News Corp shareholders lodge complaint against Rupert Murdoch' G 13-9-2011

Pleat, Zachary 'Updated: today in dishonest Fox News graphics' *MMFA* 11-9-2012

Plunkett, John and O'Carroll, Lisa '"Congrats on Brussels!" Texts reveal Hunt's close alliance with Murdoch' G 31-5-2012

Potter, Ben 'News Corp suffers post-Avatar hangover' *AFR* 5-5-2011

Price, Lance *The Spin Doctor's Diary. Inside Number 10 with New Labour* (London, Hodder & Stoughton, 2005)

—— 'Rupert Murdoch is effectively a member of Blair's cabinet' G 1-7-2006

Public Policy Polling 'Fox News' credibility declines' (Raleigh, University of North Carolina, 6-2-2013)

Ramsey, Alan *The Way They Were. The View from the Hill of the 25 Years that Remade Australia* (Sydney, UNSW Press, 2011)

Read, Donald *The Power of News. The History of Reuters 1849–1989* (Oxford, OUP, 1992)

Real, Michael R. 'Television and sports' in Janet Wasko (ed.) *A Companion to Television* (Oxford, Blackwell, 2005)

Reuters 'Murdoch's tough guy Carlucci under pressure' 2-9-2011

Rich, Frank 'Murdoch hacked us too' *New York* 31-7-2011

Richardson, Reed 'GOP-Fox circus act' *Nation* 29-4-2013

Ricketson, Matthew 'Ownership not the burning issue' *Age* 30-7-2008

Riddell, Kelly 'US network pays to stay in the game' *AFR* 1-11-2010

Robichaux, Mark *Cable Cowboy. John Malone and the rise of the modern cable business* (Hoboken NJ, John Wiley & Sons, 2002)

Robinson, James 'Scoops spur Coulson on to a red top renaissance' G 19-2-2006

—— 'Phone hacking: Steve Coogan compares NI to a "protection racket"' G 18-11-2011

Rohm, Wendy Goldman *The Murdoch Mission. The digital transformation of a media empire*

References

(New York, John Wiley & Sons, 2002)

Rooney, D. 'Thirty years of competition in the British tabloid press. The *Mirror* and the *Sun* 1968–1998' in Colin Sparks and John Tulloch (eds) *Tabloid Tales. Global Debates over media standards* (Oxford, Rowman & Littlefield, 2000)

Roshco, Bernard *Newsmaking* (Chicago, University of Chicago Press, 1975)

Rosston, Gregory L. 'Antitrust implications of EchoStar-DirecTV Proposed Merger' *Policy Brief* (Stanford Institute for Economic Policy Research, November 2001)

Rugaber, Christopher and Mayerowitz, Scott 'US unemployment: Politics, statistics morph into conspiracy' *Portland Press Herald* 6-10-2012

Rusbridger, Alan 'Introduction' in The Guardian. *How the Guardian broke the story* (Guardian Shorts, Kindle Edition, 2011)

—— 'Hackgate "reveals failure of normal checks and balances to hold power to account"' in Richard Lance Keeble and John Mair (eds) *The Phone Hacking Scandal. Journalism on Trial* (2012)

Rushe, Dominic 'News Corp shareholders renew push for Rupert Murdoch to resign' G 19-7-2012

Rushton, Katherine 'Big sister tell the bad News' AFR 25-8-2012

Sabbagh, Dan 'MPs' News Corp report will be hard to dismiss' G 1-5-2012

—— '12 things the Leveson inquiry has taught us' G 27-11-2012

Sabbagh, Dan and Halliday, Josh 'Rupert Murdoch deemed "not a fit person" to run international company' G 1-5-2012

Sabbagh, Dan and O'Carroll, Lisa 'Harold Evans tells Leveson of conflict and "vindictive" atmosphere at *Times*' G 17-5-2012

—— 'Rebekah Brooks took £10.8m compensation from News Corp' G 12-12-2012

Sabbagh, Dan and Wintour, Patrick 'Rebekah Brooks turns screw on Jeremy Hunt with "hacking advice" email' G 11-5-2012

Samuelson, Robert J. 'Are you better off now than four years ago?' WP 7-9-2012

Schudson, Michael *Discovering the News: A Social History of American Newspapers* (New York, Basic Books, 1978)

—— *Watergate in American Memory. How We Remember, Forget and Reconstruct the Past* (New York, Basic Books, 1993)

Schultz, Julianne *Reviving the Fourth Estate. Democracy, Accountability and the Media* (Melbourne, CUP, 1998)

—— (ed.) *Not just another business. Journalists, Citizens and the Media* (Sydney, Pluto Press, 1994)

Senate Select Committee on Certain aspects of Foreign Ownership Decisions in Relation to the Print Media *Percentage Players. The 1991 and 1993 Fairfax Ownership Decisions* (Canberra, Commonwealth of Australia, 1994)

Seymour-Ure, Colin *The British Press and Broadcasting Since 1945* (Oxford, Basil Blackwell, 1991)

Shafer, Jack 'Rupert Murdoch's favourite lie' *Slate* 24-4-2008

Shawcross, William *Rupert Murdoch. The Making of a Media Empire* (New York, Simon & Schuster, 1997)

—— 'Rupert Murdoch' *Time* 3-11-1999

Sheridan, Greg 'The power of one' *Australian*, 26-4-2003

Sherman, Gabriel 'The elephant in the green room' *New York* 30-5-2011

—— 'Rupert Murdoch wants stricter gun laws after Newtown, but Fox News doesn't get the memo' *New York* 17-12-2012

Shoebridge, Neil 'News Corp sells MySpace at $US540m loss' AFR 30-6-2011

Silverman, Craig 'Connecting the dots: why doesn't the public trust the press any more?' *Poynter* 19-4-2012

Simpson, Kirsty 'Let's have it on: Murdoch hits back' *SMH* 29-3-2012

Sloan, Allan 'Missing from Murdoch's family deals: News Corp shareholders' *CNN Money* (finance.fortune.cnn.com) 24-2-2011

Smith, Anthony *The Age of Behemoths: The Globalisation of Mass media Firms* (New York, Priority Press Publications, 1991)

Sorkin, Andrew Ross and Schiesel, Seth 'GM Agrees to sell its satellite TV unit in $26 billion deal' *NYT* 29-10-2001

SourceWatch 'Fox News' (sourcewatch.org)

Souter, Gavin *Company of Heralds. A Century and a Half of Australian Publishing* (Melbourne, MUP, 1981)

Sparrow, Andrew 'Vince Cable feels "vindicated" over handling of News Corp bid for BSkyB' *G* 6-5-2012

—— 'Cabinet Office backs Gordon Brown over Murdoch phone call' *G* 15-6-2012

Starr, Paul 'Governing in the age of Fox News' *The Atlantic Online*, Jan-Feb 2010

Statista 'DirecTV's revenue from 2006 to 2012 (in billion US dollars)' *Statista* (www.statista.com/statistics/195726/revenue-of-directv-since-2006/) February 2013

Stein, Sam '*New York Post* lawsuit: shocking allegations made by fired employee Sandra Guzman' *Huffington Post* 25-11-2011

Stephens, Mitchell 'Clout: Murdoch's political *Post*' *Columbia Journalism Review* July/August 1982

Stoeffel, Kat 'Col Allan denied "editorial privilege", ordered to dish on boss Rupert Murdoch and racist cartoon' *Observer.com* 4-7-2012

Suich, Max 'Uncut: the thoughts of Chairman Murdoch' *AFR* 5-11-2010

Sun editorial 'Don't you know there's a bloody war on?' 28-8-2009

Sweney, Mark 'News Corp paid Elisabeth Murdoch almost $4m for running Shine' *G* 5-9-2012

Swint, Kerwin *Dark Genius. The Influential Career of Legendary Political Operative and Fox News Founder Roger Ailes* (New York, Union Square Press, 2008)

Sykes, Trevor 'Murdoch bows out … but he'll still visit' *AFR* 27-10-2004

Tempest, Matthew 'Heseltine demands fresh inquiry into Westland affair' *G* 12-1-2006

Thatcher, Margaret *Margaret Thatcher. The Autobiography* (London, HarperCollins, 1993)

Theel, Shauna '10 dumbest things Fox said about climate change in 2012' *MMFA* 31-12-2012

Thomas, Laurie and Litman, Barry R 'Fox Broadcasting Company, why now? An economic study of the rise of the fourth broadcast "network"' *Journal of Broadcasting and Electronic Media* 35(2), 1991

Thompson, Jeremy 'Conroy steps up attack on *Daily Tele*' *ABC News* 18-7-2011

Tiffen, Rodney 'The Dynamics of Dominance. Wran and the media, 1981' in Ernest Chaples, Helen Nelson and Ken Turner (eds) *The Wran Model* (Melbourne, OUP, 1985)

—— 'Quality and bias in the Australian Press: News Limited, Fairfax and the Herald and Weekly Times' *The Australian Quarterly* 59(3–4), 1987

—— 'The *Sun* also sets. *Mirror* monopoly shock!' *Media Information Australia*, 52, May 1989

References

—— *News and Power* (Sydney, Allen & Unwin, 1989)

—— 'Media Policy' in Judith Brett, James Gillespie and Murray Goot (eds) *Developments in Australian Politics* (Melbourne, Macmillan, 1994)

—— 'The Labor-Packer Alliance, 1978–1995. RIP' *Media International Australia*, 77, 1995

—— *Scandals. Media, Politics and Corruption in Contemporary Australia* (Sydney, UNSW Press, 1999)

—— 'From technological abundance to commercial monopoly in Australian pay TV: key relationships in institutionalising subscription television' in Andrew Kenyon (ed.) *TV Futures. Digital Television Policy in Australia* (Melbourne, MUP, 2007)

—— 'UK phone hacking victims' lawyer Charlotte Harris in conversation: full transcript' *The Conversation* 22-11-2012

Toohey, Brian 'Super funds sue Murdoch over poison pill' *AFR* 8-10-2005

Toynbee, Polly 'How the badly maimed BBC can stand up to parasitic Sky' *G* 3-1-2012

Travis, Alan 'Murdoch did meet Thatcher before *Times* takeover, memo reveals' *G* 17-3-2012

Tuccille, Jerome *Murdoch: A Biography* (London, Judy Piatkus Publishers, 1989)

Tumber, Howard 'Scandal and media in the United Kingdom: From Major to Blair' *American Behavioural Scientist* 47, 2004

Tunstall, Jeremy *Journalists at Work* (London, Constable, 1971)

—— *Newspaper Power: The New National Press in Britain* (Oxford, Clarendon Press, 1996)

Turner, Barry 'The key questions: have they been answered?' in Richard Lance Keeble and John Mair (eds) *The Phone Hacking Scandal. Journalism on Trial* (2012)

UK Parliament 'MPs debate News Corporation bid for BSkyB' *UK Parliament* (www.parliament.uk) 13-7-2011

Vander Hook, Sue *Rupert Murdoch. News Corporation Magnate* (North Mankato MN, ABDO Publishing, 2011)

Vaughn, Stephen L. *Encyclopaedia of American Journalism* (London, Routledge, 2007)

Walker, Martin *Powers of the Press: The World's Great Newspapers* (London, Quartet Books, 1982)

Wallace, Christine 'The bad old days of webs of influence are long gone' *AFR* 10-6-1994

Wallis, Holly 'Archived papers reveal Thatcher secrets' *BBC News* 17-3-2012

Walsh, Maximilian '"Dries" think that media are just business' *SMH* 23-4-1987

Watson, Tom 'News International – ruthless, without conscience or morality' *Open Democracy* 8-7-2011

Watson, Tom and Hickman, Martin *Dial M for Murdoch. News Corporation and the Corruption of Britain* (London, Allen Lane, 2012)

Weir, Stuart 'Government by corporate text messages: what is left of the British constitution after Leveson?' *Open Democracy* 27-5-2012

Welch, Dylan 'New to twitter: the tweet Murdoch took down ... fast' *Age* 2-1-2012

West, Michael 'Like it or lump it – Murdoch bats away calls for reform' *SMH* 17-10-2012

Wheatcroft, Geoffrey 'The truth about Murdoch' *NYRB blog* 14-3-2012

Whitbourn, Michaela 'How to cook up a carbon tax story' *AFR* 14-9-2011

Williams, Pamela 'Canberra bristles as media moguls stir' *AFR* 7-10-2012

Wintour, Patrick 'David Cameron forced to answer Jeremy Hunt questions' *G* 30-4-2012

Wintour, Patrick and Sabbagh, Dan 'News Corp dossier appears to show contacts with minister over BSkyB bid' G 24-4-2012

Wolff, Michael *The Man Who Owns the News. Inside the Secret World of Rupert Murdoch* (New York, Knopf, 2008)

—— 'How bad is News Corp?' *Adweek* 8-8-2011

—— 'Why I love Fox News' *GQ* 5-1-2012

—— 'The News Corp split and Rupert Murdoch's rearguard action' G 28-6-2012

—— 'Rupert's challenge: the new News Corp' *AFR* 7-1-2013

Yelland, David 'I was drunk every night for nearly 24 years but I was saved by the love of my son' *Mail Online* 27-3-2010

Young, Hugo *One of Us. A biography of Margaret Thatcher* (London, Macmillan, 1989)

Young, Sir Norman *Figuratively Speaking. The Reminiscences, Experiences and observations of Sir Norman Young* (Adelaide, published by the author, 1991)

Younger, Ronald *Keith Murdoch: founder of an empire* (HarperCollins, Sydney, 2003)

Index

Index

Index

Index

Index